EAR

Zulu

To renew this book take it to any of
the City Libraries before
the date due for return

Coventry City Council

By the Same Author

Churchill's Sacrifice of the Highland Division: France 1940
Mutiny at Salerno: An Injustice Exposed
The Homicidal Earl: The Life of Lord Cardigan
Military Blunders
Prince of Pleasure: The Prince of Wales and
the Making of the Regency
The Indian Mutiny: 1857

Zulu

*The Heroism and Tragedy
of the Zulu War of 1879*

SAUL DAVID

VIKING
an imprint of
PENGUIN BOOKS

VIKING

Published by the Penguin Group

Penguin Books Ltd, 80 Strand, London WC2R 0RL, England
Penguin Group (USA) Inc., 375 Hudson Street, New York, New York 10014, USA
Penguin Books Australia Ltd, 250 Camberwell Road, Camberwell, Victoria 3124, Australia
Penguin Books Canada Ltd, 10 Alcorn Avenue, Toronto, Ontario, Canada M4V 3B2
Penguin Books India (P) Ltd, 11 Community Centre, Panchsheel Park, New Delhi – 110 017, India
Penguin Group (NZ), cnr Airborne and Rosedale Roads, Albany, Auckland 1310, New Zealand
Penguin Books (South Africa) (Pty) Ltd, 24 Sturdee Avenue, Rosebank 2196, South Africa

Penguin Books Ltd, Registered Offices: 80 Strand, London WC2R 0RL, England

www.penguin.com

First published 2004
1

Copyright © Saul David, 2004
Maps copyright © Reg Piggott, 2004

Endpapers: *front*, sketch plan of the Battle of Isandlwana published
in the *Royal Engineers Journal*, 1 June 1879 (Natal Government Archives,
photograph South Wales Borderers Museum); *back*, sketch map of
Rorke's Drift by Lieutenant Chard (South Wales Borderers Museum)

The moral right of the author has been asserted

Set in 12/14.75 pt Monotype Bembo
Typeset by Rowland Phototypesetting Ltd, Bury St Edmunds, Suffolk
Printed in Great Britain by Clays Ltd, St Ives plc

A CIP catalogue record for this book is available from the British Library

ISBN 0-670-91474-6

For Johanna

Contents

Acknowledgements

First and foremost I must thank my editor at Penguin, Eleo Gordon, for allowing me to replace the book I was originally contracted to write with this one. The Zulu War has long been a favourite subject of mine, and the 125th anniversary of the conflict seemed too good an opportunity to miss.

Many people assisted with my research in Britain and South Africa. I am particularly grateful to: Denis Barker, Pamela Clark, Ricky Crathorne, Major Martin Everett, Ken Gillings, Dr Adrian Greaves, Ian Knight, Roger Lane, Dr Alistair Massy, Ms T. Mhlongo, Themba Mthethwa, Dalton Ngobese, Jeff Rice, John Roberts and Nellie Somers.

I was given invaluable help by the staffs of the following institutions: the British Library, Devon Record Office, Gloucestershire Record Office, Killie Campbell Africana Library (Durban), KwaZulu-Natal Archives (Pietermaritzburg), London Library, National Army Museum, The National Archives (Kew), Royal Archives (Windsor), Royal Engineers' Museum (Chatham) and South Wales Borderers' Museum (Brecon). I am extremely grateful to Her Majesty Queen Elizabeth II for permission to quote from the Royal Archives.

Last year, in a classic case of putting the cart before the horse, I was the programme consultant for a BBC *Timewatch* documentary, 'Zulu: The True Story'. That experience benefitted this book hugely, and I would like to thank John Farren, Tim Robinson, Mina Panic, Elieen Inkson, Neville Kidd and Brian Howell.

The production of the book by everyone at Penguin has, as usual, been superb. Particular thanks to Eleo, Juliet Annan, Julie Duffy, Sarah Day, Donna Poppy, Andrew Smith, Reg Piggott and Douglas Matthews.

Finally I must mention the two people who continue to indulge my uncertain but enjoyable career: my agent, Julian Alexander, and my wife, Louise. Thank you.

List of Illustrations

The author and publishers are grateful to the following for permission to reproduce illustrations: John Young Collection (JYC); South Wales Borderers' Regimental Museum, Brecon (SWB); The Director, National Army Museum, London (NAM); and Sherwood Foresters' Museum, Nottingham (SFM)

List of Maps

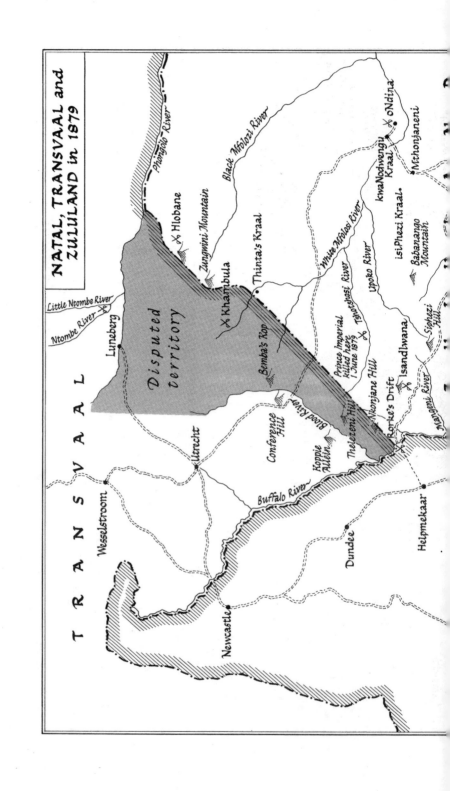

NATAL, TRANSVAAL and ZULULAND in 1879

T R A N S V A A L

Phongolo River

Black Mfolozi River

oNdina

Mthonjaneni

kwaNodwengu Kraal.

Hlobane

Zungwini Mountain

White Mfolozi River

Thinta's Kraal

isiPhezi Kraal.

Babanango Mountain

Little Ntombe River

Khambula

Ntombe River

Disputed territory

Upoko River

Luneberg

Bemba's Kop

Tshotshosi River

Prince Imperial killed here 1 June 1879

Nhlonjane Hill

Siphezi Hill

Mangeni River

isandlwana.

Conference Hill

Blood River

Thelezeni Hill

Nhonjane Hill

Rorke's Drift

Utrecht

Koppie Allein

Wesselstroom

Buffalo River

Dundee

Helpmekaar

Newcastle

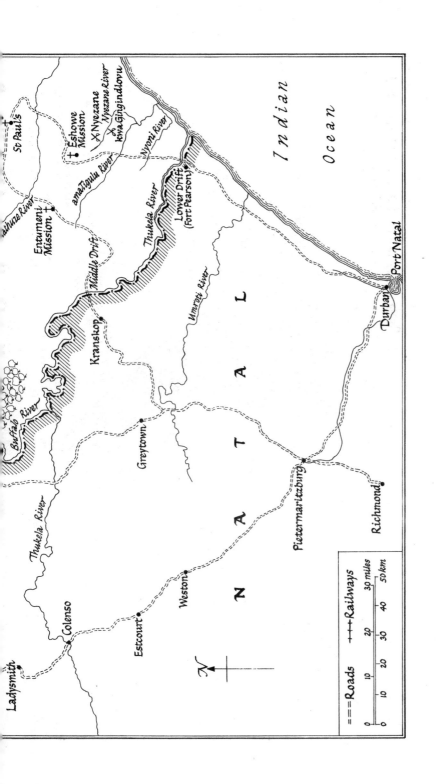

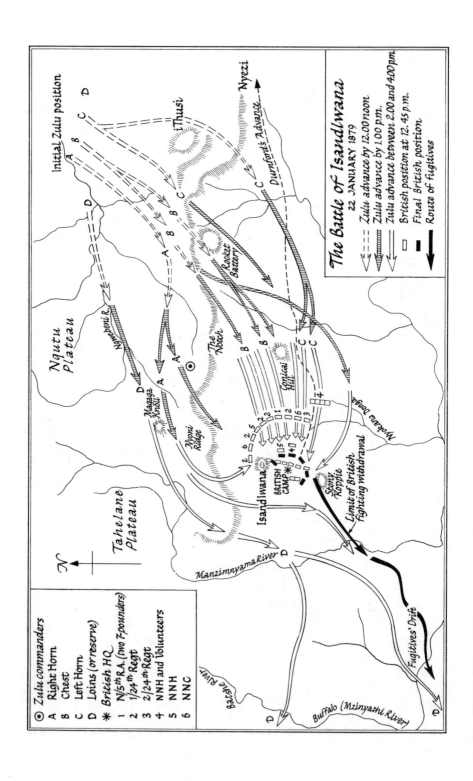

The Battle of Isandlwana
22 JANUARY 1879

Zulu advance by 12.00 noon
Zulu advance by 1.00 p.m.
Zulu advance between 2.00 and 4.00 p.m.
British position at 12.45 p.m.
Final British position
Route of fugitives

Zulu commanders
A Right Horn
B Chest
C Left Horn
D Loins (or reserve)
British HQ
*
1 N/5th R.A. (two 7-pounders)
2 1/24th Regt
3 2/24th Regt
4 NNH and Volunteers
5 NNH
6 NNC

Initial Zulu position

Ngutu Plateau

Tahelane Plateau

Ngwebeni R.

iThusi

Dartnford's Advance

Nyezi

Rocket Battery

The Notch

Magaga Knoll

Nyoni Ridge

Conical Hill

Isandlwana

BRITISH CAMP

Stony Koppie

Mpezane Donga

Limit of British fighting withdrawal

Manzimnyama River

Batshe River

Buffalo (Mzinyathi River)

Fugitives' Drift

N

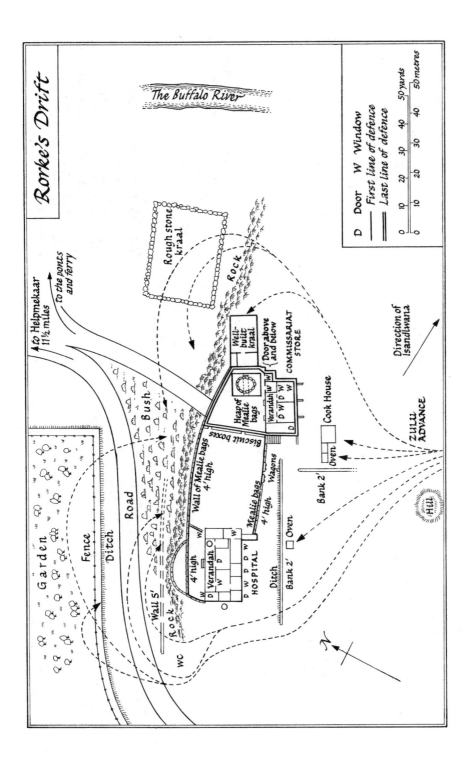

Rorke's Drift

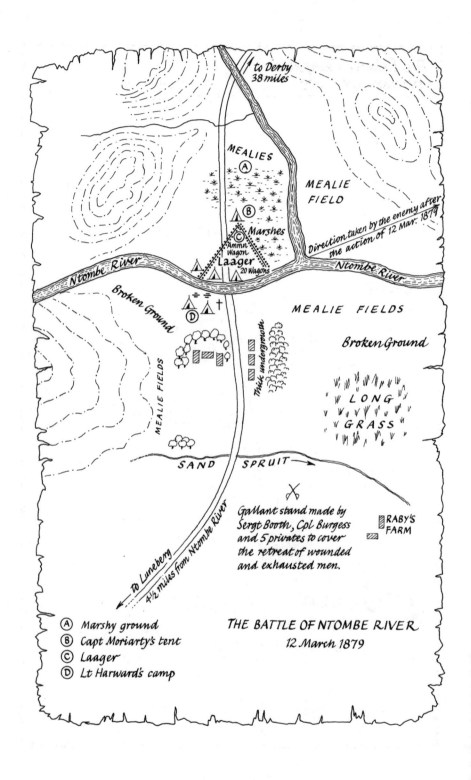

to Derby
38 miles

MEALIES
Ⓐ

MEALIE
FIELD

Ⓑ

Ⓒ Marshes
Ammn
Wagon
Laager
20 Wagons

Ntombe River   Ntombe River

Direction taken by the enemy after
the action of 12 Mar. 1879

Ⓓ †

Broken Ground

MEALIE FIELDS

Broken Ground

Thick undergrowth

MEALIE FIELDS

LONG
GRASS

SAND   SPRUIT →

Gallant stand made by
Sergt Booth, Cpl Burgess
and 5 privates to cover
the retreat of wounded
and exhausted men.

RABY'S
FARM

To Luneberg
4½ miles from Ntombe River

Ⓐ Marshy ground
Ⓑ Capt Moriarty's tent
Ⓒ Laager
Ⓓ Lt Harward's camp

THE BATTLE OF NTOMBE RIVER
12 March 1879

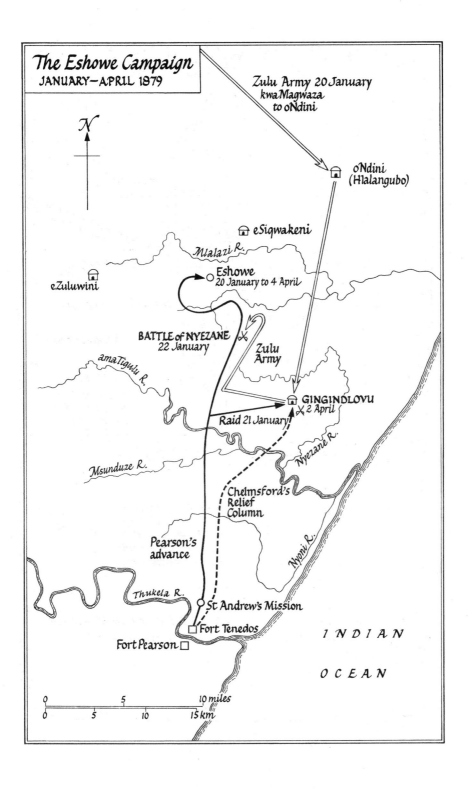

The Eshowe Campaign
JANUARY–APRIL 1879

N

Zulu Army 20 January
kwaMagwaza
to oNdini

oNdini
(Hlalangubo)

eSiqwakeni

Mlalazi R.

Eshowe
20 January to 4 April

eZuluwini

BATTLE of NYEZANE
22 January

Zulu
Army

amaTigulu R.

GINGINDLOVU
2 April

Raid 21 January

Msunduze R.

Nyezane R.

Chelmsford's
Relief
Column

Pearson's
advance

Nyoni R.

Thukela R.

St Andrew's Mission

Fort Tenedos

INDIAN

Fort Pearson

OCEAN

| 0 | | 5 | | 10 miles |
| 0 | 5 | | 10 | 15 km |

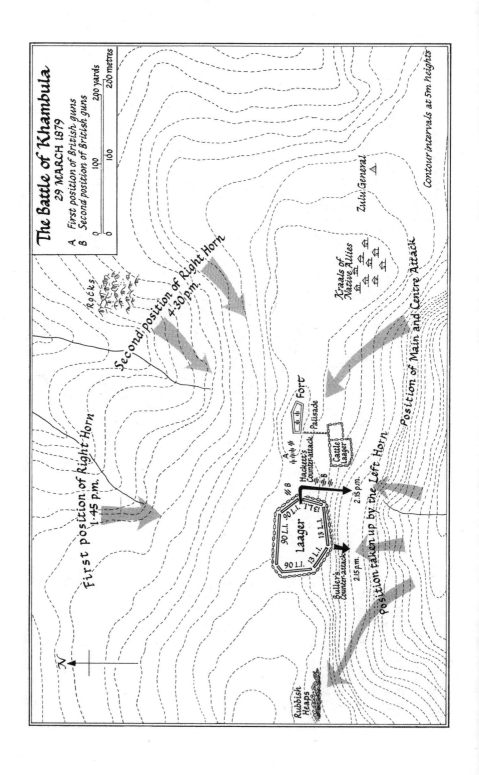

The Battle of Khambula
29 MARCH 1879

A First position of British guns
B Second position of British guns

0   100   200 yards
0   100   200 metres

Contour intervals at 5m heights

Rocks.

Second position of Right Horn
4.30 p.m.

First position of Right Horn
1.45 p.m.

Zulu General

Kraals of Native Allies

Fort
Palisade
Cattle Laager

Hackett's Counter-attack
A
B

Laager
90 L.I.   13 L.I.
90 L.I.   13 L.I.
90 L.I.

Buller's Counter-attack
2.15 p.m.

2.15 p.m.

Position taken up by the Left Horn

Position of Main and Centre Attack

Rubbish Heaps

N

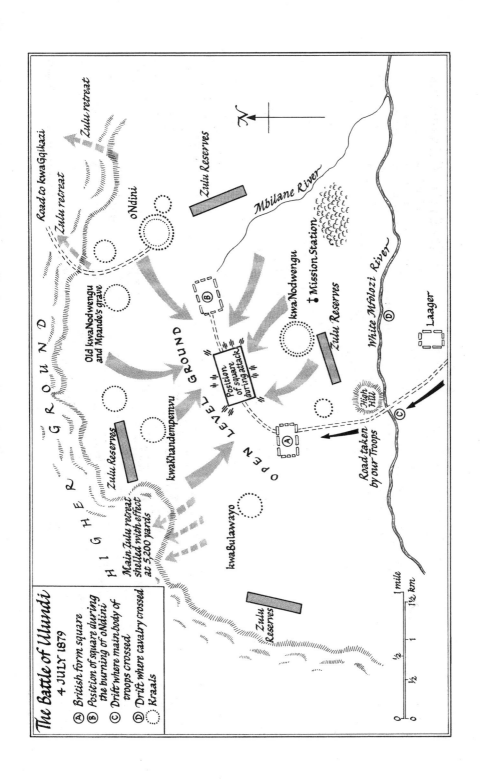

The Battle of Ulundi
4 JULY 1879

Ⓐ British form square
Ⓑ Position of square during
  the burning of oNdini
Ⓒ Drift where main-body of
  troops crossed
Ⓓ Drift where cavalry crossed
◌ Kraals

Road to kwaGqikazi

Zulu retreat
Zulu retreat
Zulu retreat

Zulu Reserves

Mbilane River

oNdini

Old kwaNodwengu
and Mpande's grave

HIGHER GROUND

Ⓑ

Zulu Reserves

kwaNodwengu

† Mission Station

Zulu Reserves

kwaKhandempemvu

Position of square
during attack

OPEN LEVEL GROUND

Ⓐ

High
Hill

Ⓒ

White Mfolozi River

Ⓓ

Laager

Zulu Reserves

Main Zulu retreat
shelled with effect
at 5,200 yards

Road taken
by our Troops

kwaBulawayo

Zulu
Reserves

N

0   ½   1   1 mile
0   ½   1½ km

Prologue
'Here they come!'

Wednesday, 22 January 1879, promised to be another hot, uneventful day at Rorke's Drift on the Buffalo River. Eleven days earlier Lord Chelmsford's main invasion column had splashed across the drift and invaded Zululand. Hampered by minor skirmishes and poor tracks, however, the column's camp had only advanced eleven miles to the rocky lower slopes of a striking, sphinx-like hill called Isandlwana.

The officer in charge of the two ponts★ at the drift was 31-year-old Lieutenant John Chard of the Royal Engineers. Born in Devon to a gentry family said to be descended from Cerdic, king of the West Saxons, Chard had had an uneventful career since struggling to pass out of the Royal Military Academy, Woolwich, in 1868. He had spent most of his service constructing forts in Malta and Bermuda, and had yet to hear a shot fired in anger. He was not even a particularly good engineer, one superior describing him as 'a most useless officer, fit for nothing'; nor did his quiet manner and unprepossessing appearance – short, bearded and 'stupid-looking' – help to compensate for his professional failings. It was perhaps fortunate, then, that his duties at Rorke's Drift were far from arduous.

On reaching Durban with his company of Royal Engineers in early January, Chard had been sent ahead with some tools and a small detachment of sappers to assist the main invasion force. At last, it seemed, he would soldier for real. But on 20 January, the day after his arrival at Rorke's Drift, he was left behind when Chelmsford moved his camp from the Zulu bank of the Buffalo to Isandlwana. During the evening of 21 January, an ambiguous order arrived from Isandlwana. 'The party of R.E. now at Rorke's Drift,'

★ Floating bridges: one was supported by barrels and the other by boats.

it read, 'are to move at once to join the Column under the charge of the NCO.' As there was no mention of an officer, Chard got permission from Major Henry Spalding, commanding the supply depot at Rorke's Drift, to go to Isandlwana the following morning to query the order.

Riding ahead of his men – crammed with their kit into a small wagon – Chard reached the huge tented camp at Isandlwana at around 9.30 a.m. It was already uncomfortably hot, and Chard was perspiring freely beneath his cork sun-helmet and tight-fitting blue patrol jacket. He made straight for the huge Union Jack that hung limply from its pole outside the column office and was given a copy of his orders. He read them with glum resignation: while others would have the chance of glory, his duties were confined to the right, or Natal, bank of the Buffalo, maintaining both the ponts and the road between Rorke's Drift and Helpmakaar. Chard was doubly disgusted when he learnt that Chelmsford and more than half his command had left the camp early that morning to engage what they thought was the main Zulu Army in hills to the southeast. In the meantime large bodies of Zulus, up to a thousand strong, had been seen on high ground to the north-east of the camp, and most of the fighting men were manning a defensive perimeter about half a mile away. Those left in camp were seemingly unconcerned: some were dismantling tents, while others – cooks, bandsmen, farriers and hospital orderlies – went about their business as if on a field day. Borrowing a pair of binoculars, Chard could clearly see 'the enemy moving on the distant hills, and apparently in great force'. Large numbers of them were moving round the back of Isandlwana, in the direction of Rorke's Drift, and it occurred to Chard that they might be planning 'to make a dash at the Ponts'. He decided to head back down the wagon track while he still could and, at the foot of the slope behind Isandlwana, met his small detachment. Ordering the men to continue on foot, he returned to Rorke's Drift with the wagon and its driver.

Spalding, alarmed by Chard's news, decided to ride the ten miles to Helpmakaar to see what had happened to the additional infantry company that was daily expected. He could easily have sent a galloper but, for some unexplained reason, chose to go himself. Before leaving, he checked his copy of the Army List to see who was senior: Chard or Lieutenant Gonville Bromhead, the popular but unexceptional and partially deaf commander of the company of British infantry that been left to guard the supply depot. Having ascertained that Chard had gained his lieutenancy first, Spalding uttered the immortal words: 'You will be in charge, although, of course, nothing will happen, and I shall be back again this evening early.' It was around 2 p.m.

Less than fifteen minutes later, Chard was writing a letter in his tent at the drift, sheltering from the glare of the fierce African sun, when a sentry reported that two riders were approaching from the Zulu side of the river. Once across, they blurted out that the camp at Isandlwana had been attacked and taken by thousands of Zulus. The Zulus, moreover, were heading towards Rorke's Drift. At that moment a message arrived from Bromhead, requesting Chard's presence at the nearby supply depot, a requisitioned Swedish mission at the foot of a large hill known as the Oskarberg.

Chard arrived at the gallop to find the camp being put into a state of defence. Bromhead had received a separate message from a staff officer at Isandlwana that the mission was to be held 'at all costs'. But, after a brief conversation with Chard, orders were given to evacuate the garrison. It was now that Acting Assistant Commissary James Dalton intervened. An experienced former NCO who had been commissioned during the recent Cape Frontier War, he cautioned against flight. The fleet-footed Zulus, he said, would surely catch them in the open. Swayed by Dalton's warning, Chard countermanded the previous order and gave instructions for the defence work to continue.

A little later a colonial officer and eighty black horsemen in the pay of the British appeared from the direction of the river. They had survived the Zulu encirclement at Isandlwana and were willing to help defend the mission. A grateful Chard asked the officer to post his men as mounted scouts and to oppose any Zulu advance for as long as possible. Along with Bromhead's B Company and a detachment of 100 African infantry (only ten of whom were armed with rifles; the rest had spears and shields), Chard now had around 300 able-bodied men under his command and was feeling reasonably confident. This all changed at 4.15 p.m., when shots were heard from behind the Oskarberg and the colonial officer galloped up, saying a huge force of Zulus was on its way and his men were leaving for Helpmakaar. He then rode off himself. Seconds later the 100 African infantry followed suit, leaping over the defences and melting into the surrounding countryside. Their officer and two white NCOs went with him, prompting a fusillade from the outraged British defenders that killed one of the NCOs. The garrison was now reduced to around 100 able-bodied British soldiers and those amongst their thirty-five hospitalized comrades who had been issued with rifles and were willing to fight.

At 4.30 p.m. a lookout on the roof of the storehouse reported the approach of a huge Zulu force. 'How many are there?' asked an anxious Bromhead. At least 4,000, came the response.

The spellbound redcoats were almost relieved when the Zulu vanguard finally appeared: 600 glistening warriors with animal-tail kilts and ostrich-plume headdresses. Carrying rifles, rawhide shields, knobkerries and short stabbing spears, they appeared at the run from the back of the Oskarberg, drove in the thin line of British skirmishers and made straight for the south wall. 'Here they come!' shouted one defender as the mission exploded in a crash of volley fire. The Battle of Rorke's Drift had begun.

1. The Zulus

The Zulu kingdom lasted for just sixty years. At its zenith, in the early decades of the nineteenth century, it covered a huge swathe of south-east Africa: from the borders of modern-day Swaziland and Mozambique in the north to central Natal in the south; from the dramatic cliffs of the Drakensberg Mountains in the west to the golden beaches of the Indian Ocean in the east. Though smaller by the time its last king, Cetshwayo kaMpande, was crowned in 1873, it was still 'the most politically sophisticated, administratively integrated and militarily powerful' black state in sub-Saharan Africa.

Its rise had been meteoric. Until the turn of the nineteenth century, there was no dominant power in the region. Most tribal chiefs were grouped under a paramount chieftain who exercised a loose, almost nominal overlordship. But a combination of increased population, destructive farming methods and competition for European trade put pressure on these paramountcies to centralize and expand. Two of the most successful were the Ndwandwe to the north of the Black Mfolozi River and the Mthethwa to the south. Among the Mthethwa's fifty subordinate chiefs was Senzangakhona of the Zulu.

The founder of the Zulu tribe was a Nguni* chieftain called Mandalela, who, in the late seventeenth century, migrated with a handful of followers from upper Natal to a small patch of land on the Middle White Mfolozi River. His clansmen took their name from his son and successor, Zulu, and were henceforth known as amaZulu ('People of the Heavens'). When Senzangakhona became chief in 1781, the Zulu tribe had swelled to 1,500 people whose kraals†

* A subdivision of the Bantu people, several hundred clans strong, that slowly spread across south-east Africa in the sixteenth and seventeenth centuries.
† Traditional Zulu settlements consisting of a cattle enclosure ringed by huts.

were spread over ten square miles of rolling grassland; but it was still no match for the powerful Mthethwa to the south-east. All this would change during the rule of Senzangakhona's eldest son, Shaka.

Born in 1787 to the Zulu chief's third wife, Nandi, of the neighbouring Langeni tribe, Shaka was never recognized as Senzangakhona's heir because he was conceived before his mother had been taken as an official wife. The Zulu elders tried to excuse the inopportune pregnancy by saying that Nandi was suffering from an intestinal beetle, or *shaka*, and the name stuck. So too did the stigma of his ill-timed birth: Shaka and his mother, a quarrelsome and headstrong woman, were never accepted by the Zulus. In 1794 the pair were sent to live with the Langeni after Nandi is said to have attacked one of her husband's headmen with a knobkerrie. Shaka did not stay long. A well-developed boy with more than his share of Nandi's aggression, he clashed with the chief's son and was packed off to a subclan of the Mthethwa. There his martial abilities brought him to the notice of the paramount chief, Jobe, and, after Jobe's death in 1807, to that of his successor, Dingiswayo. For nine years Shaka served in Dingiswayo's army as it subdued tribe after tribe (including the Zulu). It was during this period of almost ceaseless war that he devised the ruthless political and military philosophy that would transform the fortunes of his father's clan. Previously tribal conflict had been little more than a ritual show of force with few casualties, leaving the 'defeated' clan in a position to restart hostilities at a later date. Shaka changed all this by fighting wars of annihilation in which the surviving warriors were incorporated into their victors' military system. He also revolutionized the weapons and tactics of war. Fighting at a distance with light throwing spears was rarely decisive, so he introduced a short, stabbing *assegai** with a broad, heavy blade that could be used only at close quarters. He turned the traditional cowhide shield into an offensive weapon by instructing his men to hook its left edge over

---

* Called the *iKlwa* (the sucking sound it made as it was withdrawn from flesh). Some historians have suggested that the *iKlwa* was modified from a stabbing spear already in use by the Mthethwa (see Laband, *Rise and Fall*, 37).

the left edge of an opponent's shield; a powerful backhand sweep would then expose the left side of the enemy to an assegai thrust. And, crucially, he introduced the tactics of envelopment by dividing his army into three parts: a central column to pin down an opposing force, and two flanking parties to surround it. As Zulu king he would refine these tactics further into the standard formation known as *izimpondo zankomo* ('the horns of the buffalo'). It required four distinct elements: the 'chest' that closed with the enemy and held it fast; the two 'horns' that raced either side of the enemy and, having met, fought their way back towards the 'chest'; and the 'loins', or reserve, which was placed behind the 'chest' and deployed only in an emergency.

When his father, Senzangakhona, died in 1816, Shaka used Dingiswayo's support to seize the Zulu chieftainship. The designated heir was quietly murdered and Shaka installed in his place. He wasted no time introducing the military system he had developed with the Mthethwa and, within a year, the Zulu lands had quadrupled in size.* Shaka, however, was still Dingiswayo's vassal. This all changed in 1817, when the Ndwandwe decisively defeated the Mthethwa and killed Dingiswayo. Shaka could have intervened in the battle but chose not to, possibly seeing an opportunity to throw off the Mthethwa yoke. If so, it was a risky strategy, because the victorious Ndwandwe now marched against the Zulus. Shaka's numerically inferior *impi*† met them at kwaGqokli Hill in 1818 and won a close-run victory. Within a year, through a combination of diplomacy and military conquest, he had brought all the tribes between the White Mfolozi and Thukela rivers under his control. This augmentation of force enabled him to rout the Ndwandwe again in 1819, compelling the defeated tribe to move its power base north of the Phongolo into what is now southern Swaziland.

As Shaka's authority increased, so did the size of his army, with

---

* One of the first tribes to be absorbed was his mother's, the Langeni, who had cast him out as a boy.

† Zulu army, made up of several *amabutho*, or age-grade regiments.

military conscription compulsory for all adult males. For two to three years, boys from as young as fourteen lived in *amakhanda* (military kraals), where they herded cattle, tended crops and received military instruction. They were then formed into *ama-butho*, or age-grade regiments, and spent another eight months together before returning to their homes, where, for a quarter of the year, they served as Territorials in the district amakhanda. Only for national festivals and in times of war would they remobilize as a regiment. Shaka even brought girls into the military system by grouping them in amabutho for the purpose of marriage. Not only did they have to wait for Shaka's permission to wed, they also had to choose their partners from those male amabutho who had been given leave to wear the *isicoco*,★ or headring, a privilege rarely granted before the age of thirty-five. The award of the isicoco marked the attainment of adulthood, full acceptance into the village community and the right to marry and set up home. By withholding it until a relatively late age, Shaka was trying to keep young Zulu men more firmly under the authority of their tribal elders and, by extension, their king.

Within a few years Shaka's army had increased from its original nucleus of 350 to 20,000 men, his territory from one hundred square miles to 11,500. The many tribes he subdued began to refer to themselves as Zulus, so that the original clan of 3,000 had soon swelled to a nation of a quarter of a million. Shaka was no longer fighting wars of survival but of conquest, and the Zulus, a pastoral people who measured their wealth in terms of cattle, grew rich on the huge herds they looted from their victims. By 1824 the Zulus had laid waste much of modern Natal and, in the process, set off a stampede to the south† that consumed clan after clan, until it petered out on the borders of Britain's Cape Colony.

Shaka was just as brutal at home, ordering random executions

★ A fibre circlet sewn into the hair, coated with gum and then greased and polished.

† Known as the *mfecane*, or the 'crushing', though in its widest sense the term applies to *all* the wars and migrations caused by rival emergent states north of the Thukela and not just to Zulu aggression.

for 'offences' as insignificant as sneezing while he was eating. A click of his fingers and the unfortunate sneezer would be brained with a knobkerrie. It was, perhaps, inevitable that such a violent ruler would die violently. Before that could happen, an event took place that would, ultimately, spell doom for the Zulu nation. In 1824, two years after a Royal Navy expedition first surveyed the coast of south-east Africa, a Cape Town trading company established a settlement at Port Natal.* Later that year some of the settlers visited Shaka in his vast royal kraal at kwaBulawayo, 120 miles inland from Port Natal, and were given permission to remain on what was, technically, Zulu land. One of the settlers, a young English freebooter by the name of Henry Francis Fynn, stayed on at kwaBulawayo at Shaka's request and, as luck would have it, was still there when a Ndwandwe assassin narrowly failed to kill his host. Fynn helped to nurse Shaka back to health and, as a reward, he and his trading company were granted title to Port Natal and 3,500 square miles of hinterland.

Despite the arrival of the white settlers, who kept in regular contact with kwaBulawayo, Shaka's depredations continued. They reached their climax with his hysterical reaction to the death of his mother, Nandi, in October 1827. Up to 7,000 mourners were killed in the general massacre that followed several indiscriminate executions. On Shaka's instructions, Nandi was buried with ten handmaidens – still alive, and with their arms and legs broken – to keep her company. Twelve thousand warriors were left to guard the grave for a year, supplied with cattle from every kraal in the land. Shaka also issued edicts that no women were to get pregnant (on pain of death), no crops were to be planted and no milk drunk for a year. As sour milk (*amasi*) and maize were the two staples of the Zulu diet, this was tantamount to a starvation order. Fortunately Shaka came to his senses and revoked the edicts after three months. But the damage to his prestige had been done. His people had always respected his single-minded purpose, if not his violent

* Renamed Durban in 1835 after the governor of the Cape Colony, Sir Benjamin D'Urban.

methods; now that violence had gone too far and he would have to go. The question was: who would have the courage to assassinate him?

The conspirators emerged, not surprisingly, from his own family: partly because they could get close to him, and partly because they had the most to gain. The chief plotters were his aunt Mkabayi, his half-brothers Dingane and Mhlangana, and his personal attendant Mbopha, whose mother, it was said, had been executed on Shaka's orders. The act was carried out on 24 September 1828 at Shaka's kwaDakuza homestead. The army was away campaigning and Shaka was virtually unprotected. Emerging from his hiding place, Mhlangana stabbed Shaka in the shoulder. As Shaka turned to face his assailant, Dingane stepped forward and stabbed him in the side. 'What is the matter, children of my father?' implored Shaka, before stumbling to the entrance of his kraal, where he collapsed. His cries for mercy went unheeded, and he was finished off in a flurry of thrusts from the weapon he had invented.

Dingane succeeded Shaka, but only after killing his rival and fellow assassin Mhlangana.* Crucially he gained the support of the army by allowing all the regiments to endulge in pre-marital intercourse – Shaka had limited their carnal pleasures to *hlobonga*, or non-penetrative sex – and by permitting a number of the senior ones to marry. He also reduced their military obligations by ending Shaka's ceaseless wars of conquest. Yet the amabutho were still regularly called on to subdue unruly tribes on the fringes of Zulu territory.

A far greater threat to Dingane's authority, however, was the gradual encroachment of white settlers. Port Natal was growing in size, as was the number of Zulu refugees who sought white protection. By the mid 1830s more than 2,500 malcontents were living in kraals close to the port. When the white settlers refused to repatriate them, Dingane severed all trading links. But it was the

---

* A further twelve half-brothers were murdered after Dingane invited them to make free with the women of his *isiGodlo*, or harem. The following day they were bludgeoned to death.

arrival of the Voortrekkers in 1837 that posed the most serious challenge to the Zulu state. Between 1834 and 1840 around 15,000 Boers★ left the eastern Cape in their ox-drawn wagons and trekked north in search of new territory. They did so to escape hostile black Xhosa tribes and, more importantly, British colonial authority, which was keen to limit their independence but did not have the means to guarantee their security. They particularly resented the Cape Colony's emancipation of slaves in 1828 and its insistence on equality of both black and white before the law. There was also – since the consolidation of the eastern Cape frontier in the 1820s – a perceived shortage of land.

The Voortrekkers moved in two main directions: north beyond the Vaal River, with the intention of establishing trading links with the Portuguese at Delagoa Bay; and north-east towards Natal and its own sea outlet at Durban (as Port Natal became in 1835). The majority – under Piet Retief, the chief commandant of the Burgher Council – headed for Natal, and by the end of 1837 had reached the Drakensberg passes. They were welcomed by the settlers at Durban as potential neighbours and allies. Dingane was not so accommodating. When Piet Retief and a party of seventeen men arrived at his capital at uMgungundlovu in early November, Dingane was outwardly friendly and hinted that the Boers might be allowed to settle in Natal if they recovered cattle stolen from a client tribe, the Hlubi. Retief and 109 armed followers returned with the cattle in early February 1838 and, as a reward, were given a document that ceded to them much of Natal. But it was a ruse, and on 6 February, the day of their departure, Retief and his men were seized during a celebratory breakfast and dragged to the execution hill, where, one by one, they were bludgeoned to death. Retief was forced to watch until all his men had been killed. Then he too shared their fate. Dingane now sent his impis against the unsuspecting Boers camped in the foothills of the Drakensberg. On the 16th, camps along the Bloukrans and its tributaries were surprised and whole families massacred. These attacks gave the

★ Dutch-speaking farmers.

other Boer camps time to form their wagons into laagers,* from which, on 17 February, they launched a mounted counter-stroke. The Zulus were driven back with heavy losses, though they took with them 25,000 Boer cattle and thousands of sheep and horses.

The Boers responded with a raid across the Mzinyathi (or Buffalo) River in April, but they were ambushed near eThaleni Hill by a powerful Zulu force and forced to withdraw with the loss of ten men, including their leader Piet Uys, and his fourteen-year-old son. The white settlers at Durban, meanwhile, launched attacks of their own using African auxiliaries. Some early successes made them overconfident, and in mid April, during a foray across the Lower Thukela, a large settler-led force was cut off by a Zulu impi and destroyed almost to a man. A week later, as the surviving white settlers took refuge on a ship in the bay, the Zulus sacked Durban.

In August a three-day Zulu assault on a heavily fortified Boer laager at Veglaer, in the Bushman's River Valley, was beaten off. Again the Zulus retired with most of the Trekkers' livestock. Short on food, crowded in laagers that were rife with disease, the Boers were forced to take the initiative. That December a fighting column of sixty-four wagons, under the new chief commandant, Andries Pretorius, crossed the Ncome River and, warned by scouts of the imminent arrival of the Zulu Army, formed a defensive laager on a spit of land near the west bank. There, on 16 December 1838, the 600 or so defenders fought for two hours to repulse wave after wave of charging Zulus. So devastating was the fire from the Boers' muzzle-loading muskets that not a single Zulu got within ten yards of the laager. By the time the mounted pursuit was broken off, a quarter of the Zulu force of 12,000 lay dead, most of them 'heaped like pumpkins' on the killing ground between the banks of the river and a neighbouring donga.† The water is said to have run red with Zulu blood, and ever since the Ncome has been called Blood River by the Boers. Their casualties were confined to four

---

* A defensive circle of wagons, lashed together end-to-end with the shaft of each wagon fitting under its neighbour's chassis.
† Dry watercourse running only in times of heavy rain.

men wounded in the chase, including Pretorius, who was speared in the hand.

The Boers followed up their victory by firing Dingane's capital and returning to Natal with 5,000 cattle. The majority then settled with their families on the central plateau, fifty miles inland from Durban, where they traced out the beginnings of a town called Pietermaritzburg in honour of their fallen leaders, Piet Retief and Gerrit Maritz. It was here that the Boers proclaimed the 'Free Province of New Holland in South East Africa'* with a Volksraad, or 'People's Assembly', led by Pretorius. But, hamstrung by internal wrangling, a lack of money and – ultimately – the hostility of the British, this nascent Boer state would not stay independent for long. Its short life, however, was enough to cause Dingane's downfall. On becoming king in 1828, Dingane murdered those half-brothers he saw as a threat to his rule. Of the four he allowed to live, the senior was Mpande, an amiable, unaggressive and intelligent man who exercised little authority. In the autumn of 1839, fearing assassination, Mpande fled to Natal with 17,000 followers and was given the Volksraad's permission to settle south of the Thukela. Within a few months he was back in Zululand with a large impi and a Boer commando at his back. His emigrant warriors defeated the main Zulu Army in a bloody battle in late January 1840, causing Dingane to flee to the north, where he was eventually murdered by local tribesmen. The Boers proclaimed Mpande king of the Zulus on 10 February and, in return, were allowed to take away 36,000 head of cattle.

The British authorities in Cape Town observed these developments with growing unease. The Punishment Act of 1836 meant that even Voortrekkers were technically under British jurisdiction, and their actions towards Dingane – an independent chieftain who had recently signed a treaty with the British – were seen as unwarranted aggression. Boer high-handedness continued with the extermination of the amaBaca, a small bandit clan that lived on the edge of the Drakensburg, and the expulsion of most of the tribal

* Also known as the Republic of Natalia.

fragments that had survived Shaka's holocaust to a reserve in the south. To curb the Boers, the governor of the Cape sent British troops to Durban in 1842. The inevitable clash took place in May, when a British night attack on Boer positions at Congella, near Durban, was beaten back with heavy loss. The victorious Boers proceeded to besiege the hastily improvised British laager, which was packed with 500 men, women and children and low on food and water.

This action, which was seen by the Cape authorities as an act of rebellion, was to seal the Boer Republic's fate. All available British troops were ordered to Durban, and, in late June 1842, the 34-day siege was lifted by five companies of the 25th Foot, who went on to secure Pietermaritzburg. A year later – chiefly to put an end to land squabbles among the Boers, the British settlers and the African tribes – Natal was annexed by the British Crown. One of the first acts of the new high commissioner was to sign a treaty with King Mpande that fixed the Natal–Zululand border along the line of the Thukela and Buffalo rivers.

In 1845, after much consultation, the British government organized Natal not as a separate colony but as a province of the Cape Colony, with its own lieutenant-governor and executive council of five members. Many Boers had already left for their territories – later the Transvaal and the Orange Free State* – to the north. Others now followed, and by 1848 there were fewer than a hundred Boer families in the whole of Natal. Their places were taken by European settlers, returning African clans who had fled from Shaka's rule and refugees from Zululand. By the mid 1850s there were 150,000 so-called 'Natal Kaffirs', and their numbers would swell to a quarter of a million by 1879.

Mpande was not, as some historians have suggested, a peace-loving monarch who ruled with a light touch. But, given the choice, he preferred feasting, dancing and the pleasures of his

---

* The Sand River Convention of February 1852 released the Boer settlers north of the Vaal from their status as British subjects. Two years later the British abandoned their sovereignty over the Boer-settled territory north of the Orange River, which became the Orange Free State.

isiGodlo to the rigours of a campaign. The dissipation told in the end: he grew so fat that, in later life, he had to be transported about his kraal in a small cart. He also fathered twenty-three sons. The eldest to survive was Cetshwayo, who, like Shaka before him, was not expected to succeed his father. A Zulu of rank tended to marry a junior wife when still young. This meant that his first-born was rarely his heir; that position was reserved for the eldest son of his Great Wife, who was usually chosen relatively late in life to reduce the risk of usurpation. Though Mpande never took an official Great Wife, he still did not confirm Cetshwayo as his heir, because he feared a weakening of his authority. Instead he let it be known that Mbuyazi, the eldest son of his second wife, was his favoured successor.

Cetshwayo was not a man to submit without a fight. Born in 1832 to Mpande's first wife, Ngqumbazi, of the Zungu clan, his name means 'The Slandered One' and probably refers to some gratuitous slight by Dingane at the time of his birth. Like his father, he lived in constant fear of Dingane and may even have welcomed his brief exile in Natal from 1839 to 1840. It was there that his father acknowledged him – albeit temporarily – as his heir to appease the ruling Volksraad. After the Boers had been driven out of Natal by the British, Mpande was free to renounce his earlier decision; but Cetshwayo never forgot his father's endorsement. In 1851, along with Mbuyazi and six other princes, he joined the newly formed uThulwana ibutho and fought with distinction the following year in Swaziland. His *induna*, or regimental commander, was Chief Mnyamana of the powerful Buthelezi clan. A respected, clever and politically astute man, he became Cetshwayo's mentor and would prove a powerful ally in his conflict with Mbuyazi.

Even at the age of twenty, Cetshwayo was an impressive sight: tall, broad-chested and handsome, with the regal bearing that he would retain for the rest of his life. He had, at the same time, slightly bandy legs and the immense thighs typical of the Zulu royal house. Later in life he grew fat, but the muscles beneath remained firm and he kept fit by walking up to six miles a day. In his prime his bearded face was broad and unmarked, with large eyes and a pleasing countenance. He was darker than most Zulus and flushed easily when angered or embarrassed. An intelligent man with a good memory, he was a 'walking repository of Zulu lore'. To his inferiors, he was genial and open; to his friends, faithful and considerate. But he could also be autocratic, headstrong and ruthless when the occasion demanded. Cetshwayo was a dangerous man – which is why his father tried to sideline him. He failed.

By the mid 1850s Cetshwayo had built up a sizeable following among the leading princes, chiefs and amabutho. The trial of strength with his brother Mbuyazi took place at Ndondakusuka, not far from the Lower Thukela River, on 2 December 1857. Cetshwayo's army of 20,000 uSuthu warriors greatly outnumbered his brother's much smaller force of 7,000, and the battle should have been a foregone conclusion. But Mbuyazi's army had been stiffened by a small force of Natal policemen and white hunters, under an assistant border agent called John Dunn,★ and its firepower helped to repulse Cetshwayo's right horn. The respite was temporary, because Cetshwayo's commanders shifted the main weight of the uSuthu attack to its left horn and, when it broke through, Mbuyazi's army disintegrated. No quarter was given, as the defeated warriors and their families were pursued to the banks of the Thukela. Five thousand of Mbuyazi's soldiers and a further 9,000 non-combatants are said to have perished. Mbuyazi and five of his brothers were among the slain.

Cetshwayo, still only twenty-four, had removed the chief obstacle to his succession. A further five years would elapse before Mpande formally recognized him as his heir. But in 1857 the king initiated a partial reconciliation by pledging him a major role in the government of the country in return for keeping the peace. For the remaining years of his rule, Mpande continued to officiate at the great national festivals and to oversee his army. Only he could authorize the formation of new regiments and the marriage of existing ones. For all intents and purposes, however, Cetshwayo was the real power in the land.

★ Dunn survived the battle to become Cetshwayo's white induna.

A complicating factor in the uneasy relationship between father and son was the Boer pressure on Zulu territory. In 1852 a small number of Boer families began to settle in the narrow wedge of fertile land between the Buffalo and Blood rivers. According to the boundary agreement between Mpande and the Natal authorities of 1843, these acres were part of Zululand. But the flight of Chief Langilabele's Hlubi clan to Natal in 1848 had left a vacuum that the Boers were anxious to fill. Unwilling to take on these well-armed settlers, Mpande ceded the land in 1854 and the Boers named their tiny state the Republic of Utrecht. There the matter might have ended, had the Boers, hungry for more land, not started to infiltrate east of the Blood River. The issue was further complicated when the Utrecht Republic was voluntarily absorbed by the neighbouring Transvaal Republic★ in 1859; it was henceforth known as the Utrecht District, with a *landdrost*, or district magistrate, chosen by Pretoria. Now the Utrecht Boers' land claims had become those of the much more powerful Transvaal Boers, who, at the same time, were moving into the Disputed Territory at the source of the Phongolo River ruled by Cetshwayo's half-brother and rival Hamu. Aware that Cetshwayo was anxious to neutralize any rivals for the throne, the Boers were keen to do a deal. The opportunity arose when two young Zulu princes, sons of Mpande's favourite wife, fled to Utrecht. The Boers offered to hand over the princes and support Cetshwayo's claim to the Zulu throne in return for his recognition of their unspecified claims to land east of the Blood River. Cetshwayo agreed and, in March 1861, signed the Treaty of Waaihoek.

Three months later, encouraged by the British, who were against Boer expansion, Cetshwayo renounced the treaty. But the Boers continued to settle east of the Blood River and, for a time, war was the likely outcome. It was prevented by the Natal authorities; fearing a Zulu invasion, they moved troops to their northern border. Anxious to avoid a war with Britain, Cetshwayo kept his dogs of war on the leash. Mpande completed his humiliation when

★ From 1860 also known as the South African Republic.

he agreed, in August 1861, to honour the Treaty of Waaihoek. It was a concession that would return to haunt Cetshwayo and, ultimately, cost him his kingdom.

Mpande died in September 1872* and Cetshwayo was, at last, the undisputed ruler of Zululand. One of his first acts was to invite a representative of the Natal government for talks. He hoped that the backing of the British would strengthen the position of the monarch, which had been weakened by the power-sharing of the previous sixteen years. The regional barons, in particular, had taken advantage of the 'dual monarchy' to reassert their local authority. They were unwilling to allow any central interference in the running of their chiefdoms and had even begun to exercise the royal prerogative of life and death. Cetshwayo's great fear was that a group of these chiefs might unite to promote the cause of one of his brothers, no fewer than five of whom were living in exile in Natal. It was with the aim of counterbalancing these regional chiefs and undermining his rivals to the throne, as well as eliciting support against Boer land claims, that Cetshwayo invited Theophilus Shepstone, the secretary for Native Affairs in Natal, to attend his coronation.

The son of a Wesleyan missionary, Shepstone had been brought up among the African tribes of the eastern Cape, where he became fluent in Xhosa. He first arrived in Durban in 1838 when, as the interpreter to a British mission, he was sent to negotiate with Dingane. The talks led to the signing of a peace treaty with the Zulus, and, with his task completed, Shepstone departed for the Cape. He returned to the then British colony in 1845 as diplomatic agent to the Native Tribes, a post upgraded to secretary for Native Affairs in 1851. His task was to regulate the lives of the African tribes within Natal and to maintain diplomatic links with all black states in the region. His so-called 'Native Policy' was to concentrate the Natal tribes in 'locations' where they could live in kraals under the authority of traditional chiefs who would, in turn, be overseen

---

* The exact date is obscure because the Zulus did not officially acknowledge his death until many months later.

by white officials. The long-term plan was to erode the authority of the hereditary chiefs by introducing 'Western' methods of agriculture and trade. The system was funded by a hut tax, which had the bonus of pushing men out of the locations and into the wage market. The disputed north-western frontier of Zululand entered Shepstone's thinking at this stage only as a possible outlet for Natal's growing African population.

When Cetshwayo's invitation reached Pietermaritzburg, the capital of Natal, in the spring of 1873, Shepstone was quick to accept. His aim was to secure British influence over Cetshwayo by 'crowning' him and thereby legitimizing his rule. This, he hoped, would not only safeguard Natal's inhabitants but would also open up valuable trade routes into the African interior. Shepstone entered Zululand on 8 August with an escort of 110 white troops of the various Natal volunteer corps and 300 African auxiliaries. Finally, on 28 August, after much delay, he met with Cetshwayo at a military kraal in the Mahlabathini Plain. During the two-day discussions, Cetshwayo insisted that all Boer settlements below the Drakensberg, including the whole of the Utrecht district, were rightfully part of Zululand. To prevent further encroachment, he offered to cede all the Disputed Territory to the British. Shepstone could not accept, knowing that the home government would not wish to upset the Boers. His hope that Cetshwayo might want to create a buffer zone between the Zulus and the Boers by ceding some undisputed land to the British was not realized. Instead Cetshwayo suggested an offensive/defensive alliance; but Shepstone was unwilling to tie Britain to Zululand's quarrels. So it was agreed that relations would continue on the 'same footing' as before. Common ground was reached on a handful of other issues: no existing missionaries to be expelled from Zululand without the permission of the Natal government; migrant labourers to be given safe passage through Zululand; and new laws to be promulgated at the coronation ceremony.

Shepstone was impressed by his host's powers of negotiation. He reported:

Cetywayo is a man of considerable ability, much force of character, and
has a dignified manner; in all conversations with him he was remarkably
frank and straightforward, and he ranks in every respect far above any
Native Chief I have ever had to do with. I do not think that his disposition is very warlike; even if it is, his obesity will impose prudence;
but he is naturally proud of the military traditions of his family, especially
the policy and deeds of his uncle and predecessor, Chaka, to which he
made frequent reference. His sagacity enables him, however, to see clearly
the bearing of the new circumstances by which he is surrounded, and the
necessity for so adjusting his policy as to suit them.

The coronation* took place on 1 September in a large marquee
erected by the British. Shepstone began by addressing the large
audience of councillors, chiefs and amabutho in perfect Zulu,
setting out the terms of British support and gaining Cetshwayo's
verbal assent. Then he led Cetshwayo into the marquee, where he
placed a scarlet mantle on his shoulders and a gaudy crown (got up
by the master-tailor of the 75th Foot) on his head. At a signal, the
Natal band struck up and the artillery fired a seventeen-gun salute.

The terms Shepstone read out – later known as the 'coronation
laws' – were as follows: an end to indiscriminate bloodshed in
Zululand; no one to be condemned without trial or appeal to the
king; no life to be taken without the king's consent; fines to replace
the death sentence for minor crimes. Cetshwayo had agreed to
these laws as a means of reasserting the monarch's power over his
great chiefs. In this he was to be disappointed, because the chiefs
continued to execute on their own authority. Furthermore,
Cetshwayo's rule was hampered by his *iziKhulu*, the great chiefs
who made up his council of state. Sometimes they frustrated his
plans; sometimes he got his way. He was, as a result, more a
constitutional than an absolute monarch.

Shepstone's motive for promoting the 'coronation laws' was a
mixture of philanthropy and expediency. On the one hand he

---

* Cetshwayo had already gone through a Zulu coronation ceremony, much to
Shepstone's irritation.

wished to 'civilize' Zululand by introducing Western-style laws; on the other he knew that any breach of this verbal covenant would provide a convenient excuse for colonial intervention in the future. So it proved.

2. Confederation

In February 1874, not long after Theophilus Shepstone's 'coronation' report reached London, William Gladstone's Liberal government was defeated in the General Election and replaced by Benjamin Disraeli's Tories. The 64-year-old Liberal prime minister had shocked the political world in January by announcing the immediate dissolution of Parliament in an attempt to secure a clear mandate for his most radical reform yet: the abolition of income tax. But the British people were tired of 'being improved' by Gladstone's reforming administration and were suspicious of its anti-imperial fringe. The Tories – who offered stability at home and the protection of British interests abroad – won 350 seats to the Liberals' 245, and enjoyed an outright majority in the House of Commons for the first time since 1841. No one was more delighted than Queen Victoria. She had admired the Whig★ government of Lord Melbourne in her youth but had since reverted to her essentially conservative type. She regarded Gladstone, in particular, as a dangerous reformer who lacked sufficient regard for either Britain's institutions or its prestige. Disraeli, on the other hand – despite his Jewish antecedents† – she saw as both a patriot and a passionate supporter of monarchy. For his part, he knew that she was susceptible to flattery and laid it on with a shovel. 'I plight my troth to the kindest of *Mistresses*,' he declared on kissing hands at Windsor.

The new colonial secretary was Henry Herbert, fourth earl of Carnarvon. Capable and hard-working – but sensitive to criticism and known to colleagues as 'Twitters' – Carnarvon had served in the post during Lord Derby's government of 1866–7, when, as a

---

★ The Whigs were the forerunners of the Liberals.
† He had converted to Anglicanism at the age of twelve.

35-year-old, he had introduced the bill for the confederation★ of Canada. He would eventually propose a similar scheme for South Africa. But his initial reaction to Shepstone's foray into Zululand was unfavourable. 'I greatly doubt the wisdom of the expedition,' he minuted, since it 'pledges us to a protectorate or something very like it.' This, in turn, might bring Britain into conflict with the Transvaal. But, having met Shepstone during the latter's visit to London in autumn 1874, Carnarvon was partially won over, telling Sir Benjamin Pine, lieutenant-governor of Natal, that he placed 'much confidence in [Shepstone's] belief that it was very important not to lose this opportunity of causing his influence to be asserted and recognised'.

The Langilabele† affair of 1873/4 – when the Natal authorities used excessive force to punish the Hlubi clan for not giving up its firearms – eventually cost Pine his job. He was replaced as lieutenant-governor in 1875 by Major-General Sir Garnet Wolseley, the darling of the Victorian public and known to them as 'our only General'. Born in Dublin in 1833, to an Anglo-Irish family that traced its Saxon descent from before the Conqueror, Wolseley was a talented, vain and fiercely ambitious officer who had proved his courage and genius for organization in countless campaigns. He had been wounded as an infantry officer in Burma and the Crimea, served on the staff during the Indian Mutiny and the China War of 1860, and commanded his own force during the Red River Expedition of 1870 and the Ashanti War of 1873–4. During this last campaign his logistic arrangements had enabled a British column to penetrate the jungles of the Gold Coast and burn the Ashanti capital of Kumasi. He was rewarded with a knighthood, £2,500 a year and promotion to major-general. But Wolseley's talents were not confined to war. He was also a keen military theorist and reformer who had written the seminal *Soldier's Pocket-Book for Field Service* in 1869 and, as assistant adjutant-general at the War

---

★ A union of separate states into a single political entity.
† The same Chief Langilabele of the Hlubi who fled with his clan from Zululand to Natal in 1848.

Office in 1871, had worked with Secretary of State Cardwell to introduce a host of military reforms. His reputation as a reformer had earned him the lifelong enmity of the 'conservative' clique at the Horse Guards,★ led by HRH the duke of Cambridge, the commander-in-chief of the British Army. Cambridge was Queen Victoria's first cousin – a grandson of George III – and a dangerous enemy, not least because he had the ear of the monarch. 'The Queen,' wrote Wolseley, 'naturally leans upon the opinions on military subjects expressed by Her Royal Cousin, & when it is impressed upon Her that those holding opposite views are not loyal subjects, their advice is naturally disregarded.' Wolseley was too famous an officer for Cambridge to destroy out of pique. But one professional slip and his career would be over.

Wolseley's task in Natal was to reform Shepstone's 'Native Policy'. Carnarvon had come to the conclusion that the tribal chiefs in Natal were too independent and insubordinate. The colonists were in constant fear of an uprising and so tended to regard any sign of disaffection as an excuse for repressive measures. The upshot was a general lack of control leading to the occasional savage crackdown such as that of Langilabele's Hlubi. What was needed, Carnarvon thought, was the scrapping of the lieutenant-governor's arbitrary power as 'supreme chief', and the replacement of the tribal system by individual citizenship, of chiefs by white magistrates, and of native law by the colony's common law. But Wolseley was unable to institute these reforms because of Shepstone's 'objection that we are too weak to run the risk of the excitement that any such attempt on my part to carry out existing laws would occasion'.

In Wolseley's opinion, the proximity of the Zulu kingdom made it even more difficult to introduce reforms in Natal with the existing military presence. The solution proposed by Wolseley and Shepstone was to annex Zululand. It would solve the problem of Natal's surplus population; it would make it easier to introduce a

---

★ The original headquarters of the British Army in Whitehall. In 1871 the headquarters were moved to the War Office but Cambridge continued to write letters on paper headed 'Horse Guards'.

'new native policy' in Natal; it would end the threat of a Zulu invasion of Natal; and it would facilitate the eventual confederation of South African states by preventing the two independent Boer republics – the Transvaal and the Orange Free State – from gaining independent access to the sea. Nor would annexation be difficult to attain. According to Shepstone – an acknowledged expert in 'native' matters – it would take only a thousand British soldiers to win over Zululand because Cetshwayo was a murderous tyrant whom his subjects could not wait to see the back of. This assessment could not have been further from the mark, but Wolseley, a newcomer to the region, was convinced.

Carnarvon's response to Wolseley's promptings was not enthusiastic. As colonial secretary, it was his job to see the wider picture, and it had never been imperial policy to expand British possessions in South Africa beyond the strategically placed ports of Cape Town and Simonstown. Most of the acquisitions since had come about as a result of local pressure from land-hungry Boers, unruly tribes, white traders and Christian missionaries. They had been sanctioned by the 'man on the spot' – the governor or high commissioner – and only after the event by the British government. Gladstone's Liberal administration of 1868–74 took this 'static' imperial policy one step further by encouraging Britain's white colonies to become self-governing and self-sufficient so as to allow the withdrawal of costly imperial garrisons. The prerequisite to such a withdrawal in South Africa was, as far as the Liberals were concerned, the confederation of the various colonies and republics into a single political entity. Carnarvon also supported confederation: not as a cost-cutting exercise – he strongly opposed the removal of British troops from South Africa – but as a way of spreading British influence and civilization throughout the region without the need for direct rule.

Carnarvon's initial attempt to hold a confederation conference in Cape Town failed, because the Cape government of J. C. Molteno*
– unwilling to share the security expenses of the other colonies –

* The Cape Colony had been self-governing since 1872.

refused to attend. A second conference in London in 1876 was also boycotted by the Cape government and that of the Transvaal. It went ahead none the less – with representatives from Natal, the Orange Free State and Griqualand West★ – and, not surprisingly, achieved nothing. Realizing that the colonies and states of South Africa would not embrace confederation by choice, Carnarvon opted for coercion. The first state that needed to be brought to heel, he decided, was the Transvaal. 'The Transvaal . . . *must* be ours,' he wrote in late 1876. It was not only an integral part of the hoped-for confederation of South Africa, but a country rich in farm, trading and mineral potential. Gold, it is true, was not discovered on the Witwatersrand until 1886. A decade earlier, however, a senior engineer had noted that 'the resources of the Transvaal are greater and more varied' than those of any other South African state.

Carnarvon's biggest fear was that the Transvaal would develop with the aid of foreign capital and governments – it had already had an agreement with the Portuguese to build a railway from Pretoria to Delagoa Bay – and would therefore remain outside Britain's sphere of influence. But he could hardly use that as an excuse for annexation. A less self-serving reason had to be found, and it arose in 1876 when the Transvaal declared war on its northern neighbour, the rapacious Pedi tribe of Chief Sekhukhune. Shepstone happened to be in London at the time – to receive a knighthood and attend the abortive confederation conference – and no sooner had news of a Boer defeat reached England in September than he was on his way back to South Africa 'with a secret dispatch empowering him to take over the Transvaal Govt. & Country and to become the first English Governor if circumstances on his arrival render this in any way possible'. Ideally he was to accomplish this task peacefully and with the consent of the Transvaal government; if this was not forthcoming, then by force.

Arriving back in South Africa in October 1876, Shepstone learnt to his disappointment that the Boers had recovered from their

---

★ Annexed by Britain in 1871, four years after the discovery of the Kimberley diamond fields.

earlier setback and were gaining ground in the fight against the
Pedi. He needed an alternative pretext for annexation and so turned
to the republic's parlous finances. The original loan to build the
Pretoria to Delagoa Bay Railway had been seriously under-
subscribed and the interest payments were crippling the Transvaal
treasury, which was in debt to the tune of £250,000. Extraordinary
taxes had been voted but were proving difficult to collect. With
the government on the verge of bankruptcy, unable to pay its
officials, Shepstone decided to act. On 12 April 1877, four months
after entering the Transvaal with his personal staff and a small escort
to inquire into the 'origin, nature and circumstances' of the war
with the Pedi, he declared that no internal reforms could save the
republic and that henceforth it was annexed to the British Crown.

There was little protest. Shepstone had taken an escort of just
twenty-five mounted policemen, but imperial troops were waiting
on the frontier, and behind them lay the almost limitless resources
of the British Empire. The inhabitants of the Transvaal, by contrast,
were impoverished and divided. Most of the English-speaking
mining and commercial community, and some of the frontier
Boers, embraced British rule as the surest way to provide financial
and physical security. The majority of Boers were, contrary to
Shepstone's claims, not supportive of the takeover, but with President Burgers and the republic discredited, there seemed to be no
alternative. Armed resistance was still a possibility, until Burgers
declared that any violent acts would jeopardize the success of the
deputation that he and his outgoing Executive Council had sent to
London to seek a reversal of the British government's decision. It
helped too that there had recently been a number of aggressive
Zulu acts in the Disputed Territory that Shepstone was able to cite
as evidence of Cetshwayo's desire for war with the Boers. In truth
Cetshwayo had no intention of attacking the Boers – not least
because he feared British retaliation – but Shepstone was able to
convince many in Britain and South Africa that only annexation
had saved the Transvaal from the Zulu.

It was at this point that a new actor entered the stage of South
African politics: Sir Bartle Frere. Born in Breconshire in 1815, the

descendant of an old East Anglian landowning family that had close ties to Cambridge University, Frere was the sixth of nine sons. In 1832 his desire for foreign travel was satisfied when a family friend nominated him for a writership in the service of the Honourable East India Company, the London trading house that governed much of India on behalf of the British government. He graduated first in his class at Haileybury, the Company's college for budding civil servants, and chose to join his brother William in the Bombay Presidency in western India. A talented draughtsman and a brilliant linguist, Frere passed his examination in Indian languages in just three months and was posted to Pune as a junior official. Thereafter he rose rapidly in the Indian service and by 1842 was private secretary and son-in-law to the governor of Bombay. In 1850, at the age of thirty-five, he was appointed governor of the backward but strategically important frontier province of Sind. His finest hour came during the Indian Mutiny of 1857, when – despite the danger of a rising in Sind – he sent almost all his available British troops to the seat of the rebellion in the Bengal Presidency. His outward sang-froid was in marked contrast to the panic displayed by many other British officials during the Mutiny, and he was rewarded in 1859, after the rebellion had been suppressed, by the thanks of both houses of Parliament and the award of a CB. In 1862 he became governor of Bombay and, after five years in the post, returned to England to serve on the India Council. A successful mission to Zanzibar to persuade the sultan to end the slave trade was undertaken in 1873. Two years later he accompanied the prince of Wales on his state visit to India and became an intimate of the Royal Family. By 1876, when he was first approached by Carnarvon to serve in South Africa, he was a baronet, a member of the Privy Council and looking forward to retirement.

Ordinarily the minor governorship of the Cape would not have interested an imperial administrator of Frere's stature. But Carnarvon managed to seduce him into accepting the post by setting him the challenge of confederation. If successful, he would become South Africa's first governor-general and almost certainly – Carnarvon hinted – a peer. In the meantime he would not only be governor of the Cape but also high commissioner of Native Affairs for South Africa – giving him a say in the other British territories of Natal, Griqualand West, Basutoland and the Transkei – on a salary of £7,000 a year, rising to £10,000 after confederation. It was all too much for a man of Frere's vanity, ambition and impecunity to resist. Carnarvon made the appointment on his own authority – selecting Frere on the basis of his expansionist, or 'Forward', approach to Empire – but not all his Cabinet colleagues approved. Lord Salisbury, the Indian secretary who had served with Frere on the India Council, found him 'quarrelsome and *mutinous*'. A decade earlier he had noted how 'Impatience of control is a common defect in men of [Frere's] able and fearless character and his impetuosity of disposition.'

Frere arrived in Cape Town in mid April 1877, shortly after Shepstone's annexation of the Transvaal, and was at once assailed with accounts of Cetshwayo's cruelty towards his own people, particularly Christian converts. Most were without foundation and had been propagated by missionaries and Natal newspapers in the hope of provoking a British invasion – and eventual annexation – of Zululand. But a new arrival like Frere was hardly in a position to judge. So when Shepstone confirmed the veracity of the accounts, and the border agent F. B. Fynney warned of the dangers of Zulu aggression, Frere was wholly convinced. He could not, he informed Shepstone in October 1877, see how the 'present state of things' in Zululand could last. He added: 'To maintain a standing army of 40,000 unmarried young men, would task the resources of a country as rich & populous & industrious as Belgium, & if Cetywayo can manage it, without a constant succession of conquests, he is fit to be War Minister to any great military power in Europe.'

Shepstone – who had come to the conclusion that only the annexation of Zululand would solve Natal's overpopulation and security problems – was forced to reply that Cetshwayo did not have 40,000 *unmarried* soldiers and that they provided their own food when serving the king. He might have added that the Zulu force was in no way a 'standing' army. Its members were part-time soldiers – the equivalent of Territorials – who spent most of the year at home. Their so-called 'military' service was largely spent working for the king: tilling his fields, tending his herds and building his amakhanda. This unpaid labour was the equivalent of taxation and enabled the central government to exist. The amabutho system was, therefore, a help rather than a burden to the Zulu state, which did not need a foreign war to maintain its army.

That Frere never saw this was partly because he based his understanding of the Zulu Army on his experience of India. He wrote to Shepstone in July 1877:

We have always been quite as much harassed in our Indian conquests, as here, by the inordinate numbers of the hereditary classes who swallowed up all the resources of a native state. There, as in Kaffraria & Zululand, all the best muscle, as well as money, of the country was absorbed by idle warriors who found but scanty provision in the smaller but more compact Sepoy armies of their English conquerors.

Even at this early stage, Frere was contemplating the annexation of Zululand so that its people could take to 'honest work'. This was in no way contrary to official policy. Carnarvon had envisaged 'taking Cetywayo and his Zulus under our protection' as early as the summer of 1876. A year later, the permanent under-secretary at the Colonial Office was urging caution. 'H. M. Govt. are rather nervous as to the probability of their being pressed to take Zululand also immediately,' he informed Shepstone. It would be better to postpone any 'actual annexation' of Zululand for a 'year or so'. This was chiefly because a significant body of opinion in Britain, particularly in Parliament, was wary of imperial expansion on the grounds of expense and possible diplomatic repercussions. Any further annexations in South Africa, therefore, would have to be carefully timed. The annexation of Zululand 'must & ought to come eventually', minuted Carnarvon in June 1877, 'but not just now'.

In the meantime Shepstone, the new administrator of the Transvaal, had to deal with the thorny issue of the Disputed Territory. Previously he had sided with the Zulus as a means of keeping the Boers as far from the sea as possible. But now the Boers were British subjects and their border dispute had become Britain's. Having toured the Transvaal's eastern frontier with Zululand, almost all of which was in dispute, Shepstone continued on into Zululand to negotiate with Cetshwayo's prime minister, Chief Mnyamana of the Buthelezi. The meeting – on 18 October 1877 at a large flat-topped hill, henceforth called Conference Hill, west of the Blood River – was a bad-tempered affair. Shepstone asked Mnyamana to state what he thought was the rightful boundary. He eventually named the line of the Buffalo as far as the Drakensberg, and the Drakensberg as far north as the sources of the Vaal. Shepstone rejected this as impossible, and suggested the Blood River and the Lynspruit to its source. He also suggested leaving an unoccupied strip on the Zulu side of this line that would be administered by a British agent and eventually, after five years or so, awarded to one side or the other. On the surface this was a generous offer. But the Zulus were in no mood to compromise: they wanted an investigation into years of Boer encroachment. Without it there could be no agreement.

Cetshwayo later modified the Zulu demands. But by then Shepstone had hardened his own position by claiming for the Transvaal all the land allegedly ceded by the Treaty of Waaihoek in 1861, including unspecified land east of the Blood River. Since the 18 October meeting he had, he claimed, seen 'the most incontrovertible, overwhelming and clear evidence' to support the Boer case. He later sent this evidence to Carnarvon; but it consisted mainly of statements made long after the event and was far from convincing. The truth is that Shepstone was not in a position to make an unbiased judgement: Boer opposition to his rule was growing and he could not afford to increase his unpopularity by appearing to side with the Zulus on the issue of the Disputed Territory.

With tensions rising on both sides of the frontier, and many Boer settlers abandoning their farms, Sir Henry Bulwer, the lieutenant-governor of Natal, decided to intervene. Bulwer did not believe that the Zulus were intent on war; nor did he agree with Shepstone that the Zulus were deeply divided and would disintegrate as a nation if attacked. He was, in addition, deeply suspicious of the new 'evidence' that Shepstone had produced to support the Boer claims. So, on 8 December 1877, in an attempt to defuse a dangerous situation, he sent a message to Cetshwayo, offering to write to the British government to ask it to nominate an independent arbitrator. The relieved king accepted the principle of arbitration, but suggested a preliminary investigation by Natal commissioners, which Bulwer agreed to.

But time was running out, because Shepstone had begun to see war as the only solution. 'I am fully satisfied,' he told Frere on 8 January 1878, 'that no permanent peace can be hoped for until the Zulu power has been broken up.' He, Frere and Carnarvon had long believed that the annexation of Zululand was simply a matter of time. From his new perspective as Transvaal administrator, there was no longer the possibility of delay. To convince Frere, Shepstone insisted that the war that had recently broken out on the eastern Cape border – between the British and their Fingo allies on the one side, and the Gaika and Gcaleka tribes on the other – had been inspired by the Zulu king. He told Carnarvon, 'Cetywayo is the secret hope of every petty independent chief hundreds of miles away from him who feels a desire that his colour should prevail.' Bulwer was horrified by Shepstone's warmongering and outlined the difference between their two approaches to the disputed border in a letter of 16 January 1878:

You make no reference to the possibility of this question being settled by peaceful means in any one way or another, but are giving reasons for the destruction of the Zulu power, and for the Zulu Nation ceasing to exist as an independent Nation . . . We are looking to different objects – I to the termination of this dispute by a peaceful settlement, you to its termination by the overthrow of the Zulu kingdom.

Frere was largely in agreement with Shepstone but supported Bulwer's attempt at arbitration because it would allow time for the build-up of British forces and make it easier to justify the conflict that was bound to follow. Senior officials at the Colonial Office were of a similar opinion. 'Nobody seems to think that the arbitration or enquiry will be much more than a farce,' noted an assistant under-secretary. 'It is clear that directly a decision is given we must be prepared to support it . . . We have however now gained time & have sent out to S. Africa a force sufficient to deal with the Zulus. The Authorities will therefore now probably hasten on the crisis.'

The Boundary Commission – made up of three nominees* of the Natal government and assisted by Boer and Zulu delegates – began its deliberations on 12 March 1878 at Rorke's Drift on the Buffalo River. Most people in South Africa and Britain assumed that the commission would rule in favour of the Boers and that a Zulu war would be the result. But they failed to take into account either the integrity of the commissioners or the fact that, by the time the commission presented its report, the British government might still be embroiled in other overseas ventures that made it particularly unwilling to sanction a war in South Africa. There was also the small matter of a new, less Afro-centric colonial secretary. Carnarvon, the architect of confederation, had resigned from the Cabinet in February 1878 over the Eastern Question (Russia was winning its war with the Ottoman Empire, and Carnarvon objected to the aggressive measures the British government was taking to deter the Russians from entering Constantinople). His replacement was Sir Michael Hicks Beach, Bt., a rising Tory star who had represented the seat of East Gloucestershire since 1864. Tall, dark and choleric, 'Black Michael' was respected – if not liked – in the House of Commons for his lucid, no-nonsense speeches. Colleagues found his quick temper less appealing. 'Hicks Beach,' wrote one, 'is the only man I know who habitually thinks angrily.' A former Irish secretary and a staunch anti-Russian, Hicks Beach

---

* M. H. Gallwey, the attorney-general; John Shepstone, the acting secretary for Native Affairs (and brother of Sir Theophilus); and Lieutenant-Colonel Anthony Durnford, the colonial engineer.

knew little about African affairs and even less about Carnarvon's plans for confederation. The effect was twofold: Frere's bold moves would no longer receive the automatic support of the colonial secretary; and the British government generally would pay increasingly less attention to events in South Africa over the coming months.

On hearing of Carnarvon's resignation, Frere was distraught, because he understood the implications. The news had, he told his former boss, 'utterly taken the heart out of me' and his 'hopes of carrying through' confederation had 'sadly diminished'. He added: 'It is peculiarly trying to us just now, when there seems at last a prospect of a break in the clouds.' Frere was referring to two recent bits of good news: his success in dismissing the obstructive Cape government of J. C. Molteno and replacing it with one led by J. C. Sprigg from the eastern Cape that was more amenable to confederation; and the prospect of a successful conclusion to the Cape Frontier War, which had been all but guaranteed by the bloody repulse of a combined attack by Gaikas and Gcalekas on an outpost of the 1/24th Regiment at Kentini on 7 February. In describing the battle to Carnarvon, Frere laid particular stress on the destructive power of the new breech-loading Martini-Henry rifle against the massed rushes of the 'Kaffirs' – tactics that he assumed the Zulus would repeat in any future war. 'They came on in four divisions very steadily,' he wrote, 'and in the days of Brown Bess would certainly have closed, and being eight or ten to one would possibly have overwhelmed our people. They held on after several shells had burst among their advanced masses, but they could not live under the fire of the Martini-Henry. The 24th are old, steady shots, and every bullet told.'

But Frere was right to suspect that government support for a war with the Zulus – in his opinion a prerequisite for confederation – was less likely with Carnarvon gone. Hicks Beach confirmed as much in his first private letter to Frere of 7 March 1878:

I presume that the presence of a considerable force in Natal, with some (not too large) augmentation of that in the Transvaal would not be without its useful effect on Cetywayo: though I think Shepstone would have to be discouraged from taking the opportunity to make war. The negotiations, through Bulwer, with Cetywayo should be pushed on, and the dwellers on the disputed territory be protected from aggression meanwhile; but our power should not make us relax our best efforts to obtain a peaceful solution.

Hicks Beach went on to say that he mistrusted the 'fairness of the Boer treaties' and was not surprised that the Zulus had rejected Shepstone's arbitration, given his new role as administrator of the Transvaal. It would not do, on the other hand, to alienate the Boers further by appearing to ignore their 'just rights'. Perhaps the answer, he suggested, was to give the Transvaal that part of the Disputed Territory that was occupied by Boers and the rest to the Zulus.

Frere would have liked the support of Hicks Beach and the home government, but did not see it as essential for policy-making, any more than he had in India. The responsibility of officials to their superiors 'should always be retrospective in the shape of praise or blame for what is done', he once wrote, 'and should never involve the necessity for previous sanction'. As governor of Bombay he had occasionally fallen out with the viceroy and home government over his unilateral initiatives. But they had generally borne fruit. When, for example, the sultan of Zanzibar refused to halt the slave trade, Frere told him without authority that British ships would intercept slavers and the British consul would supervise his customs service. This had the desired effect, and, because his mission had been successful, Frere escaped criticism. He carried the same self-confidence with him to South Africa; but the political situation there – particularly the role of the white colonists – was a far more complicated one than he had been used to.

Nevertheless he, like Carnarvon, was committed to creating a vast confederation of South African states that would enable the Empire to exploit the huge mineral, labour and trading potential of the region. As early as January 1874, well before his appointment to the Cape, he had spoken of the discrepancy between Africa's resources and its relatively small trade. He also referred to African labour as a 'mine of wealth to the employer' and suggested 'welding together the loose elements of a great South African Empire'. In 1878 he told Hicks Beach: 'You must be master, as representative of the sole sovereign power, up to the Portuguese frontier, on both the E. & W. coasts. There is no escaping from the responsibility which has already been incurred, ever since the English Flag was planted on the Castle here.' However, the annexation of Zululand and the other independent black states in the region was not just a means to an end but an end itself. He regarded black Africans as less 'civilized' than Indians – or Asians generally – and their rulers as less deserving of preservation. Only by ending their 'reign of barbarism' could trade and civilized life flourish. For all these reasons as he saw them – political, commercial and humanitarian – Frere wished to provoke a war with Zululand that would result in its defeat and annexation. But to achieve the first part of his grand scheme he had to contend with a distinct lack of enthusiasm from the Colonial Office and the Cape and Natal governments.

The most serious blow to his plans was the report of the Boundary Commission, which he received in July. It ruled largely in favour of the Zulus, on the grounds that the documentary evidence supporting the cessions of both 1854 and 1861 was defective and that, in any case, the Zulu king had no right to relinquish land without the consent of his people (represented by the Council of Chiefs, or iziKhulu). However, the Transvaal was awarded the territory to the west of the Blood River because it had long exercised sovereignty over it with the tacit acceptance of the Zulus; but this was hardly likely to satisfy the many Boers who had farms to the east of the river. Frere was aghast. Not only would the report infuriate the Boers; it would also lessen the chance of war with the Zulus. Yet he could hardly set it aside. Instead he decided to 'make the best of it' by granting Cetshwayo a nominal sovereignty over the Disputed Territory, while allowing the Boer settlers to keep their farms under a British guarantee. One senior Colonial Office official likened it to 'giving the shells to the Zulus and the oysters to the Boers'. But Frere knew that it would satisfy neither and that only the replacement of Zulu with British rule would suffice. So he delayed the announcement of the Boundary Commission's award until he had worked out the best way to bring on a war.

Until now the staunchest supporter of Frere's anti-Zulu policy in South Africa had been Sir Theophilus Shepstone. But Shepstone had alienated the restive Boers by his high-handed manner and become something of a political liability. Even Frere had to admit this, and, in August 1878, he asked Hicks Beach to recall him to Britain on the pretext of discussing the Transvaal's new constitution. Shepstone was eventually replaced as acting Transvaal administrator by Colonel Lanyon in January 1879.

No sooner had one supporter of war been discredited than another appeared in the form of the new commander-in-chief of British forces in South Africa: Lieutenant-General the Honourable Sir Frederic Thesiger. The eldest son of the first Baron Chelmsford, a former Tory Lord Chancellor, Thesiger was descended from a Saxon gentleman who emigrated to England in the mid eighteenth century and became secretary to the influential second Marquess of Rockingham. Thesiger's father – a midshipman in the Royal Navy before becoming a successful lawyer – had sent him to Eton and then bought him a commission in the British Army. Young Frederic joined the Rifle Brigade in 1844 and later exchanged to the Grenadier Guards and the 95th Regiment, with whom he saw action in the Crimea and the Indian Mutiny. He was able to use his father's influence and money to purchase a lieutenant-colonelcy by the age of thirty. But most of his service since had been on the staff: as Sir Robert Napier's deputy adjutant-general, for example, during the brilliantly executed Abyssinian campaign of 1868; and as adjutant-general in India from then until 1874. On returning home, he was put in charge of the Shorncliffe Camp and had only recently been appointed to the Aldershot Command with the rank of brigadier-general when the War Office recalled Lieutenant-General Sir Arthur Cunynghame from South Africa in early 1878. The obvious replacement was Sir Garnet Wolseley, Britain's most experienced commander, who had recently served as lieutenant-governor of Natal. But Wolseley was about to become Britain's

first high commissioner of Cyprus and was, in any case, not high
in the duke of Cambridge's favour. Thesiger, on the other hand,
was seen as a safe pair of hands: a talented staff officer, if light on
active service and seniority, who would prove more than a match
for any recalcitrant African tribe. It helped that he was a Tory, an
aristocrat (albeit recently) and a former aide-de-camp to the queen.

Thesiger was just fifty when he arrived in South Africa in
February 1878. A tall, handsome man with an immaculate spade
beard, he possessed a robust physique that was ideally suited to the
taxing African climate. He did not drink, ate sparingly and could
rough it with the best. Like so many of his class, he was a skilled
horseman and could spend hours in the saddle. To his subordinates
he was the perfect gentleman: modest and courteous. He was
particularly interested in the welfare of the ordinary soldier –
discouraging drunkenness, for example – and was calm under fire,
which always helped. For all these reasons he was well liked by
those who served under him. (His personal staff remained especially
loyal.) But he could be sharp and even vindictive towards those
who crossed him, delivering stinging rebukes in public, and was
offhand to the point of rudeness when dealing with colonial officers.
As a field commander he found it difficult to delegate and would
interfere in petty administrative details at the expense of the wider
strategic picture. More seriously, he was often swayed by contrary
advice, and the result was frequent vacillation. Lacking command
experience, he tended to rely on outmoded tactics that were not
particularly applicable to African warfare. In Zululand he would
neglect, in particular, the need for constant and detailed reconnaissance. To sum up, then: a conscientious, hard-working officer
but one lacking in 'flair, intuition, breadth of vision and military
acumen', and therefore hopelessly out of his depth when it came
to fighting the Zulus.★

Thus far, however, Thesiger's appointment had been a relative

★ Thesiger shared many of the personal and professional characteristics of Lord
Raglan of the Charge of the Light Brigade infamy, and it may be no coincidence
that the pair presided over two of the most famous military disasters in British
history.

success. Since arriving in South Africa, he had brought the Cape Frontier War – known to contemporaries as the 'Ninth Kaffir War' – to a satisfactory conclusion in a little over two months. Frere was impressed, telling Hicks Beach in April 1878:

The newspapers will . . . give you a very imperfect idea of what Genl. Thesiger has been doing, & of the degree of success which has attended his operations . . . he has really done all that regular troops can do in such warfare. He has broken up every strong hold in which the Kaffirs have tried to rally. He has cut off their supplies of food and ammunition, & some very important chiefs have been captured, & others killed. In no previous war have the Kaffirs been so signally, speedily & completely defeated & the disturbance brought within the limits the police can manage.

This easy victory – due in no small part to the groundwork laid by General Sir Arthur Cunynghame, Thesiger's predecessor – would have unfortunate consequences for Frere and Thesiger because it would blind both to the far more formidable challenge posed by the well-drilled Zulu Army.

Having concluded operations in the eastern Cape, Thesiger stayed for a time as Frere's guest at Government House in Cape Town. It was during this period that Frere managed to convince him of the threat posed by the Zulu kingdom and the need to remove it. A successful campaign also held out the prospect of fresh laurels for Thesiger (he had been knighted at the close of the Cape Frontier War) and might even result in a lucrative senior command in India.* Frere's plan was to send Thesiger and all available troops to Natal to prepare for the coming war. He justified the move to Bulwer and Hicks Beach by insisting that Thesiger was simply taking defensive precautions. For a time even Thesiger appeared to be taken in. 'The Zulus have been very kind to us to abstain from any hostile movements during the time we were so busily engaged

---

* Thesiger was relatively strapped for cash and made a number of unsuccessful applications for Indian commands after the Zulu War.

in this colony,' he wrote to Shepstone on 8 July. 'If they will only wait until next month I hope to have the troops somewhat better prepared than they are at present.' But a subsequent letter to Shepstone, written by Thesiger shortly before his departure for Natal, was far more pugnacious and reeked of the overconfidence that was to cost the British so dear:

If we are to have a fight with the Zulus, I am anxious that our arrangements should be as complete as it is possible to make them. Half measures do not answer with natives. They must be thoroughly crushed to make them believe in our superiority, and if I am called upon to conduct operations against them, I shall strive to be in a position to show them how hopelessly inferior they are to us in fighting power, altho' numerically stronger.

3. The Road to War

General Thesiger arrived in Natal with his staff in early August and was soon at loggerheads with the governor, Sir Henry Bulwer, over the military build-up. Bulwer did not share Frere's conviction that the Zulus were about to invade and felt, on the contrary, that the massing of troops would simply make matters worse. Only later did he realize that Frere's intention all along had been to prepare an invasion. In the meantime he had some success with Thesiger. 'It is possible,' Thesiger reported to the Horse Guards on 12 August, 'that the anticipated disturbance may yet be brought to a peaceful issue.'

Bulwer would later claim that Frere, Thesiger and the latter's military secretary, Colonel Crealock, all arrived in Natal in late 1878 'fully determined' on war with the Zulus; yet of the three, Thesiger was the 'least anxious for it'. If that was true, it did not last. It was, after all, Thesiger who urgently requested Frere's presence in Natal because Bulwer would not allow him to take even 'the most ordinary measures of precaution for fear lest they should be misconstrued by Cetewayo and the Zulus'. On 24 August, within two weeks of that request, Thesiger threw off all remaining pretence by submitting to Bulwer a memorandum entitled: 'Invasion of Zululand; or, Defence of the Natal and Transvaal Colony from Invasion by the Zulus'. The second part of the title was no more than a sop. Instead the memo concentrated on Thesiger's intention to place five separate columns – on lines of advance 'equally adapted for attack or defence' – at various points along the Zulu border. It was very similar to the invasion plan that Thesiger eventually adopted and could not have worked as a defensive measure because it left too many parts of the frontier unguarded.

On 14 September Thesiger sent a similar memorandum to

Colonel the Honourable Frederick Stanley,* the secretary of state for War, setting out his plan of campaign 'in the event of an invasion of Zululand being decided upon'. It repeated his intention to advance with five columns, each consisting of at least one infantry battalion. He would keep an extra battalion in reserve and two for garrison duties. This meant a minimum of eight battalions. As there were only six battalions available in Natal and the Transvaal, he asked for two more to be sent out, as well as two companies of Royal Engineers and a number of Special Service officers for staff work. Frere, on his own initiative, had asked Hicks Beach for more troops on 10 September, but only one infantry battalion and six staff officers, with another battalion 'in readiness to follow if required'. He explained: 'Every thing I read & hear confirms my belief that the Natal believers in Ketchwayo's peaceful intentions are dreaming, & that those who . . . forbear to prepare, entirely mistake the way of inducing gentlemen like Ketchwayo to keep the peace.'

Frere arrived in Durban on 23 September, having been urged to make the trip by both Thesiger and Bulwer. Thesiger needed his 'support', Frere told Hicks Beach, to overcome the Natal government's opposition to a military build-up; Bulwer did not want the 'responsibility' of announcing the report of the Boundary Commission without him present. On the day of his arrival, Frere repeated his request for reinforcements in a telegram to the Colonial Office. A week later, in a private letter to Hicks Beach, he stressed the seriousness of the situation. 'The people here are slumbering on a volcano,' he wrote, '& I much fear you will not be able to send out the reinforcements we have asked, in time to prevent an explosion . . . The Zulus are now quite out of hand, & the maintenance of peace depends on their forbearance.' Thesiger had used a similar argument in a memorandum to Stanley of 28 September, noting that an invasion of Natal by the Zulus was more 'imminent' than it had been for many years. In Thesiger's opinion the security of Natal and the Transvaal now required three

---

* Later the sixteenth earl of Derby.

extra infantry battalions: one from the Cape and two from Britain. He also outlined his intention to organize the Natal Africans – who were liable to be mobilized for defensive duties by the civil authorities – into British-style battalions, commanded by European officers and with every tenth man armed with a rifle.

Thesiger had clearly come round to Frere's way of thinking that the Zulus posed a considerable security threat to their white neighbours and would have to be dealt with sooner or later; far better, then, to launch a pre-emptive strike. But as this would be unlikely to gain the sanction of the British Cabinet, they justified their preparations for war by stressing the danger of an imminent Zulu invasion. Thesiger may even have believed in such a threat. Frere almost certainly did not. He was, however, prepared to use alarmist language to prepare the British government and public for a Zulu war. The first hint of how he might provoke it was contained in a private letter to Hicks Beach of 14 October. There was, he wrote, 'no way of settling' the frontier dispute except by an 'arbitrary line' like the one proposed by the Boundary Commissioners. Had Transvaal still been independent, he might have hesitated before adopting a line 'less advantageous' to the Transvaal than the Boers might have expected. But as British and Transvaal interests were 'now identical', he had thought it wise to adopt the line as the best the Zulus could reasonably hope for, and one that would put the British 'in a stronger position when we demand those further securities for peace, without which we can never be safe'.

What 'further securities for peace' Frere had in mind would become clear to the British government only when it was too late to prevent war. To prepare the ground further, however, Frere mentioned in the same letter that he was waiting to hear Cetshwayo's reply to a demand for an 'explanation regarding violations of the frontier already reported'. He was referring to two recent border incidents. The first had taken place in late July, when two wives of Chief Sihayo of the Qungebe clan, based in the Batshe Valley opposite Rorke's Drift, fled to Natal with their lovers. The wives were pursued by one of Sihayo's brothers and two of his sons at the head of a large war party, dragged back to Zululand and

executed. No one else was harmed, but settler opinion was outraged, and Bulwer at once demanded that the ringleaders be handed
over for trial. Cetshwayo did not take the demand seriously, not
least because a similar incident had occurred in 1876 without
causing a diplomatic crisis. Moreover, the Natal police had often
arrested criminals on Zulu soil without permission. His response,
therefore, was to offer £50 in compensation.

The second incident happened in late September, when a Natal
surveyor and his friend were apprehended by Zulus as they
inspected a drift across the Thukela near Fort Buckingham. The
surveyor had been asked by the colonial engineer's department to
report on what would need to be done 'to make the drift passable
by wagons, etc.', and his presence was bound to be viewed with
suspicion by the Zulus, who were keeping a constant watch on
their borders. The pair were interrogated for a couple of hours and
then released, minus a few minor items from their pockets. So
insignificant did the surveyor consider the matter that he did not
bother to report it. But the friend did, and Frere was quick to
capitalize on the incident by telling Hicks Beach that the surveyor
had been 'seized & assaulted by an armed party of Zulus which
crossed to our side of the river'. He had, actually, been arrested in
midstream, but Frere was not about to let facts spoil his portrayal
of the Zulus as itching for a fight. Bulwer, on the other hand,
blamed the colonial engineer's department for dispatching such a
provocative mission in the first place. He thought the Zulus'
response – at a time when British troops were pouring into the
Natal with the thinly disguised intention of invading Zululand –
was 'not to be wondered at'.

Yet another border 'violation' took place in early October, when
Mbilini kaMswati, a chief of Swazi descent who was living in
northern Zululand under Cetshwayo's protection, raided a group
of Swazi refugees on the Ntombe River near the disputed Boer
settlement of Luneberg. The local magistrate was at first convinced
that Mbilini had acted on orders from the Zulu king, and described
the raid as 'a feeler and of great significance'. But a fortnight later,
with no more attacks having taken place, he reported the rumour

that Cetshwayo was very angry with Mbilini and had given orders for his arrest. This intelligence did not deter Frere, who later characterized all three border clashes as 'not accidents, but acts . . . to keep up the terror [Cetshwayo] believed he had inspired, and to try how far he might go'.

This was very far from the truth. Cetshwayo was anxious to avoid a war he knew he could not win and was understandably alarmed by the military preparations across the border. He told Bulwer:

I hear of troops arriving in Natal, that they are coming to attack the Zulus, and to seize me; in what have I done wrong that I should be seized like an 'Umtakata' [wrongdoer], the English are my fathers, I do not wish to quarrel with them, but to live as I have always done, at peace with them.

Back in London the news that storm clouds were gathering over South Africa was an unwelcome distraction from more pressing affairs. For much of the early part of the year it had seemed likely that Britain would go to war with Russia to protect Constantinople. Even when Russia drew back from attacking the Ottoman capital and concluded her war with Turkey in March 1878, Disraeli's government considered the terms of the resultant Treaty of San Stefano far too harsh. So too did the other European powers, and it was Otto von Bismarck, the architect of recent German unification, who suggested an international congress to discuss the issue. It took place in Berlin in July and – with Bismarck playing the role of 'honest broker' and Disraeli★ ably fighting Britain's corner – made considerable revisions to the original treaty.

But by September Russia had yet to fulfil all the terms of the treaty – in particular the withdrawal of troops from Bulgaria – and was threatening British interests in a quite separate quarter: Afghanistan. For much of the nineteenth century Britain had feared a Russian invasion of India. The obvious route was through

★ He had been raised to the peerage as the earl of Beaconsfield in 1876 but is better known as Disraeli.

Afghanistan, and Britain had already fought one war there, in 1839–42, to forestall Russian encroachment. In July 1878 the threat returned when Sher Ali, the amir of Afghanistan, welcomed a Russian mission to Kabul. Lord Lytton, the viceroy of India, was determined to force Sher Ali to replace the Russian mission with a British one. He asked London for authority to send an envoy to Kabul, and it was duly granted in early August. But Lytton failed to inform the home government that he intended to make the dismissal of the Russian mission a prior condition of sending his own; nor did he heed the instruction to send his mission via Kandahar rather than through the Khyber Pass. The British mission – under Lieutenant-General Sir Neville Chamberlain – set off up the pass on 21 September, despite Lytton having been told to delay its departure until St Petersburg had responded to the home government's official protest. If the mission had succeeded, all might have been well. But it did not. Chamberlain was refused passage and war was inevitable. 'When V-Roys and Comms-in-Chief disobey orders, they ought to be sure of success in their mutiny,' commented a furious Disraeli. 'Lytton by disobeying orders had only secured insult and failure.' An ultimatum was duly dispatched in early November, and when it expired without adequate response on the 20th, Britain was at war with Afghanistan.

Under the circumstances, the British government was determined to avoid further complications in South Africa. Disraeli had hitherto paid very little attention to the colonies, describing them in a moment of petulance as 'millstones round our neck'. But by September 1878, with war looming against Afghanistan, he was forced to take notice of events in South Africa. 'If anything annoys me more than another,' he informed Lady Bradford, 'it is our Cape affairs, where every day brings forth a new blunder of Twitters. The man he swore by was Sir T. Shepstone . . . We sent him out entirely for Twitters' sake, and he has managed to quarrel with Eng., Dutch, and Zulus; and now he is obliged to be recalled, but not before he has brought on, I fear, a new war.' In truth it was another Carnarvon appointee, Sir Bartle Frere, who was the chief proponent of war. He, like Lytton, was quite willing to ignore instructions from London if they contradicted his 'forward' policy: to bring about a short, successful war that would receive retrospective sanction. He may well have been right. But his war would neither be short nor – initially – successful.

The main obstacle to establishing control over unruly proconsuls was the time it took to send instructions. In South Africa's case, the telegraph cable from London went only as far as St Vincent in the Cape Verde Islands; from there messages had to be carried to Cape Town by steamer. The fastest telegram on record took sixteen days, with letters and dispatches at least three weeks in transit, often a month. Thus Frere was able to argue that he had to respond to events and could not afford to wait for government approval of every decision he made. He would have had a point, had the British government not repeatedly warned him to do everything he could to avoid war. On the other hand, the Colonial Office had made it quite clear since Frere's arrival in South Africa that Zululand needed to be dealt with sooner or later. It was just a matter of timing – when, not if – and Frere had simply put the good of Empire as he saw it ahead of London's other diplomatic considerations.

Frere's request for reinforcements reached London in early October. Hicks Beach's response – having consulted his colleagues, who expressed 'considerable exception' to the 'great expense already being incurred' – was to postpone his decision until he had heard the result of the meeting between Frere, Thesiger and Bulwer at Pietermaritzburg in late September. At this stage he was under the impression that Thesiger 'did not want reinforcements' and that Bulwer 'did not believe in the imminence of a Zulu war'. But he was quickly disabused of the former notion when Thesiger's memorandum of 14 September arrived in London. If Frere and Thesiger persisted in their demands after meeting in Natal, he told Disraeli on 15 October, 'we cannot refuse to send them'. Two days later, having spoken to those members of the Cabinet still in London, Hicks Beach informed the prime minister* of their collective decision:

---

* Disraeli was at his country home of Hughenden Manor in Buckinghamshire.

We decided to send out the 'special service' officers asked for . . . but no more troops at any rate for the present. And I have sent by to-night's mail a despatch to Frere to this effect, throwing as much cold water as possible upon his evident expectation of a Zulu war, and telling him that the imperial forces now in South Africa . . . should suffice for all other necessities. I much fear, however, that before this can reach him, we may hear of the beginning of a fight with the Zulus; and then the troops will probably have to go.

Hicks Beach's suspicions were not that far off the mark. On 1 November he received Frere's letter of 30 September, repeating the demand for reinforcements and warning that the people of Natal were 'slumbering on a volcano'. The appeal was 'so urgent', he told Disraeli, that it had to be reconsidered by the Cabinet. He added: 'I am by no means satisfied that a Zulu war is necessary, or that if one should break out, a sufficient force out of the 6000 imperial troops now in South Africa, could not be concentrated in that particular part of the country to bring it to a successful termination.' The Cabinet duly met, but its decision, Hicks Beach wrote to Frere on 7 November, remained the same:

The Government are not prepared to comply with the request for more troops. The fact is, that matters in Eastern Europe & India, of which you have by this time heard, wear so serious an aspect that we cannot now have a Zulu war in addition to other greater and too possible troubles . . . You will, I hope, before this, have been able to take some steps towards the arbitration in the Boundary dispute; and these – looking to the facts reported by the Commission – can hardly fail to dispose the Zulus towards the maintenance of peaceful relations with us . . . The only serious recent act on the part of the Zulus . . . as giving ground for complaint on our part, is the taking and killing the two refugee Zulu women . . . This can surely be settled without war.

By late November the Cabinet had changed its mind and agreed to send two battalions to South Africa. It had heeded Frere's warning that if war did break out and it went badly for the British,

the government would be blamed for refusing to send reinforcements. But, as Hicks Beach told Frere in a private letter of
28 November, it was particularly anxious to avoid a war at that
moment. Russia had yet to fulfil all the terms of the Treaty of
Berlin, he said, and would be less likely to do so if she knew that
Britain was 'fully occupied elsewhere'. He added: 'The Afghanistan
affair has therefore arisen at a most unfortunate time: and you will
see how much the risk arising from this would be increased by the
addition of a Zulu war. Therefore . . . [the Cabinet] wished me to
impress upon you most strongly the necessity of avoiding aggression, and using all proper means to keep out of war.'

These two letters can have left Frere in no doubt that the British
government was opposed to a Zulu war while its resources – men
and money – were required elsewhere. But the second letter, in
particular, had hinted that a pre-emptive war per se was not out of
the question; it was rather the timing that was the problem. 'I can
quite understand,' Hicks Beach wrote, 'that there must be in the
Colony a strong desire to take the present opportunity of putting
an end to such a state of things as that which you have described,
by teaching Cetywayo a "lesson" which may prevent him from
future aggression. But taking a wider view . . . we are most anxious
not to have a Zulu war on our hands just now.'

And yet the same letter had confirmed that two battalions were
to be sent anyway. If Lord Chelmsford – Thesiger had become the
second Baron Chelmsford on the death of his father on 5 October
– really could conquer Zululand with just eight battalions,★ as he
had claimed in his memo of 14 September, there would be no need
to tap the British government for any further resources. Frere was
convinced that he could and that a successful war, even against
the government's advice, would quickly be forgiven. He admired
Chelmsford's efficient handling of the recent Cape Frontier War
and trusted his judgement. The conclusion both Frere and Chelmsford had drawn from the earlier campaign was that no tribal force
could live with the breech-loading rifle. 'I am inclined to think,'

★ These two battalions plus the six already in Natal and the Transvaal.

Chelmsford wrote to a subordinate in late November, 'that the first experience of the power of the Martini Henrys will be such a surprise to the Zulus that they will not be formidable after the first effort.' Such overconfidence was to have fatal consequences.

In the meantime, Frere was able to use the time lag between London and South Africa as an excuse for ignoring official instructions. Hicks Beach's letter of 7 November did not reach Pietermaritzburg until 13 December, by which time the die was almost cast, though a summary arrived by telegram on 30 November. The second letter followed a few weeks later. Both letters arrived after Frere had delivered an ultimatum to Cetshwayo that was designed – successfully as it turned out – to start a war.

Most historians have accused Frere of provoking an iniquitous and unnecessary war – and so he did, though the Natal settlers would not have described the conflict as either. But a large slice of the responsibility for the war must also go to the British politicians and officials in London who, since his appointment, had continually reminded Frere that the neutralization of Zululand was a virtual prerequisite for confederation. Admittedly the new colonial secretary, Hicks Beach, was less committed to confederation than his predecessor Carnarvon had been. But even Hicks Beach was sending Frere mixed messages by authorizing more troops on the one hand and advising caution on the other. It must have seemed, to a seasoned proconsul like Frere, that he was being urged to use his own judgement as to whether the war could be won with the troops then in South Africa. He was convinced that it could.

Sir Bartle Frere knew that both the Transvaal and the Cape were unlikely to agree to confederation until the threat from the Zulu kingdom had been removed. He was determined to fight the Zulus for the good of Empire, but had to make it look as though it was being fought for 'local, defensive reasons'. It did not help, therefore, that all the noises coming out of Zululand were essentially pacific. On 5 November, for example, the same day that Frere urged Hicks Beach to send reinforcements to prevent a 'war of races', a message reached Pietermaritzburg from Cetshwayo to the effect that he wanted to 'sit down and rest and be peaceful'.

Frere ignored the message and continued to exaggerate the threat posed by the Zulus. 'Even the most blind optimists out here are now seeing the truth,' he wrote to Hicks Beach on 10 November, '& realizing the fact that if, after repeatedly insulting us, & refusing reasonable demands for redress, Cetywayo cannot quite make up his mind to attack, we owe our immunity to his want of resolution, or fears of internal revolution, & to no want of settled determination on his part to get rid of all his white neighbours . . . The only safe course is immediate action, to secure the earliest & most assured peace possible.' What type of 'immediate action' he did not say, and it would be some time before the Cabinet learnt the truth: that Frere had decided to deliver an ultimatum so harsh that Cetshwayo could not possibly accept it. War would be inevitable, and the responsibility for starting it would lie with the Zulus. Or so Frere hoped.

His plan was to sugar the pill by delivering the ultimatum and announcing the award of the Boundary Commission at the same time. That way the expected Zulu rejection of the ultimatum could be portrayed as doubly uncooperative. The terms of the ultimatum were drawn up in late November. A long, rambling hypocritical document that ran to 5,000 words, it contained thirteen key demands. The first three related to the recent border outrages and insisted on:

(1) The surrender of Sihayo's brother and sons – the men responsible for the kidnap and murder of the chief's errant wives in July – and the payment of a fine of 500 cattle within twenty days.

(2) A further fine of one hundred cattle as recompense for the 'unwarrantable' treatment of the surveying party in September, also to be paid within twenty days.

(3) The handing over of Mbilini and others for their part in the raids across the Phongolo in October. No time limit was specified.

None of these demands was impossible to comply with, though Cetshwayo would have had trouble persuading his favourite Sihayo to surrender his relatives and the unruly Mbilini to surrender himself. The same could not be said of the next ten demands, which required the king's response within thirty days:

(1) The present military system to be abolished and replaced with one sanctioned by the Council of Chiefs and British officials.
(2) The army to be disbanded and the men returned to their homes.
(3) All able-bodied men still liable for military service in the defence of their country; but, until then, they should be allowed to live quietly at home.
(4) No man to be called up without the sanction of the Council of Chiefs and British officials.
(5) Every man to be free to marry 'when he pleases'.
(6) No Zulu to be punished for any crime unless convicted by a court of 'properly appointed Indunas'.
(7) No one to be executed without a fair and open trial and the right of appeal to the king.
(8) A British resident to reside in or near Zululand to enforce the above regulations.
(9) All missionaries and converts who had fled Zululand since 1877 to be allowed to return.
(10) No one to be expelled from Zululand unless the British resident has given his permission.

The demands were mixed with wordy passages that sought to justify them: Cetshwayo had not kept the promise he made at his coronation in 1873 to introduce certain laws 'for the better Government of the Zulu people'; the military system 'was destroying the country' by not allowing men to 'labour for themselves' and 'to live in quiet and in peace, with their families and relatives'; the army was not for self-defence but an instrument for the 'oppression of the people'. But all these issues were internal to the Zulu nation and did not provide a genuine reason for British intervention.

So Frere added the question of security. While Cetshwayo kept such a huge standing army, said the ultimatum, it was 'impossible for his neighbours to feel secure'. The British government was forced to keep large numbers of imperial troops in Natal and the Transvaal to guard against 'possible aggression by the Zulu King', and this was a state of affairs that could not be allowed to continue. Frere knew that Cetshwayo could not possibly comply with such harsh demands and keep his throne. The terms relating to the military system alone would have deprived him of most of his power and rendered him little more than a cipher. He was bound to resist, and that is exactly what Frere wanted him to do.

The ultimatum was written in Frere's name but endorsed by Sir Henry Bulwer. According to Bishop Colenso of Natal, a staunch opponent of the war, Bulwer agonized long and hard before putting his name to the document, commenting later, 'That's, I fear, the worst thing I ever did in my life.' Bulwer later confirmed Colenso's account when he told Sir Garnet Wolseley that he was 'very sore at having been induced by Frere to sign the ultimatum' and that 'much pressure' had been 'brought to bear upon him to make him do so'. In his opinion Frere had 'forced on' an 'unnecessary' war. The Zulus had 'always been our best friends', he said, and would have remained so if they had not been attacked. But in a letter to his brother, written a few days after signing the ultimatum, Bulwer gave a very different version of events. He described the demands made upon Cetshwayo as 'absolutely necessary and just'. He doubted they would be accepted and that war was the most likely outcome. 'However,' he added, 'there is no help for it. It is impossible to allow the king to keep up a standing army of thirty or forty thousand warriors – a perpetual menace – and without necessity, for there are no enemies to fear.' As for Frere, he wrote: 'I get on very well with him. We have not always agreed upon all points, but I am able to agree with what he has now asked and consider he has asked no more than necessary.' In truth Bulwer had caved in to Frere's relentless pressure and was probably embarrassed to admit as much to his own brother. He may have been hedging his bets: if the campaign went well, it made sense to be seen as a proponent of war; if it did not – as would prove to be the case – then he could always claim to have opposed the war from the start. But he may also have realized that Britain could not simply withdraw its troops from the border without doing irreparable damage to its prestige.

The boundary award and ultimatum were delivered by John Shepstone – brother of Sir Theophilus and acting Natal secretary for Native Affairs – to a deputation of Zulu indunas at the Lower Thukela Drift on 11 December. The announcement was made on the Natal bank of the river, beneath an awning shaded by a large fig tree, just below the recently constructed earthwork known as Fort Pearson. Shepstone and his assistants sat at a table, the Zulus in a rough semicircle at their feet. First Shepstone announced the boundary award; his words were translated into Zulu by F. B. Fynney, the local border agent. The Zulu response was typically non-committal. After a break for lunch – the Zulu indunas and their escort consuming the ox provided for the occasion – Shepstone read out the terms of the ultimatum. Again the indunas kept their composure, though they were clearly shocked. But one could not help growling, as Shepstone read through the litany of Cetshwayo's misrule, 'Have the Zulus complained?'

When Shepstone finished, the Zulu delegates responded by denying that the coronation laws had been broken. They could not understand, they added, why the disbandment of such an ancient and necessary institution as the army was necessary. Because, said Shepstone, it posed a serious threat to the subjects of Natal, whereas Cetshwayo knew that the British government presented no threat to the Zulus. What about them? asked one induna, pointing to Shepstone's escort. They were for defence, replied Shepstone, and were only there because of Cetshwayo's actions. Realizing that further discussion was pointless, the indunas requested an extension to the deadline on the grounds that thirty days was not enough time to discuss and respond to the ultimatum. Shepstone refused.

Fearful of Cetshwayo's reaction to the news, the indunas took their time returning to the royal kraal at oNdini, situated on a slight elevation of the Mahlabathini Plain between the White and Black

Mfolozi rivers. But John Dunn – a settler who had acted for many years as Cetshwayo's European adviser and been rewarded with a sizeable chiefdom in southern Zululand – intercepted them en route and sent the details of the ultimatum on ahead by his own messenger. The messenger returned on 18 December with Cetshwayo's response and Dunn forwarded it to Pietermaritzburg. The king was prepared to surrender Sihayo's sons and pay the fine, but needed more time to discuss the other demands with his council. He also asked Frere not to take any action if the men and cattle had not arrived within twenty days because the recent heavy rains had made travel difficult. Frere refused to allow any leeway, informing Dunn that 'the word of the Government as already given cannot now be altered unless the prisoners and cattle are given up within the time specified'. If they were not, he would order his troops to cross the Zulu border and halt at 'convenient posts'. There they would await the expiry of the thirty-day deadline and not take any 'hostile action' unless provoked.

A few days later a second letter arrived from Dunn, dated 24 December. It said that Cetshwayo was still collecting cattle, but that he did not attach much importance to the time limit and 'it will be impossible now for them to be up in time'. Dunn had therefore decided to seek refuge in Natal. He knew full well that the Zulus could not win a war with Britain and, with some of Cetshwayo's advisers accusing him of treason, had decided to cut his losses. On 30 December he informed John Shepstone that Cetshwayo had 'quite changed his tone' and was now 'determined to fight, as he says that, for what he hears of the Forces that are to be sent against him, he can easily eat them up one after the other'. The following day Dunn began to cross over into Natal with 2,000 retainers and 3,000 cattle. When the Zulus learnt of his betrayal, they looted and burnt his kraals. But Dunn had escaped and, as the campaign progressed, would provide Lord Chelmsford with much useful intelligence.

By late December, Cetshwayo had come to the reluctant con-clusion that war could not be avoided. If Frere would not even give him more time to pay the fines, he reasoned, what hope was there of persuading him to drop the ultimatum's more extreme demands? And yet to agree to dismantle the amabutho system was tantamount to accepting the abolition of monarchy. Cetshwayo would never do that. So he gave orders for his regiments to assemble for the annual First Fruits Ceremony★ at his kwaNodwengu military kraal on 8 January without their usual 'ornaments and badges' and to come 'with only their arms and ammunition prepared for immediate active service'.

In Natal, meanwhile, the first deadline expired on 31 December 1878 without the appearance of either Sihayo's relatives or the cattle. The following day Chelmsford, who had moved his headquarters to Greytown, warned Frere that 'any delay' in the advance of his invading columns 'would be very disadvantageous' and might 'tempt the Zulus to make a raid into Natal'. Frere's response, on 4 January, was to put the 'further inforcement' of the ultimatum's demands into Chelmsford's hands. That same day Chelmsford ordered Colonel Evelyn Wood's No. 4 Column at Utrecht to cross the Blood River but not to 'push on too far'. He was, he said, 'very anxious for Sir Bartle Frere's sake that no shot be fired by us' before the second deadline had elapsed. Wood advanced on 6 January. Five days later, Fynney received word from Cetshwayo that the 'Zulu nation' had gathered with him to listen to the British demands. It was too late. That morning the main invasion column had splashed across the Buffalo at Rorke's Drift. A day later another column, under Colonel Charles Pearson, crossed the Lower Drift of the Thukela. Frere's war had begun.

For fear of being countermanded, Frere had deliberately kept the British government in the dark for as long as possible. But in early December 1878 Hicks Beach managed to get his hands on a copy of a letter Frere had written to Theophilus Shepstone a month earlier, asking for the latter's opinion of the course he intended to

★ The festival, known as the *umKhosi*, took place in December/January when the moon was at its fullest. During the three days of ceremonies, the king and his regiments were ritually strengthened and cleansed of evil influences.

pursue. 'It seems to contain proposals which I don't understand,' wrote Hicks Beach to Frere on 11 December, the day the ultimatum was delivered, 'and the precise nature of which you have not yet, either officially or privately, explained to me ... Your letter to Shepstone speaks of "final proposals" and an "ultimatum". I really do not know at all what you contemplate in this direction, nor do I at present see the necessity for such an ultimatum ... As you will see from my dispatch, we entirely deprecate the idea of entering on a Zulu war *in order to settle the Zulu question.*'

As that was exactly what he was planning to do, Frere had to tread carefully. But the time lag between Britain and South Africa made it almost impossible for the government to intervene. Hicks Beach's letter of 11 December, for example, did not reach Frere until after the war had begun. In the meantime Frere continued to skirt round the issue. In a letter of 8 December he said that messengers were about to give Cetshwayo details of the boundary award and 'further communications' on 'our relations, past & future'. There was no mention of an ultimatum. He was more open in a letter to Hicks Beach of 23 December because he knew that by then the Cabinet was powerless to prevent war. He wrote:

I hope that Chelmsford's plans for moving in three converging columns on the royal kraal will go far to paralyse opposition, & to ensure success, with as little sacrifice as possible ... The die, for peace or war, had been cast long before I, or Bulwer, or even Sir Garnet Wolseley came here.

On Christmas Day, having at last received information about some of the demands in Frere's ultimatum in an official dispatch,* Hicks Beach penned an indignant response:

When I first came to the Colonial Office I told you you might rely on my support: and so you may. But (bearing in mind all I have written to you against the Zulu war, at the instance, remember, of the Cabinet) I

---

* The dispatch referred to enclosures that contained the full text of the ultimatum. They had not yet arrived and had probably been held back on Frere's orders.

think you will see how awkward a position you may have placed me in by making demands of this nature without my knowledge or sanction ... Cetywayo may very possibly prefer fighting to accepting them, and then, if the Cabinet should not be satisfied that you were right in making them, it will be too late to draw back, and we shall find ourselves involved in this war against our will.

The full text of the ultimatum finally reached Britain on 2 January 1879. It was followed on 13 January by a telegram from Frere. Cetshwayo, it said, had agreed to some of the demands but needed time to consider the others. Frere had refused to give him any. Hicks Beach knew this meant war and assumed – rightly – that it had already broken out. His only hope, he told Disraeli, was that it would be as 'short and successful' as the recent Afghan campaign had been. It was wishful thinking. The speed with which the British had defeated the Afghan Army, captured Kabul and forced Sher Ali into exile was mainly thanks to the brilliant generalship of Sir Frederick 'Bobs' Roberts. Chelmsford was no Roberts, while the Zulus were if anything more formidable – and certainly more disciplined – than the Afghans.

4. Preparing for War

Since arriving in Natal in early August 1878, Chelmsford had worked tirelessly to prepare for war. One of his first acts had been to ask F. B. Fynney, the border agent for the Lower Drift, to provide an assessment of the Zulu Army's capabilities. Fynney's report was detailed but concise. He explained how boys as young as fourteen were recruited into age-grade regiments and trained at military kraals; how each regiment or corps – a formation of two or more regiments – was divided into two wings and subdivided into companies of sixty men (the number of companies depending on the size of the regiment or corps); and how each regiment or corps, possessing its own military kraal, had one commanding officer, one second in command, two wing officers and a further three officers per company. He also explained how only married regiments were allowed to wear the headring and carry white shields; unmarried regiments were distinguished by black shields. The size of the Zulu Army he estimated at thirty-three regiments: eighteen married and fifteen unmarried. But, as seven were composed of men over sixty, that left 'for practical purposes' only twenty-six able to take the field: a total of 40,400 men.

Drill in the European sense, wrote Fynney, was 'unknown among the Zulus'. Their battlefield synchronization, as a result, was restricted to a number of 'simple movements' such as 'forming a circle of companies or regiments' and 'breaking into companies or regiments from the circle'. Zulu skirmishing, on the other hand, was 'extremely good' and could be performed under heavy fire 'with the utmost order and regularity'. Officers had clear responsibilities and were readily obeyed.

As for commissariat and transport, the Zulu Army had little need of either. The former consisted of 'three or four days' provisions, in the form of maize or millet, and a herd of cattle'; the latter of 'a number of lads who follow each regiment, carrying the sleeping mats, blankets, and provisions, and assisting to drive the cattle'. To the end of the report Fynney appended a list of more than a hundred of Cetshwayo's indunas, giving their personal details and a brief assessment of character and political affiliation. Overall the report was remarkably accurate, and Chelmsford recognized its worth by having it printed and distributed to every officer of the rank of company commander and above.

He also seems to have taken on board some of its implications as he formulated his plan of invasion. He wrote to Colonel Stanley:

In conducting operations against an enemy like the Kaffir or the Zulu, the first blow struck should be a heavy one, and I am satisfied that no greater mistake can be made than to attempt to conquer him with insufficient means. He has the advantage of being able to march in one day at least three times as far as the British soldier, and has no commissariat train to hamper him.

Chelmsford was wrong, however, to assume that the Zulu Army would seek to avoid a set-piece battle in favour of guerrilla warfare. Since Shaka's day its mindset had been aggressive. The young warriors, in particular, were anxious to 'wash their spears' in the blood of their enemies. They could hardly achieve this by operating 'hit and run' tactics. Nor did they want to. They had been trained to fix, surround and annihilate an enemy force. The tactic of envelopment introduced by Shaka – the 'horns of the buffalo' – was still the only one in use. But so confident was Chelmsford of the killing power of his infantry and artillery, and so dismissive of the threat posed by a mass Zulu attack, that he deliberately divided the relatively small force at his disposal to lure the Zulus into fighting a set-piece battle he was sure he would win.

His initial plan – as outlined to Colonel Stanley in his memorandum of 14 September – was to advance into Zululand with five small columns that would converge on the royal kraal at oNdini. Small columns, he reasoned, would be more flexible and easier to resupply. Their wide dispersal would also help to block a Zulu counter-invasion of Natal or the Transvaal. The points of advance were chosen because of their proximity to existing wagon tracks. They were (from south to north): the Lower Drift of the Thukela; the Middle Drift upstream; Rorke's Drift on the Buffalo; Utrecht near the Blood River; and Derby near the Phongolo.

Each invading column would be composed of a mixed force of British infantry, artillery and, in the absence of regular cavalry, mounted infantry and colonial volunteers. These European troops would be supported by a large force of African auxiliaries. For a time, Sir Henry Bulwer did everything he could to prevent the mobilization of Natal's blacks, many of them Zulu refugees, on the grounds that it would provoke the Zulus. He was also worried – rightly as it turned out – that Chelmsford would use the auxiliaries in an offensive rather than a defensive capacity and was wary of the long-term consequences of arming Natal's African population. Backed by Frere, Chelmsford eventually got his way. But it was not until late November 1878 that Bulwer finally authorized the raising of three regiments of infantry, five troops of horse and a force of 300 pioneers.

The man given the task of recruiting and organizing the auxiliaries was Lieutenant-Colonel Anthony Durnford, one of the three Natal representatives on the Boundary Commission. Born in Ireland in 1830, Durnford had followed family tradition by joining the Royal Engineers. He was a model pupil, graduating from the Royal Military Academy, Woolwich, in 1848 with first-class passes in mathematics, fortification and French, and completing his specialized instruction at Chatham with a commendation for his 'intelligence, abilities, zeal and high principles'. But his subsequent career had not lived up to this early promise. It began well with a posting to Ceylon and an appointment as civil engineer. His marriage in 1854 to the daughter of a retired colonel of the Ceylon Rifles, however, was not a success. Two of their three children were lost in infancy and they separated in 1860.★ Divorce was out of the question: a lengthy, public ordeal would have ended Durnford's career.

In 1872, still only a captain, he arrived in South Africa anxious to further his career and, if possible, test himself in battle. Eight years earlier – having missed out on all the major wars of the 1850s, including the Crimea (where he was transferred too late to take part) and the Indian Mutiny – he had set off for China in the hope of joining his old friend Charles 'Chinese' Gordon, who had just concluded a brilliant campaign against the Taiping rebels. But he fell ill en route and had to return to England. He had yet to see action when he landed at Cape Town.

This would all change with his posting, as a newly promoted major, to Natal in 1873. Appointed to Theophilus Shepstone's staff, he was an enthralled onlooker at King Cetshwayo's coronation on 1 September. 'They sang a war song,' he recalled, 'a song without words, wonderfully impressive as the waves of sound rose, fell and died away, then rose again in a mournful strain, yet warlike in the extreme.' A month later, having returned from Zululand, he took part in the expedition to prevent Chief Langilabele's rebellious Hlubi tribe from leaving Natal. Langilabele had persistently refused to register the guns paid to his people for work in the Kimberley diamond fields and, when Lieutenant-Governor Pine summoned him to Pietermaritzburg to explain himself, the chief made preparations to escape with his tribe over the Drakensberg Mountains into Basutoland. Durnford had been given the task of preventing him, and on 2 November, accompanied by just fifty-five members of the Royal Natal Carbineers and thirty mounted Basutos, he began the long and dangerous climb up to the Bushman's River Pass. A Carbineer recalled:

★ Durnford's most recent biographer has suggested that he may well have 'blamed his wife for the death' of his second child and 'that this brought about their separation' (Droogleever, 18).

Everyone was too tired to give more than a passing glance at the stupendous masses of projecting rock above us like a rugged wall, half a mile high. We would scramble up 20 or 30 yards then sit down, scramble another 20, and sit down again, leading our horses, which made it much more tiring than it would have been without them, for in keeping out of their way we would slip down at almost every step.

Despite falling badly on the ascent, dislocating his shoulder and gashing his head, Durnford eventually made it to the top during the early hours of 4 November. Warned by scouts that the Hlubi were approaching, he immediately deployed his reduced command – now just thirty-six Carbineers and fifteen Basutos – across the top of the pass. What Durnford did not know, however, was that Langilabele and the majority of his people had already crossed into Basutoland. The approaching Hlubi were the cattle guard: just a few hundred warriors. But even this small force was more than a match for Durnford's exhausted party. Ordered by the lieutenant-governor not to fire unless fired upon, Durnford could only watch in helpless fury as more and more Hlubi outflanked his position. Urged by Captain Barter,★ the commander of the Natal Carbineers, to withdraw his 'dispirited' men to a less exposed position, he assembled the troop and asked: 'Will no one stand by me, then?'

Only five troopers stepped forward: included amongst them were Robert Erskine, the son of Natal's colonial secretary, and Charlie Raw, who came from a farming background. The rest wanted to retire. With no option, Durnford gave the order to withdraw to higher ground. But, as the men did so, they were fired on by the Hlubi and chaos quickly ensued. Erskine and two other members of the rearguard were killed. Somehow Durnford survived. At one point, as he tried to rescue his mortally wounded Basuto interpreter, he was surrounded by Hlubi warriors, who grabbed his bridle and thrust at him with their assegais. One blow severed the nerve in his left elbow and wounded his side. But he managed to shoot two of his assailants with his revolver and escape

★ A farmer in his fifties and a member of Natal's executive council.

on his trusty Basuto pony 'Chieftain', his useless left arm hanging by his side.★

The operation had been a fiasco and many colonists blamed Durnford and his faulty planning. The *Natal Witness*, a newspaper generally supportive of Durnford, claimed that his 'pride in his profession as a soldier was buried in the grave of the 3 carbineers'. Durnford denied this and insisted that he was 'blameless'. His only regret was that he had lived when others died. In his official report, however, he criticized the lieutenant-governor's order not to fire first and questioned the courage of the Carbineers ('two or three shots were enough to send them into headlong flight'). All parties were exonerated by a Court of Inquiry: Durnford was praised for his courage and devotion to duty; 'extenuating circumstances' were used to excuse those who fled. But those connected to the Carbineers – including many of Natal's leading families – were unable to forgive Durnford's accusations of cowardice.

It did not help that, since arriving in Natal, Durnford had become a regular guest at the Bishopstowe Mission of John Colenso, the controversial bishop of Natal. Since taking up his post in 1853, Colenso had spent many years fighting colonial mismanagement and championing the cause of black Africans, who called him *Sobantu* ('The Father of His People'). He had also made a number of attacks on High Church orthodoxy that led, in 1869, to the appointment of a rival Anglican bishop of Maritzburg. For all these reasons Colenso was unpopular with Pietermaritzburg society and Durnford was damned by association. But, though he liked Colenso and shared many of his humanitarian views, Durnford had another motive for visiting Bishopstowe: to see Colenso's daughter Frances Ellen (or 'Fanny', as her family knew her). A handsome and head-strong woman, born in 1849, Fanny was the second of the bishop's five children. Like her two sisters she taught at her father's mission school and never married. Shortly before meeting Durnford she had broken off a relationship with a young man called Louis

---

★ He never regained the full use of his left arm and would tuck it into the front of his tunic.

Knollys. Durnford, with his handsome regular features, old-fashioned courtesy and high principles, may have helped to lessen the pain of that break-up. That she fell in love with Durnford is not in question; her ferocious defence of his posthumous reputation is proof enough of that. Whether they consummated their relationship is another matter. Durnford was, after all, unavailable for marriage.

The Colensos as a family were opposed to war with the Zulus because they saw it as unwarranted aggression. Durnford took a more detached, professional view. He did not seek war, but when it became inevitable he did everything he could to see that it was brought to a speedy and successful conclusion. It offered, after all, the chance to remove any lingering doubts about the quality of his leadership at Bushman's River Pass. So when Chelmsford asked Durnford, one of the few senior British officers in Natal with any experience of African levies, to raise a body of black auxiliaries, he readily agreed.

The infantry, known collectively as the Natal Native Contingent (NNC), totalled 7,000 men: the 1st Regiment of three battalions, each of 1,000 men, and the 2nd and 3rd Regiments of two battalions each. Each battalion was composed of ten companies of three white mounted officers, six white NCOs and one hundred Africans. The companies were organized on a tribal basis, each having a nickname and a small flag. But the battalions as a whole were tribally diverse, and this did not help to foster *esprit de corps*. Nor did the fact that only white NCOs and one African in ten were armed with firearms: outdated Snider breech-loading rifles and even older muzzle-loading Enfields. Durnford had wanted every man to be given a Snider rifle. But Bulwer was wary about arming Africans with guns, and there were, in any case, only a limited number of rifles available. So the rest of the contingent had to make do with billhooks and their traditional weapons of assegai and shield. Dress was also a matter of controversy. Durnford had been keen to clothe the contingent in scarlet tunics to impress the enemy and 'to ensure safety from the English side'. He was overruled by Chelmsford, who thought the men would move more freely as scouts and skirmishers if not encumbered by uniforms. The contingent's only distinguishing mark from Zulu warriors, therefore, was a red bandana. It was not enough to prevent many being mistaken for Zulus during the campaign and shot as a consequence.

Most of the contingent's senior officers – regimental and battalion commanders – were experienced soldiers. Commandant Rupert Lonsdale of the 3rd Regiment, for example, was an ex-imperial officer who had distinguished himself as a leader of Fingo levies in the recent Cape Frontier War. Lonsdale's staff officer, Captain Henry Harford, was a former adjutant of the 99th Foot who had grown up in Natal and spoke fluent Zulu. But decent junior officers and white NCOs were harder to find. Most of the best colonials had already volunteered for mounted units such as the Royal Natal Carbineers and Natal Native Horse (NNH). The contingent had to make do with the residue, with many of the NCOs recruited from unemployed drifters in the eastern Cape, few of whom could speak Zulu. The role of the NNC, as specified in Chelmsford's instructions to column commanders of 23 December 1878, was to protect the flanks of the columns and to help the wagons when they were in 'difficulties'. In the event of a Zulu attack they were to form up in echelon on the flanks of the British line, with the mounted troops protecting their rear. Once the charge had been stopped by rapid rifle-fire, their speed over broken ground would make them ideally suited for pursuit. It was never envisaged that the NNC would stand up to a full-blooded Zulu assault.

The mounted auxiliaries, the Natal Native Horse, were a much more effective force. Personally trained by Colonel Durnford – who described them in a letter to his mother as 'full of ardour' – they were mounted on sturdy Basuto ponies and each issued with a Martini-Henry carbine and a yellow cord uniform. Their officers were mostly from established colonial families like the Hendersons, Bartons and Raws. Three of the five troops – 150 men – were recruited from Chief Zikali's Amangwane tribe from the Upper Thukela and known as Zikali's Horse; though Zulu-speaking, they were traditional enemies of the Zulus. The two remaining troops were made up of Chief Hlubi's Basutos – 'old friends' of Durnford from Bushman's River Pass – and Christian converts from the Edendale Mission near Pietermaritzburg.

The creation of the Natal Native Pioneers was also Durnford's brainchild. In a memorandum of September 1878, he had argued that each column needed a force of pioneers to repair roads and throw up earthworks. Bulwer eventually agreed, and 300 were raised from Zulu refugees for distribution amongst the three Natal columns. Equipped with tools, rifles and a semblance of a European uniform, they were the pick of the African foot soldiers.

It was later claimed by friends of Durnford, notably Fanny Colenso, that Chelmsford originally offered him command of all the African levies and then changed his mind, reducing Durnford's command to one regiment of the NNC – the 1st – and the Native Horse. 'At first,' wrote Fanny, 'the General promised him the control & command in chief of the *whole* of the native force – & I *know* that the whole matter was talked over between them & settled, *but not on paper.* Consequently Col. Crealock [Chelmsford's military secretary] was able to over-persuade that weak General into altering everything, & giving only a third to him.' This scenario is certainly possible. Chelmsford would offer Major John Dartnell of the Natal Mounted Police, another British officer with extensive colonial experience, overall command of the mounted troops before giving the post to a better connected colleague.★

But even if Chelmsford did go back on his original promise to Durnford, he more than made up for this by giving him command of one of the five columns. 'I shall have some 3000 men, infantry, cavalry and a rocket battery,' Durnford informed his parents on 11 November, 'so the command is at least a respectable one for a Lieutenant-Colonel.'

One of Chelmford's chief handicaps – given the nature of the terrain he would be fighting on – was his lack of trained horsemen. He did not have a single regiment of British cavalry when the war began and would have to rely on mounted infantry, volunteers and

★ Brevet Lieutenant-Colonel Cecil Russell.

police. The Imperial Mounted Infantry (IMI) – descendants of a force raised by Lieutenant Carrington of the 1/24th Regiment for service on the Cape frontier in 1877 – were volunteers from most of the imperial battalions in South Africa. A hundred men in total, they were indifferent horsemen and armed with unwieldy Martini-Henry rifles instead of carbines. Their original commander was Lieutenant Edward Browne of the 1/24th. But towards the end of 1878 Browne was superseded by Lieutenant-Colonel Cecil Russell of the 12th Lancers, a special service officer recently arrived from England. Russell had served on the staff during the 1873 Ashanti Expedition and was a member of the Wolseley 'Ring' of talented young staff officers. He also owed his appointment to the fact that he was a former equerry to the prince of Wales and knew Chelmsford socially. But he had no experience of leading cavalry in war and his elevation above Browne caused much disgruntlement in the IMI. His subsequent promotion to commander of all mounted troops would – as we shall see – spark a far more serious disturbance among the colonial troops.

The oldest unit of volunteer horse was the Royal Natal Carbin-eers, first raised in 1855. Loosely organized and with elected officers, the Carbineers provided their own uniforms and horses but drew pay, weapons and ammunition from the government. They mustered quarterly for drill but had rarely seen action: Bushman's River Pass was an exception, and not a particularly glorious one. They were, however, mostly established colonials: excellent riders and crack shots with a good knowledge of the country. Their pre-eminence in Natal was underlined by the fact that their com-manding officer was Captain 'Offy' Shepstone, son of Sir Theo-philus. Other Natal units that contributed to Chelmsford's mounted force were the Natal Hussars, the Newcastle Mounted Rifles and the Buffalo Border Guard. In all, about 290 Natal volunteers were available for service in Zululand. They were supplemented by a smattering of tough volunteer units from across South Africa.

The final component of Chelmsford's irregular cavalry was a small paramilitary force known as the Natal Mounted Police (NMP). It had been raised in the wake of the Langilabele rebellion in 1874 by John Dartnell, a former major in the British Army who had resigned his commission to become a Natal farmer. Dartnell, a veteran of the Indian Mutiny, had by force of personality turned an unpromising bunch of raw recruits – absconded seamen, ex-soldiers and jobless vagrants – into a smart and well-drilled outfit of 110 men. Manning small posts across the colony, they assisted the local magistrates and apprehended gun-runners and cattle thieves. Their pay of 5s. 6d. a day was, on the surface, a handsome sum; but out of this they had to provide their own uniforms and food, and also pay back an advance for their horses and equipment. They were only too happy to volunteer for service in Zululand when they heard that the British government would provide their rations. What they could not stomach, however, was Chelmsford's cavalier treatment of their chief. According to Inspector George Mansel of the NMP, Chelmsford originally put Dartnell in command of all mounted troops with the central column. This was in accordance with the wishes of all the Natal volunteers, who had agreed to serve in Zululand only on the condition that they approved of their commander. Shortly before the invasion, however, Chelmsford changed his mind and put his favourite Cecil Russell, soon to be promoted to brevet lieutenant-colonel, in charge instead. Dartnell was 'shunted' on to the staff as Chelmsford's cavalry adviser. When Dartnell's men learnt of the switch, they were outraged. Mansel recalled:

I tried in every way to get Major D. to make a stand & fight [against] such injustice. I got all the officers of the Police to put their resignations in my hands, & went & tendered them & my own but they were not accepted. The reason why we continued to serve was that Major Dartnell asked us as a personal favour to himself not to resign our commissions.

The Carbineers too had been ready to put up a fight. Asked by their commanding officer, 'Offy' Shepstone, whether they were prepared to serve under Russell, they had answered no. As with the police, the incipient mutiny was nipped in the bud when Dartnell told them that he was happy with the new arrangement. But the resentment caused by Chelmsford's unjustified elevation of Russell above both Browne and Dartnell, two officers with extensive experience of South African warfare, would not go away.

Chelmsford's eight battalions of imperial infantry formed the backbone of his invading columns. Five were veterans of South Africa warfare: the 1/24th and 2/24th (Royal Warwickshire) Regiment and the 90th (Perthshire) Light Infantry had fought Kreli and Sandili in the eastern Cape; the 1/13th (Somerset) Light Infantry and 80th (South Staffordshire) Regiment had recently served against Sekhukhune's rebels in the Transvaal. The 2/3rd Foot (The Buffs) had seen no action but had been stationed in Natal for some time. Only the two battalions sent out from Britain as reinforcements – the 4th (King's Own) and 99th (duke of Edinburgh's) regiments were new to the African climate.

Each imperial battalion was commanded by a colonel and comprised eight companies – A to H – of a hundred men each. All of the senior officers were products of the purchase system – in which commissions were bought for a fixed price★ – and many had fought in the Crimean War and Indian Mutiny of the 1850s. Some captains too would have bought their first commission and served in the various imperial conflicts of the 1860s and 1870s: China, New Zealand, Abyssinia and Ashanti. But the junior officers, ensigns and lieutenants who had joined the army after the abolition of the purchase system in 1871 were selected, in theory, on the basis of merit. In reality breeding and money still mattered, and the majority of British officers continued to be drawn from the 'gentlemen' of the upper and upper-middle classes. Ordinary soldiers seemed to prefer it this way. One officer recalled a conversation with his colour-sergeant on the eve of his departure for England. 'Oh, sir,' said the colour-sergeant, 'what will the company do now you are going to leave us?' The officer replied: 'You have got a smart officer, Mr B——, to look after you all.' 'Yes, sir,' came the response, 'but he is not a gentleman.'

★ Though in reality many sold for well above the official price, particularly those for the smarter infantry and cavalry regiments.

However, other reforms introduced by Edward Cardwell, the Liberal secretary of state for War, in the early 1870s did alter the demographics of the ordinary soldier. Previously a recruit signed on for life (meaning, in practice, until his services were no longer required or he was no longer physically capable to perform his duties). This all changed with the introduction of short service in 1870, whereby recruits spent six years in the regular army and six in the reserve. The scheme was designed to create a large pool of trained reservists (who could be called up in time of war), to reduce the length of time served abroad and to save money. In 1872 it was complemented by the creation of linked battalions: one recruiting at home while the other served abroad, so ensuring that only experienced troops guarded the Empire. But in practice the steady increase of colonial commitments meant that a growing number of 'green' battalions were sent abroad. By 1879 eighty-two battalions were stationed abroad and only fifty-nine at home. To cater for the large turnover of men caused by short-term enlistment, physical standards had to be lowered. Younger, less hardy recruits were the result. The conservative duke of Cambridge had opposed the reforms on the ground that they would weaken the fighting capacity of the army. With the war under way and not going well, he would comment, 'Now we want *men* & have nothing but *boys* to send out & not half enough even of them.' Colonel Wood was even more critical of the reinforcements sent from Britain, telling the queen that 'these poor young fellows had not the metal nor the health & strength to make them really good soldiers, & this was the reason why so many officers were killed'.

Chelmsford had been appalled by the quality of the recruits with whom he had travelled out to South Africa in February 1878. Over 60 per cent of them, he told the duke of Cambridge, had less than four months' service, had not completed a musketry course and were still learning recruit's drill. The 2/24th Regiment, which arrived in South Africa at around the same time, also contained a relatively high proportion of young recruits. But three months on active service in the Perie Bush, followed by six months under canvas – or, more frequently, the stars – had turned these rookies into hardy soldiers with lean bodies and tanned, bearded faces. The 1/24th – the 2/24th's sister battalion – had been in South Africa since 1875 and was fully acclimatized long before the recent Cape Frontier War in which the 'old, steady shots' of the battalion had distinguished themselves in numerous actions, notably the defence of Kentini on 7 February 1878. 'In the British Army it would have been impossible,' recalled one officer, 'to pick a body of men fitter for such work. The majority were old soldiers of 10 years service and over, of grand physique, self confident and fresh from the successful campaign in the old Colony.'

The British Army had come a long way since Wellington's famous 'scum of the earth' jibe in 1813. Improved food, uniforms, education, barracks and leisure facilities had made the army a less forbidding place. Gone were the days when it was dominated by paupers and ex-convicts. But most recruits still came from the lower echelons of the agricultural and urban poor, were barely literate and had enlisted as something of a last resort. This was reflected by the low esteem in which the army was still held by the Victorian public. 'It was not uncommon,' wrote one senior officer, 'to hear people speak, perhaps in ignorance, but sometimes in contempt, of the "common soldier". He was, in their view, a creature to be shunned by the good and virtuous of society . . . an outcast not to be thought of or considered until his services were required to fight his country's battles.' Yet this same officer had been associated with the private soldier for nearly forty years and had found him, as a rule, 'truthful, generous, and chivalrous, grateful for any kindness' and quick to repay 'those who think of and care for him with gratitude and affection'. Rudyard Kipling summed up the ambivalent attitude of the public in his poem 'Tommy': 'For it's Tommy this, an' Tommy that, an' "Chuck him out, the brute!" / But it's "Saviour of 'is country" when the guns begin to shoot.'

To keep the 'brutes' in order, harsh punishments were still considered necessary – even flogging. Parliament had debated the abolition of flogging since the 1820s and progressively reduced the number of lashes that could be awarded from a thousand to fifty. But conservative officers had prevented outright abolition by insisting that army discipline depended upon the ultimate sanction of flogging. Without it, said Wellington, 'We might as well pretend to extinguish the lights in our houses or theatres by extinguishers made of papers as to maintain the discipline of the army.' Chelmsford's men paid the price. 'They are very strict out here, and flog men for very little,' wrote one private during the campaign. 'There were two of the Engineers flogged this morning for stealing gin.' An officer described the flogging of two of his men for drunkenness on a ship bound for South Africa:

There was a large plank fastened up, the man was stripped of his clothes down to his hips, his hands and legs secured by ropes to the plank, and then came the sickly horrible sight; the cat was produced. 9 lashes of whipcord with knots, and two of the strongest men in the Regiment, the Farrier and the Trumpeter, were selected. They each gave 5 lashes in turn, relieving one another. At each stroke, blood came up. It was a beastly sight. I turned away. The man merely groaned a little and winced as the stroke fell, but no flinching, no speaking or murmur. . . I hope there will be no more flogging. It does not bring credit to a regiment.

On land a prisoner was tied to an iron triangle or, if one was not available, a wagon wheel. The barbaric practice of flogging was finally abolished in 1881.

Army pay in 1879 was meagre: a private soldier was due a shilling a day, but, after deductions for necessaries, washing, haircutting and damages, he rarely received more than eight pence. A few pennies more were earned for long service, good conduct and marksmanship. But it was not a lucrative career. Food, however, was plentiful and of reasonable quality. The staples of 1 lb of bread and ¾ lb of meat a day were supplemented by tea, coffee, sugar, milk, preserved potatoes and any other vegetables that were available. The meat was either salt beef or pork, supplied in barrels, though slaughter herds followed the troops when on active service. Field bakeries were present in the main camps; detached troops had to make do with hard tack. The only constant was the rum ration of half a gill a day.

Infantry uniforms were not ideal but better than they had been.

Gone were the restrictive shakos, leather stocks and double-breasted coatis of pre-Crimean days. In their place were shorter, single-breasted scarlet tunics and cork sun-helmets covered with white canvas. Blue trousers and heavy ammunition boots completed the get-up. Equipment too had been rationalized. In the Crimea a fully laden soldier would carry up to sixty-eight pounds, including rifle, knapsack, water-bottle, blanket and webbing. By 1879 – thanks to the recommendations of Garnet Wolseley's *Soldier's Pocket-Book* – this burden had been reduced to fifty-seven pounds; it included a rifle and bayonet, two pouches, an ammunition bag, a haversack, a water-bottle, a mess-tin, a greatcoat and two days' rations. Everything else was thrown into a company wagon.

The standard infantry rifle in 1879 was the excellent breech-loading Martini-Henry. The first breech-loader, issued in 1865, was the Snider conversion of the old muzzle-loading Enfield rifle. But the Snider–Enfield was only a stopgap, and the War Office looked at 120 different actions before adopting the Martini-Henry in 1871. It fired a black-powder, centre-fire, brass .45 cartridge with a heavy lead bullet that could stop a buffalo and knock a man back in his tracks. It was loaded by depressing the lever behind the trigger guard, which emptied the chamber. A fresh cartridge was then placed on the exposed breech-block and thumbed home. There was no safety catch.

So quick and efficient was the rifle's action that some regarded it as the first firearm to compare with the longbow of the Hundred Years War in terms of range, rapidity of firing and robustness. In an expert's hands it was accurate up to 1,000 yards; battalion volley fire began at 600 to 800 yards. Even an average shot could score hits at 300 yards. But it had two serious defects: it was liable to jam when sand got into the breech mechanism or excessive firing melted the thin brass cartridge and made it difficult to extract; and the deep, square-cut grooves of the barrel tended to foul. This made its kick even more vicious than usual, resulting in bruised shoulders and even nosebleeds. During a lengthy firefight the barrel – despite the protection of a wooden forestock – became too hot to touch, and so veterans sewed cowhide covers around it to protect their hands. The only other weapon carried by the infantry was a 21½-inch triangular bayonet known as a 'lunger'. When fixed, it increased the rifle's reach to just under six feet – a handy weapon for close-quarter fighting.

Rifle ammunition came in paper packets of ten rounds. Each man carried two packets in each of his leather ammunition pouches, ten rounds loose in his small canvas expense pouch and a further two packets in his haversack – seventy rounds in all, though few battles required such expenditure. Nevertheless each battalion had a reserve of 30,000 rounds – enough for thirty per man – that it kept with it at all times in two wagons. A column would carry a huge field reserve of almost 500 rounds per man. This reserve ammunition was packed in strong wooden boxes that each contained 600 rounds. Two feet long, seven inches wide and nine inches deep, each hefty box was made of solid teak or mahogany planks, almost an inch thick, and weighed eighty pounds when full. They were strengthened by a copper band at either end and carried by rope handles. Access was gained by a central tongue-and-groove sliding lid that was held in place by a single two-inch brass screw. Once opened, the protective tin lining could be removed and the paper packets handed out.

Officers wore uniforms similar to those of the men, though members of the Royal Artillery, Royal Engineers and staff, including Chelmsford himself, preferred dark blue Norfolk jackets in the field. They carried swords – but rarely used them – and Adams or Webley centre-fire .45 revolvers. In an emergency they would often grab a rifle. Many had telescopes, though these were being replaced by binoculars.

The most destructive firepower available to Chelmsford was his three batteries of light field artillery. Each battery consisted of six 7-pounder muzzle-loading field guns.★ Originally designed as

★ A breech-loading piece with a wrought-iron reinforced, rifled barrel – known as an Armstrong gun, after its inventor, William G. Armstrong – had been introduced in the wake of the Crimean War. But it was difficult to load and expensive to produce, and in 1866 a select committee ruled in favour of muzzle-loaders. They remained in use until 1886.

mountain guns, they were specially mounted on light 'Kaffrarian' carriages with 5-ft-diameter wheels that gave a total weight of just 200 pounds. This made them easier to transport over the broken African terrain, though they gave 'rather a queer dwarfed appearance mounted on their long axles, between their tall wheels'. On the move each gun carriage was attached to a limber and drawn by a team of six horses, the near-side horses ridden and the off-side horses controlled with whip and rein by the drivers on the limber. With their steel-rifled barrels, these powerful guns could fire explosive shells up to 3,000 yards; shrapnel was used at close range.

Additional artillery came in the form of a 9-pounder rocket battery that could propel a small iron projectile, seventeen inches long and two and a half inches in diameter, to a maximum range of 1,500 yards.* Fired by a hand-lit fuse from a V-shaped iron trough, the rocket made a hideous shrieking noise in flight and left behind a thick trail of white smoke and yellow sparks. Its effect was as much psychological as practical. Chelmsford also had a handful of hand-cranked Gatling guns – the forerunner of the machine-gun – each of which could fire up to 600 rounds a minute from its ten barrels.

The nerve centre of Chelmsford's army – any Victorian army for that matter – was a small coterie of staff officers. The British had yet to adopt the Prussian model of a General Staff: a corps of highly trained staff officers responsible for war planning and organization, which would provide assistance to commanders in the field. British generals used their staff more like a personal secretariat. Wellington's staff work had been divided amongst three senior officers: a military secretary, an adjutant-general and a quartermaster-general. Such an ad hoc system was still largely in operation during the Crimean War. Only fifteen of the 221 staff officers with Lord Raglan's army had gained any theoretical knowledge of staff work

* The original rocket, invented by William Congreve in the early 1800s, had used a long wooden stick to stabilize it in flight. But these were notoriously inaccurate and by the Zulu War the rocket had been steadied by three metal vanes in its exhaust nozzle.

by studying at the Senior Department of the Royal Military College, Sandhurst. Most staff appointments were made entirely upon the basis of 'influence' rather than ability: all four of Raglan's aides-de-camp, for example, were relatives. The inadequacy of such a system was highlighted by the acute supply problems in the Crimea and resulted in the establishment of the Staff College at Camberley in 1858. But the hostility of the duke of Cambridge towards the creation of a professional staff corps meant that Camberley graduates did not begin to flourish until the 1870s, when Sir Garnet Wolseley, the pre-eminent British general, favoured them as staff for his various expeditions. More conservative commanders like Chelmsford, however, continued to recruit their staffs from those officers they knew and liked, rather than choosing those with experience and training. His key staff officer, Brevet Lieutenant-Colonel John North Crealock, is a case in point. A veteran of the Indian Mutiny, Crealock had served with Chelmsford at Aldershot before receiving a plum staff appointment at the Horse Guards. On hearing that Chelmsford was to be sent to South Africa as Cunynghame's replacement, Crealock had applied to join his staff and was eventually appointed 'assistant military secretary'. A clever, abrasive man – if not a particularly efficient staff officer – Crealock was the ideal lightning rod for a commander of Chelmsford's geniality. 'He had not a very good manner and Chelmsford had,' recalled one of his subordinates, 'so that all disagreeable orders were supposed to emanate from Crealock which was rather unfair on him.' Wolseley, on the other hand, described Crealock as 'that arch-snob' and Chelmsford's 'evil genius'. Another senior officer agreed, telling the duke of Cambridge that, in his opinion, Chelmsford was 'governed by Crealock & kept in ignorance of all going on about him'. He was, at the same time, a skilled watercolourist and would leave a unique pictorial record of the Zulu War.

Crealock became, by default, Chelmsford's acting chief of staff. He did not appoint an official chief of staff, because 'he had confidence in his own organizational abilities and was reluctant to delegate'. But, as operations during the Zulu War became more complicated, his poorly trained and badly structured staff organization became more of a handicap. He did not, for example, feel the need to appoint a properly trained intelligence chief. Instead he selected a Natal civil servant with experience of Zululand.* It was not until Wolseley took the field – in August 1879 – that intelligence was put in the hands of a graduate of the Staff College.†

Other areas of Chelmsford's staff would also prove deficient. His most experienced staff officer was his deputy adjutant-general, Colonel William Bellairs, who had served with Chelmsford on the Cape frontier. But because Chelmsford 'did all his work as Adjt. Genl.', this capable officer would be sidelined in Pietermaritzburg for much of the early part of the war. As for Chelmsford's three aides-de-camp, not one had any formal staff training: Major Matthew Gossett of the 54th Regiment had sailed out with him from England; Captain Ernest Buller‡ of the Rifle Brigade had recently arrived as a special service officer; and Lieutenant Berkeley Milne, RN, had been attached to his staff as a courtesy to the Naval Brigade, who were serving with Pearson's column.

Chelmsford was not in any doubt that the 17,000 troops and twenty guns available to him in January 1879 would prove more than a match for the Zulus. His biggest headache was finding a way to supply them in the field. First he had to stockpile food and ammunition; then arrange for it to follow the invading columns in ox-wagons and mule-carts. This was a huge logistical effort that ultimately required the purchase and hire, often at exorbitant prices, of more than 27,000 oxen, 5,000 mules and 2,500 wagons and carts. The ox-wagon had been developed by the Boer Voortrekkers and was ideally suited to carrying heavy loads over difficult terrain. But it was neither a cheap nor a swift mode of transport. Each covered wagon was twenty feet long and six wide, with huge iron-rimmed wheels as tall as a man. It was drawn by a span of not less than

* The Honourable William Drummond, younger son of the earl of Strathallen.
† Captain J. F. Maurice.
‡ No relation of Lieutenant-Colonel Redvers Buller.

sixteen oxen, whose lead beasts, usually the most experienced, were guided by a *voorlooper*★ (often a teenager) with a stick. The driver, meanwhile, stood at the front of the cart and controlled the team with a long whip that he could crack at will above the head of any beast that slacked. No fodder was required but plenty of grazing. Oxen took literally hours to eat and would tire fast if they did not get their fill. Their pace, when on the move, was little more than two miles an hour; and that was before the inevitable hold-ups crossing rivers and broken ground. An army that relied on ox-wagons was not in a position to launch a campaign of surprise.

The supply process might have been easier, and considerably cheaper, had Chelmsford been on better terms with the Natal government. But he was not, and Bulwer was deaf to his appeal for transport to be requisitioned. The cost of transport became, as a result, the biggest single expense of the war. But transport considerations had a far more serious strategic consequence in that Chelmsford's reliance on slow-moving and vulnerable supply trains limited both his manoeuvrability and the size of his invading columns.

His original plan to invade with five columns was partly a response to the problem of supply. Small columns would have more forage at their disposal and be easier to manoeuvre. They would also cover more of the enemy's territory, reduce the risk of being outflanked and deter a counter-invasion of British territory. But by late December 1878 Chelmsford had modified his plan. Now he would invade with just three columns: the right column – No. 1 under Colonel Pearson – would cross the Thukela at the Lower Drift and make for Eshowe, fifteen miles to the north; the centre column – No. 3 under Colonel Glyn – would cross the Buffalo at Rorke's Drift and move east; and the left column – No. 4 under Colonel Wood – would march south-east from Utrecht. All three columns would then converge on Cetshwayo's capital at oNdini. No. 2 Column under Colonel Durnford had been scheduled to cross the Thukela at Middle Drift. Now it would play a supporting role to Pearson's column and not advance until the

★ Team leader.

invasion was well under way. The remaining column – No. 5 under Colonel Rowlands – had failed to put down the rebellion by Sekhukhune's Pedi and so was left in a defensive role on the Phongolo River, both to protect the Transvaal from the Pedi and to cover No. 4 Column's open left flank from the Zulu and the equivocal Swazi.

On 8 January 1879, just three days before the second and final ultimatum was due to expire, Chelmsford wrote a cautious letter to the duke of Cambridge:

Our movements will all be made in the most deliberate manner. There is nothing to be gained by a rapid forward movement, and if I wished to make a rush I should be unable to carry it out, consequent upon the great difficulties of supply and transport . . . We are now also in the most rainy season of the year, and convoys are sadly delayed by the state of the roads. I may possibly therefore be unable to finish the war with the rapidity which, under the present aspect of affairs in Europe, is evidently so desirable.

He would, however, do his best to bring the war to 'a speedy close' so that he could return some of his troops to Britain.

Chelmsford could not say when the war would end, but he was certain he would be victorious. This sense of superiority – even contempt for his foe – was felt by the British troops massed on the Zulu border. One private in the 1/24th Regiment told his mother: 'I suppose we will give the natives a dreadful thrashing when we commence.' A colleague was more dismissive still. 'I can tell,' he wrote, 'although large and powerful, they have not the pluck and martial spirit of Englishmen.' Occasionally a warning note was sounded. 'I think we shall lose a good many,' wrote a sergeant of the 2/24th, 'for they are too strong for us.' But such lone words of caution were lost in a chorus of optimism. All three of the above correspondents – optimistic and pessimistic alike – would die in the opening battle.

Officers were just as dismissive of the Zulu threat and could not wait for the fighting to start. 'We are longing for the war to begin,' wrote 31-year-old Lieutenant Henry Curling of N/5 Battery, Royal Artillery, in late November, 'it seems as if it never would.' A couple of weeks later Curling could breathe again. 'Our ultimatum has been sent to the Zulu king,' he told his mother, 'but it asks so much that he cannot, even if he wishes, give in. The only thing the natives understand is force. They will promise anything but always break their promises, so the only thing to be done is to take all their cattle, burn all their huts and kill a few thousand of them; if they make a fight and get beaten, so much the better.' Lieutenant Nevill Coghill of the 1/24th Regiment had considered war to be both inevitable and necessary since being given the plum appointment of aide-de-camp to Sir Bartle Frere in September 1878. 'The Zulus are ready to fight,' he wrote on 3 November. 'They have called up all their regiments and may any day commence aggressive action in which case we shall have to go in at them and treat them as we did the Kaffirs in Cape Colony.' Another officer recalled: 'We all thought and so did nearly everyone that they would come once at us and after getting most frightfully smashed, all organised resistance would be at an end and that the old hunting business would have to go on.' He could not have been more wrong.

—

5. Invasion

The invasion of central Zululand began shortly after dawn on 11 January 1879, when the lead troops of Colonel Richard Glyn's No. 3 Column took advantage of patchy mist to cross the Buffalo River at Rorke's Drift. A short, pugnacious officer with a waxed moustache and an evil temper, Glyn had been blooded during the brutal suppression of the Indian Mutiny and later purchased the colonelcy of the 1/24th, which he brought to South Africa in 1875. He had done well in the recent Cape Frontier War as commander of the Transkei and received the thanks of Sir Bartle Frere and a CB from the queen. Then his battalion had formed part of his command; now it did so again, less three companies that were on detached garrison duty. He also had with him seven companies of the 1/24th's sister battalion, the 2/24th, a battery of Royal Artillery, a mixture of European horse (mounted police and volunteers), two battalions of the Natal Native Contingent (1/3rd and 2/3rd NNC) and a company of Natal Native Pioneers: a grand total of 1,891 European and 2,400 African troops. Staff officers and civilian support brought the total to more than 4,700 men. To drag the guns, transport the supplies and provide food were more than 2,000 oxen, 67 mules, 220 wagons and 82 carts.

The first man from the column to set foot in Zululand was not a soldier but a journalist, Charles Norris-Newman of the London *Standard*, who was also stringing for two Cape newspapers. So oblivious was the British press to events in South Africa at this stage that Norris-Newman, a talkative ex-British officer known affectionately as 'Noggs',* was the only correspondent covering

---

* Lonsdale had nicknamed him 'Noggs' after Newman Noggs in Dickens's *Nicholas Nickleby*. Another officer described him as 'an excellent and garrulous companion in our Mess' (*Harford Journal*, p. 12).

the war. He had attached himself to the headquarters of Colonel Rupert Lonsdale's 3rd NNC and was proudly wearing the contingent's distinguishing mark, a red scarf tied round his sun-helmet like a puggaree, as he urged his horse through the girth-deep water of the old drift. He was soon joined on the Zulu bank by Major A. W. Cooper's 2/3rd NNC and the rest of the mounted men, who spurred towards the high ground and established an uneven line of vedettes.* Most of the British infantry and the 1/3rd NNC crossed a couple of hundred yards upstream at the new drift, the British using two ponts and the Africans wading across. Here the eighty-foot wide stretch of water was neck-deep and fast-moving, and, despite linking arms, several Africans were swept away and drowned. How many was impossible to tell: they had never been properly counted.

The crossings continued throughout the day, and by evening most of the combat troops were over. Glyn had set up camp on the banks of the river and posted a semicircular chain of picquets a mile and a half to the front. Of hostile Zulus there was no sign. The only Zulu encountered was a lone herdsman who was swiftly relieved of his cattle by a mounted patrol.

While Glyn supervised the siting of the camp, Chelmsford and his staff rode north to Nkonjane Hill to consult with Colonel Wood. Three days earlier, acting on intelligence that Chief Sihayo planned to oppose the crossing with 8,000 men, Chelmsford had asked Wood to create a diversion by marching part of his force towards Rorke's Drift. Wood had done just this – establishing his base at Bemba's Kop on the Blood River – and the two met, as planned, at Nkonjane Hill at 9 a.m. on 11 January. They talked for three hours on a variety of subjects, including Frere's suggestion that Wood should become resident of Zululand after the war. Wood replied that a resident 'ought to speak the language', which he could not, and that he was 'too fond of soldiering to leave the 90th Light Infantry for Political Employment'. Wood then said that, according to his spies, the 'first serious Zulu attack' would fall

* Cavalry outposts.

on No. 3 Column. Chelmsford thanked him for his assistance and told him not to advance for a few more days, because Colonel Pearson, who was due to cross the Lower Drift that day, had the furthest distance to cover. He then returned to the Natal bank to spend the night.

The following morning Chelmsford joined Glyn's camp in Zululand and, to all intents and purposes, took command of the column. Major Francis Clery, Glyn's principal staff officer, wrote to a fellow officer:

That he should take command was of course to be expected, but it had the effect of practically effacing the nominal Commander of the Column (Colonel Glyn, 24th Regt) and his staff. You know the General so well you will understand all this, and how his energetic, restless, anxious temperament, led him into very minor matters. For he used even to detail himself the patrols & constantly gave orders direct to Commanders of Corps. Beyond placing one in an uncertain and sometimes anxious position in thinking what remained for one, as Staff Officer of the Column, to do, and what the General had left undone, or how far any orders one may issue would be running counter to those he may have issued etc. etc. I did not see any objection whatever to the General taking the whole thing into his hands. The only thing I thought of importance was that he should do so, *thoroughly*.

Clery's letter is important because it contradicts Chelmsford's claim – made later in an effort to deflect the blame for Isandlwana – that he had nothing to do with the day-to-day running of the column.

Chelmsford's intention was to advance up the old track that ran from Rorke's Drift to Cetshwayo's capital of oNdini, sixty or so miles to the east. But he knew that the kraal of Sihayo – the local chief and favourite of Cetshwayo, whose sons had committed the recent outrage in Natal – was in the Batshe Valley to the left of the track and so proceeded with caution. During the morning of the 12th, he led a reconnaissance in force up the track and before long had spotted a herd of cattle below one of Sihayo's hilltop strongholds. Orders were given to four companies of the 1/24th and the whole of the 1/3rd NNC to capture the cattle and, as they approached, a steady fire was opened on them by Zulus hidden in caves. The auxiliaries were in front and a handful was hit. After a momentary pause, their officers persuaded them to continue their advance and, assisted by the 1/24th, they managed to clear the caves and kill about a dozen Zulus. Their own casualties were two killed and twenty wounded, including two officers. Despite the doubters, the NNC had performed well in its first engagement.

Chelmsford now ordered Colonel Henry Degacher, who had just arrived from camp with four companies of his 2/24th and a portion of the 2/3rd NNC, to capture Sihayo's main kraal, which was a little further up the valley under a steep krantz.* Having 'skirmished or rather clambered up the steep mountainside', Degacher's men found all the caves empty. The kraal – 'picturesquely situated in an angle of the hills, 200 feet above the level of the valley' – was also empty but for three old women and a girl who told the British that the inhabitants had left the day before. Frustrated by Sihayo's narrow escape, Chelmsford ordered the kraal to be burnt before returning to the drift with 500 head of cattle. There he learnt of another minor success. During the operation the mounted troops had been told to secure a nearby hill and, as they neared the crest, they were engaged by about sixty Zulus. The riders dismounted and returned fire, killing '9 or 10 of the enemy amongst whom was one of Sirayo's sons'. His name was Mkhumbikazulu and he had not taken part in the kidnap and execution of Sihayo's errant wives. That act was chiefly the responsibility of his eldest brother, Mehlozkazulu, who had accompanied his father to oNdini to attend the general muster. Mkhumbikazulu had been given the thankless task of defending the family homestead with just two or three hundred warriors. His resolute conduct cost him his life, but Chelmsford failed to draw the obvious conclusion: the Zulus *would* stand and fight.

That evening he wrote to Frère in buoyant spirits: 'I am in great hopes that the news of the storming of Sirayo's stronghold & the

---

* Rocky outcrop.

capture of so many of his cattle . . . may have a salutary effect in Zululand & either bring down a large force to attack us or else produce a revolution in the country. Sirayo's men have I am told always been looked upon as the bravest in the country & certainly those who were killed today fought with great courage.' Yet Chelmsford knew that severe logistical problems lay ahead. He added:

The country is in a terrible state from our rain, and I do not know how we shall manage to get our wagons across the valley near Sirayo's Kraal. A large working party will start tomorrow to dig deep ditches on each side of the road which runs across a broad swamp – and I hope that under this treatment it may consolidate. 16 Oxen is too few to draw even 4000 lbs and I am sending an order for sufficient oxen to be sent up so as to make each span up to 20. Whether they are procurable remains to be seen. I am afraid our losses have been so heavy and the demands for draught oxen so great, that the Transport director [Captain Edward Essex] will find a difficulty in complying with the demand.

Chelmsford told Wood, in a letter on 13 January, that it would take at least a week to drain the road and build up sufficient supplies at Rorke's Drift to enable the advance to continue. Irritated by the delay, he was doubly enraged when word reached him that Colonel Durnford, whose No. 2 Column was stationed at Kranskop above the Middle Drift, had disobeyed his most recent orders. Chelmsford's original intention had been for Durnford to advance into Zululand – with a mixed force of 3,000 black levies and a European rocket battery – to cover the left flank of Pearson's No. 1 Column. But he had second thoughts, as we have seen, and, on 1 January, subordinated Durnford to Pearson: not only would Durnford forfeit a battalion of NNC when the invasion began, but he would have to wait for Pearson to clear the country ahead of the Middle Drift before he was allowed to cross the border. A week later, Durnford's command was divided again when Chelmsford ordered him to send his two strongest NNC battalions to Sandspruit on the Buffalo to block a possible Zulu counter-invasion. From there they could, if necessary, cooperate with Glyn's column; the rest of Durnford's force would remain at Kranskop until Pearson had occupied Eshowe. By 13 January, however, Durnford had still not dispatched the two battalions. Instead, acting on a tip-off, he informed Chelmsford that he was about to move his entire force down to the Middle Drift to oppose a possible Zulu invasion. He was forming up his men for the descent, in the early hours of 14 January, when Chelmsford's response brought him up short. 'I saw a change in his face at once,' recalled one of Durnford's officers. 'Suddenly he gave the word to retrace our way to camp and I well remember the look of disgust that crossed his countenance as he read the order.' It stated:

Unless you carry out the instructions I give you, it will be my unpleasant duty to remove you from your command, and to substitute another officer for the command of No. 2 Column. When a column is acting *separately* in an *enemy's country* I am quite ready to give its commander every latitude, and would certainly expect him to disobey any orders he might receive from me, if information which he obtained, showed that it would be injurious to the interests of the column under his command. Your neglecting to obey my instructions in the present instance has no excuse ... If movements are to be delayed because report hints at a chance of an invasion of Natal, it will be impossible for me to carry out my plan of campaign. I trust you will understand this plain speaking & not give me any further occasion to write in a style which is distasteful to me.

Chelmsford's censure was justified. Durnford had used unconfirmed – and, as it turned out, inaccurate – reports as an excuse for not sending the two battalions to Sandspruit. No doubt he was smarting from the break-up of his command. But this cannot excuse disobedience. However, Chelmsford had left open the possibility of an officer disobeying orders in Zululand if, in his opinion, they were 'injurious to the interests of the column under his command'. It granted an officer of Durnford's independent stamp far too much freedom of manoeuvre – as events would prove.

On 15 January Durnford was ordered to move towards Rorke's Drift with a battalion of infantry, the Natal Native Horse and the rocket battery. Two weak battalions – the 1/1st and 3/1st – were to be left at Kranskop. The obvious assumption is that Chelmsford did not trust Durnford and wanted to keep a closer eye on him. This was partly true. But he had already envisaged that Durnford's and Glyn's columns might work together, and his brush with Sihayo's men may have convinced him that the central column would have the hardest fighting. He was also woefully short of cavalry for reconnaissance purposes and would have welcomed the assistance of Durnford's excellent Native Horse. There is no suggestion, at this stage, that Durnford had ceased to operate as an independent column commander.

On 16 January Chelmsford outlined his new strategy in a letter to Colonel Wood, who was still at Bemba's Kop, though his mounted irregulars had made good use of the intervening period by capturing more than 2,500 Zulu cattle, many of them owned by Cetshwayo himself. His intention, he told Wood, was for the invading columns to 'push everyone slowly before us towards the King's kraal, or otherwise disarm the tribes and take their chief and some of their headmen as hostages for good behaviour'. His horsemen had scouted as far as Siphezi Hill, twenty-two miles towards oNdini, but had found the road 'quite unfit for convoys to pass'. He intended, therefore, to establish an intermediate camp at Isandlwana Hill,★ where there was 'wood and water'. From there he could clear the Qudeni Forest of Chief Matshana's tribe, before moving on to the open ground between the Siphezi and Mhlabamkhosi hills. His final objective, prior to reaching oNdini, was the mission station on the Little Itala Hill, where he 'hoped to establish Durnford'. Pearson, meanwhile, was to leave part of his force at Eshowe and take the rest to the Entumeni Mission. All three southern columns – Glyn's, Durnford's and

---

★ Isandlwana in Zulu means 'little hut'. It was so named because the top of the hill looks like a traditional Zulu beehive hut. Some British commentators have erroneously called it Isandlana, which translates as 'little hand'.

Pearson's – would then be in a position to clear the country along the Buffalo and Tugela rivers before continuing their advance across the Mhlathuze River towards oNdini. 'By this plan,' he wrote, 'we shall oblige Cetywayo to keep his force together, when it will suffer from want of food and become thoroughly discontented, or we shall oblige him to attack which will save us going to find him.' While the three southern columns were thus engaged, Wood was advised not to advance his column further than Ingwe Mountain on the Sand River; though he could, if he wished, 'find wood and a military position by moving further north'.

In formulating his new plan, Chelmsford had been heavily influenced by his political adviser, Henry Francis Fynn Junior. The son of the original Natal settler who had become a confidant of King Shaka, Fynn had grown up among the Zulu and was fluent in their tongue. He had succeeded his father as the magistrate of M'singa, the border district that included Rorke's Drift, and in that capacity had attended Cetshwayo's 'coronation'. His knowledge of the people and terrain on both sides of the Buffalo was unrivalled. So when he informed Chelmsford, soon after the invasion had begun, that his spies had knowledge of Cetshwayo's strategy, he was listened to at once. This was, he said, to 'shelter' in the Mangeni Hills until the British column 'had moved forward sufficiently to enable the Zulu army to creep round from the [Mangeni] valley, up the Buffalo River, and so cut off the column in the rear and close in upon them'.

All Chelmsford's subsequent movements were influenced by this report. A bold commander might have ignored it and headed straight for the Zulu capital. But Chelmsford – fearful of his rear and anxious to prevent any raids into Natal – wanted to clear the border region first before driving the Zulus towards oNdini for the final showdown. By assuming that Cetshwayo would do everything he could to avoid a pitched battle, Chelmsford betrayed his ignorance of Zulu warfare. The Zulus knew only one way to fight: aggressively. Chelmsford thought they would behave much as the Cape Xhosas had done and fight only as a last resort. It was a misapprehension he would live to regret.

Chelmsford reconnoitred the new camp ground at Isandlwana
in person on 16 January and four days later, by which time the road
was at last passable after sterling work by four companies of 2/24th
and the Natal Pioneers, the column began the ten-mile march from
Rorke's Drift. As the track climbed out of the wet lowlands of the
Batshe Valley, it crossed a small stream, the Manzimnyama, and
then crested a broad saddle between a stony koppie* on the right
and Isandlwana Hill on the left. It then wound its way south-east
towards Siphezi Hill through an undulating plain, five miles wide
and twice as long, strewn with rocks and criss-crossed with narrow
watercourses and deep dongas. To the south of the plain lay the
Malakatha Hills, the Mangeni Valley and, beyond it, the broken
country of the Qudeni Forest that led down to the Buffalo; to the
north was a steep escarpment known as the Nyoni Ridge, which
led, via the Nqutu Plateau, to the hidden Ngwebeni Valley beyond.
This plateau could be reached by several steep ravines, the biggest
of which began just beyond a large conical koppie that rose from
the plain one and a half miles to the front of Isandlwana. The hill
itself lay north to south, with a broad spur running from its lower
northern end up to the Nqutu Plateau. The open ground in front
of Isandlwana fell gently away to a wide, shallow donga that cut
across the plain. It was here, in the shadow of the mountain, that
the British set up camp.

One officer described the hill as a 'very steep, stocky eminence,
6 to 700 feet high, rising boldly from the surrounding undulating
country'. In shape, he added, 'it is like a *sphinx*, or Lion, and it is
accessible, and that with difficulty, at one or two points only'. The
hill's similarity to a sphinx was seen by many members of the
24th as auspicious. For the regiment had worn the sphinx as part
of its regimental badge since the victorious Battle of the Nile
against the French in 1800. But it had not brought it luck. In
1810, en route to attack Mauritius, the colonel and half the 1/24th
were captured when the French boarded their transports; the
Colours were saved from capture but only by being dropped into

* Small hill.

the sea. In 1849, at the Battle of Chilianwalla during the Second Sikh War, the regiment was cut to pieces in a bungled assault and one Colour lost. The Zulu War would not prove any kinder to the 24th.

The site for the camp at Isandlwana was selected by Major Clery. He had asked Inspector George Mansel of the Natal Mounted Police for advice; but, as the pair reached the eastern slope of the hill, where the ground levels off with the plain, Clery had announced: 'I think this will do.'

Mansel 'did not like it one bit', warning Clery that the site was commanded by both the stony koppie and the shoulder of the hill.

'No,' said an irritated Clery, 'this will do.'

Fynn, who had also been asked for his opinion, preferred the open ground two miles further on. He too was ignored.

With the site chosen, Clery instructed Mansel to post mounted picquets in front of the camp. Mansel did so, placing four at various intervals along the Nqutu Plateau to the left front* and more to the rear of the hill. Later that day, on Clery's orders, those to the front were withdrawn closer to the camp and those behind the hill removed altogether on the grounds that 'the rear always protects itself'. As the former were being brought in, they spotted and captured a lone Zulu. An old man, he claimed that a big impi was on its way from oNdini. This intelligence was passed on to Clery and, presumably, to Chelmsford himself.

Meanwhile infantry picquets had been placed about a mile from the camp: NNC detachments to the north and north-east; the south and south-east approaches, leading to the Mangeni Valley where Fynn had predicted the Zulu Army would gather, were guarded by British troops. Even so, a number of officers – colonial and imperial – were sufficiently worried about the vulnerability of the camp to raise the issue with their superiors. Sub-Inspector Phillips of the NMP, Mansel's deputy, made his fears known to Colonel Crealock. Chelmsford overheard the conversation and

---

* The furthest on high ground, five miles distant, was clearly visible from the camp.

called out: 'Tell the police officer my troops will do all the attacking, but, even if the enemy does venture to attack, the hill he complains about will serve to protect our rear.'

A major of the 2/24th, who complained to Crealock about the absence of sentries behind the hill, was given equally short shrift. 'Well, sir,' came Crealock's sarcastic reply, 'if you are nervous, we will put a picquet of pioneers there.' But nothing was done. Nor did Chelmsford comply with his own field regulations – issued to column commanders in December 1878 – which stated that all permanent camps should be both entrenched and laagered. He later claimed that the ground was too stony to dig and that the wagons were 'under orders to return to Rorke's Drift on the 22nd January in order to bring up more supplies and were therefore not available for use as a laager'. Neither explanation is convincing. Rocks could have been used to construct a redoubt and not all the wagons were required for resupply on the 22nd. Chelmsford did not take the necessary precautions because he did not think he needed to. His mindset was fixed on the Mangeni Valley to the south-east, where, Fynn had told him, a strong Zulu force would gather. It was his intention to get there first.

He had outlined his strategy to Durnford, who was still en route to Rorke's Drift, in a letter of 19 January:

No. 3 column moves tomorrow to Isalwana Hill and from there, as soon as possible to a spot about 10 miles nearer to the [Qudeni] Forest. From that point I intend to operate against the two Matyanas [Matshanas, both local chiefs] if they refuse to surrender. One is in the stronghold on or near the Mhlazakazi Mountain, the other is in the [Qudeni] Forest . . . I have sent you an order to cross the river at Rorke's Drift tomorrow with the force you have . . . I shall want you to operate against the Matyanas, but will send you fresh instructions on this subject.

A separate order reached Durnford at Vermaak's Farm on the same day. It instructed him to take his mounted men, two companies of the 1/1st NNC and the rocket battery across Rorke's Drift and camp on the Zulu bank. Major Bengough, commanding the 2/1st

NNC, was also to march down to the Buffalo and be ready to cross by the 22nd.

Clearly Chelmsford envisaged using Durnford's troops to help clear the broken ground between Isandlwana and the Buffalo. But first he had to locate the main Zulu strength in the area and, to that end, he and his staff went on a long reconnaissance during the afternoon of 20 January in the direction of the Mangeni Gorge, where, it was rumoured, 'the two Matyanas' were concentrated. He wrote to Frere:

At 1 pm I started off to reconnoitre what is called the Zulu stronghold which is almost ten or twelve miles from here. Our road lay over a hard rolling plain, cut up at long intervals by deep watercourses which however will not be difficult to get waggons over . . . The so-called stronghold is a precipitous valley with krantzes on each side in which there are caves. The [Mangeni] river which runs through it tumbles over a precipice at the upper end, and the valley is thus closed in on three sides. The fourth opens out into lateral valleys some three miles down and the main valley continues on until it reaches the Buffalo river, close under the [Qudeni] bush. No sign of Zulus or cattle could be discovered . . . A few kraals were visible and from some we saw a few women running away with bundles on their heads, but otherwise the country was deserted.

Among the officers who took part in the reconnaissance was Lieutenant Nevill Coghill of the 1/24th, Frere's former aide-de-camp, who shortly before the war began had requested a transfer back to his regiment. A handsome, ambitious and well-connected officer – his father was an Anglo-Irish baronet – Coghill had passed the new examination for direct appointment to the army in 1871 and, after two years at Sandhurst, was gazetted to the 1/24th. A combination of his own ability and his father's 'influence' had secured him a succession of staff posts since his arrival in South Africa in 1875: first as aide-de-camp to General Cunynghame, Chelmsford's predecessor, with whom he returned briefly to England; then as aide-de-camp to Frere. Even his transfer back to the 1/24th did not last long, as Colonel Glyn, his former commanding officer, made him his orderly officer (or extra aide-de-camp). It was in this role that he had accompanied Glyn on the patrol. But on the way back he stopped at a deserted kraal and, while trying to catch a chicken for the pot, badly twisted his knee. The injury was serious enough to confine him to his tent for the next two days. By such cruel twists of fate are the fortunes of soldiers decided.

The layout and mood of the camp on 20 January were later described by Captain Penn Symons of the 2/24th:

The camp was pitched at the front of the hill, facing South-East. In front a broad valley, on either side ridges of hills. The 1/24th was on the right, the different mounted corps next, then the Artillery, next the 2/24th Regiment and the NNC on the left. The whole occupying a frontage of about 800 yards. Most of the wagons were scattered about the ridge on our right rear, preparatory to being sent back to Rorke's Drift for further supplies. The General's Camp was pitched in rear of the centre, close under the scarped face of the hill. Every one turned in early that night, not dreaming even of what was in store for the morrow. Indeed so far the invasion had been as autumn manoeuvres in pleasant but hot weather in England. Officers with permission went out alone shooting and prospecting miles from the camp, with no thought of risk or danger.

★

King Cetshwayo's initial response to the invasion was cautious. Much of his army had been mobilized since 8 January when it had gathered at the kwaNodwengu military kraal, near oNdini, to celebrate the annual First Fruits Ceremony. But he was anxious not to take the initiative for fear of provoking the British. 'My troops,' he wrote, 'although many with me at my kraal, have not yet taken up arms, but are simply waiting for some settlement. The Zulus now, when they hear that the troops are laying waste their country, take the alarm and arm themselves . . . I am still telling my troops not to fire or throw an assegai; my people are simply firing and stabbing to defend themselves.'

He was referring, of course, to small local skirmishes like the one fought by Chief Sihayo's tribe on the 12th. But, as news of the

British advance reached oNdini, the younger Zulu warriors demanded a response, and Cetshwayo felt compelled to call up his remaining regiments. A member of the iNgobamakhosi Regiment remembered: 'We had scarcely got home when a special messenger came from oNdini telling us to go there immediately as Cetshwayo, our King, had need of us. The white men were even then in their tents at Isandlwana.'

All new arrivals were given their fill of beef and beer. Their arms were then inspected by the king himself. A warrior of the uVe regiment recalled: 'Cetshwayo came out of the inner gate of oNdini. He said, "Is this the whole impi then? Lift up your guns." We did so. "So there are no guns?" Each man with a beast from his place must bring it up next day and buy guns.'

Thanks to the activities of European gun-runners like John Dunn, firearms had been freely available in Zululand since the 1830s. Up to 20,000 guns had been smuggled into the country by the 1870s, mainly through the Portuguese port of Delagoa Bay. But by 1879 most were outdated muzzle-loading muskets and rifles that were no match for the Martini-Henry. Nor were Zulu tactics adapted to suit firearms. Instead those warriors with guns would fire a ragged volley at distance before closing with the assegai.

Cetshwayo's military strategy was essentially one of aggressive self-defence. He knew from his spies that the British had invaded his country at three separate points and that the biggest force had come over Rorke's Drift. He and his council decided, therefore, to send the pick of his army against this central column with the intention of catching it in the open. If successful, his best warriors could then take on the other columns. He later explained this strategy to Captain Ruscombe Poole, who wrote:

Cetshwayo hoped to be able to crush the English columns, drive them out of the country, defend the border, and then arrange a peace. He knew the English in Natal could not bring a very large force into the field; but he had often been told by white men (traders in the country) that they had a very large army beyond the sea. He knew that if the English persevered in the war, he would get the worst of it in the end.

'It seems,' noted Poole, 'that Cetshwayo believed in his power to crush the English columns, and that then, by increasing his army on the frontier, and so menacing Natal, he might force the English to make peace before reinforcements arrived from across the sea.'

His other obvious option was guerrilla warfare. But the militia nature of his army made a short successful campaign imperative so that the men could be released for everyday tasks like collecting the harvest; nor was Cetshwayo prepared to risk the devastation of his country over a long period. Perhaps the clincher was that Zulu military tactics – enveloping an enemy and destroying it in close-quarter fighting – were only really suited to pitched battles in the open field.

On 17 January the main Zulu Army was formed into a huge circle at kwaNodwengu. Twenty thousand strong, it was sprinkled with the ashes of burnt medicines as part of its ritual purification. Nzuzi, a warrior of the uVe, recalls the speech that Cetshwayo made from the centre of the circle:

I have not gone over the seas to look for the white man, yet they have come into my country and I would not be surprised if they took away our wives and cattle and crops and land. What shall I do? I have nothing against the white man and I cannot tell why they came to me. They want to take me. What shall I do?

'Give the matter to us,' replied his warriors. 'We will go and eat up the white men and finish them off. They are not going to take you while we are here. They must take us first.'

Having selected the regiments that would go against the centre column, Cetshwayo gave them their final instructions. They were, according to a Zulu deserter, as follows: 'You are to go against the column at Rorke's Drift, and drive it back into Natal; and if the state of the river will allow, follow it up through Natal, right up to the Drakensberg. You will attack it by daylight, as there are enough of you to "eat it up", and you will march slowly, so as not to tire yourselves.'

Other accounts insist that the army was forbidden to cross into Natal, and it may be that the Honourable William Drummond, the officer who took this statement after the battle, added in the bit about an invasion of Natal to make the subsequent defence of Rorke's Drift seem more important than it really was.

Nzuzi claimed that the king gave a timely warning: 'If you come near to the white man and find that he has made trenches and built forts that are full of holes, do not attack him for it will be of no use. But if you see him out in the open you can attack him because you will be able to eat him up.'

The instructions that Cetshwayo gave to his commander, Chief Ntshingwayo kaMahole, were rather less forthright. 'I told Ntsing-wayo,' he recalled, 'not to go to the English troops at once, but to have a conference and then send some chiefs to ask the English why they were laying the country waste and killing Zulus, when they had plainly said they had not entered the country to fight, but to talk about the settlement.' Other than that, his commanders were left to act 'independently as they thought best'.

The main army left kwaNodwengu in the late afternoon of Friday, 17 January, and, in accordance with its orders not to tire itself out, marched just seven miles to its bivouac on the west bank of the White Mfolozi River. It consisted of the cream of the Zulu Army, including young unmarried men in their twenties and thirties from the uVe, iNgobamakhosi, uMcijo, uKhandempemvu, uMbonambi, uNokhenke, iMbube, uDududu and iSangqu regiments. But it also contained married men in their forties and fifties from the regiments attached to the royal kraal at oNdini – the iNdluyengwe, uDloko, iNdlondlo and uThulwana – and a handful of sexagenarians who had fought against the Voortrekkers in the 1830s. Most of the younger men had discarded their regimental regalia and were naked but for their breech-clouts and headdresses. Accompanying the warriors, one to every three or four, were thousands of *udibi* boys whose job it was to carry cooking pots, sleeping mats and dismantled shields. The army would live off the land, with scouts driving in sheep and cattle each evening for slaughter. Left behind at oNdini to protect the king from a surprise

attack by British horsemen was a small reserve of a couple of
thousand veteran warriors in their fifties and sixties.

Chief Ntshingwayo, the senior army commander, was almost
seventy, a short muscular man with a pot belly and huge thighs. He
owed his appointment to his deserved reputation as a military
tactician and the fact that he was second only to Chief Mnyamana
of the Buthelezi clan on the king's council. His co-commander was
Mavumengwana, the senior induna of the uThulwana Regiment
and an old friend of Cetshwayo from his military days. He was the
brother of Chief Godide kaNdlela, a member of the king's council,
who would lead a much smaller army south to confront Pearson
the following day. Other Zulu luminaries present with the main
army were: Princes Dabulamanzi and Nugwende kaMpande,
younger brothers of the king; Chief Zibhebhu kaMaphitha of the
Mandlakazi, induna of the uDloko; Chief Sihayo, in whose territory
the army would operate, and his eldest son, Mehlokazulu, a junior
induna of the iNgobamakhosi.

On day two of its march, the huge army covered nine miles to the
isiPhezi military kraal near the Mpembeni River. Even five months
later its route was still evident from the huge swathe of trampled grass.
On 19 January the army split into two columns that marched 'parallel
to and in sight of one another'. Ntshingwayo commanded the left
column and Mavumengwana the right. Both commanders accompanied their troops on foot; only the scouts provided by Sihayo were
mounted. That evening, having covered another nine miles, the
army camped on tableland east of Babanango Mountain. 'On the
20th,' recalled the deserter, 'we moved across open country and slept
by the [Siphezi] hill. We saw a body of mounted white men on this
day to our left.' They had had their first contact with the British in
the form of Chelmsford's Mangeni patrol. A battle could not be
long delayed, though Cetshwayo later insisted that negotiation
was still on the agenda. 'The officers of the different regiments
assembled,' he told the governor of the Cape, 'in order to come to
an agreement as to which chiefs they should send to confer with
the English . . . to settle matters by words and not by arms.'

★

At dawn the following day – 21 January – Chelmsford sent a third of his force to explore 'more thoroughly' the broken country to the south-east of Isandlwana that he had reconnoitred the day before. Major Dartnell and most of the NMP and mounted volunteers were to follow in his footsteps along the rough track that led to the Mangeni Falls.* Meanwhile Commandant Rupert Lonsdale would take both battalions of his 3rd NNC –1,600 men in all – through the Mala-katha and Hlazakazi hills before linking up with Dartnell near the falls and returning to camp. 'I shall know by evening therefore,' wrote Chelmsford, 'whether anybody is left in the country.'

Chelmsford also sent a small patrol of mounted infantry, under Lieutenant Edward Browne, to patrol up the oNdini road as far as Siphezi Hill. 'On his way home,' recorded the lame Nevill Coghill, 'an attempt was made to cut him off by some 30 [Zulus] on foot and eight on horseback. Some shots were exchanged, one of the enemy killed another badly wounded and Browne and his men returned safely to Camp.' Browne could not know it but he had made contact with scouts from the main Zulu impi.

If he had been more receptive, Chelmsford might have taken note of the many hints he received that day that a Zulu army was approaching from the east. In the morning he rode to the kraal of Gamdana, a brother of Sihayo, who had indicated his willingness to treat with the British. Gamdana had left – frightened by the sight of Lonsdale's battalions marching past his homestead – and so Chelmsford returned to the camp empty-handed. He had not been back long when Gamdana and another local chief arrived to tender their submission with a collection of firearms. When Chelmsford pointed out that most of them were obsolete, and that the best weapons must have been kept by their warriors, Gamdana's indig-nant response was that 'Cetshwayo had sent an impi to eat him up, for surrendering his arms to the British.' He had expected it 'that morning but it had not arrived'. He had heard, however, that 'Zulus

* On hearing that the popular Dartnell was to command the patrol, instead of Brevet Lieutenant-Colonel Russell, the police and volunteers let out a spon-taneous cheer.

were in force to the right of Isipezi [Siphezi Hill].' Chelmsford was unconvinced and told the Zulu chiefs to leave the camp, thereby giving them an opportunity to see – in Crealock's words – '*whether it was defended or not by earthworks or waggons*'.

Late that afternoon Chelmsford and his staff left to reconnoitre the Nqutu Plateau to the left of the camp. He had planned to go straight after lunch but was delayed by Gamdana's arrival. On the way, at about 4 p.m., he was met by his two aides, Major Gossett and Captain Buller, who had accompanied Dartnell's patrol. Colonel Glyn recalled: 'These officers brought the Lt. General information that Major Dartnell with the mounted troops had come up with a body of the enemy, but he did not consider he was strong enough to attack them until Commandant Lonsdale's force arrived. Further that Major Dartnell intended to remain out that night and watch the enemy.' Chelmsford at once sent a messenger to Dartnell with orders 'to attack if and when he thought fit'. He also arranged for rations to be sent on pack-horses.

Neither Glyn, the column commander, nor Clery, his senior staff officer, had had anything to do with the decision to send Dartnell and Lonsdale on their reconnaissance in force. 'The instructions to both these commanders,' recalled Clery, 'were given personally by the General himself, and this was absolutely necessary . . . as neither Colonel Glyn nor myself knew in the least where they were being sent to or what they were being sent for.' Yet Dartnell's report confirmed Clery's worst fears:

I had felt from the first very much averse to this movement of sending out irregulars under command of irregular officers, amounting to half the force, on a roving commission of this sort. And when word came that they were going to bivouac out, I could not help speaking strongly to Colonel Glyn on the possibility of this sort of thing dragging the rest of the force into any sort of compromising enterprise that these people may get messed up in.

Glyn, however, preferred to keep his own counsel. Chelmsford's presence had reduced him to little more than a cipher and he did not feel he had the authority to interfere with operational matters.

With his orders dispatched, Chelmsford continued his patrol along the plateau to the crest of iThusi Hill, about two and a half miles from the camp. From there he could see Hlazakazi Mountain to the south, where Dartnell and Lonsdale were preparing to spend the night; Siphezi Hill to the east; and a plateau to the north-east on which Lieutenant Milne 'counted fourteen Zulu horsemen watching us at the distance of about four miles'. The vedettes on iThusi 'said they had seen these men several times during the day, and had reported the fact'. Yet Chelmsford took no action beyond a verbal intention 'to reconnoitre there the next day'. He never did.

Chelmsford arrived back at camp as the picquets were being relieved. No one was more surprised than Lieutenant Henry Mainwaring of F Company, 2/24th. He had been on outpost duty with his men to the south-east of the camp since six in the morning and had not expected to be relieved for another twelve hours. But at 6 p.m., 'for some unaccountable reason', Lieutenant Pope appeared with G Company and told him to return to camp. Mainwaring recalled:

Extending his men on his line for night outpost nearer to the Camp, [Pope] signalled to me to 'close' which I did, passing through his sentries about 100 yards from where he was standing and talking with Lieut. Austin [Godwin-Austen]. I regretted afterwards that I did not go up and speak to him, but I was tired with my day's work.

Later that evening a second message arrived from Dartnell. He had not yet received Chelmsford's response to his initial report and, with the number of Zulus in his immediate vicinity having risen to several thousand, he wanted to know if it was wise to attack the following morning. At first Chelmsford assumed that his initial response would suffice. Then it occurred to him that Dartnell might be under the impression that he was not at liberty to attack 'without instructions'. So the messenger was roused from his sleep and told to return to Dartnell with authorization for him to use 'his own judgement as to whether he should attack or not'. When Chelmsford was asked by his own staff whether part of the imperial infantry should be ordered to 'move out' and support Dartnell, he replied: 'No.' The distance was too far and it was too late in the day.

For the two battalions of Lonsdale's 3rd NNC, in particular, it had been an exhausting day. They had set off at dawn and after a march of several hours, having covered about seven miles of mostly level country, reached the base of the Malakatha hills. It was, wrote Lieutenant John Maxwell of the 2/3rd NNC, 'covered pretty well with thorns, and as we found out afterwards rather difficult to get through owing to the thickness of the thorns and the very broken country'. They proceeded in skirmishing order and, by noon, had arrived at the southern end of the range, having 'scoured the western side'. Their only reward, so far, was to have seen 'some old men and women' and captured 'thirty or forty head of cattle', which had been escorted back to the camp by a company of NNC. Commandant G. A. Hamilton-Browne's 1/3rd NNC had had more success: his men had captured two Zulu warriors who, under torture, admitted that they had left the Zulu Army in the vicinity of the Siphezi Hill that day to visit their mother. The intelligence was sent back with the cattle but – like the other snippets of information that contradicted Chelmsford's belief that the Zulus would gather to the south-east of Isandlwana – was not acted upon. Meanwhile the NNC had continued their march. Lieutenant Maxwell wrote:

We now started to scour the other or eastern side of the ridge and on arriving at the northern end about 2 p.m., we halted for a little rest before starting on our march back to the camp, where we were expected in time for dinner, having left camp in light marching order, no blankets, cooking utensils, food or other impedimenta . . . We were about falling in for this purpose, when Inspector Mansell [*sic*] of the NMP appeared on the scene with a request that we should march eastward instead. He stated the enemy were in sight some five miles off, and that the NMP, Carbineers and Newcastle [Mounted] Rifles . . . requested our support. So instead of marching back to our dinners, we took the opposite direction . . . We soon sighted the enemy, they gradually retiring, keeping some two to three miles from us, and we following until dark. Word in the meantime had been sent to the General.

Dartnell's mounted troops first spotted the enemy in late morning as they approached the Mangeni River. The Zulus, several hundred strong, were gathered half a mile to the east in the Magogo Hills. They had detached themselves from the main army, which had spent the previous night near Siphezi Hill, with the intention of drawing as many British troops as possible from the camp at Isandlwana. Aware that their numbers were steadily increasing, Dartnell ordered up the NNC in support and sent off the first of his messages to Chelmsford. While he awaited the response, he formed his command into a hollow square: the NNC forming three sides and the mounted troops the fourth, 'horses in rings in the centre, also some fires'. Two companies of the NNC were put on picquet duty. Their morale, however, was dangerously low: they had marched more than twenty miles over difficult terrain and through the heat of the day; now, having not eaten since breakfast and with no supplies in sight, they were expected to sleep rough in sight of a large and ever-growing force of their mortal enemy. The NNC officers were also unhappy, despite the fact that they were mounted. 'There was some grumbling among the officers of the Native Contingent, who were tired out, at having to bivouac without food, forage or blankets (the Natives all carried their blankets on their persons),' noted Captain Henry Harford, Lonsdale's staff officer, in his journal. 'Two young officers, Lieutenants Avery and Holcroft, went off without leave, evidently to ride back to camp, but were never seen or heard of again.'

As dusk was falling, a small detachment of IMI reached Dartnell with four pack-horses and Chelmsford's response. Neither was satisfactory. The supplies – blankets, tea, biscuits and tinned meat – were not enough to go round the white troops let alone the Africans; and Chelmsford's authorization for a dawn attack had been overtaken by events. With the Zulus' strength growing by the minute, Dartnell now felt that any attack without British infantry support would be suicidal. So he sent the IMI detachment back with a request for reinforcements. Slowed by darkness and the broken terrain, the message did not reach Isandlwana until the early hours of 22 January. In the meantime Dartnell and Lonsdale's men did their best to sleep. Lieutenant Maxwell recalled:

About 2 a.m. I awoke suddenly and to my astonishment heard a frightful noise some distance from me, and found myself alone . . . Our natives instead of being in front of me were now in my rear and must have jumped over me in the alarm and I slept through it all . . . After some three or four minutes I made out from the shouting that it was an alarm and that the enemy had not yet put in an appearance . . . It would appear that the enemy were heard or seen by the outlying companies, who immediately retired upon the square, firing in the direction of the enemy and by the time they arrived found the square in a state of panic.

Fortunately the mounted troops kept their composure while the NNC officers and NCOs, with a liberal use of both oaths and knobkerries, managed to get their men back into some semblance of order. But hardly anyone could sleep after the rumpus, and the remaining hours of darkness slowed to a suspense-ridden crawl. Fortunately the Zulus chose not to attack. If they had, a mounted policeman wrote later, 'not a man would have escaped, for our natives were panic stricken and would have caused the greatest confusion in the dark'.

Major Clery was sleeping soundly in his tent when he was woken at 1.30 a.m. and handed Dartnell's message. It said 'that the enemy had shown in increased force and that it would not be prudent to attack them in the morning without some white troops'.* For form's sake he took the message to Glyn, who, after reading it, told him to give it to Chelmsford. Clery recalled:

* Glyn remembered the note asking for 'two or three companies of the 24th Regiment' (Glyn to the DAG, 6 February 1879, SWB, 1983.13).

1. Sir Bartle Frere, governor of Cape Colony

2. Lieutenant-General Lord Chelmsford, the British commander in South Africa

3. King Cetshwayo at his 'coronation', 1 September 1873. A European armchair serves as his throne, and he wears the scarlet and gold mantle and gaudy crown provided by his British guests

4. Chief Ntshingwayo, the senior Zulu commander at Isandlwana

5. A wagon and oxen crossing the Thukela River by pont

6. Fort Pearson on the Natal bank of the Thukela. Zululand is visible
in the distance

7. A unit of the Natal Native Contingent, a force of black auxiliaries raised in
the autumn of 1878 to assist the British invasion of Zululand. Only one in ten
was armed with an outdated firearm; the rest had to make do with billhooks,
assegais and shields

8. *At Bay* by W. H. Durand, depicting the desperate last stand of the
24th Regiment at Isandlwana on 22 January 1879

9. Brevet Lieutenant-Colonel Henry Pulleine, 1/24th Regiment, with his wife

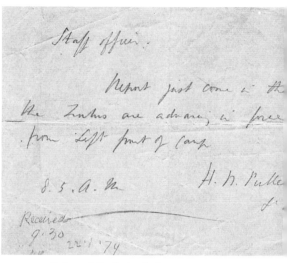

10. Colonel Pulleine's famous message to Lord Chelmsford, timed at 8.05 a.m. on 22 January 1879, and warning of a Zulu advance 'in force from left front of camp'

11. Lieutenant-Colonel Anthony Durnford, RE, who became the posthumous scapegoat for Chelmsford's defeat at Isandlwana

12. Watercolour of Colonel Richard Glyn, commanding No. 3 Column, by Lieutenant-Colonel J. N. Crealock, Chelmsford's talented but unscrupulous military secretary

13. W. H. Durand's graphic drawing of the Zulu charge at Isandlwana

14. Pen and ink drawing by Crealock of Chelmsford's column returning to the shattered camp at Isandlwana during the evening of 22 January 1879

15. Abandoned wagons on the nek at Isandlwana, with bones clearly visible in the foreground. The picture was taken in May 1879, four months after the battle, when the British at last returned to bury their dead

16. Lieutenant Nevill Coghill, 1/24th,
orderly officer to Colonel Glyn

17. Lieutenant Teignmouth
Melvill, adjutant of the 1/24th

18. The spot where Lieutenants Melvill and Coghill were killed, with Zululand
in the distance. The point at which the fugitives crossed the Buffalo River can
just be seen to the left of the picture

19. The laager method of repelling a Zulu attack, by W. H. Durand

20. The mission station at Rorke's Drift before the war, with the
Oskarberg hill behind

The General's tent was close by, so I roused him up. Lying on my face and hands close to his camp bed, I can still remember how I read out from that crumpled piece of note-paper, written *across* in pencil, word after word what I just previously had such difficulty in deciphering in my own tent. The General did not hesitate much. He said 'Order the 2/24th, 4 guns and all the mounted troops remaining, to get ready to start at daybreak.' He also added: 'Order up Colonel Durnford with the troops he has to reinforce the Camp.'

This last comment was overheard by Colonel Crealock in the next tent. He at once appeared and asked Chelmsford: 'Is Major Clery to issue orders to Colonel Durnford?'

Clery thought the question very proper. Durnford was, after all, an independent column commander and only answerable to the general and his staff. Chelmsford took the point. 'No,' he replied to Crealock, 'but you do it.'

Crealock at once began to write out the order to Durnford, which he copied in his order book. For some time after the battle neither the original order nor the order book could be found. Crealock's recollection of the order – in early February 1879 – was as follows:

Move up to Sandhlwana at once with all your mounted men and Rocket Battery – take command of it. I am accompanying Colonel Glyn, who is moving off at once to attack Matyana and a Zulu force said to be 12 or 14 miles off, and at present watched by Natal Police, Volunteers, and Natal Native Contingent. Colonel Glyn takes with him 2–24th Regiment, 4 guns R.A., and Mounted Infantry.

In his journal entry for 22 January Crealock wrote: '[I] was told to order Durnford up from Rorke's Drift with 250 mounted men and 200 infantry to take command of the camp, as Col. Glyn with the 2/24th was to move out with 4 guns to attack Zulus.' In both these versions – written by Crealock from memory – Durnford is ordered to 'take command' of the camp. Crealock had, as shall become clear, a very good reason to make that claim. But it was not true. The actual order – recovered from the battlefield and suppressed for a number of years – stated:

You are to march to this camp at once with all the force you have with you of No. 2 Column. Major Bengough is to move to Rorke's Drift as ordered yesterday. 2/24th, Artillery and mounted men with the General and Colonel Glyn move off at once to attack a Zulu force about 10 miles distant.

There was no reference to Durnford taking command of the camp. He was simply ordered to move his men to Isandlwana where, he must have assumed, further instructions would await him. He might have inferred from the message that Chelmsford wanted him to reinforce the camp; but equally he could have taken it to mean – particularly in the light of his previous order – that Chelmsford expected him to take part in the battle. The order lacked clarity and, like the famous Fourth Order at Balaclava,★ left its interpretation open to the officer who received it. A man of Durnford's history was bound to take advantage of this ambiguity. A battle was pending and he would not want to miss out.

Crealock entrusted the order to Lieutenant Horace Smith-Dorrien, a young officer on the transport staff, and told him to leave 'as soon as he could see his way'. Smith-Dorrien chose to leave at once. 'It ought to have been a very jumpy ride,' he recalled, 'for I was entirely alone and the country was wild and new to me, and the road little better than a track; but pride at being selected to carry an important dispatch and the valour of ignorance (for I only realised next day that the country was infested with hostile Zulus) carried me along without a thought of danger.'

Clery, meanwhile, had carried out Chelmsford's original order. He wrote later:

As I did not want to give any warning to the enemy or disturb the Camp I went direct to each of the Commanders & gave the General's orders.

★ The wrongful interpretation of which resulted in the tragic Charge of the Light Brigade.

This took some time and the General was soon dressed and impatient to be starting. The troops too, turned out well. The General had given no orders about the camp except that Colonel Durnford was to move his troops up there. But in trying to gather my wits together, after giving out the different orders for the march, personally myself, as to what further should be cared for before marching off, it occurred to me that some instructions should be left to the officer left in charge of the camp. It was too late to refer to Colonel Glyn, who of course, would only have referred me to the General, so I ventured on the responsibility of issuing them myself.

According to Clery, the order he wrote to Lieutenant-Colonel Pulleine, commanding the 1/24th, was as follows:

You will be in command of the camp in the absence of Colonel Glyn. Draw in your line of defence while the force with the General is out of the camp. Draw in your *Infantry* outpost line, in conformity. Keep your Cavalry vedettes still well to the front. Act strictly on the defensive. Keep a waggon loaded with ammunition ready to start at once, should the General's force be in need of it. Colonel Durnford has been ordered up from Rorke's Drift to reinforce the Camp.

The order was sent by a runner and, just before leaving the camp, Clery visited Pulleine's tent to make sure he had received it. He had, but Clery repeated the gist of it, 'laying stress on the point that his mission was simply to hold & keep the Camp'.

Henry Pulleine had only recently rejoined the 1/24th. Born in Yorkshire in 1838, the eldest son of a vicar, he obtained his original commission without purchase. In 1858, after three years in the 30th Regiment, he transferred to the newly raised 2nd Battalion of the 24th. Thirteen years later he bought a majority in the 1/24th, but, on arriving in South Africa in 1879, had no experience of war. Even his service during the Cape Frontier War was not with his regiment but with an irregular corps that he raised in Kingwilliam's Town: a band of hard-drinking former railroad workers known as Pulleine's Rangers (or 'Lambs' to those with a sense of irony).

Pulleine is often portrayed as a talented administrator but an inexperienced commander. There is some truth in this. He had, for
example, been highly commended for his work in the Commissariat
Department in the 1860s. But he had also done well on the Cape
frontier and was not as ineffective a commander of troops as some
suppose. He did, on the other hand, have the major handicap of
not knowing the officers and men of the 1/24th as well as some
long-serving colonels. He had only been with the 1/24th for a total
of eight years and had spent much of the previous twelve months
on detached duty: first with the irregulars and then, on returning
to Natal, as commandant of Durban and Pietermaritzburg respectively. Of course none of this mattered to Chelmsford because he
did not expect Pulleine to see action during his absence. When
Pulleine was left in command, recalled Clery, 'nobody from the
General downwards had the least suspicion that there was a chance
of the enemy attacking the camp'.

Unbeknownst to the British, a huge Zulu army was now concentrated in the hidden folds of the Ngwebeni Valley, about six miles
to the north-east of the camp. The initial strategy of its commanders
had been to advance down the Mangeni Valley to the Buffalo
River, from where it could fall on the British rear. While still
paying lip-service to Cetshwayo's demand for negotiations, they
were searching for a way to outmanoeuvre the British. To this end,
the assistance of Chief Matshana of the Sithole was crucial because
he and his men could guide the army through Mangeni's difficult
terrain. Up until 21 January, therefore, the intelligence that Fynn
gave to Chelmsford had been correct. But on that day, as Matshana
conferred with Ntshingwayo and Mavumengwana at Siphezi, Zulu
scouts reported the presence of British horsemen and foot soldiers
in the Mangeni area. This changed everything. With his route
south blocked, Ntshingwayo decided to outflank the British from
the north instead. He therefore gave orders for the bulk of his army
to move in 'small detached bodies' from Siphezi to the Ngwebeni
Valley. At the same time he sent Matshana and a couple of thousand
warriors south to distract the British columns and keep them away

from their camp at Isandlwana. These were the Zulus that Dartnell spotted in the Magogo Hills during the afternoon of 21 January. They kept fires burning all night to convince Dartnell that the main Zulu Army was near. But by morning most of them had left to rejoin Ntshingwayo.

At dusk on the 21st, meanwhile, mounted Zulu scouts on a hill above the Ngwebeni Valley had spotted 'videttes of the English force' on high ground to the south-west. The fourteen Zulu horsemen were noticed, in turn, by Chelmsford and his staff, who were visiting the sentries on iThusi Hill. However Chelmsford – as we have seen – failed to deduce their significance.

At this stage it is unlikely that Ntshingwayo intended to attack the camp the following morning. The 22nd of January was, after all, the day of a 'dead' moon and therefore an inauspicious day for a battle. 'That day the moon had waned,' explained a warrior of the uVe. 'It was not customary to fight at such a time . . . A young woman does not dance that day . . . A garden is not reaped, a hunting party is not sent out. It is our equivalent of Sunday.' Most of the Zulu sources agree that the army planned to rest on the 22nd and attack either that night or the following morning. Even as the 22nd was dawning – claimed Cetshwayo – 'my chiefs were again consulting about sending to the English before fighting'. But events would soon conspire to make a battle inevitable.

6. 'There is nothing to be done'

It was barely light when the vanguard of Chelmsford's relief column left Isandlwana camp by the oNdini road. The Imperial Mounted Infantry were in the lead, followed by six companies of the 2/24th, four guns of N/5 Battery and a company of NNP. The foot soldiers were in light marching order, without greatcoats or blankets, and carried one day's rations and the usual seventy rounds of ammunition per man. There was no regimental reserve.

Chelmsford and his staff cantered ahead with a small escort and, having taken the right fork to Mangeni, reached Major Dartnell's bivouac in the Hlazakazi Hills at around 6.30 a.m. Chelmsford recalled:

I at once ordered [Dartnell] to send out his mounted men to gain intelligence of the enemy, whose whereabouts did not appear to be very certain. The enemy shortly after showed in considerable strength on some heights opposite to the [Malakata] range, but at some distance and appeared to be advancing to take possession of a projecting spur which ran out into the plateau beneath, and completely [commanded] it.

These were, in fact, Chief Matshana's men. Most of the Zulus who had confronted Dartnell the previous day were by now on their way back to the main impi. But Chelmsford could not have known this. Assuming he had located a major Zulu force, he ordered Lonsdale's two battalions of NNC 'to move across and occupy the spur in question and sent word to Colonel Glyn to move with the guns and 2/24th right up a valley which lay to the left of the spur'. The Mounted Infantry would cover the left flank; the NMP and mounted volunteers the right. Chelmsford continued:

A general advance was then made, and the enemy retired without firing. On the extreme right, however, the Natal Carbineers under Captain Shepstone managed to cut off about 300 who took refuge in a difficult hill, and in some caves. These were finally dislodged with the assistance of some of the Native Contingent and fifty were killed. The main force of the enemy returned to Isipezi Hill which was about six miles off on the flank being threatened by the [advance] of the mounted corps.

The withdrawal of the Zulus was, of course, deliberate. 'We marched 12 miles,' recalled Captain Penn Symons of the 2/24th. 'We then saw the enemy in scattered bodies of from 10 to 500 dispersing and retreating in front of us in all directions. We followed them. It was hunting a shadow, or worse than a shadow, as men, who well knew the Zulus, their character and tactics, declare that the cattle which had been seen, and the retreating bodies of men, were simply a decoy to entice us away from the camp.' According to Major Clery, Chelmsford 'was from the first much disappointed and annoyed at what was taking place, as he saw soon enough that beyond killing a certain number of these fellows, we were going to have our day's work for nothing'. Not for a minute, however, did Chelmsford suspect that the camp might be in danger.

The first hint came at 9.30 a.m. Chelmsford and his escort were on a knoll in the Magogo Valley, watching a party of Zulus being pursued towards Siphezi Hill by Colonel Russell and his Mounted Infantry, when a galloper rode up with a message from Pulleine. He handed it to the nearest staff officer, who happened to be Captain Hallam Parr, Glyn's aide-de-camp. It was written on a half-sheet of light blue paper and read:

Staff Officer – Report just come in that the Zulus are advancing in force from the left front of the camp. (8.5 a.m.). H. B. Pulleine, Lt Col.

Having noted on it the time of receipt – 9.30 a.m. – Hallam Parr gave it to Major Clery, who at once showed it to Chelmsford. Clery recalled:

He returned it to me without a word. I said: 'What is to be done on the subject?' He said: 'There is nothing to be done on that.' So I took myself off, and *only then* showed it to Colonel Glyn. You may perhaps be surprised from what you know of me . . . that I said nothing more; but the fact is that, whether from over-work or other causes, the General has got rather irritable since we knew him, and particularly touchy about suggestions being made to him. So the General gave some directions about following up the people we had been engaged with & turned his glass on the Camp which we could plainly see, though 12 miles off.

Chelmsford could see nothing out of the ordinary but, to make sure, he sent Lieutenant Milne, his naval aide-de-camp, and Captain Penn Symons up the nearby Silutshana Hill with two powerful telescopes. At the same time he dispatched Captain Alan Gardner, another of Glyn's aides-de-camp, back to the camp with orders for Pulleine 'to send on the camp equipage and supplies of the troops camping out, and to remain himself at his present camp'. Gardner was accompanied by a handful of officers – including Major Stuart Smith of the artillery and Adjutant Henry Dyer of the 2/24th – who would supervise the striking of their respective camps.

While he waited for Milne and Symons to return, Chelmsford called a halt for breakfast. The meal was interrupted by the arrival of Commandant Hamilton-Browne and his weary battalion of 1/3rd NNC, who had just returned from fighting Matshana's men. Hamilton-Browne was offered some food but tactfully declined. His own men had not eaten for more than twenty-four hours. 'I shall never forget the sight of that peaceful picnic,' he wrote later:

Here were the staff quietly breakfasting and the whole column scattered over the country! Over there the guns unlimbered, over the hills parties of mounted infantry and volunteers looting the scattered kraals for grain for their horses, a company of the 24th one place and another far away.

Hamilton-Browne was ordered to return to Isandlwana and assist Pulleine in striking part of the camp. On the way he was to skirmish through the many dongas and ravines on the plain 'in case any

Zulus were hanging about near the camp'. He left shortly after the departure of Lieutenant-Colonel Arthur Harness and his four guns, who, with an escort of two companies of the 2/24th, had been ordered to march back down the Magogo Valley to a new campsite near the Mangeni Falls. To save time Hamilton-Browne struck out across country and, after a mile or so, he and his adjutant came across two Zulu scouts, killing one and capturing the other. The terrified prisoner admitted to having come from the main impi of twelve regiments that was positioned above the Isandlwana camp. An officer was sent back to Chelmsford with this startling intelligence, but its receipt was never acknowledged.

Milne and Symons, meanwhile, had reached the top of Silutshana. Through their powerful telescopes they could clearly see Isandlwana and the camp at its base, ten miles to the northwest. 'Beyond noticing that some of the oxen seemed to be collected about the wagons,' recalled Symons, 'all seemed quiet in camp, and at that time it is certain that no fighting was going on.' If there had been a serious threat, the tents would have been struck to provide a clear line of fire. And yet they were all still standing. But large bodies of Zulus were visible: a group of 500 'retreating away from the camp' and another column at the foot of the Siphezi Hill. This latter group withdrew as Colonel Russell and the Mounted Infantry approached. Russell wrote later: 'This hill was covered with the enemy in very large numbers and we saw the spoor in the valley where the masses had come down from the hills where they had been in front of the General in the morning.' The spoor headed towards the Ngwebeni Valley – in the general direction of Isandlwana – but Russell failed to report this.

Having spent almost an hour on Silutshana, studying the camp, Milne and Symons descended the hill to make their report. It was now a little before 11 a.m. Convinced that the camp was not in danger, and that any Zulus in the vicinity were pulling back, Chelmsford decided to head for the Mangeni Valley 'to fix upon a site for our main camp which I had determined to shift the next day'. He and his staff decided to take a short cut through the hills, and not to follow Harness back down the valley, and for the next crucial hour or so were effectively incommunicado.

During that time – between 11.30 a.m. and noon – Harness's column of guns and infantry heard the sound of firing from the direction of the camp. 'I galloped up the hill in order to get a better view,' recalled Lieutenant Mainwaring of the 2/24th, 'and then distinctly saw the firing and the shells bursting on the western slopes of the [Nqutu] range.' On the way back to the column Mainwaring spotted a large black mass in the plain below and, when he reported this, Captain Hugh Church of the 2/24th volunteered to go and find out who they were. Meanwhile the firing at Isandlwana continued, and Lieutenant George Banister of the 2/24th could see through his field glasses 'where our lines of skirmishers were by the puffs of smoke and could also distinguish Kaffir lines'. He added: 'We all watched with the keenest interest never doubting the result and only cursing our luck being out of it.' Ten minutes later, Captain Church was back. At the foot of the hill he had met an English sergeant with a message from Commandant Hamilton-Browne: 'For God's sake send every man back to the camp, it is surrounded and will be taken unless helped at once.' Hamilton-Browne's hungry and dispirited battalion of NNC had got within six miles of Isandlwana when it encountered, in the distance, three columns of Zulus 'marching from his right to his left, stopping his advance, and cutting him off from the camp'. So he had taken up a defensive position and sent for help.

On hearing the news, Colonel Harness 'at once turned back, and the men of the 24th on being told that the camp was in danger, and that they must push on with all speed, gave a cheer, and set off home with a will'. They had gone less than half a mile when they were 'stopped by a Staff-officer of Lord Chelmsford, who ordered us to again return and join the main body'. The staff officer was Major Gossett and, according to Lieutenant Banister, he 'wanted to know what we meant by moving' and 'utterly ridiculed the idea of any assistance being necessary' at Isandlwana. He also told Harness 'that he would have to take the responsibility of disobeying orders if he continued marching in the direction of the camp'. Harness wisely decided to halt while an officer, Lieutenant C. S. B. Parsons of the artillery, was sent to update Chelmsford with this new intelligence. He soon returned with orders for the column to retrace its steps towards the Mangeni River. The last opportunity to save the camp – or at least a portion of it – had been thrown away.

Chelmsford never admitted countermanding Harness's return to Isandlwana. Nor did he mention any conversation with Parsons.★ His official report makes it clear that he had no fears for the camp and only began his ride back – between 2 and 3 p.m. – after he had ordered the infantry to bivouac at the new campsite. The account given by Colonel Crealock, his senior staff officer, is a little more revealing. The first suspicion Crealock had that the camp might be in danger was at 1.15 p.m., when George Drummond, Chelmsford's intelligence chief, said 'he had heard (and that the natives were certain of it) two cannon shots'. Crealock added:

We were then moving back to choose a camp for the night, about twelve miles distant from Isandhlana. About 1.45 p.m., however, a native appeared on a hill above us, gesticulating and calling. He reported that heavy firing had been going on round the camp. We galloped up to a high spot, whence we could see the camp perhaps 10 or 11 miles distant. None of us could detect anything amiss; all looked quiet. This must have been 2 p.m. The General, however, probably thought it would be well to ascertain what had happened himself, but not thinking anything was wrong, ordered Colonel Glyn to bivouac for the night where we stood; and taking with him some forty Mounted Volunteers proceeded to ride into camp.

★

No sooner had Chelmsford's column left the camp, at around 4.30 a.m., than Colonel Pulleine drew in his line of infantry outposts in accordance with Clery's instructions. He did, however, leave some on the Tahelane Ridge to the north of the hill, 'and some men were stationed on the top of Isandlana, from which point a good view of the country would be obtained'.

★ In a letter to Glyn, dated 4 March 1879, he claimed that 'none of the messages sent by Browne were received by me' (SWB, 1983.13).

The cavalry vedettes remained in their advanced positions. Furthest from the camp was the one on Nyezi Hill, six and a half miles due east. It had a bird's-eye view of the entrance to the Ngwebeni Valley and, like the other vedettes, was made up of a pair of Natal Carbineers (one of whom was called Trooper Whitelaw). Other vedettes were stationed on the Nyoni Ridge, on the Conical Hill in the plain, and on a low ridge halfway along the track to Mangeni known as Qwabe. They had marched out at daybreak, under the command of Lieutenant F. J. D. Scott of the Carbineers, to relieve the night vedettes. All had missed accompanying Dartnell and the rest of their unit on 21 January because of illness, vedette duty or unfit horses.

The vedette on Qwabe was composed of nineteen-year-old Trooper Walwyn Barker and his 'bosom friend', Villiers Hawkins. They had not been there long when they noticed horsemen approaching from the east. At first they assumed they were British and did nothing. But as the riders got closer they could see they were Zulus and, having circled their horses as a signal, retired off the hill 'post haste' to avoid being cut off. They met Lieutenant Scott in the plain, two miles closer to the camp, and told him what they had seen. Scott decided to ride back to the camp with them, but before they had gone far they 'saw Zulus on the hill we had just left, and others advancing from the left flank where two other videttes, Whitelaw and another, had been obliged to retire from'. Barker added: 'Whitelaw reported a large army advancing, "thousands" I remember him distinctly stating, and he was immediately sent back to camp with the report.'

Whitelaw delivered his report to Lieutenant Coghill, who, despite his bad knee, was on duty at the column office. Coghill immediately informed Colonel Pulleine. It was this report that caused Pulleine to send the hasty message to Chelmsford, timed at 8.05 a.m., warning of Zulus 'advancing in force from the front left of the camp'. Unfortunately Pulleine made no mention of the 'thousands' that Whitelaw had seen – and this encouraged Chelmsford to dismiss the message as unimportant. It is of course possible that Pulleine thought he had enough firepower to deal with anything the Zulus could throw at him. He may even have welcomed a general action and did not want to share the expected victory with his superiors. Or he may have felt that Whitelaw was exaggerating and that a verbatim account would have been seen as alarmist. Either way, his message did not convey the urgency that it should have.

But Pulleine was wary enough to send Whitelaw back to Scott with a message 'to watch the enemy carefully and send back reports of their movements'. He also ordered the rest of his fighting troops to fall in. His total command consisted of five companies of his own regiment, the 1/24th (now in the temporary charge of Captain William Degacher, brother of the 2/24th's Colonel Henry); G Company of the 2/24th, which had been on outpost duty; four companies of the 3rd NNC; the remaining two guns of N/5 Battery; a composite squadron of mounted troops; and a handful of Natal Native Pioneers. A grand total of 891 European and 350 African troops: 1,241 in all. Camp followers and wagon drivers brought the total garrison to almost 1,600. But even many of the soldiers were not frontline troops, including as they did farriers, bandsmen, cooks and clerks. Lieutenant Henry Curling, commanding the two 7-pounder guns, remembered how few combat troops were actually available:

I got a message to turn out at once and we got ready in about 10 minutes, forming up by the 1/24th on their parade ground. The companies were very weak, no more than 50 in each, and there were only 6 of them in all. We congratulated ourselves on the chance of our being attacked and hoped that our small numbers might induce the Zulus to come on. They were then 1,000 or 2,000 strong on some hills about 2 miles off. I suppose that no more than half the men left in camp took part in its defence as it was not considered necessary and they were left as cooks etc.

Pulleine's lack of concern is reflected in the rather lackadaisical manner in which he disposed of his troops. 'Column Alarm was sounded and the troops told to fall in,' recalled Private John Williams, Colonel Glyn's groom. 'The [men were] then marched below the Native Contingent Camp where they waited for orders for about half an hour. They were then sent back to their own Camp where they stood under arms about three quarters of an hour.'

All the while reports kept coming in of large formations of Zulus to the left of the camp. Lieutenant the Honourable Standish Vereker, the son of Lord Gort, was on outpost duty with Captain A. J. Barry's company of 2/3rd NNC on Magaga Knoll when he noticed that Zulus were 'appearing on the extreme left and nearly opposite his outlying picket'. The Carbineer vedettes in the plain could see 'numbers of Zulus' on 'all the hills to the left and front'. These warriors were even visible from the camp itself. 'Zulus showed in considerable force at the southeast end of [Nqutu Plateau],' wrote James Brickhill, Glyn's civilian interpreter. 'Shortly afterwards another force came in sight at about the middle of Nqutu, and the intervening space was speedily filled in.' Lieutenant Chard, RE, who arrived at the camp from Rorke's Drift at 9.30 a.m., remembered seeing 'the enemy moving on the distant hills, and apparently in great force'.

The most alarming report was brought by Trooper Arthur Adams of the Buffalo Border Guard. Adams later claimed that 'he and his half-section, when on vedette duty early on January 22, saw from a high hill overlooking a deep valley, the Zulu army, which they estimated to be between 25,000 and 30,000'. They 'immediately returned to camp and reported to an Imperial officer, who was still in bed in his tent'. But the officer – who may have been Coghill, which would explain why he was lying down – 'pooh-poohed the idea that the Zulus would attack the camp'. He may also have disbelieved their estimate of numbers. When Adams and his comrades realized that 'practically no heed was being taken of what they had seen and reported', they made up their minds to slip away at the first sign of a Zulu attack.

But so conflicting were some of the reports – as Zulu formations kept appearing and then disappearing – that Pulleine became confused. The only extra precaution he took was to order the wagon drivers and voorloopers to 'collect all their oxen (which were then scattered all around the camps and might impede the action of the troops) and tie them to the yokes, but not inspan them'. It was not his intention, at this stage, to form a wagon laager. Why? Because he did not believe an attack was imminent, and, if it had been, a laager might have deterred it. Pulleine's chief concern was not how to prevent an attack but how to encourage it.

The arrival of Colonel Durnford, shortly after 10 a.m., changed everything. He had been absent from his camp near the Zulu bank of Rorke's Drift, on a foraging mission, when Lieutenant Smith-Dorrien arrived with the ambiguous order for him to march to Isandlwana 'with all the force you have'. But he was quickly located and, having read Crealock's order, he exclaimed: 'Just what I thought, we are to proceed at once to Isandhlwana. There is an *impi* about eight miles from the camp, which the General moves out to attack at daybreak.'

He gave the necessary orders and hastened back to his camp. His command, by now, had been whittled down to just five troops of Natal Native Horse, two companies of 1/1st NNC and the European rocket battery: a total of just 526 men. He rode ahead with the horsemen; next came the mule-drawn rocket battery and the two companies of NNC; the slow-moving ox-wagons brought up the rear.

An old African hand, Durnford was in his usual distinctive garb: blue serge patrol jacket, scarlet waistcoat, dark cord breeches, boots and spurs; over one shoulder and around his waist he wore two broad belts, attached to 'the former a revolver and to the latter a hunting knife and ammunition'; and topping off his 'stage brigand' costume was a 'wide-awake soft felt hat with wide brim, one side turned up and a crimson turban wound around the hat'. He was also sporting the magnificent droopy moustache that had become his trademark. As he climbed the final hill to the camp, he met Lieutenant Chard moving in the opposite direction. Chard told him that he had seen Zulus in hills to the north of the camp and that they were moving in the direction of Rorke's Drift. Fearing for the safety of his wagons, Durnford asked Chard to take a message to his two companies of NNC, ordering Captain Walter

Stafford's E Company to remain with the wagons while Captain Cracroft Nourse's D Company accompanied the rocket battery to Isandlwana without delay.

Lieutenant Charlie Raw, commanding No. 1 Troop (Zikali's Horse) of the NNH, was with Durnford as he rode into the sprawling encampment. As one of the five Carbineers who had stood by Durnford at Bushman's River Pass, he probably owed his commission to his courage on that occasion. He wrote later: 'We found the troops drawn up in front of the camp and the oxen inspanned. There were a few Zulus on the ridge in front of the camp about two miles off.' Having ordered his men to dismount in front of the NNC tents, but not to offsaddle, Durnford, accompanied by a number of his officers, set off for the column office at the rear of the camp. Just as he reached the office, he 'saw a small body of Zulus on a ridge of hill to the right, & at the same time a sentry brought word to the Colonel that there were Zulus upon the ridge, & that they seemed to be running away'. On asking the sentry how many Zulus, he was told about 400. 'He at once sent out 6 scouts in all directions,' remembered Jabez Molife, his Basuto sergeant-major, 'to find out whether any larger army was at hand.'

Durnford then entered the bell tent that served as the column office and was met by Colonel Pulleine. The detail of their conversation is much disputed. What is not in doubt is that Durnford quickly established his superior rank – he was a substantive lieutenant-colonel, Pulleine only a brevet – and, in effect, took command. That is not to say that he felt bound to carry out Pulleine's orders and defend the camp; simply that he regarded all the troops at Isandlwana at his disposal.

One eyewitness to the conversation between the two colonels was Lieutenant Francis Cochrane of the 32nd Regiment, a special service officer in charge of Durnford's transport. 'Colonel Pulleine,' recalled Cochrane, 'gave over to Colonel Durnford a verbal state of the troops in camp at the time, and stated the orders he had received, viz., to defend the camp. These words were repeated two or three times in the conversation.' Cochrane added in a separate account:

The news was that a number of Zulus had been seen since an early hour on top of the adjacent hills, and that an attack had been expected. In consequence the following disposition of troops had been made: the natives of Lonsdale's contingent were on outpost duty on the hills to the left; the guns were in position on the left of the camp; the infantry were turned out, and formed in column in the open space in front of the General's tent. The wagons, etc., were inspanned. Constant reports came in from the scouts on the hills to the left, but never anything from the men on the top of the Isandhlwana hill, that I heard. Some of the reports were: 'The enemy are in force behind the hills on the left', 'The enemy are in three columns', 'The columns are separating, one moving to the left rear, and one towards the General', 'The enemy are retiring in every direction'.

This last message was brought by Lieutenant Walter Higginson of the 1/3rd NNC. Durnford had earlier asked him to send men to the top of Isandlwana Hill 'to keep a look out'. They had reported back that the Zulus were 'retreating'. When Higginson told Durnford, his reponse was: 'Ah! Is that so? Well we will follow them up.'

Cochrane's version of events is similar: on hearing that the Zulus were 'retiring', Durnford said that he 'would go out and prevent' them from joining the force opposed to Lord Chelmsford. He also asked Pulleine if he would give him two companies of the 2/24th to support his column. According to Cochrane, 'Pulleine objected, stating that he did not think he would be justified in sending away any men, as his orders were "to defend the camp".'

Durnford replied: 'Very well; perhaps I had better not take them. I will go with my own men.'

Durnford's decision to take the initiative was to leave him open to the charge of disobeying orders. As the new senior officer at Isandlwana, so the argument goes, he had inherited the orders given to Pulleine to 'act strictly on the defensive'. Yet it probably never entered his head that he was expected to take command at Isandlwana and was therefore bound by Pulleine's instructions. He had not received any clear orders to that effect. Instead he had simply been instructed to move his force to Isandlwana. He must have been expecting to find fresh orders from Chelmsford waiting for him there. If so, he was to be disappointed. But, given the tenor of his previous orders – particularly the one on 19 January, which had outlined Chelmsford's plan to use him 'against the Matyanas' – it was only logical for him to assume that Chelmsford expected him to play an active part in the anticipated battle at Mangeni. There was, of course, a more pressing reason – or, to the cynical, a more convenient excuse – to go on the offensive: to intercept the Zulu column that was said to be moving in Chelmsford's direction.

Durnford had at this point just four troops of NNH at his disposal: he had sent a troop of Zikali's Horse back to provide additional security for the wagons; the rocket battery and Captain Nourse's D Company of 1/1st NNC had yet to appear. So he dispatched his two remaining troops of Zikali's Horse – under the overall command of Captain William Barton* – up on to the Nqutu Plateau with orders to 'drive the enemy into the valley below'. Barton was accompanied by Captain George Shepstone, Durnford's political officer and the son of Sir Theophilus. Durnford's intention was to proceed up the oNdini track with his remaining horsemen in the hope of catching the Zulus as they debouched into the plain. But he knew that Barton's men had more ground to cover and so had time to snatch a quick bite with Pulleine. As Durnford took his leave, he said, almost as an afterthought: 'If you see us in difficulties you must send and support us.' Pulleine promised he would.

Before setting off, Durnford ordered Major Francis Russell, R A, who had just arrived with his rocket battery and its escort of NNC, to 'advance from the Camp towards the right front, saying that the Zulus were retiring and he must make haste and outflank them'. He then mounted his trusty grey pony, 'Chieftain', and rode out of camp at the head of his Edendale and Basuto troops. It was now about 11.30 a.m. Barton and Shepstone had left twenty minutes earlier.

---

* A shadowy Irish soldier of fortune who had spent seven years fighting in South America.

As he rode up the valley, Durnford could see Zulus retreating along the Nqutu Plateau, causing him to remark: 'If they are going towards the General we must stop them at all hazards.' But when he and his horsemen had covered about four miles, they were overtaken by a scout from the Carbineers, who told them that 'it was a ruse on the part of the Zulus, as the great army was now appearing, & would attack the camp'. It had been discovered by a small patrol of Carbineers, including Trooper Barker, who recalled:

About two hundred [Zulus] advanced to within three hundred yards of us, but on our advancing they retired out of sight, and a few of us went up to this hill where the Zulus had disappeared, and on a farther hill, at about six hundred yards' distance, we saw a large army sitting down. We returned to Lieut. Scott, who was then about three miles from camp, and reported what we had seen.

Durnford was furious at the turn of events. He knew he had been outwitted and blamed the scouts he had sent out earlier, asking Jabez Molife what they were 'about'. There was nothing for it but to fall back on the camp. As he and his men turned their horses, they heard a burst of gunfire from up on the Nqutu Plateau. Barton's horsemen had engaged the Zulus. The accepted version of events is that members of Charlie Raw's troop stumbled across the Zulu impi as it lay silently waiting in the Ngwebeni Valley; if it had not been discovered, it would not have attacked that day. Great cinema: but not the truth.

7. Isandlwana

It was not Chief Ntshingwayo's intention to fight on 22 January 1879 – the day of a 'dead' moon – but the opportunity presented to him that morning was too good to miss. The British had split their force not once but twice. The sight of a column leaving the camp at dawn that day must have convinced the Zulu general that he would never get a better chance to secure the type of crushing victory that might lead to a negotiated peace. He may also have been influenced by the aggression of his younger warriors. This was the claim made by an iNgobamakhosi warrior to the Natal settler T. E. Newmarch after the battle. 'He said,' wrote Newmarch,

that their scouts had been out early and had returned to report to the leaders that the White People were scattered about on the hills around the camp like a lot of goats out grazing and that they were convinced that the 'spirits' (*amadhlozi*) of the Zulu nation had put them into their hands to be killed and that they should attack whether they had been doctored or not that day. In the end the young men prevailed against their more cautious leaders and were given the order to attack, especially as they knew that the greater part of the British forces had gone further into the country.

Having made up his mind, Ntshingwayo spent the early part of the morning moving his regiments across the broken ground that lay between their bivouac in the Ngwebeni Valley and the Nqutu Plateau above Isandlwana. He was not in any particular hurry: partly because he wanted to avoid detection; and partly because he was waiting for the return of those warriors who had been used to entice Chelmsford's column ever deeper into the Malakatha Hills. The bulk of his army had reached the valley behind iThusi Hill when it was spotted by Barker's patrol. Minutes later it was 'discovered' by Raw and his men.

The two troops of Zikali's Horse had ascended the Nqutu Plateau by the broad Tahelane Spur that connected it to the north end of Isandlwana Hill. Once on the plateau they picked their way east, through broken terrain strewn with rocks and boulders, supported by Captain Barry's company of 2/3rd NNC that had been on outpost duty on Magaga Knoll. Raw's troop hugged the edge of the Nyoni Ridge; half a mile further on to the plateau, but moving in the same direction, was the troop under Lieutenant J. A. Roberts. Raw recalled:

We left camp proceeding over the hills, Capt. George Shepstone going with us, the enemy in small clumps retiring before us for some time, drawing us over five miles from the camp when they turned and fell upon us, the whole army showing itself from behind the hills in front where they had evidently been waiting.

According to James Hamer, Durnford's commissariat officer, who accompanied the sweep along the ridge, he and George Shepstone had been about to capture some cattle the Zulus were driving before them when 'they disappeared over a ridge'. He added: 'On coming up we saw the Zulus, like *ants* in front of us, in perfect order, quiet as mice and stretched across in an even line. We estimated those we saw at 12,000.'

Zulu accounts of the encounter with Raw's troop are roughly in agreement. 'A small herd of cattle came past our line from our right,' recalled a warrior of the uNokhenke who later deserted to the British, 'being driven by some of our scouts, and just when they were opposite to the uMcijo Regiment, a body of mounted men, on the hill to the west, were seen galloping, evidently trying to cut them off.' The deserter added:

When several hundred yards off, they perceived the uMcijo, and, dismounting, fired one volley at them and then retired. The uMcijo at once jumped up and charged, an example which was taken up by the uNokhenke and uNodwengu [Corps] on their right, and the iNgobamakhosi and uMbonambi on the left, while the uNdi Corps and the uDloko formed a circle [in reserve] – as is customary in Zulu warfare when a force is about to be engaged – and remained where they were.

Uguku, a member of the uMcijo, remembered seeing 'a body of horse coming up the hill towards us from the Isandhlwana side'. His regiment opened fire, and then the 'whole of our army rose and came up the hill'.

The original Zulu order of battle had the uNodwengu Corps* and the uNokhenke and uMcijo regiments on the right; the iNgob-amakhosi, uVe and uMbonambi regiments in the centre; and the uNdi corps† and the uDloko Regiment on the left. But the precipi-tate action by the uMcijo altered this. The commanders were able to hold back only the uNdi and the uDloko, which became the reserve. The missing left horn was formed by a portion of the iNgobamakhosi,‡ about 1,500 strong, which moved off to the left of iThusi towards Qwabe. It was eventually joined by the rest of the iNgobamakhosi, the uVe and the uMbonambi regiments, which had emerged from the right of iThusi and swept towards the British camp around the left of the Conical Hill. The Zulu chest was now made up of the uMcijo, uMhlanga, uKhandempemvu and iNgakamatye regiments; the right horn formed from the uNodwengu Corps and part of the uNokhenke.

Faced with the sight of this huge Zulu army on the move, George Shepstone told Barton to conduct a fighting retreat along the plateau with his two troops of Zikali's Horse, while he and Hamer galloped back to warn Pulleine. The black horsemen duly opened fire. But the appearance of so many of their mortal enemies was too much for Captain Barry's supporting company of NNC, most of whom were armed with just spear and shield, and they

* The uDududu, iMbube and iSangqu regiments.
† The uThulwana and iNdluyengwe regiments.
‡ The iNgobamakhosi regiment, at 6,000 strong, was the largest in the Zulu Army. The uVe and uMbonambi – the other two regiments at the centre of the original Zulu order of battle – were, at 1,000 men and 2,000 respectively, too small to be split.

turned and fled back to the camp, leaving their officers to retire on foot beside the horsemen. It was around 11.45 a.m.

On hearing the sound of gunshots, Durnford and his men turned towards the Nqutu Plateau and were momentarily transfixed by the appearance of warriors to their left and front. Members of the uVe and iNgobamakhosi regiments – now part of the Zulu left horn – had debouched from the valley behind iThusi and were coming on 'in skirmishing order but ten or twelve deep, with supports close behind'. At 800 yards the Zulus opened fire. Durnford's men responded, before conducting a staggered withdrawal, one troop firing while the other passed through it.

The rocket battery, meanwhile, had also come into action. On reaching the Conical Hill, about two miles to Durnford's rear, Major Russell met a scout from the Natal Carbineers, who told him that the NNH were heavily engaged on the ridge above. The scout also offered to show Russell a short cut on to the ridge up a re-entrant (later dubbed 'the Knotch'). But as the men and mules of the rocket battery and their escort of NNC began to struggle up the re-entrant, they were stopped in their tracks by the sight of Zulus lining the crest. Russell at once shouted: 'Action front!' But his men had time only to set up the iron trough and fire one badly aimed rocket – which exploded harmlessly into the side of the ridge – before the Zulus charged down and fired a volley at a range of about 100 yards. Three of the eight gunners were killed instantly, and Russell was mortally wounded. Most of the battery's horses and mules bolted in panic, as did the NNC escort after firing a few shots. The remaining gunners also fled: some on foot, others leading artillery horses. Most were saved from almost certain death by the timely arrival of Durnford's horsemen. 'There was a hand-to-hand engagement going on with those that remained,' recalled Lieutenant Cochrane. 'As the mounted men returned towards them, the Zulus ran back to their cover.' Durnford then continued his retreat until he came to a deep watercourse known as the Nyokana Donga, parallel to and half a mile from the front of the camp. There he decided to make a stand.

★

Durnford had not been gone long when Pulleine, in a change of heart, sent Lieutenant Charles Cavaye's E Company, 1/24th, up the Tahelane Spur so that it was in a position to support the two troops of Zikali's Horse. But he did not expect a fight and marched the rest of the fighting troops to their parade grounds, where they were dismissed with orders not to take off their accoutrements. They were told to get their dinners 'as quick as possible and to be in readiness to fall in at any moment'. Lieutenant Curling, commanding the guns, was invited to join the officers of the 1/24th in their regimental mess. 'Not one of us dreamt that there was the least danger,' he wrote later, 'and all we hoped for was the fight might come off before the General returned. In the meantime, our dinner had been cooked and as there seemed no chance of our being attacked, we broke off and went into our tents.'

The illusion was shattered by the sound of gunfire from the Nqutu Plateau as Raw's men engaged the Zulus. Ten long minutes later, with all eyes turned towards the plateau, Shepstone and Hamer galloped down the Tahelane Spur and into the camp with the startling news that a huge Zulu army was on its way. They met James Brickhill, who showed them the way to Pulleine's tent in the 1/24th camp. 'But before Capt. S. could sufficiently recover his breath to speak to him,' wrote Brickhill, 'Capt. Gardner of the General's staff rode up with a letter from the General which the Col. read aloud, only four of us being present.' It was the order to strike part of the camp and entrench the remainder. Pulleine was perplexed. Four hours earlier he had warned Chelmsford that a large Zulu force was threatening the left of the camp. He had been expecting to hear that the rest of the column was on its way back; not that its camp should be sent on. Seeing Pulleine hesitate, and realizing that every second was crucial, Shepstone said calmly: 'I'm not an alarmist, Sir, but the Zulus are in such black masses over there, such long black lines, that you will have to give us all the assistance you can. They are now fast driving our men this way.'

Gardner now intervened, advising Pulleine that under the circumstances he should ignore Chelmsford's order. 'The General knows nothing of this,' he added, 'he is only thinking of the cowardly way in which the Zulus are running before our troops over yonder.' Reluctantly Pulleine agreed. Gardner wrote later:

We both went to Colonel Pulleine, to whom I delivered the order. Colonel Pulleine at first hesitated about carrying out the order, and eventually decided that the enemy being already on the hill on our left in large numbers, it was impossible to do so. The men of the 24th Regiment were all fallen in, and the Artillery also, and Colonel Pulleine sent two companies to support Colonel Durnford, to the hill on the left, and formed up the remaining companies in line, the guns in action on the extreme left flank of the camp, facing the hill on our left. Shortly after, I took the mounted men, by Colonel Pulleine's direction, about a quarter of a mile to the front of the camp, and left them there under the direction of Captain Bradstreet, with orders to hold the spruit.*

Pulleine had also dashed off a quick note to Chelmsford, which read: 'Staff Officer. Heavy firing to the left of our camp. Cannot move camp at present.' Gardner did not consider it sufficiently informative and so sent a message of his own by a separate galloper: 'Heavy firing near left of camp. Shepstone has come in for reinforcements and reports that Zulus are falling back. The whole force at camp turned out and fighting about one mile to left flank.' Where Gardner got the impression that the Zulus were retiring is anyone's guess; certainly not from Shepstone. The result of this misapprehension would be to convince Chelmsford, when he received the two messages shortly after 2 p.m., that the camp was still not seriously threatened. Yet by then it had almost been overrun.

If Pulleine, on first hearing of the Zulu attack, had struck his tents and concentrated all his available troops in a tight defensive formation with its rear protected by Isandlwana Hill, he might well have saved the camp. Instead he did almost the opposite, sending out infantry companies in penny packets to support Durnford's horsemen, and deploying the rest of his command along a huge defensive perimeter away from the camp. Why? First, because, like

* Another name for a donga or shallow watercourse.

most of the men under him, he underestimated the threat the Zulus posed; second, because he had promised Durnford, his superior, that he would assist him if he got into trouble; and third, and perhaps most important, because he was acting in accordance with the tactical disposition recommended by Chelmsford in the event of a Zulu attack. This document – entitled 'Instructions . . . for the Consideration of Officers Commanding Columns when Entering Zululand' and dated 23 December 1878 – made the point that any Zulu attack would threaten 'one or both flanks, as well as the front'. The best formation '*to meet* such an attack' was to have 'British infantry in the Front Line, deployed or extended, with one or both flank companies thrown back'. The guns should be slightly forward of the centre of the front line and an infantry reserve well behind. Supporting the British infantry, but in echelon to the rear and 'well clear of each flank', should be the Native Contingent. Finally the Mounted Infantry were to be placed to the rear of each flank, 'ready to move round the flanks, and rear, of the enemy'. This suggested formation is remarkably similar to the one adopted by Pulleine at Isandlwana when he made his final dispositions (as we shall see).★

Up on the Tahelane Ridge, Lieutenant Cavaye had deployed his men along the rocky crest line at intervals of five yards. The first sight they got of the advancing Zulus was not the chest of the army, which had swept over the Nyoni Ridge and into the gap between the ridge and the Conical Hill, but part of the Zulu right horn, which had bypassed the retreating horsemen and suddenly came into view about 800 yards to the north of the crest line. Cavaye ordered his men to open fire and, shortly after, sent his second-in-command, twenty-year-old 2nd Lieutenant Edward Dyson, with part of the company to a position 500 yards to the left, from where they could engage the Zulus as they reappeared beyond a small ridge. Despite volleys from both positions causing a number

★ A copy of these 'Instructions' was found on Durnford's body after the battle by a Trooper A. Pearse of the Natal Carbineers and eventually sent to the editor of the *Natal Witness*, who was trying to clear Durnford's name. It was later deposited in the Royal Engineers' Museum at Chatham, where it still resides.

of casualties, the Zulu right horn continued its march eastwards through the broken ground to the north of the camp. It rapidly became clear that the British position was being outflanked.

Captain Edward Essex of the 75th Regiment, Glyn's transport officer, arrived on the ridge about this time:

At about twelve o'clock, hearing firing on the hill where the company of the [1/24th] was stationed, I proceeded in that direction . . . On arriving at the far side of the crest of the hill, I found the company in charge of Lieutenant Cavaye, a section being detached about 500 yards to the left, in charge of Lieutenant Dyson. The whole were in extended order engaging the enemy, who was moving in similar formation towards our left, keeping about 800 yards from our line. Captain [William] Mostyn moved his company into the space between the portions of that already on the hill, and his men extended and entered into action. This line was then prolonged on our right along the crest of the hill by a body of native infantry. I observed that the enemy made little progress as regards his advance, but appeared to be moving at a rapid pace towards our left.

Extending the line to the right of Cavaye's E Company was Captain Walter Stafford's company of 1/1st NNC and Lieutenant Vause's troop of Zikali's Horse. Having brought Durnford's wagons in safely, they had been led up the Tahelane Ridge to support the British infantry by George Shepstone. Vause's dismounted troopers were 200 yards to the right of Stafford's men. They had not been there long when they were joined by some of Barton's Zikali Horse, mostly men of Raw's troop; the rest had taken the shortcut back to the camp via the Nyoni Ridge. 'By the time these dispositions had taken place,' Stafford wrote later, 'there was a force of some 2,000 Zulus steadily advancing 700 yards off.' They were part of the Zulu right horn, which had followed Barton's men along the plateau. Stafford added:

My first shot at 800 yards went over the enemy, and I distinctly recollect the second shot, with my sight at 700 yards, to have got on target . . . I ran over to Barton and asked him to let Colonel Durnford know that a large force of the enemy was in front of us. [Barton duly sent off a message by rider.] Barton then suggested that we close up our forces, which we did, and the firing now became general. The Zulu impis continued their steady advance, splendidly the savages pressed forward and when within 300 yards the native Contingents began to waver and bolted.

The auxiliaries did, however, reform at the bottom of the spur, where they were joined by C Company of the 1/24th, under Captain Reginald Younghusband, and the survivors of Mostyn and Cavaye's companies which had received an order from Lieutenant Teignmouth Melvill, adjutant of the 1/24th, to withdraw closer to the camp. Dyson's small party never received the order and were speared to a man. The defensive line facing the Tahelane Ridge was now composed of three companies of the 1/24th – Young-husband's on the left, Mostyn's in the centre and Cavaye's on the right – with Stafford's company of NNC and the remnants of three troops of the NNH interspersed between them. For a time their combined firepower managed to drive part of the Zulu right horn – mainly the uNokhenke Regiment – back over the ridge. But the respite would be temporary.

Meanwhile the two 7-pounder guns – under the command of Major Stuart Smith, who had returned to the camp with Gardner – had taken up a position on high ground about 1,000 yards to the left of the camp, facing the Nqutu Plateau. From there they opened fire on the Zulu chest at a range of about 1,000 yards, throwing shells 'into a huge mass of the enemy that remained almost stationary'. According to Uguku, a warrior of the uMcijo, 'the first shell took effect in the ranks of my regiment, just above the kraal of Baza'. It was not long before the seventy or so artillerymen were joined by the remaining two companies of the 1/24th – A and F under Captains Porteous and Wardell respectively – which lay down in skirmishing order on both flanks, ten yards between each man. Lieutenant Pope's G Company, 2/24th, was a further 800 yards to the right, protecting the front of the camp and firing over the top of Durnford's horsemen in the Nyokana Donga.

Lieutenant Henry Curling of the artillery recalled: 'The Zulus soon split up into a large mass of skirmishers that extended as far around the camp as we could see. We could get no idea of numbers but the hills were black with them. They advanced steadily in the face of the infantry and our guns, but I believe the whole of the natives who defended the rear of the camp soon bolted and left only our side of the camp defended.'

As the Zulus moved closer, Smith took one of the guns a little to the right and fired a few rounds, one of which landed in the midst of a nearby kraal, before returning to his original position. Some of the warriors noticed that the artillerymen stood aside when the gun was ready to fire; so when that happened they threw themselves to the ground, avoiding the worst of the explosion. But the combination of shell and rifle-fire was beginning to cause serious casualties among the regiments of the Zulu chest, particularly the uMcijo, and for a time its advance began to falter. Warriors sought cover in the many dips and folds that covered the terrain, and their indunas tried desperately to rally them. One named Undhlaka shouted: 'Never did his Majesty the King give you this command, to wit, "Lie down upon the ground!" His words were: "Go and toss them into Maritzburg."' This seemed to have the desired effect, as a number of warriors rose to their feet, only to be driven to ground moments later by a hail of bullets.

The left horn too was finding it difficult to get beyond the withering fire of the dismounted horsemen in the Nyokana Donga. As well as Durnford's two troops of NNH – Lieutenant Alfred Henderson's Basutos and Lieutenant Harry Davies's Edendale Contingent – the donga contained the thirty or so volunteers under Captain Bradstreet and the remnants of the NMP and the Natal Carbineer vedettes: about 150 men in all. According to Jabez Molife of Henderson's troop, Durnford inspired by example:

Here we made a long stand, firing incessantly. The Colonel rode up and down our line continually, encouraging us all; he was very calm & cheerful, talking & even laughing with us. 'Fire my boys,' 'Well done my boys', he cried. Some of us did not like his exposing himself so much to the enemy, & wanted him to keep behind us, but he laughed at us, &

said, 'All right! Nonsense!' Sometimes as he passed amongst us one of the men brought him his gun with the old cartridge sticking, & he dismounted &, taking the gun between his knees, because of only having one hand with the strength in it, he pulled the cartridge out & gave back the gun.

The deadly effectiveness of the fire from the donga was later acknowledged by Mehlokazulu, Sihayo's son and a junior induna of the iNgobamakhosi Regiment. 'On the side of [the Conical] hill there is a donga into which the mounted men got and stopped our onward move there,' he stated. 'We could not advance against their fire any longer. They had drawn their horses into this donga, and all we could see were their helmets. They fired so heavily we had to retire. We kept lying down and rising again.'

But eventually, not just in the donga but right along the extended British line, the defenders began to run low on ammunition. The infantry had marched out with their usual seventy rounds: four packets of ten bullets each in their ammunition pouches and a further thirty rounds loose in their canvas expense bags. If fired at a rapid rate of six rounds a minute, this personal supply would have been used in under twelve minutes. This, of course, did not happen at Isandlwana, because the Zulus kept dropping to the ground and did not always present the soldiers with a target. But after the battle had been raging in front of the camp for about half an hour, many soldiers began to shout to their officers and NCOs that they were running short. Fortunately some of the staff officers in the camp had already anticipated their needs. Bandsman Wilson of the 1/24th was on his way back from the firing line to the hospital tent when he noticed that 'ammunition was beginning to be brought to the Companies'. Among those organizing the supply to the companies on the extreme left was Captain Essex:

The companies . . . first engaged were now becoming short of ammunition, and at the request of the officer in charge I went to procure a fresh supply, with the assistance of Quartermaster 2nd/24th and some men of the Royal Artillery. I had some boxes placed on a mule cart and sent it off to the companies engaged, and sent more by hand, employing any men without arms. I then went back to the line, telling the men that plenty of ammunition was coming. I found that the companies [of the 1/24th] . . . had retired to within 300 yards of that portion of the camp occupied by the Native Contingent. On my way I noticed a number of native infantry retreating in haste towards the camp, their officer endeavouring to prevent them but without effect.

Essex had gone to the 2/24th camp for ammunition because its tents and wagons were much closer than those of the 1/24th on the far side of the oNdini track. Quartermaster Bloomfield of the 2/24th, a former NCO who had been in the battalion since its formation in 1858, has been condemned by history for refusing – in true jobsworth's style – to give bullets to men from different corps. Presumably he made an exception when Essex came calling because the supply was intended for the 2/24th's sister battalion.

Another officer who helped dole out bullets – only this time to the three companies on the right of the British line – was Lieutenant Horace Smith-Dorrien, back from his night ride to Rorke's Drift. He wrote: 'I, having no particular duty to perform in camp, when I saw the whole Zulu Army advancing, had collected camp stragglers, such as artillerymen in charge of spare horses, officers' servants, sick, etc., and had taken them to the ammunition-boxes, where we broke them open as fast as we could, and kept sending out the packets to the firing line.' As the heavy ammunition boxes had a sliding lid that was secured by a single two-inch screw, and screwdrivers were in short supply, Smith-Dorrien took to smashing the lids with rocks, rifle butts, anything heavy that came to hand.

But this trickle of bullets could not hope to meet the ever-increasing demand, and it was not long before a steady stream of runners and horsemen was besieging the various quartermasters with requests for more bullets. Some, like Quartermaster London of the Natal Carbineers, were happy to serve 'all who asked for it', no matter their corps; others like Bloomfield were more pedantic. Smith-Dorrien was busily trying to break open a box when Bloomfield piped up: 'For heaven's sake, don't take that, man, for it belongs to our Battalion.'

'Hang it all,' was Smith-Dorrien's angry reply, 'you don't want a requisition slip now, do you?'

When Durnford realized his men were running out of ammunition, he sent 'a messenger back to the camp for more, but none came'. So he sent an officer, Lieutenant Henderson, who managed to locate the column's supply wagons on the other side of the nek.★ But by then the troops in the donga had fired virtually all their bullets, and the Zulu left horn was moving far to the south in an effort to outflank the donga. Durnford ordered an immediate withdrawal. 'On seeing us retire towards the Buffalo,' recalled Mehlokazulu, 'they retired on the camp, fearing lest we should enter the camp before they could get to it, and that the camp would not be protected.' At the entrance to the camp, Durnford's troopers were met by Henderson, who led them to their wagons so that they could replenish their ammunition. The volunteers and mounted police sought out their own supplies. Trooper Sparks of the NMP wrote later:

There seemed to be still a great deal of confusion, no kind of formation being made for the defence of the camp, and it was only after some considerable time that we were able to procure any ammunition, as the boxes in which it was packed were all screwed down, and we had no tools to open them. I noticed Quartermaster London, of the Natal Carbineers, opening one of these boxes, and he was killed by a bullet wound in the head while doing so. By this time the Zulu Army had thrown out wings on our flanks, so that we were hemmed in on three sides and in a very short time the camp was invaded by vast numbers of Zulus, and owing to every one of us being more or less in skirmishing order it was impossible to make any effective defence.

The speedy collapse of the camp's defences has generally been attributed to a lack of ammunition. If the soldiers in the firing line had not run out of bullets, so the theory goes, the Zulus would

★ Boer name for a pass between two hills: in this case Isandlwana and the stony koppie.

never have broken in. Certainly Durnford's withdrawal from the donga was partly caused by low ammunition; but he was also aware that the Zulu flanking manoeuvre was about to make that position redundant. Captain Gardner met some of the mounted volunteers as they reached the camp and asked them why they were retiring. They had been ordered to by Colonel Durnford, they said, because 'the position taken up was too extended'. Gardner added: 'The same remark was made to me by Colonel Durnford himself immediately afterwards.'

Durnford's withdrawal from the donga, however, had exposed the left flank of Lieutenant Pope's G Company, 2/24th. Well aware of this, Durnford sought out Pulleine so that orders could be issued to 'collect all the troops together'. But he failed to find him and instead asked Essex to take as many men as he could to the right of the British line 'to hold the enemy in check'. Pulleine, meanwhile, belatedly recognizing the danger, had ordered all his companies to withdraw closer to the camp and nearer their ammunition supplies. This was the critical moment. But no sooner had H and A Companies of the 1/24th, flanking the guns, begun to retire, than the Zulus leapt to their feet and charged. Their inspiration, according to one warrior, was the Biyela chief Mkhosana kaMvundlana, an induna of the uMcijo, who ran down from the Nyoni Ridge, where Ntshingwayo and Mavumengwana were directing the battle, 'and rallied them, calling out that they would get the whole impi beaten and must come on'. He added: 'Then they all shouted "uSuthu!" and waving their shields charged the soldiers with great fury. Mkhosana was shot through the forehead and dropped down dead, but the uMcijo rushed over his body and fell upon the soldiers, stabbing them with their assegais and driving them right in among the tents.'

The two guns had only managed to fire a round of caseshot* each by the time Major Smith, already wounded in the arm, received the order to retire. 'We limbered up at once,' recalled

* Containing hundreds of small lead balls for use at close quarters, similar to a shotgun.

Lieutenant Curling, 'but were hardly in time as the Zulus were on us at once and one man was killed (stabbed) as he was mounting the seat of the gun carriage. Most of the gunners were on foot as there was not time to mount them on the guns.' Smith and Curling escaped on their chargers, followed by the two guns, which bounced and crashed their way over the broken ground in front of the camp. Those on foot had no chance. Curling added: 'We trotted off to the camp thinking to take up another position but found it in possession of the enemy, who were killing the men as they ran out of their tents. We went right through them [the tents] and out the other side, losing nearly all our gunners in doing so, and one of the two sergeants.'

A black auxiliary named Malindi was with his company of NNC in support of the British troops:

Our ammunition failed once but we got more from the camp, and remained firing until the Zulus were within 100 yards of us. We were then ordered to retire as we were also threatened to our rear by the advancing left of the Zulus . . . The company of soldiers was with us and on nearing the tents knelt down and commenced firing at the enemy. Below them, some distance to the west, was another company or more of soldiers, also kneeling down, and firing. Our Captain now got off his horse and gave it to me, telling me to take it to the ammunition wagons, and, turning back . . . he joined the red soldiers who were firing and I never saw him again.

The company 'some distance to the west' was probably Pope's. His men had also fled their earlier position, but many were overtaken by the fleeter-footed warriors of the uMbonambi Regiment, who were later credited as the first Zulus to enter the camp. 'The British soldier,' wrote an officer with Chelmsford's column, 'his feet encased in heavy boots, carrying a rifle, his body hampered with straps and pouches, had no chance in a race with the naked savage, his dress a feather or two, and his weapons a slight shield and spear.'

Mehlokazulu, son of Sihayo, recalled: 'When the soldiers retired

on the camp they did so running, and the Zulus were then intermixed with them, and entered the camp at the same time . . . things
were then getting very mixed and confused . . . what with the
smoke, dust, and intermingling of mounted men, footmen, Zulus
and natives.' Pope himself – the 29-year-old son of a vicar, handsome, popular and a crack shot – was finally brought to bay on
the nek between Isandlwana Hill and the stony koppie. A
graphic account of his death, and that of his second-in-command,
Lieutenant Frederick Godwin-Austen, was provided by a Zulu
induna who remembered engaging two officers with pieces of
glass in their eye: Pope and Godwin-Austen both wore monocles.
One was felled by a rifle shot but the other continued to fire his
revolver, grazing the induna's neck with one bullet and wounding
him in the leg with another. The induna retaliated by hurling his
throwing assegai into the officer's chest. He tried to pull it out, and
almost succeeded; but the induna closed and finished him with his
iKlwa.

Pope may have been supported by Quartermaster Pullen of the
1/24th. He was distributing ammunition at the top of his battalion's
camp when the line began to disintegrate. 'Follow me,' he shouted
to a group of soldiers near him, 'and let us try to turn the enemy's
flank.' At the same time he turned to Glyn's interpreter, who
happened to be passing on horseback, and said: 'Mr Brickhill do go
to Colonel Pulleine and ask him to send us help, as they are
outflanking us here on the right.' Then he ran off in the direction
of the stony koppie, followed by 'several' soldiers, and was never
seen again.

The British left flank, meanwhile, had also collapsed. It too had
been withdrawn closer to the camp to prevent it from being
outflanked by the Zulu right horn, which had advanced beyond
the Tahelane Ridge and up the Manzimnyama Valley. Charlie
Raw recalled the suddenness of the rout:

The enemy attacked in great force in front of the camp or I should say to
the left. I turned my troop and engaged them, the troops drawn up in
the camp firing over us. We took up the left of a company of the 24th

Regiment having on our left a troop of Lonsdale's men. The company
of the 24th then retired towards the tents and the enemy following close
after cut them up before they could rally, killing them close into the tents.
We were driven through the camp and found the right had also been
driven in and the camp surrounded.

'In a moment all was disorder,' wrote Captain Essex,

and few of the men of the [1st/24th] had time to fix bayonets before the
enemy was among them using their assegais with fearful effect. I heard
officers calling to their men to be steady; but the retreat became in a few
seconds general, and in a direction towards the road to Rorke's Drift.
Before, however, we gained the neck near the Isandula Hill, the enemy
had arrived on that portion of the field also, and the large circle had now
closed in on us.

James Brickhill was in the 2/24th's camp, still looking for Pulleine,
when panic set in. Men were running in all directions but there
was no sign of an officer. In the distance he could see the Zulus
coming on in a determined walk. Suddenly they roared 'Suthu'
and charged. Brickhill rode back to the top of the 1/24th camp, on
the far side of the oNdini road, to see if he could find Quartermaster
Pullen. There was no sign, and as 'Zulus were already stabbing in
this camp as well as the others', he joined the stream of fugitives
making for the nek. So too did James Hamer, who, minutes earlier,
had been firing away with George Shepstone on the left flank. As
he galloped through the camp, he noticed that the escape route
over the nek was being kept open by a company of the 24th –
probably Pope's – and 'good Colonel Durnford making a heroic &
most gallant stand to cover the retreat'. He added: 'The scene at
the top of the camp baffles description, oxen yoked to wagons,
mules, sheep, horses & men in the greatest confusion, all wildly
trying to escape.'
   A warrior of the uMbonambi witnessed the meeting of the two
Zulu horns that sealed the camp's fate:

I saw several white men on horseback galloping towards the neck, which was the only point open; then the *uNokenke* and *uNodwengu* regiments, which had formed the right horn of the *impi*, joined with the *inGobamak-hosi* on the neck. After that there was so much smoke that I could not see whether the white men had got through or not. The tumult and the firing was wonderful, every warrior shouted 'Usutu' as he killed anyone, and the sun got very dark like night.★

Thanks to the sacrifice of those who decided to fight on rather than flee – particularly those with horses, like Durnford and the Natal volunteers – scores of others were given the opportunity to escape. An eyewitness to the exodus was a warrior of the uNokhenke:

We worked round behind Isandhlwana under cover of the long grass and dongas, intending to join with the *inGobamakhosi* on the neck and sweep in upon the camp. Then we saw white men beginning to run away along the road to Rorke's Drift; many of these were cut off and killed, down in the stream which flows along the bottom of the valley. More and more came over, some mounted and some on foot. When they saw that the valley was full of our warriors, they turned to the left and ran off along the side of the hill towards the Buffalo; those who had not got horses were soon overtaken. The *uNodwengu* pursued the mounted men, numbers of whom were killed along the thorns and dongas, but I heard that some escaped.

Among the first to try were the two artillery officers, Major Smith and Lieutenant Curling. When they reached the saddle, the guns trailing in their wake, they found the road to Rorke's Drift 'completely blocked up by Zulus'. Just then Lieutenant Nevill Coghill, Glyn's aide-de-camp, appeared on his roan charger. Could they not rally some men and make a stand? asked Curling. Coghill 'did not think it could be done'. So they left the road and followed a crowd of 'natives, men left in camp, and civilians' down 'a steep ravine towards the river'. Curling recorded:

★ There was an eclipse of the sun during the afternoon of 22 January 1879.

The Zulus were in the middle of the crowd, stabbing the men as they ran. When we had gone about 400 yards, we came to a deep cut in which the guns stuck. There was, as far as I could see, only one gunner with them at this time, but they were covered with men of different corps clinging to them. The Zulus were in them almost at once, and the drivers pulled off their horses. I then left the guns. Shortly after this I again saw Lieutenant Coghill, who told me Colonel Pulleine had been killed.

On the fugitives pressed, over six miles of steep, rocky ground, harried all the way by the fleeter warriors of the uNodwengu Corps. There was no path. Instead the riders were forced to pick their way down a rock-covered slope to a small stream at the base of a deep donga. Its steep sides were covered with dense scrub, making it impossible for horsemen to cross, and most escapees were forced to follow the stream's twisting course for a mile or so down to the marshy bed of the Manzimnyama, a tributary of the Buffalo. From there the river flowed over the open spur of a hill before falling away to a final ridge that led down to the high wooded banks of the Buffalo. Those on foot had no hope and were rapidly overtaken and killed. The last to perish was a group of sixty foot soldiers under 27-year-old Lieutenant Edgar Anstey, Mostyn's second-in-command, which got as far as the banks of the Manzimnyama before it was surrounded. One warrior remembered the British soldiers pleading for their lives. 'Have mercy on us,' said one, 'What wrong have we done to Cetshwayo?' 'How can we give you mercy,' replied the warrior, 'when you have come to us to take away our country and eat us up? uSuthu!'

Even the mounted men were vulnerable as the rugged terrain made it difficult for their horses to rise above a walk. One lucky rider, the interpreter James Brickhill, provided a graphic account of the horrific, interminable flight to the river over six miles of treacherous ground:

No path, no track, boulders everywhere – on we were borne, now into some dry torrent bed, now weaving our way amongst trees of stunted growth . . . Our way was already strewn with shields, assegais, blankets, hats, clothing of all description, guns, ammunition belts, saddles (which horses had managed to kick off), revolvers and I do not know what. Whilst our stampede was composed of mules, with and without pack saddles, oxen, horses in all stages of equipment and fleeing men all strangely intermingled – man and beast, apparently all infected with the danger which surrounded us. One riderless horse that ran up alongside of me I caught and gave to a poor soldier, who was struggling along on foot, but he had scarcely mounted before he was knocked down by a Zulu bullet.

Moments later Brickhill came upon Band Sergeant Gamble of the 1/24th, 'tottering and tumbling about the stones'. Gamble implored: 'For God's sake give us a lift.'

Brickhill, however, had performed his Good Samaritan's act for the day. 'My dear fellow, it is a case of life and death with me,' he replied as he spurred his horse forward. Gamble was never seen again. Further down the trail Brickhill spotted, 200 yards ahead, Lieutenants Coghill and Melvill of the 1/24th riding together. Melvill was carrying the cased Queen's Colour★ of his battalion. After the battle a story was circulated by the officers of the 24th Regiment that, when all was lost, Pulleine ordered Melvill to save the Colour and prevent the disgrace of it falling into the hands of the enemy. But there is no first-hand evidence of this and, in any case, Pulleine was probably dead by the time Melvill took the Colour – mounted on an eight-foot-long wooden staff but still in its leather case – from the battalion's guard tent. Melvill could, of course, have been intending to use the Colour to rally the remnants of his battalion; that, after all, was its main use on the battlefield. But if that had been his purpose, as some historians have suggested, why did he not unfurl it and ride towards one of the points of resistance? A more cynical assessment of his action is that he took the Colour to provide himself with an excuse for leaving the

★ All British infantry battalions had two gold-fringed silk standards that they carried into battle: the Queen's Colour, which consisted of a large Union Jack with the Crown and regimental title at its centre; and the Regimental Colour, which was dark blue and decorated with the regimental crest and battle honours.

battlefield. Apart from Coghill, who was attached to the staff, he appears to have been the only officer of the 24th who chose to abandon his men.

Both Melvill and Coghill are credited with the attempt to save the Colour. But there seems little doubt that Coghill left the camp first – at around 1 p.m. Lieutenant Smith-Dorrien, one of only five imperial officers to escape the carnage, remembered seeing Coghill – 'wearing a blue patrol jacket and cord breeches and riding a red roan horse' – shortly after passing the overturned guns. Further down the trail, and by now 'at least half a mile behind Coghill', Smith-Dorrien was passed by Melvill, 'in a red coat and with a cased Colour across the front of his saddle'. Melvill eventually caught up with Coghill, whose horse had been partially disabled by an assegai thrust as he left the camp, and the pair continued together. 'When I got down to the drift,' recalled Private Williams, Glyn's groom who escaped on one of his master's horses, 'I saw Lieutenants Melvill and Coghill coming down the rocks to it.'

For those lucky enough to reach the clifftops above the Buffalo River, then in spate due to the recent rains, fresh horrors were in store. Natal and safety beckoned. But they could only descend the precipice in single file, leading their horses, and this produced a bottleneck at the top. Smith-Dorrien took advantage of the delay to get off his horse and help a mounted infantryman who had been assegaied in the arm and was 'unable to move'. He managed to make a tourniquet from his handkerchief to stop the bleeding, and had got him halfway down the cliff, when a shout came from behind: 'Get on with it, man, the Zulus are on top of you!'

Smith-Dorrien recalled: 'I turned round and saw Major Smith, R.A. . . . as white as a sheet and bleeding profusely; and in a second we were surrounded, and assegais accounted for poor Smith, my wounded M.I. friend, and my horse. With the help of my revolver and a wild jump down the rocks, I found myself in the Buffalo River, which was in flood and eighty yards broad.' Carried away by the current, he was seconds from drowning when he managed to grab the tail of a loose horse, which towed him across to the far bank. But he was too exhausted to hold on to the horse and was forced to continue on foot up the steep hill beyond. All around were 'friendly natives', both horse and foot, but only one European: James Hamer. He had been kicked by his horse and was lying on the ground, 'unable to move'. So Smith-Dorrien helped him mount his horse and, in addition, lent him his knife. Hamer promised, in return, to catch him a horse. But 'directly he was up he went clean away'.

Smith-Dorrien struggled on as the Zulus poured in a 'very heavy fire from the opposite bank', hitting 'several friendly natives' as they climbed the hill. Even at the top he was far from safe: he could see that 'a lot of Zulus' had crossed further upstream and were running over to cut him off. So he veered to the left and for three miles was chased by about twenty Zulus. But a combination of his revolver and some mounted Basutus – members of Davies's troop of NNH – managed to hold them off. Eventually the Zulus gave up and Smith-Dorrien was able to continue his march to Helpmakaar, arriving 'at sundown, having done twenty miles on foot from the river, for I almost went to Sandspruit'. At Helpmakaar he met up with about thirty European survivors who had helped the inhabitants form a wagon laager. 'We sat up all night,' he recalled, 'momentarily expecting attack.'

Coghill and Melvill – the latter gamely clinging to the Queen's Colour – were not so lucky. The only British eyewitness to their fate was Lieutenant Walter Higginson of the 1/3rd NNC; but the veracity of his account, as will become clear, is not to be trusted. According to Higginson, the three of them tried to cross the river at the same place, but he and Melvill were thrown from their horses. Higginson was washed up against a large rock and Melvill, as he was being swept past, shouted for him to grab hold of the Colour. 'I did so,' claimed Higginson, 'and the force with which the current was running dragged me off the rock . . . but fortunately into still water. Coghill, who had got his horse over alright came riding back down the bank to help Melvill.* As he put his horse in

---

* Coghill's action was doubly gallant in that, thanks to his bad knee, he had little chance of escaping without a horse.

close to us the Zulus who were about 25 yards from us on the other bank commenced firing at us in the water. Almost the first shot killed Coghill's horse and on his getting clear of him we started for the bank.' But without the Colour, which was too heavy to swim with and had to be abandoned.

Higginson claimed that the three of them made it to the river bank – exhausted but alive – and, having crossed about 200 yards of level ground, began to climb the steep hill beyond. They were followed by two Zulus, who, having approached to within thirty yards, were shot at and killed by Melvill★ and Coghill. Higginson did not have a revolver and had lost his rifle in the river. A few yards further on, 'Melvill said he could go no further and Coghill said the same.' So Higginson left them, ostensibly to find some horses. Having succeeded in his aim – thanks to the generosity of some Basutos – he returned to find Coghill and Melvill surrounded by Zulus and beyond help. At which point he mounted one of the horses and escaped to Helpmakaar. That, at least, is the version of events that Higginson gave in a letter to Lord Chelmsford.

But a very different account emerges from the pen of Trooper Walwyn Barker of the Natal Carbineers. He had reached the top of the hill on the Natal bank – assisted by covering fire from black troopers of Zikali's Horse – and was about to ride off with Charlie Raw and a fellow Carbineer named Tarboton when he spotted a lone figure scrambling up the bank on foot. Thinking it might be his best friend, Villiers Hawkins, whom he had not seen since leaving the camp, Barker rode back to investigate. It turned out to be Lieutenant Higginson. 'As my horse was too tired to carry two,' recalled Barker, 'I assisted him to mount, and he rode away leaving me to follow on foot.'

In his written account, Barker was too discreet to specify the details of Higginson's desertion. Higginson was, after all, a superior officer. But he told his family and they, recently, have chosen to

---

★ Brickhill said later that, during the ride to the river, Melvill asked him if he had seen the cylinder to his revolver, which he had lost (Brickhill Report, SWB, ZC 2/4/1).

set the record straight. The conversation between the two men, according to Barker's grandson, went like this: 'Look, sir,' said Barker, 'my horse is dead beat – we've been on the go since four o'clock this morning. He's fallen twice already coming down to the river. He will never get us both back up the hill. You get going on your own, and wait for me at the top.'

But Higginson did not wait. Knowing that Zulus were near, and that Barker was unlikely to reach the top alive, he spurred on towards Helpmakaar. Unfortunately for him he was intercepted four miles further on by Tarboton and Raw, who were waiting for Barker and wanted to know what Higginson was doing on their friend's horse. Higginson's response was that he had found it abandoned near the river. They had no way of knowing that Higginson was lying – Barker could well have been thrown or killed on his way back down the hill – so they gave him a Basuto pony in place of their friend's horse and returned to look for Barker. A mile down the trail they came across him: exhausted, angry, but relieved. He had run three miles, pursued for most of the way by Zulus. When Higginson was later confronted by Barker, he broke down and said that he 'could not have walked any further' and that his intention was to 'send the horse back' for him. He was not believed and was later seen at Helpmakaar with a black eye. This rough justice may have encouraged him to decamp that night to Ladysmith. He returned two days later – ostensibly in charge of wagon stores – and managed to salvage his reputation by omitting all mention of the Barker incident in an account of the battle he wrote for Lord Chelmsford on 17 February 1879. So convincing was his account that the duke of Cambridge later suggested Higginson as a possible VC recipient for assisting 'Melville [*sic*] & Coghill in saving the colours of the 24th'. Fortunately the hint was not taken up by Lord Chelmsford who, by then, may have known the truth.

In complete contrast to Higginson's disgraceful behaviour is the selflessness of 22-year-old Private Samuel Wassall of the 80th Regiment, attached to the Mounted Infantry. Wassall did not have any specific duty during the battle and was still in his shirtsleeves when he made his escape down to the Buffalo on a stray Basuto pony. He was halfway across the raging torrent when he heard a colleague, Private Westwood, cry for help. Westwood had been unhorsed and was being swept round a whirlpool. Wassall at once turned his horse and headed back to the Zulu bank. There he calmly tied his horse to a branch and waded in to rescue Westwood. The pair mounted Wassall's pony and, despite a hail of Zulu bullets, managed to reach the Natal bank and safety.

They were two of just fifty-five Europeans and 350 African auxiliaries to survive the carnage at Isandlwana out of a total garrison of 1,762 troops.* Of the Europeans, only five were imperial officers: Captains Essex and Gardner, and Lieutenants Curling, Cochrane and Smith-Dorrien. Before leaving the camp, Gardner had 'sent an order by a Basuto to the officer on Rorke's Drift, telling him to fortify and hold the house'. A similar order was sent to Helpmakaar. Curling was the only imperial officer to escape from the firing line; the other four were all staff officers. It is probably no coincidence that all five were wearing blue patrol jackets. No officer clad in the scarlet tunic of the British infantry at Isandlwana would live to tell the tale: partly because they were more conspicuous, and partly because Cetshwayo had told his warriors to concentrate on the British redcoats.

The only front-line soldiers to avoid the initial Zulu encirclement were Durnford's two troops of NNH, who had gone to replenish their ammunition from wagons that, by a great stroke of fortune, had been left on the far side of the saddle. 'The Zulu army swept down,' recalled Jabez Molife, 'shutting us out, but our leader was within, & we saw no more of him. We were only a few, & the Zulus were too many to count. What could we do?' The answer was not a lot. To attempt to re-enter the camp would have been almost certain death. But their officers, Davies and Henderson, appear to have done so a little earlier – presumably to find Durnford – and they were loath to abandon them. At last Henderson appeared, having successfully run the gauntlet with Davies, who recorded:

* 922 Europeans and 840 black auxiliaries. These figures do not include the 350 or so wagon drivers and camp followers.

One fellow seized hold of my horse's bridle and I made a stab at him with my rifle (a foolish thing that has a nine-inch knife attachment); but the man caught hold of it and pulled it out of my hand, which at the same time made my horse rear and shy and cleared me of the man. I then only had my revolver, and I saw a Zulu right in my course, and rode at him and shot him in the neck. My horse got a stab, and many assegais were thrown at me; but as I was lying on my horse, they did not hit me.

Davies took the same route as the majority of fugitives: down the rocky valley to the left of the Rorke's Drift track that led, eventually, to the Buffalo River. Henderson continued along the track and soon met up with the remnants of his and Davies's troops, about eighty men in all, including a few survivors of the NMP. For a short time – in shocked silence and from a safe distance – they watched as the Zulus dragged the two artillery guns up from the ravine and into the camp. Then they turned and rode towards Rorke's Drift. They were not the first to carry the news of the disastrous defeat to the supply depot: that dubious honour was reserved for a shadowy figure called Lieutenant G. Adendorff of the 1/3rd NNC.★ A fellow officer wrote: 'His escape must have been most miraculous – that is according to his account. But considering he managed to get along the road to Rorke's Drift, it was the opinion of most of us that he left the field rather early.'

George Shepstone's body was found on the western slopes of Isandlwana Hill in a clump of about thirty corpses. It seems that he took a reserve company of NNC – possibly Captain Walter Erskine's No. 4 Company, 2/3rd NNC – round the back of the hill to try to hold back the Zulu right horn. For a time he succeeded. But his small party was eventually overwhelmed by Zulus, probably from the uNodwengu Corps. A Zulu source recorded: 'We were told . . . that there was present a son of Somseu.† He fought very

---

★ Who, by coincidence, was from the same company – No. 6 – as that other disreputable survivor, Lieutenant Higginson.
† Correctly *Somtseu*, the Zulu honorific for Theophilus Shepstone, meaning 'Father of the Nation'.

bravely. He killed our people. The others feared to approach him. Suddenly there dashed in our brother Umtweni before he could load, and killed him.'

Another pocket of resistance was provided by Captain Younghusband's C Company, 1/24th, which had been on the extreme left of the British line. As the Zulus closed in on the camp, Younghusband and his men retreated in good order along the eastern slopes of the hill and made their last stand on a rocky shelf above the nek. Sixty-eight bodies were later discovered there. There were no survivors to tell the tale, but a warrior of the uNokhenke Regiment had this to say: 'They fought well, a lot of them got upon the steep slope under the cliff behind the camp, and the Zulus could not get at them at all; they were shot or bayoneted as fast as they came up.' Only when their ammunition ran out – possibly as late as 3 p.m. – did some of them charge down the hill in an attempt to join another group that was still holding out on the nek. At the head of this suicidal charge was 'an *induna*' with a 'flashing sword, which he whirled round his head as he ran'. The officer may well have been Younghusband. But the charge was in vain. 'They killed themselves by running down,' observed the warrior, 'for our people got above them and quite surrounded them; these, and a group of white men on the neck, were the last to fall.'

The identity of those who made the last stand on the nek has never been satisfactorily proven. It might have been the remnants of Pope's G Company;* or it might have been the mixed body of troops who rallied round Colonel Durnford. Having failed to find Pulleine, Durnford is said to have made a stand on the edge of the stony koppie with about forty white horsemen and another thirty redcoats, possibly stragglers from G Company. The willingness of Lieutenant Scott and fifteen of his Natal Carbineers to stand by an officer whom, owing to bad blood over the Bushman's River Pass controversy, they despised is nothing short of remarkable. They

---

* Among the dead of G Company was Private William Griffiths, an old sweat in his forties, who had won a VC in 1867 for risking his life to rescue seventeen comrades from almost certain death in heavy surf off the island of Little Andaman.

were all excellent horsemen and crack shots, and could easily have escaped as a group, yet incredibly they chose a hero's death. Durnford, this time, was an inspiration. A Zulu eyewitness claimed that a one-armed officer killed four Zulus with his revolver as his party was forced by weight of numbers up the slope of the stony koppie. 'It was a long time before they were overcome,' said Mehlokazulu, who took part in the fight. 'They threw down their guns, when their ammunition was done, and then commenced with their pistols . . . and then they formed a line, shoulder to shoulder, and back to back, and fought with their knives.' For once the Zulus chose not to fight at close quarters:

Some Zulus threw assegais at them [claimed Mehlokazulu], others shot at them; but they did not get close – they avoided the bayonet; for any man who went up to stab a soldier was fixed through the throat or stomach, and at once fell. Occasionally when a soldier was engaged with a Zulu in front with an assegai, another Zulu killed him from behind.

A warrior named Kumbeka did just this to one British officer. 'Dum! Dum! went his revolver as he was firing from right to left,' claimed Kumbeka, 'and I came beside him and stuck my assegai under his right arm, pushing it through his body until it came out between his ribs on the left side. As soon as he fell I pulled the assegai out and slit his stomach so I knew he should not shoot any more of my people.'

The act of disembowelment, carried out on most of the British dead at Isandlwana, was in fact a Zulu ritual to release the spirit of their victims. If it had not been done, explained Mehlokazulu, 'the Zulus would have become swollen like the dead bodies'. It was also part of the post-battle rite to strip the dead and stab the victims of other warriors. In this way all Zulu got the opportunity to 'wash their spears' in blood. Some body parts were removed by *izinyanga* (war-doctors) seeking powerful charms: jawbones, with the beard still attached, were a particular favourite. Inevitably these practices were condemned by the Victorian public, when it got to hear about them, as needless savagery. But there is no evidence that any of the mutilations took place while the victim was still alive, though the bodies were undoubtedly still warm.

The fate of Colonel Pulleine is a mystery. The last definite sighting of him was near his tent in the 1/24th camp by Captain Gardner shortly before Durnford's retreat from the donga. One source – unattributed – claims that he died 'early' in the battle. If by early the source means before the final collapse, then it would explain why Durnford was unable to locate him after his return to the camp, and why there was no sighting of him thereafter. It also fits with Coghill's comment to Curling, as the pair tried to escape to the Buffalo, that Pulleine was already dead.

The last soldier to die at Isandlwana is said to have been a redcoat who took refuge in a small cave on the southern face of the hill, above the shelf where Younghusband's C Company was wiped out. Every Zulu who tried to approach the entrance was shot. Eventually a volley was fired into the cave and the resistance ceased. This could have been as late as 3.30 p.m. Months later, as he was surveying the battlefield, an officer of the 2/24th came across the cave and found its floor 'strewn with empty cartridge cases' and 'shreds of a red serge jacket'. A hundred yards below he found the soldier, now just a skeleton with a rope round its neck.

With all organized resistance at an end, the Zulus ransacked the camp. The highest premium was on guns and more than a thousand Martini-Henry rifles and 250,000 rounds were captured. 'Maize, bread stuffs and stores of all kinds' were also taken. But there was far too much to carry and, in any case, some Zulus feared the food had been poisoned. So grain bags were cut open, tins stabbed and biscuit boxes smashed, their contents thrown all 'over the veldt'. Everything else not wanted was left strewn around the camp: camp beds, boots, bellows, sponges, books, photographs, papers and even cricket-pads. The warriors were not so discerning when it came to drink, particularly alcohol. 'Some of our men got very drunk,' remembered a warrior of the uMbonambi. 'We were so hot and thirsty that we drank everything liquid we found, without waiting to see what it was.' This included paraffin; but not ink – 'black stuff in bottles' – which was left well alone.

Once the tents had been looted of anything useful, particularly clothes, the ropes were cut and the canvas slashed to ribbons. Most of the livestock had been stabbed or shot during the first mad rush into the camp. Those bullocks and mules that survived were rounded up and used to transport the booty, particularly the ammunition. But all horses were killed 'because they were the feet for the white men and we had not been ordered to take those back to the king'. As the sun began to set, the bulk of the Zulu Army – many of its warriors drunk, all laden with booty – moved off towards its bivouac in the Ngwebeni Valley, 'hastened by having seen another English force approaching from the south'. It was Chelmsford returning to the camp; but far too late to save its garrison.

Commandant Rupert Lonsdale was in an 'absent state of mind' as he rode slowly into the camp at Isandlwana during the early afternoon of 22 January. He had returned to inquire about rations for his men – who had hardly eaten for thirty-six hours – but a combination of overwork and lack of sleep had dulled his senses. He was vaguely aware of the bustle of the camp and redcoats all around him. Then, suddenly, he noticed a figure appearing from a tent with a blood-smeared assegai and, as his eyes began to focus, he saw with horror that 'every redcoat had a black face above it.' The urge to flee was overwhelming. Instead, with remarkable presence of mind, he slowly turned his pony round and gently dug in his heels. But the exhausted pony refused even to break into a trot, and the Zulus near by, alerted to his presence, broke off from their plunder and began to give chase. In desperation he slammed his heels into the pony's flanks and at last it broke into a canter. 'Had the Zulus thrown nothing but their assegais at me I should have been done for,' he recalled, 'but the majority fired rifles and missed.'

After what seemed like an age, but was probably less than a minute, he cleared the outer limit of the camp and was in open country. No Zulus pursued him; they preferred to plunder. At last he came across a European sergeant of Hamilton-Browne's battalion of NNC, which, having witnessed the latter stages of the

Zulu attack, had taken up a defensive position about six miles from the camp. The sergeant led him back to the battalion, where he was he met by Chelmsford and his staff, who had just ridden in from the new campsite. It was around 4 p.m. 'The Zulus have the camp,' said Lonsdale wearily.

'How do you know?' asked an incredulous Colonel Crealock.

'Because I have been into it.'

A stunned Chelmsford could only lament: 'But I left 1,000 men to guard the camp.'

Then he turned to his staff and said, 'Glyn must return at once.' Gossett volunteered to carry the message, taking care to slacken his pace as he neared the new camping site so as not to 'alarm Glyn's men'. Unaware of the real reason for their recall, some cheered.

Chelmsford, meanwhile, had advanced closer to the camp, with the battalion of NNC deployed in three ranks – 'the first being formed of white men and those natives who had firearms' – and the Mounted Infantry and volunteers on the flanks. About two miles from the camp he sent Colonel Russell forward to investigate. 'All was as bad as it could be,' reported Russell. An estimated 7,000 Zulus were in possession of the camp.

It was 6 p.m. and almost dark when Glyn arrived with the infantry and guns. Though fatigued, they had covered more than ten miles in under two hours. Rumours were rife that the camp had been attacked. Chelmsford now confirmed them. 'Twenty-fourth,' he said, 'whilst we have been out yonder the enemy has outflanked us and taken our camp. They are probably holding it now. At any cost we must take it back tonight and cut our way back to Rorke's Drift tomorrow. This means fighting, but I know I can rely upon you.' The men answered with a cheer.

As the nervous British soldiers advanced, they could see, on the skyline to the camp's right, 'dense masses' of Zulus retiring with herds of cattle and wagons. Half a mile from the camp the column was halted and formed into line: guns in the centre on the road; three companies of British infantry, an NNC battalion and a portion of cavalry on each flank; Mounted Police in reserve. The guns then came into action, throwing shells on to the nek while

Major Wilsone Black advanced with the right wing to seize the stony koppie.* 'It must have been about 7 p.m.,' recalled Lieutenant Mainwaring, 'when amidst the gathering gloom, stumbling over rocks, debris of the camp, and a few bodies, we at length gained the top of the kopje, and then by a cheer, we signalled to the remainder of the force to advance.'

Captain Harford, who advanced on the right with the 2/3rd NNC, noticed that the grass had been 'trampled quite flat and smooth by the Zulu army' and that there was little sign of their dead. But on the left, towards the nek, 'where the 24th and others of our men made their stand, the dead lay thick, and it was a ghastly sight'. His men were in a 'most awful funk' and had to be literally 'driven along'. Harford added: 'Nothing on earth could make those who were armed with rifles keep their place in the front rank, and all the curses showered on them by their officers could not prevent them from closing in and making up in clumps.' The darkness spared the soldiers the magnitude of the disaster but not the detail. Captain Penn Symons remembered the horror of constantly stumbling 'over the naked, gashed and ghastly bodies of our late comrades'. Harford, who visited his tent to see if he could recover any of his belongings, recorded:

Everything had gone, and the same with Lonsdale's tent, which was next to it. Between our tents lay the bodies of two artillery men, disembowelled and terribly mutilated. Within a few yards of where our wagon had been drawn up I found the dead bodies of our two drivers, with their faces blackened, and it struck me at the time that they must have done this themselves in the hope of being able to escape. On passing the hospital wagon from whence all the abominable stench came [from the smashed medical bottles], I came across the body of Surgeon-Major Shepherd . . . He was lying face downwards, and had been stabbed in the neck.

By far the most traumatic discovery, however, was made by Colonel Henry Degacher of the 2/24th whose brother William

---

* Known thereafter by the British as Black's Koppie.

had commanded the 1/24th during the battle.★ In the gloom Degacher almost rode over his brother's body. 'I did not feel it much,' he wrote later, 'for I never expected to see day light and said to myself, "Old Boy, I shall be with you in half an hour." None of us thought our lives worth two minutes purchase.'

The troops were bivouacked in a large hollow square on the saddle with the guns and horses in the centre. Black's men remained on the stony koppie. It was a miserable, bitterly cold night. On the hills all around could be seen hundreds of Zulu campfires. As the troops settled down to a nervy, sleepless night – punctuated by false alarms and NNC panics – they could hear the sound of firing, and see intermittent flashes of light from the direction of Rorke's Drift. 'Everyone felt very anxious for the fate of the little garrison after what had happened in the camp,' recalled Harford, 'and longed for daylight to march to their relief.' None more so than Chelmsford, who visited the NNC sector during the night and asked Harford if he thought the Zulus would attack their column. Yes, replied Harford, as soon as it was daylight. The general had already made up his mind to abandon the camp before it got light. He was later criticized for not staying long enough to bury the dead and salvage what he could from the wrecked camp. He explained:

The troops had no spare ammunition and only a few biscuits, a large portion of it had had no other food for 48 hours; all had marched at least 30 miles the day before, and had passed an almost sleepless night on the stony ground. No one was fit for any prolonged exertion, and it was certain that daylight would reveal a sight which could not but have a demoralizing effect upon the whole force. I determined therefore to reach our supply depot at Rorke's Drift as quickly as possible.

An early-morning fog obscured the worst of the carnage. But the sights that greeted the soldiers were bad enough. 'Most of the bodies were more or less stripped,' recorded Captain Penn Symons. 'One little Band Boy of the 2/24th Regiment, a mere child, was

★ On account of Colonel Pulleine being left in charge of the camp.

hung up by his heels to the tail of an ox wagon, and his throat cut. Even the dogs and goats about the camp, and the horses and mules tied to the picket ropes, were butchered. Further details would be too sickening.' An artillery sergeant was reduced to tears by the sight of his mutilated comrades. 'There were bullocks, horses, and mules lying dead all over the place,' he wrote home, 'waggons thrown down very deep precipices, and smashed all to bits; ammunition and medicines of all descriptions lying all about, our tents burnt and torn up to ribbons.' Some Carbineers, looking for their comrades, discovered one of the Tarboton brothers 'with his head cut clean off' and surmised that another trooper, Swift, had 'died hard' because he had been finished off with knobkerries.

No one was sorry to leave the dismal scene, but the march to Rorke's Drift was not without its alarms. Lieutenant Maxwell, with the 2/3rd NNC at the front of the column, recalled: 'The road wound through a valley for some distance, and the enemy appeared in great numbers on the ridge to our right as we marched along. It is a narrow valley, and they appeared in some places not more than 300 yards from us and far outnumbering us. Had they charged us as we were on the line of march, covering about half a mile or more in length, we must have been beaten, our ammunition being, with the exception of a few rounds, exhausted.' But these Zulus – members of the uNdi Corps and uDloko Regiment – had sustained heavy casualties in the night attack on Rorke's Drift and had no appetite for further combat. At one point a young warrior sprang forward and tried, with gestures and shouts, to urge his comrades to attack. Having failed, he 'rushed madly down the hillside towards the centre of the column' and was shot dead at a distance of just 30 yards, 'not one of his fellows having followed or even risen from their squatting position'.

Once across the Batshe River, the troops felt 'pretty safe' and this caused Captain Hallam Parr to think of those members of his battalion left behind: 'Poor little [Lieutenant] Hodson, so simple & boylike; Coghill, who had been sharing my tent; Pulleine, Porteous, Melville [sic], Younghusband, our servants & a host of honest soldier-like faces rushed to my memory as I rode along.' For the men of the 2/24th, however, more heartache was expected. 'When we reached the top of the last rising ground between us and Rorke's Drift,' wrote Lieutenant Banister, 'our hearts again sank, for where our little camp of one Company used to be was now to be seen nothing but a column of smoke and no tents.' Fearing the worst, they pressed on.

8. Rorke's Drift

Rorke's Drift was named after an early settler, James Rorke, the son of an Irish ex-soldier who had acquired the 3,000-acre farm on the right bank of the Buffalo in 1849. Rorke and his wife built their modest homestead half a mile from the drift on a terrace of flat land at the foot of the Shiyane Hill. A thatched, single-storey house of home-made bricks and stones, it contained eleven rooms: five could be accessed only from the outside of the building and the remaining six were split into two self-contained suites. Rorke not only had an aversion to inside doors but to windows: five of his rooms were windowless. A covered veranda at the front of the house, overlooking the vegetable garden, was a rare concession to domesticity.

Over the years, as more hunters and traders used the drift, the nearby trail became a dirt road. Rorke was on good terms with the local Zulus and eventually built a small store – also thatched and fronted by a covered veranda – to which they came for trade goods. It became known as kwaJimu, or 'Jim's Place'. Rorke died childless in 1875, and three years later his farm was bought by a Swedish missionary called Otto Witt, who moved into the house with his wife and infant children. Witt left the house as it was but converted the store into a chapel and replaced the rough neighbouring cattle pen with a stout construction of breast-high stone. Witt also gave Shiyane Hill the grand new name of 'Oskarberg', in honour of the king of Sweden.

As the British prepared to invade Zululand, Witt put his property at Chelmsford's disposal. The house was converted into a makeshift hospital under the supervision of Surgeon James Reynolds – a 35-five-year-old Irishman who had arrived in South Africa with the 1/24th Regiment in 1875 – and his small medical team. By 22 January the hospital contained thirty-five patients in rudimentary beds: straw mattresses placed on wooden planks that were raised a few inches off the hard dirt floor by bricks. A few of the patients had been wounded in the fighting at Sihayo's kraal on 12 January, including a lone warrior of the NNC who had been shot in the leg; but most were recovering from the fevers, dysentery, trench foot and minor injuries that were typical of an African campaign. The most seriously ill patient, Sergeant Robert Maxfield of the 2/24th, had been given Witt's bed, as he was suffering from delirious fever. Witt slept in a small tent in the garden, but there was no room for his wife and children, who had been sent to stay with friends near Umsinga.

The chapel, on the other hand, had reverted to its original use as a store and was packed with supplies for Chelmsford's column: heavy wooden boxes of biscuit and tinned meat, and sacks of locally grown Indian corn known as mealies; so many, in fact, that the surplus mealie sacks had been stacked in front of the veranda in two large pyramids. In charge of the stores were three quasi-officers of the Commissariat Department: Assistant Commissary Walter Dunne, a 26-year-old Irishman; his deputy, Acting Assistant Commissary James Dalton, a former NCO; and Acting Storekeeper Louis Byrne, twenty-one, from Pietermaritzburg. Dalton, in his mid forties, was by far the most experienced. He had joined the 85th Regiment as a seventeen-year-old and, having served in both the Commissariat and the Army Service Corps, was discharged from the army with the rank of staff sergeant in 1871. He later emigrated to South Africa and, thanks to his efficient and hardworking reputation, was appointed to the Commissariat by his former CO during the Cape Frontier War. He did well supplying the strung-out British columns and was the only civilian to be mentioned in dispatches. He probably owed his appointment at Rorke's Drift to Glyn, the column commander, who remembered him from the previous conflict.

The nominal commander at Rorke's Drift was Major Henry Spalding of the 104th Regiment, Chelmsford's staff officer in charge of communication and supplies. Also in residence was the No. 3 Column's military chaplain, the Reverend George Smith. Tall with a long red beard, he was a popular if eccentric figure who typically wore a frayed alpaca frock that was turning green with age. A former vicar of the local Estcourt parish, Smith had helped Durnford bury his dead after the Bushman's River Pass fiasco. But he had wisely chosen not to cross into Zululand with Chelmsford's column: if he had done so, he would probably have perished at Isandlwana.

Local security at Rorke's Drift was provided by B Company of the 2/24th under Lieutenant Gonville Bromhead.★ Born at Versailles in 1845, the third son of a baronet and general who had fought at Waterloo, Bromhead had followed his elder brother Charles into the 2nd Battalion at the relatively late age of twenty-one. Five years his senior, Charles had served on the staff during the Ashanti campaign and was already a major; Gonville, on the other hand, saw no significant action in the Cape Frontier War and had languished in the same rank since 1871. His command of the company, moreover, was purely temporary and had come about because the original captain, Alfred Godwin-Austen, had been accidentally shot by one of his own men. Known affectionately as 'Gunny' by his fellow subalterns, Bromhead was a noted sportsman and popular with his men. But he was also partially deaf and not highly regarded by his superiors. Colonel Degacher, his commanding officer, condemned him in a confidential report as a 'hopeless' soldier thanks to his 'unconquerable indolence'. Another officer summed him up pithily as 'a great favourite in his regiment and a capital fellow at everything except soldiering'. This reputation for laziness and poor intellect almost certainly contributed to the selection of his company for guard duty at Rorke's Drift, where it was not likely to see action.

Contrary to the impression given by the iconic film *Zulu*, B Company was not dominated by Welshmen liable to break into a rendition of 'Men of Harlech' at the first opportunity. The misapprehension was understandable: the 24th had moved its depot to Brecon in 1873 and would be renamed the South Wales

★ Pronounced 'Brumhead'.

Borderers in the regimental reorganization of 1881. But in 1879 it was still known as the 24th (2nd Warwickshire) Regiment of Foot and, though some of its men had been recruited in the Welsh borders, most came from the industrial slums and agricultural classes of England and Ireland that provided the vast majority of Victorian soldiers. Of the 113 NCOs and men of the 2/24th who were present at Rorke's Drift on 22 January (many of them sick), only twenty-seven – or just over 25 per cent – had been born in Wales.★

The senior NCO, Colour-Sergeant Frank Bourne, was typical of the company's national diversity. Born in Sussex, the youngest of eight sons, he had left the family farm against his father's wishes and joined the army as an eighteen-year-old private in 1872. His comparatively good education – he could read and write – sobriety and natural aptitude for military life had ensured rapid promotion to colour-sergeant in under six years. At 5' 5½" and 'painfully thin', he had to rely on character rather than physical presence to command respect. 'I was only twenty-three,' he recalled, 'very nervous, sensitive, and afraid of my new responsibilities. Several men of the Company were my own age, others older, and some old enough to be my father, but after a few months I felt secure.' It helped that Bourne could act as 'unpaid private secretary' to those men who were illiterate, helping them read and write their letters. Despite the embarrassment of his nickname – 'the Kid' – he got on well with his men and regarded B Company as 'a very happy family'.

A measure of Bourne's meteoric rise is that his senior corporal, William Allen, was ten years his senior. Born in Yorkshire in 1844, Allen had signed up as a fifteen-year-old and served as far afield as Mauritius and South Africa. He was rarely out of trouble in his first five years in the battalion and served no less than seven spells in confinement. But he was a reformed man by the time he signed up for a second term of service in 1873 and, having taught himself to read, was appointed assistant schoolmaster at Brecon. He also won

★ And sixteen of those twenty-seven came from Monmouthshire, then an English county.

the battalion prize for marksmanship in 1878, a skill that would serve him well at Rorke's Drift.

Of the privates, one of the most distinctive was Henry Hook from Gloucestershire because he bore a striking resemblance to Lieutenant-Colonel Redvers Buller, commanding the irregular cavalry in Wood's column. Their backgrounds could not have been more different. Buller came from Devon gentry stock; Hook from the agricultural poor. But the portrayal of Hook in the film *Zulu* – as an old sweat who liked a drink and was constantly in trouble – is way off the mark. He was, in reality, a 28-year-old teetotaller who had been in the battalion for less than two years, though he had earlier served in the Monmouth Militia. At Rorke's Drift he was based at the hospital: not because, as the film would have us believe, he was under house arrest, but because he was working as the hospital cook.

Even the five privates called Jones in B Company were not all Welsh. Thirty-nine-year-old William Jones, for example, had been born in Worcestershire and began life as a shoemaker. Within two years of joining up, he had been both promoted to corporal and demoted to the ranks. But army life must have agreed with him because in 1868, after completing twenty-one years' service, he signed on for a second stint. His wife had accompanied him out to South Africa but fell 'dangerously ill' during 1878 and Jones was given leave to nurse her. 'Jones took a little room in a house facing the St George's Hotel tap,' reported the *Natal Mercury*, 'and there, by working night and day repairing boots and shoes, he managed to earn many comforts for his then dying wife.' She eventually died and, having buried her, a grief-stricken Jones returned to his battalion. Of the remaining four Joneses, one was born in Glamorgan and two in Monmouthshire, including Robert Jones, a personable 21-year-old former farm labourer from Raglan with just three years' service.

Bromhead's men had pitched their tents close to the store and hospital. A little nearer to the drift was camped a company of Major Cooper's 2/3rd NNC – 100 men under Captain William Stephenson – that had been left at the drift on fatigue duties. The only other military presence was Lieutenant John Chard's tiny detachment of Royal Engineers, responsible for the two ponts at the drift.

Chard returned from his morning visit to Isandlwana, where he had witnessed the ominous presence of Zulus in the hills to the north-east, at around 12.45 p.m. on 22 January. He was met at the drift by a group of seven British soldiers and fifty of Stephenson's NNC. They had been ordered by Spalding to guard the ponts until relieved by a company of British infantry, which was daily expected from Helpmakaar, ten miles to the south-west. Realizing that the guard was hopelessly inadequate, Chard continued on to the supply depot to speak to Spalding. If the Zulus attacked the ponts, he told him, the guard would be quickly overwhelmed. Spalding decided to ride to Helpmakaar to hurry up the infantry company. Why he chose to go himself, and not send a galloper, has never been satisfactorily explained; nor has his failure to return with reinforcements. There is, in any case, no excuse for an officer abandoning his post when an attack is imminent; particularly when that post is defended by just 200 able-bodied men.

Chard had mounted his horse and was about to return to the river when Spalding asked him who was senior: he or Bromhead. Chard did not know, so Spalding ducked into his tent to consult his copy of the Army List. It told him that Bromhead received his commission first, in 1867, but Chard had been a lieutenant for longer.* 'You will be in charge,' Spalding told Chard, 'although, of course, nothing will happen, and I shall be back again this evening early.' It was now 2 p.m.

Inexplicably, given his new status as temporary commander at Rorke's Drift, Chard chose to return to the ponts without informing Bromhead of the threat from the advancing Zulus. Nor did he order any defensive preparations to be made at either the

---

* Bromhead was commissioned as an ensign in 1867 and was promoted to lieutenant in 1871. Chard received his lieutenant's commission on graduating from Woolwich in 1868.

supply depot or the drift itself. Instead he enjoyed a light lunch in his tent before settling down to write a letter. He had barely begun when a sentry drew his attention to two riders galloping towards the drift from the direction of Isandlwana. From their shouts and gesticulations it was obvious that something was wrong. No sooner had they been ferried across the river than one of them rode up to Chard, dismounted and identified himself as Lieutenant Adendorff of the 1st/3rd NNC. The camp at Isandlwana, he added hurriedly, had been attacked and taken by thousands of Zulus; scarcely a man had escaped and Lord Chelmsford and the rest of the column had probably 'shared the same fate'. The Zulus, moreover, were 'advancing on Rorke's Drift'. Adendorff's companion, a private in the Natal Carbineers, confirmed his incredible story, but in such an excitable manner that Chard found it hard to believe. Had they actually stayed long enough to witness the fate of the garrison? Before Adendorff could reply, a messenger arrived from Lieutenant Bromhead, asking Chard to come to the mission without delay.

He arrived at the gallop to find the camp a hive of activity. The tents were in the process of being struck and every available man was busy barricading and loopholing the mission's two stone buildings – in use as a store and a hospital – and connecting them with a wall of wagons and mealie sacks. Bromhead showed Chard a pencil-written message he had just received from a staff officer at Isandlwana. The camp had fallen, it said, and the mission at Rorke's Drift was to be fortified and held 'at all costs'. Chard now had a brief conversation with Bromhead. Its result, according to one eyewitness, was that 'orders were given to strike the camp and make ready to go, and we actually loaded up two waggons'. Clearly neither officer thought much of the tiny garrison's chances of repelling a large-scale Zulu attack. But fortunately for the honour of the British Army, not to mention the careers of the two officers, a calmer head was close at hand: Acting Assistant Commissary James Dalton. Dalton could see no sense in flight. If they abandoned the mission, he told Chard, they would be overtaken by faster-moving Zulus and 'every man was certain to be killed'. This gloomy assessment brought Chard to his senses and, having consulted

Bromhead, he ordered the work on the defences to continue. It was supervised by Dalton, the possessor of a certificate in field works, who had come up with the idea of linking the two stone buildings with a wall of mealie sacks. Dalton's 'energy, intelligence and gallantry', recalled Chard, 'were of the greatest service to us'. In his two reports of the battle, Chard omitted to mention his moment of irresolution. Instead he gives the impression that his determination to hold on never faltered. 'Several fugitives from the camp arrived,' he wrote, 'and tried to impress upon us the madness of an attempt to defend the place. Who they were I do not know, but it is scarcely necessary for me to say that there were no Officers of HM [Her Majesty's] Army among them . . . They proved the truth of their belief in what they said by leaving us to our fate, and in the state of mind they were in, I think our little garrison was as well without them.'

Shortly after Chard's arrival, Lieutenant Henderson and his eighty black horsemen* appeared from the direction of the river. They had, Henderson explained, narrowly survived the Zulu encirclement at Isandlwana but would help to defend the supply depot. A grateful Chard asked him to post his men as mounted scouts and to oppose any Zulu advance for as long as possible. He agreed. Chard now had around 300 fit men under his command. But he could only rely on Bromhead's men and the handful of attached British troops. The mounted Basutus had gone through a terrible ordeal and were clearly jittery; so too were the poorly trained and inadequately armed NNC.

One of Chard's most useful acts during this period was to post a guard over the 'several casks of rum' in the storehouse with orders to shoot any man who attempted to get his hands on the drink. He knew the penchant that British soldiers had for alcohol and was well aware that a drunken redcoat was more of a hindrance than a help.

The first positive sighting of the Zulus was by three men – Surgeon James Reynolds, Otto Witt and the Reverend George

---

* A mixture of Henderson's Zikalis and Davies's Basutus.

Smith – who had climbed the Oscarberg after lunch to verify reports of a battle. On the summit the distant boom and crack of cannon and rifle-fire was unmistakable. Looking through a telescope, they could see Isandlwana clearly enough, seven miles away as the crow flies, but the camp beyond was out of sight. Eventually a swarm of black figures poured across the saddle to the right of the hill and disappeared out of sight. They assumed these were NNC. Even when this huge black column reappeared at the Buffalo River, half a mile below the drift, and proceeded to cross one by one, they thought they were friendly. Only when the column set fire to a Natal farm before splitting into two, one half following the course of the river and the other heading directly towards the Oscarberg, did the awful truth dawn on the onlookers. 'They now were so close to us that their bullets could easily have reached us,' recalled Witt, 'and we saw that they were all naked. Reality then also stood naked before us – the thick mass that swarmed in the camp was the Zulus who had taken possession of it . . . Those who had crossed the river and were approaching were Zulus.'

The trio could not know it but the Zulus below them were part of Ntshingwayo's reserve, which had played little part in the fighting at Isandlwana. Members of the uNdi Corps and the iNdluyengwe Regiment – all senior men associated with the royal kraal at oNdini – they had followed in the wake of the right horn, eventually cutting the road to Rorke's Drift in the region of the Manzimnyama Valley. In the excitement some of the iNdluyengwe had taken part in the pursuit to the Buffalo, crossing the river close to Fugitive's Drift. But the uNdi Corps had kept its discipline and was the body that Reynolds, Witt and Smith saw fording the river a short distance from Rorke's Drift.

Most Zulu sources agree that Cetshwayo specifically ordered his commanders not to invade Natal. He knew that such an act would make a negotiated peace much more difficult to achieve. Why, then, did the reserve commander disobey him? The original commander – the wily and resourceful Chief Zibhebhu, who was destined to become one of Chelmsford's most redoubtable opponents – had been wounded in the hand during the pursuit. His place was taken by Prince Dabulamanzi, Cetshwayo's younger brother, who had no designated military authority beyond his royal status and aggressive personality. At forty years old he was a handsome, muscular man with a well-groomed moustache and pointed beard. Intelligent and sophisticated, he liked to wear European clothes and was fond of gin. He was also an excellent shot. But, sadly for the Zulus, he was not an experienced general, and his decision to launch what became, in effect, a large-scale raid of the Natal border had no strategic value. He admitted later that he was angry at having missed out on the glory at Isandlwana and wanted to give his men the opportunity to redeem themselves. The unprotected farms and kraals along the border would provide, he assumed, an easy and rewarding target. So too would the supply depot at Rorke's Drift. 'Oh! Let us go and have a fight at Jim's!' the warriors of the royal uThulwana Regiment are said to have shouted.

Having belatedly identified the approaching column as Zulus, the British trio raced down the hill as fast as the rocky terrain would allow and were surprised to find the garrison preparing to fight. How long before the Zulus arrived? they were asked. 'In five minutes they will be here,' replied Witt.

Witt later claimed that he was keen to defend his house – now the hospital – but that his first priority was his wife and three children who were staying a 'short distance' from the drift. In reality they were at Umsinga, twenty miles to the south, and relatively safe, though Witt could not have been certain of that. The final straw was the damage done to his house. On seeing 'the best parlour paper being pulled down and loop-holes being knocked out, while splendid furniture was scattered about the rooms', he became 'excitable and, in broken English, demanded an explanation'. When someone reminded him that the Zulus were on their way, he suddenly remembered his family – 'Mein Gott, mein wife and mein children at Umsinga' – and left in a hurry. With him went a sick colonial officer who preferred the discomfort of a long ride to the dangers of a Zulu attack. Smith wanted to go too, but, on discovering that his groom had vanished with his horse, had no option but to stay.

He was not alone. A trooper of the Natal Mounted Police, in hospital with rheumatism, recognized two of his comrades among the steady trickle of breathless fugitives from Isandlwana and asked: 'Is it true?' The response from one, clearly in shock, was short and to the point: 'You will all be murdered.' Minutes later a mounted scout reported that the Zulus had closed to within a mile.

At 4.15 p.m. shots were heard from behind the Oscarberg, and Lieutenant Henderson arrived at the gallop. Thousands of Zulus were approaching, he reported, and his men would not obey orders and were 'going off to Helpmakaar'. He then rode away, ostensibly to rally his men but in truth to save his own skin. This mass desertion caused panic among the Natal Kaffirs, who had done good work on the barricade. Almost as one they vaulted the defences and melted into the surrounding countryside. Incredibly, and disgracefully, Captain Stephenson and his two white NCOs followed them.★ This was too much for some of the furious British defenders, who opened fire and killed one of the NCOs, a Corporal Anderson.

The garrison had, at a stroke, been reduced to 104 fit men and those of their thirty-five hospitalized comrades who had been issued with rifles and were willing to fight. To compensate, Chard ordered a wall of wooden biscuit boxes to be built across the middle of the compound – between the edge of the storehouse and the middle of the mealie-bag wall – so that the troops could withdraw to a smaller defensive area if necessary. It was just two boxes high, and far from complete, when Private Frederick Hitch, perched on the roof of the storehouse, reported a huge Zulu column over the brow of the hill. 'How many are there?' asked an anxious Bromhead.

Four to six thousand was the reply. 'Is that all?' muttered a private below. 'We can manage that lot very well for a few seconds.'

★ Chard never mentioned Henderson by name in either of his reports, possibly because he came from a prominent Natal family. Stephenson, on the other hand, was later arrested and dismissed from the service.

Moments later the Zulu vanguard of around 600 warriors appeared from the back of the Oscarberg and, at a signal from a mounted induna,★ ran towards the south wall between the hospital and the storehouse. 'Here they come!' shouted Sergeant Henry Gallagher, a 23-year-old Irishman from County Tipperary, in charge of the south wall. 'As thick as grass and as black as thunder!'

The defenders opened fire at 500 yards, shooting wildly at first but soon steadying their arm. Zulus fell in heaps, but their comrades kept coming, using the cover provided by the trees, banks and cookhouse ovens at the back of the post to approach to within fifty yards of the wall. There, caught in the crossfire from the two buildings, they were 'checked as if by magic' and forced to seek shelter. 'Our firing was very quick,' recalled a sick artilleryman called Howard, who had borrowed the delirious Sergeant Maxfield's rifle, 'and, when struck by the bullets, the niggers would give a spring in the air and fall flat down.'

Meanwhile an even bigger force of Zulus had veered to the left and attacked the end of the hospital and the north-west wall, where they were opposed by a group that included Bromhead, prominent with his revolver, and Commissary Dalton. So numerous were the Zulus, and so oblivious of casualties, that they got as far as the wall itself, where a fierce hand-to-hand fight ensued. Dalton, a former army marksman, saved the life of a corporal of the Army Hospital Corps by shooting a Zulu who had grabbed the corporal's rifle and was about to assegai him. For a time the pressure was so acute that the defenders were driven back from that part of the wall. Private Hitch, who had jumped down from the roof of the storehouse to join the thin layer of defenders in front of the hospital veranda, recalled:

Had the Zulus taken the bayonet as freely as they took the bullets, we could not have stood more than fifteen minutes. They pushed right up to us and not only got up to the laager but got in with us. But they

---

★ The unidentified induna was shot and killed shortly afterwards by a marksman called Private Dunbar, who went on to claim another eight victims.

seemed to have a great dread of the bayonet, which stood us from beginning to end. During that struggle there was a fine big Zulu saw me shoot his mate down – he sprang forward, dropping his rifle and assegais, seizing hold of the muzzle of my rifle with his left hand and the right hand hold of the bayonet. Thinking to disarm me, he pulled and tried hard to get the rifle from me, but I had a firm hold of the small of the butt of the rifle with my left hand.

With his right hand he was able to grab a fresh cartridge from a pile he had left on top of the mealie-bag wall, reload his gun and shoot the Zulu, who, though mortally wounded, took some time to release his grip. A combination of stout defence and supporting fire from the hospital was enough to cause the Zulus to withdraw behind the five-foot garden wall that faced the front of the hospital.

Hundreds of Zulus had, by now, lined the ledge of rocks and caves in the Oskarberg that overlooked the south of the post. From there, from the garden wall and from a position behind the rough stone kraal they kept up a constant rifle-fire that continually threatened the unprotected defenders on the far sides of the perimeter. If the Zulus had been more practised shots, the casualties would have been impossible to sustain. As it was, a mass assault from all sides would almost certainly have overwhelmed the tiny garrison at this early stage. But it never came. Dabulamanzi had advanced to within a hundred yards of the hospital. Having witnessed the death of one of his indunas, however, he took shelter behind a tree. He had, as a result, no overall picture of the battle and would have done better to position himself in a cave on the Oskarberg, from which he could have co-ordinated the assault. Instead, during the remaining hour or so of daylight, his men were left to launch a series of piecemeal attacks against the hospital – identified as the weak point in the defences – and the north wall, positioning themselves in the orchard and some brush to its front that the defenders had not had time to clear. 'Each time,' recalled Chard,

as the attack was repulsed by us, the Zulus close to us seemed to vanish in the bush, those some little distance off keeping up a fire all the time.

Then, as if moved by a single impulse, they rose up in the bush as thick as possible, rushing madly up to the wall (some of them being already close to it), seizing where they could, the muzzles of our men's rifles, or their bayonets, and attempting to use their assegais and to get over the wall. A rapid rattle of fire from our rifles, stabs with the bayonets, and in a few moments the Zulus were driven back, disappearing in the bush as before, and keeping up their fire.

Particularly prominent in the defence at this stage, according to Chard, were Colour-Sergeant Bourne, Sergeant Thomas Williams, Corporal John Lyons, various privates⋆ and Corporal Christian Schiess of the NNC. Born in Switzerland in 1856 and brought up in a municipal orphanage, Schiess had joined the French Army as a fourteen-year-old and saw action at the tail-end of the Franco-Prussian War of 1870–71. Six years later he emigrated to South Africa and served in a volunteer unit from King Williamstown on the Cape frontier. A big, powerful man, his bold exploits brought him to the notice of Colonel Durnford, who appointed him a corporal in the newly raised 2/3rd NNC. But his part in the attack on Sihayo's kraal had left him with severe blisters and he was recovering in hospital when word came of the Zulu advance. Ignoring the pain, he had taken his place on the north wall and his prowess with the bayonet was of great assistance to the defence. Padre Smith provided a rare moment of light relief – as he made his regular circuit of the firing line, handing out ammunition† – by asking the men not to swear so much. 'But the men continued to swear,' wrote Hitch, 'and fight the harder.'

At around 6 p.m., as daylight faded, Dabulamanzi ordered simultaneous attacks on the south and north walls. With the garrison in serious danger of being swamped, Dalton was an inspiration as he moved up and down the barricades fearlessly exposing himself and using his rifle to deadly effect. Not for nothing did Private Hook

⋆ McMahon of the Army Hospital Corps and Roy, Deacon, Bushe, Cole and Jenkins of the 2/24th.
† A crucial task for which he earned the affectionate sobriquet 'Ammunition Smith'.

describe him later as 'one of the bravest men that ever lived'. Another who acted with 'great coolness and gallantry' at this stage was the young storekeeper, Louis Byrne. But, on rushing over to give water to a stricken corporal of the NNC – wounded in the back by a bullet fired from the Oscarberg – he was shot in the head and killed.

Worried that the Zulus were about to get over the wall behind the biscuit boxes, Chard ordered the defenders to withdraw to the second line of defence. This reduced the defensive perimeter by about two thirds; it also marooned the six soldiers and twenty-four patients still in the hospital. The Zulus immediately occupied the far side of the walls that had been abandoned and used them to fire over. They also stepped up their efforts to take the hospital.

At the outset of the battle, Privates Henry Hook and Robert Cole – a twenty-year-old from Kent – were guarding the room on the south-east corner of the hospital with just a single occupant: the NNC warrior with the broken leg. For a time Hook and Cole blazed away from their loopholes, the outer door having been sealed with mattresses and mealie sacks. But eventually Cole lost his nerve and fled the room. 'The helpless patient was crying and groaning near me,' remembered Hook. 'The Zulus were swarming around us, and there was an extraordinary rattle as the bullets struck the biscuit boxes, and queer thumps as they plumped into the bags of mealies.' He was also struck by the 'whizz and rip' of the assegais as they flew through the air, a sound familiar to him from the Cape Frontier War.

Soon after Chard had withdrawn behind the biscuit boxes, the Zulus finally managed to set alight the western end of the hospital's thatched roof with flaming spears. It had taken some time because the thatch was damp from the recent rains. Escape was imperative for those inside, but the only unsealed external door led on to the veranda, which was swarming with Zulus. To remain, however, meant certain death from fire or assegais. As Hook's room began to fill with choking smoke, he broke through the flimsy inner door into the neighbouring room, leaving the injured African to his fate. But Hook's troubles were just beginning because in the next room he found nine unprotected sick and wounded men. Unwilling to leave them, but unsure what to do next, he barred the doorway and waited. It was not long before Zulus got into the room he had just vacated and, having dispatched the wounded warrior, tried to force the door. Hook fired to keep them back. Just then Private John Williams,* a 21-year-old former labourer from Monmouthshire, appeared through a hole he had made in the side wall and shouted: 'The Zulus are swarming all over the place. They've dragged Joseph Williams out and killed him.' The two Williamses had been detailed to defend the four patients in the room on the other side of Hook's original position. For an hour they fired away. But when their ammunition ran out, there was nowhere to go, the room having only one sealed-up door that led outside. Eventually the Zulus broke in and hauled out Joseph Williams and two of the patients. As they were butchered outside, John Williams and the remaining two patients used bayonets to break through the shoddy mud brick partition that separated their room from an empty inner room. From there they repeated the trick into Hook's room.

The situation was still desperate. Hook and Williams now had eleven patients on their collective hands and only one route of escape: through the wall and into the next room along. While Williams worked away with a pickaxe, Hook held off the Zulus, who were trying to burst through the doorway. Assegais kept whizzing past him until, finally, one struck him on the peak of his white sun-helmet, causing it to tip back and leaving him with a minor flesh wound on his scalp. Fortunately the doorway was only big enough to allow one Zulu through at a time and, as each one appeared, Hook shot or bayoneted him. Suddenly a huge warrior sprang through the entrance and grabbed Hook's rifle. In desperation he hauled it free and, having slipped in a fresh cartridge, shot the Zulu. Hook recorded:

All this time Williams was getting the sick through the hole into the next room, all except one, a soldier of the 24th named Conley [Private John

* Also known as John Fielding.

Connolly of G Company★], who could not move because of a broken leg. Watching my chance, I dashed for the doorway and, grabbing Conley, I pulled him after me through the hole. His leg got broken again, but there was no help for it. As soon as we left the room the Zulus burst in with furious cries of disappointment and rage.

And so it went on – although in the next room Hook only had to defend a hole instead of a door. Williams picked away at the far wall. Again Hook had to drag Connolly to safety, a 'terrible task because he was a heavy man'. Unwittingly they left behind Private Waters, the original occupant of the room, who was hiding in a cupboard with a wounded arm. Having shot, so he claimed, a number of Zulus, he was eventually driven out of the cupboard by the heat and smoke. Covered in a dark cloak, he escaped from the hospital and took refuge in the cookhouse, where he used soot from the chimney to blacken his face and hands. Incredibly he remained undiscovered until morning, though the Zulus were all around him and some even trod on him.

Hook and Williams then met up with Privates Robert and William Jones, whom they found guarding six more patients in the end room. While the Jones pair covered the entrances to the room with their bayonets, Hook and Williams lowered the patients out of a high window and on to the ground below. Most of them made it across the forty yards that separated the hospital from the comparative safety of the biscuit boxes thanks to the efforts of Corporal William Allen and Private Hitch, who exposed themselves to provide covering fire.† But one unfortunate, an NMP

★ Connolly, who had dislocated his left knee loading wagons on the Thukela River on 5 January, wrote his own far-fetched account of the action, in which he claimed he crawled out of a window and hid in a bush until morning (Statement by Private John Connolly, in Holme, 282).

† It is often stated that Allen and Hitch ran forward and assisted the patients across the neutral ground. But there is no evidence to support this. Hitch himself wrote: 'One by one the poor fellows scrambled out of the burning building, and ran the gauntlet. We covered them as much as we could, but many of them went under' (*Chums*, 11 March 1908).

trooper called Hunter, did not make it. Momentarily 'dazed by the glare of the burning hospital', he was repeatedly stabbed by a brave Zulu who raced out from the shadows. The warrior, in turn, was shot.

One other patient did not make it: Sergeant Maxfield. Delirious in bed, he refused to be moved and was assegaied by Zulus as Robert Jones made a final attempt to save him. Jones fled back into the end room, where he and his namesake crossed bayonets. 'As fast as they came up to the door we bayoneted them,' he recalled, 'until the doorway was nearly filled with dead and wounded Zulus.' By now Robert Jones had three assegai wounds – two in his right side and one in his left – and was weak with loss of blood. Fortunately the spreading flames forced the Zulus to draw back, which gave the pair a chance to escape through the window. No sooner had they hit the ground – the last to leave after Hook and Williams – than the roof fell in, 'a complete mass of flames and fire'. Bullets whizzed past them as they raced over the neutral ground, but none found their mark.

There was one other lucky survivor: Gunner Arthur Howard. He and another patient, Private Robert Adams of the 2/24th, had been defending a room on the north-west corner of the hospital. When the roof partially collapsed, Howard dashed outside and secreted himself in the low grass and bushes, among a pile of dead horses and Zulus. Adams stayed put and was killed.

Chard later regretted the loss of life in the hospital.* He had, he said, impressed upon the tiny garrison the 'necessity for making a communication right through the building – unfortunately this was not done'. No other witness confirms that this suggestion was ever made, and it is tempting to conclude that Chard was trying to shift the blame from himself. For, in truth, the patients should never have been left in such an exposed and inaccessible position. Far better to have removed them to inside the second line of defence before the battle began. That so many patients were ultimately saved was due, in no small part, to the gallant conduct of Surgeon

---

* Seven of the thirty men in the hospital were killed.

Reynolds, who repeatedly braved the hazardous open ground to carry ammunition to the beleaguered garrison, 'a bullet striking his helmet as he did so'.

The capture of the hospital gave the Zulus renewed confidence. While some looted B Company's abandoned camp, the majority stepped up their attacks. But the light from the burning hospital made it easy for the defenders to see them and it was this advantage, in Hook's opinion, that saved the garrison. After each repulse the warriors would retire for ten or fifteen minutes and perform a war dance. 'Then, when they were goaded to the highest pitch,' recalled Hook, 'they would hurl themselves at us again.' The storehouse's thatched roof was an obvious target but, by some miracle, it was kept intact. At one point a warrior was in the act of placing a lighted brand against it when he was shot. Chard recorded the marksman as Lieutenant Adendorff, the officer who had brought the news from Isandlwana. But no one else remembers Adendorff assisting the defence, and Chard probably mistook him for Corporal Francis Attwood of the Army Service Corps, who performed a number of gallant acts that day. Adendorff almost certainly decamped before the battle began, though to this day his name is included on some defenders' rolls.

The Zulus had more success when they targeted the stone kraal at the eastern end of the defensive perimeter, driving the British back to an inner wall and then out of the kraal completely. With the outer defences in danger of collapsing, work began on a circular redoubt in front of the storehouse, which eventually stood twenty feet tall and spanned twelve in diameter. Chard has generally been credited with this initiative. But both his reports state cryptically that 'we' converted the two heaps of mealie bags into a 'sort of redoubt'. And yet earlier, when referring to the construction of the biscuit-box wall, he claimed personal responsibility. It seems likely, therefore, that someone else came up with the idea, probably Assistant Commissary Dunne. Chard wrote: 'Dunne worked hard at this, and from his height, being a tall man, he was much exposed, in addition to the fact that the heaps were high above our walls, and that most of the Zulu bullets went high.'

One of the first men placed within the safety of the redoubt was James Dalton after he was shot in the right shoulder. He, according to Chard, 'had been using his rifle with deadly effect, and by his quickness and coolness had been the means of saving many men's lives'. On being shot, he turned and handed Chard his rifle 'so coolly that I had no idea until afterwards how severely he was wounded'. He then waited patiently while his pockets were emptied of ammunition. Dalton had been helping to defend the most vulnerable point in the reduced perimeter: an eight-yard gap in the centre of the biscuit-box wall. Others helping to plug the gap were Lieutenant Bromhead, Private Hitch and Corporal Schiess. At one point Schiess crept a short way along the abandoned mealie-bag wall to get a shot at a Zulu sniper who was proving 'particularly annoying'. But as he raised his head to fire his helmet was shot off by another Zulu on the other side. Without thinking, he vaulted the wall and bayoneted the warrior. Two more came at him and he shot one and stabbed the other, before scampering back behind the biscuit boxes. Schiess was later hit by a bullet that deflected off the back of his head and lodged in the flesh of his shoulder. But it did not prevent him from fighting on. Nor did gunshot wounds in the shoulder prevent Allen and Hitch, the pair who had helped save the patients, from continuing to assist the defence. Hitch wrote a graphic account of the events before and after his injury:

In one of these nasty rushes three Zulus were making for me . . . The first fellow I shot; the second man I bayoneted; the third man got right into the laager, but he declined to stand up against me. With a leap he jumped over the barricade and made off. A few yards from the barricade lay a wounded Zulu. We knew he was there . . . [but] were far too busy with the active members to find time to put him right out. Presently I saw him, rifle in hand, taking aim at one of my comrades. It was too late to stop him; he fired, and poor [Private] Nicholls fell dead, shot through the head.

On another occasion a Zulu was in the act of throwing an assegai at Bromhead when Hitch brought his empty rifle up to his shoulder and shouted. The Zulu fled. Later Bromhead returned the favour by shooting the warrior who had just fired a bullet into Hitch's back, smashing his shoulder blade. 'I got up again,' recalled Hitch, 'and attempted to use my rifle, but it was no use; my right arm wouldn't work, so I strapped it into my waist belt to keep it out of the way. Then Bromhead gave me his revolver to use, and with this I think I did as much execution as I had done before.' Later Hitch helped to serve out ammunition, as did the wounded Allen. He remembers Bromhead 'keeping a strict eye on the ammunition and telling the men not to waste one round as we were getting short'. Hitch eventually lost consciousness from loss of blood, four hours after being shot, and was dragged inside the mealie-bag redoubt.

The capture of the stone kraal marked the high point of the Zulu assault. Their failure either to take or burn the storehouse or to advance beyond the wall in the centre of the kraal, their dislike of night fighting and their mounting casualties all contributed to a falling off of effort. Another crucial – and yet often ignored – factor was the approach of British reinforcements. On nearing Helpmakaar, at about 3.45 p.m., Major Spalding had met two companies of the 1/24th, commanded by Major Upcher. Spalding eventually led these troops back in the direction of Rorke's Drift, and en route they came across numerous fugitives from Isandlwana. Spalding ordered several to join the column, but 'all except two slipped away when my back was turned'. Leaving the slower-moving infantry at Varmaarks, five miles from the drift, he continued on with three other riders.

My object [recalled Spalding] was to ascertain whether the post at Rorke's Drift still held out. In this case I should have sent word to Major Upcher to advance and endeavour to throw myself into it. But every single white fugitive asserted that the mission house was captured and at about three miles from the same I came across a body of Zulus in extended order across the road. They were 50 yards off; a deep donga was behind them, capable of concealing a large force . . . On reaching the summit of a hill from which the mission house is visible it was observed to be in flames;

this confirmed the statement of the fugitives, that the post had been captured.

Spalding decided to return with the whole force to Helpmakaar. He persuaded Upcher by telling him that Rorke's Drift had been 'surrounded and captured' and that his two companies would 'share the same fate' if they carried on. They duly arrived back at Helpmakaar at midnight, much to the delight of Smith-Dorrien and the handful of fugitives guarding the laager. Somehow Spalding escaped official censure for his craven acts this day: first abandoning his post when he knew that a Zulu force might be on its way; then causing the reinforcements to turn round when almost within sight of Rorke's Drift. But a fellow staff officer had no illusions, describing Spalding later as 'utterly worthless'.

Some of the defenders claimed to have actually seen the 'red-coats coming on the Helpmakaar road'. Word quickly spread and a spontaneous cheer broke out, causing the Zulus 'to pause'. But on 'seeing the hospital on fire,' wrote Hitch, the reinforcements 'came to the conclusion that we had all been annihilated, and with drooping spirits we saw our comrades turn back and retire'. Chard later queried the validity of the sightings on account of the fact that the two companies 'did come down to the foot of the hill, but not, I believe, in sight of us'.

Whatever the truth about the sightings, what is not in doubt is that reports of British troop movements made the Zulus even more loath to launch another assault. They continued to line the abandoned walls and kept firing from all sides until midnight, but no actual attempt to break into the defensive perimeter was made after about 9.30 p.m. According to Chard, there were just three serious assaults: the initial onslaught; the attack 'just before we retired behind the biscuit boxes'; and 'for a short time after it, when they had gained great confidence by their success on the Hospital'. After midnight there was desultory firing from both sides and the occasional false alarm. From 4.30 a.m. the firing stopped completely, though the garrison remained on the alert. When day finally broke the weary defenders were overjoyed to see the Zulus 'disappearing' the way they had come, round the southern shoulder of the Oscarberg. The garrison was down to its last box and a half of bullets and could not have held on for long if the Zulus had renewed their attack.

Patrols were at once sent out to collect the arms and ammunition of the dead.* Hook went out alone and almost paid the price when a wounded Zulu grabbed his rifle and tried to wrestle it from him. But after a short fight he knocked the Zulu to the ground and shot him. Fearful the Zulus might return, the garrison set about repairing its defences. But if any Zulus had been thinking about resuming the fight, the sight of Chelmsford's column returning from Isandlwana changed their minds. Most had already recrossed the Buffalo (and it was their advance guard that the column passed during its march to Rorke's Drift). Those that remained had gathered on the kwaSingindi Hill to the south-west of the post. Chard recalled:

The enemy remained on the hill, and still more of them appeared, when about 8 a.m. the Column came in sight, and the enemy disappeared again. There were a great many of our Native Levies with the Column, and the number of red-coats seemed so few that at first we had grave doubts that the force approaching was the enemy. We improvised a flag, and our signals were soon replied to from the Column. The mounted men crossed the Drift and galloped up to us, headed by Major Cecil Russell and Lieutenant Walsh, and were received by us with a hearty cheer. Lord Chelmsford, with his Staff, shortly after rode up and thanked us all with much emotion for the defence we had made.

And so he might. For the defence of Rorke's Drift would provide Chelmsford with the perfect smokescreen for Isandlwana. Yet at the time his chief emotion was one of relief: he had expected to find the post in ruins. He spoke to the two lieutenants and, on hearing of Hook's gallantry, demanded to see him. Hook was in his shirtsleeves, making tea for the sick and wounded, when a sergeant ran up and told him he was wanted by Lieutenant

---

* One hundred rifles and guns, and around 400 assegais, were eventually collected.

Bromhead. 'Wait till I put my coat on,' said Hook. 'Come as you are, straight away,' came the reply. Hook recalled: 'With my braces hanging about me, I went into the midst of the officers. Lord Chelmsford asked me all about the defence of the hospital, as I was the last to leave the building. An officer took our names, and wrote down what we had done.' Chelmsford later visited the wounded Private Hitch and told him that he would do everything in his power to get him a VC for his 'excellent services'. Already, it seems, the advantages of emphasizing the heroism at Rorke's Drift had occurred to the downcast general.

Chard celebrated the post's survival by sharing a long-forgotten bottle of beer with Bromhead. He might have offered a sip to Commissary Dalton, the man who more than any other had organized and inspired the defence. But he did not. Dalton had come up from the ranks; he also knew too much.

When Lieutenant Banister arrived at the post with the rest of the 2/24th, having crossed the Buffalo in the ponts, he found 'old Gunny as cheery as ever and not a scratch about him'; but all around 'was a scene of awful confusion', the hospital a 'misshapen mass of smoking cinders' and 'dead niggers everywhere'. Having told Lieutenant Mainwaring, another fellow subaltern, that he was 'walking on air as he never expected to see daylight again', Bromhead took him on a guided tour of the post. In front of the hospital veranda and near two blue gum trees close by, Mainwaring noticed Zulu bodies 'lying three deep'. Bromhead pointed out a young induna with a plume headdress, remarking that he was 'a very gallant man, and had headed a charge three times'. He added: 'But we got him in the end.'

Some of the wounds inflicted by the heavy .45 lead bullets were grotesque. One warrior's head was split open 'as if done by an axe'; another had been shot between the eyes, leaving a tiny entry hole and his face otherwise 'perfect', yet the bullet had carried away the 'whole of the back of his head'. As at Isandlwana, the British dead that had fallen into Zulu hands were badly mutilated. Private Hayden of D Company, 2/24th, one of the hospital casualties, had been stabbed sixteen times, 'his belly cut open' in two places, 'and part of his cheek was cut off'. A dead Zulu was found clutching 'the knife with which he had mutilated one of our poor fellows, over whom he was still leaning'.

Given the length and ferocity of the fight, the British casualties were comparatively light: fifteen dead and twelve wounded (though two mortally, bringing the eventual dead to seventeen). Of those who survived, many had bruised and badly swollen shoulders from the recoil of their rifles, 'proving to what an extent they had been firing'. So sore did both shoulders become – as they constantly switched between right and left – that some defenders were eventually forced to hold and fire their rifles at arm's length. Quite a few had powder burns on their faces★ and burnt fingers from grasping their overheated rifle barrels. Not that all the rifles worked flawlessly. As already mentioned, the Martini-Henry's chief design flaw was that its empty cartridge had a tendency to jam in the breech-block after periods of prolonged firing. After hundreds of rifles had jammed during the Battle of Abu Klea in the Sudan in 1885, a special committee concluded that this was partly because the thin brass cartridge melted and stuck to the chamber; and partly because the extractor system was not robust enough to remove the jammed cartridge. Both flaws were eventually remedied. But at Rorke's Drift, and almost certainly at Isandlwana too,† jammed rifles were a serious problem. 'We did so much firing,' recalled Private Hook, 'that [our rifles] became hot . . . and the cartridge-chamber jammed. My own rifle jammed several times, and I had to work away with a ramrod 'till I cleared it.'

The official number of Zulu dead at Rorke's Drift was put at 351. This was roughly the number of bodies that were buried by Chelmsford's men during 23 and 24 January: Lonsdale's men confined themselves to digging the huge burial pits 'on account of their prejudices against touching dead bodies'; the British soldiers had the infinitely more gruesome task of dragging the corpses to

---

★ Sergeant Henry Gallagher would retain a blue powder mark on the right side of his nose for the rest of his life.

† Though no infantry witnesses from the firing line lived to tell the tale.

the pits and tipping them in. The bodies were then covered with
wood and burnt. As Chard himself admitted, however, a number
of dead Zulus were later discovered a fair way from the post 'in the
caves and among the rocks'. They were probably wounded Zulus
who had crawled away to die. But no mention is made in any
official report of the hundreds of wounded Zulus who were brutally
dispatched by both NNC and British troops during the afternoon
of 23 January. Captain Harford of the 3rd NNC remembered it
being 'quite impossible' to keep his men in hand as they crawled
about the Zulu dead. He put it partly down to 'curiosity but I dare
say some may have been looking out to identify friends or relations'.
Maybe. But many were bent on revenge. Commandant Hamilton-
Browne of the 1/3rd NNC recorded what happened when a 'large
number of wounded and worn-out Zulus' were discovered in
nearby mealie fields:

My two companies of Zulus with some of my non-coms and a few of
the 24th quickly drew these fields and killed them with bayonet, butt and
assegai. It was beastly but there was nothing else to do. War is war and
savage war is the worst of the lot. Moreover our men were worked up
to a pitch of fury by the sights they had seen in the morning and the
mutilated bodies of the poor fellows laying in front of the burned hospital.

Inspector George Mansel of the NMP described the killings at
Rorke's Drift on 23 January: 'as deliberate a bit of butchery as I
ever saw'. He tried all he could 'to stop it' and would not let any
of his men 'join in the pursuit'. He even managed to stop two
Carbineers who were about to kill a wounded Zulu. But it was all
to no avail. All the Zulu wounded left behind at Rorke's Drift were
'butchered', he wrote, and he 'saw no attempt made to stop it'.
    How many Zulus were murdered in cold blood is impossible to
say. But some sources suggest a figure as high as 500. Lieutenant-
Colonel Crealock's journal entry for 23 January, for example, states:
'351 dead Zulus were found, and 500 wounded.' No mention is
made of the wounded Zulus' fate. They were certainly not taken
prisoner. Private Pitt, one of the defenders, provided a clue. 'In the

morning we found the ground strewn with dead and dying,' he told a newspaper reporter. 'We reckoned we had accounted for 875, but the school books tell you 400 or 500.' Also Sergeant Smith of B Company, in a letter to his wife, estimated the number of dead – 'killed and shot' – at 'over 800'. Even allowing for a little exaggeration, it is fair to assume that the number of murdered Zulus ran into the hundreds. A few, like Hook's assailant, were no doubt killed in 'self-defence'. The Zulus neither gave nor expected quarter, and even when wounded would often fight to the death. But many at Rorke's Drift were beyond resisting – and were killed none the less. The British troops, appalled by what they had witnessed at Isandlwana, were in no mood for mercy. The killing of the wounded at Rorke's Drift was the first major British atrocity of the Zulu War; but it would not be the last.

It was customary for a victorious Zulu army to return to oNdini to receive the king's congratulations. But after the twin engagements of Isandlwana and Rorke's Drift only the chiefs and a small fraction of the army journeyed to the capital. This was partly because the setback at Rorke's Drift had taken the gloss off the earlier victory; but mainly because the overall Zulu losses were so crippling. An estimated 1,000 Zulus were killed during the battle of Isandlwana; that many again may have died from their wounds.* 'Remarkably few of those wounded who reached their homes survived,' reported two Christian refugees to Eustace Fannin, border agent along the Middle Thukela. 'The Zulus imagine from this that the [British] bullets are poisoned.' But poison was not necessary: while injuries inflicted by spears could be healed with traditional remedies, bullet wounds – particularly those resulting in shattered bones and serious internal injuries – required more sophisticated care than the Zulus possessed. The bulk of the Zulu Army remained for three days in the Ngwebeni Valley, tending to the mortally wounded, amongst

---

* Though only two chiefs of any note lost their lives: Mkhosana kaMvundlana, the uMcijo induna, and Sigodi kaMasiphula of the emGazini, whose father had been King Mpande's chief induna.

whom were two of Ntshingwayo's sons. During that time the battlefield dead were buried in pits, though a number were simply covered with their shields.

On 23 January the beaten remnants of Dabulamanzi's reserve were given a derisive welcome by the main army at Ngwebeni. 'Our people laughed at them,' recalled Muziwentu, a Zulu boy whose father had fought at Isandlwana. 'Some said, "You! You're no men! You're just women, seeing that you ran away for no reason at all, like the wind." Others jeered and said, "You marched off. You went to dig little bits with your assegais out of the house of Jim that had never done you any harm!"' Having spoken to Munyu, a warrior of the uThulwana, Muziwentu gave this account of Rorke's Drift:

The white men had . . . made their preparations; they were quite ready. The Zulus arrived at Jim's house. They fought, they yelled, they shouted, 'It [the regiment] dies in the entrance! It dies in the doorway!' They stabbed the sacks; they dug with their assegais. They were struck; they died. They set fire to the house. It was no longer fighting: they were now exchanging salutations merely.

When, some years later, a member of the uNdi Corps was asked by a Cape civil servant why the Zulus did not 'make a better fight of it' at Rorke's Drift, he replied, 'The soldiers were behind a schaans (breastwork), and . . . they were in a corner.' The same reason was given for the decision not to advance deeper into Natal. 'The Zulus had no desire to go to Maritzburg,' recalled Muziwentu. 'They said, "There are strongholds there."'

Not surprisingly, the news of the defeat took time to filter through to King Cetshwayo at oNdini. According to Captain Ruscombe Poole, who had many conversations with the king in the early 1880s,

The first news that reached Cetshwayo of the doings of his three armies was by a messenger who said that the camp of the middle column from Rorke's Drift had been taken and plundered, and nearly the whole of the

English column destroyed . . . he spoke of it as a great victory . . . Of the Rorke's Drift fight Cetshwayo received the most imperfect news. Dabulamanzi reported that he had successfully stormed and taken 'the house'; he attacked and then retired, but admitted he had suffered heavily . . . It was ten days before they returned to oNdini, and then the indunas, and quite a small part of the army, was all that appeared; most had gone to their homes with their wounds or their plunder. Cetshwayo was much disturbed at finding his losses so heavy.

Once the warriors that had returned to oNdini had been ritually purified, Cetshwayo addressed them in the huge cattle kraal, congratulating them on their success at Isandlwana but warning of hard times to come: 'If you think you have finished with all the white men you are wrong, because they are still coming.' Cetshwayo then asked his indunas where the artillery pieces and plunder were, and why no officers had been taken prisoner. 'They told him,' wrote Ruscombe Poole, 'that the guns were left on the battlefield . . . as for taking officers prisoner that was impossible in the heat of the fight, and especially as the white men fought to the last.' The indunas claimed, in addition, that they 'could not tell an officer from a soldier'. Cetshwayo's response was that officers were armed with swords and soldiers with rifles. 'Don't you see how useful it would have been to me to have had some officers as prisoners?' he asked. He was very angry and sent out immediate orders for Zulus in the vicinity of Isandlwana 'to collect and bring him the two guns, and all the ammunition, etc., that was left on the ground'. He also ordered his army to reassemble at once at oNdini.

Back at Isandlwana, meanwhile, Muziwentu and some other Zulu boys had plucked up the courage to visit the corpse-littered battlefield. In amongst the wreckage of the camp, he and his brother 'took some thread for sewing and a black pocket-book'. They tried on some boots and a satchel, before throwing them away, and played for a time with the boxes and tent ropes. But Muziwentu drew the line when one of his friends offered to share some army hard tack. 'O! Sit there, if you please,' he retorted, 'with your little bits of bread smelling of people's blood!'

9. Wood and Pearson

Within days of learning of Ntshingwayo's stunning victory over the British at Isandlwana – albeit an incomplete and costly one marred by the subsequent reverse at Rorke's Drift – King Cetshwayo received less welcome news from his other two armies in the field. The northern army – composed mainly of Qulusi irregulars and the followers of Mbilini kaMswati, a rebel Swazi prince – had been sent against Colonel Evelyn Wood's No. 4 Column.

Wood's men may not have known it at the time, but it was their great fortune to be led by two of the most able officers in the British Army: Wood himself and his deputy, Lieutenant-Colonel Redvers* Buller, both protégés of Sir Garnet Wolseley. Wood was the grandson of Sir Matthew ('Alderman') Wood, the famous Radical MP and former lord mayor of London who had supported Queen Caroline in her ultimately successful fight to prevent her hypocritical husband, George IV, from divorcing her on the grounds of adultery. Wood was a short, balding man with doleful eyes and a large unruly beard; yet his unimpressive appearance belied his professional talents. He suffered, moreover, from partial deafness and was something of a hypochondriac. Not without good reason: by the age of twenty he had already suffered from typhoid fever, pneumonia, chronic indigestion, toothache, sunstroke and an ingrowing toenail. He had been clawed by a tiger and a giraffe had broken his nose with a kick. But when he spoke his sharp mind and ready wit were at once apparent. 'He is clever & amusing,' noted the queen after their first meeting, '& all he says is very interesting.'

His military career had been nothing less than extraordinary.

---

* Pronounced 'Reevers'.

Born in 1838, the son of an Essex vicar, he had entered the Royal Navy as a midshipman at the age of fourteen. Two years later, he went ashore in the Crimea with the Naval Brigade, leaving his sickbed to take part in the failed assault on the Redan of 18 June 1855. He and his sailor-nurse were the only two men of the entire column to reach the Russian entrenchment. The sailor was killed and Wood, badly wounded in the elbow, narrowly escaped capture by crawling back to the British lines. His hardest task that day, however, was persuading an army surgeon not to amputate his arm. Once recovered, he was offered an army commission and joined the 13th Light Dragoons, later transferring to the 17th Lancers so that he could fight in the Indian Mutiny. Bold and ambitious young officers like Wood had one main aim: to bolster their careers by winning the recently instituted Victoria Cross. Wood gained his during the mopping-up operation in central India, in late 1858, when he 'attacked almost single-handed a body of rebels, whom he routed'.

Back from India, he shuttled between various infantry regiments while qualifying as a barrister and graduating from Staff College. In 1873, by then a brevet lieutenant-colonel with the 90th Light Infantry, he was selected by Wolseley for his forthcoming Ashanti campaign. So began a close association with the most talented officer of his generation. He impressed Wolseley on the Gold Coast by spearheading the difficult march towards the Ashanti capital of Kumasi with a regiment of coastal tribesmen, surviving a dangerous bullet wound in the process. In early 1878 he and Buller were chosen to accompany Lieutenant-General Sir Frederic Thesiger out to South Africa as members of his staff. Both earned Thesiger's good opinion during the Cape Frontier War: Wood as commander of a column and Buller as chief of a newly raised body of irregular cavalry known as the Frontier Light Horse. It was during this period that Wood earned his African nickname 'Lukuni', after the hardwood used to make knobkerries. As well as a pun on his name, it referred to his toughness in battle. Resourceful and self-reliant, Wood was made for the sort of independent command that best suited African warfare. If he had a weakness, it was his occasional tendency to take excessive risks.

At thirty-nine, Buller was a year younger than Wood, but the two could not have been more different in appearance and character. Tall and gaunt with a long thin nose and small piercing eyes, Buller had an impressively muscular physique; yet the queen found him 'reserved & shy, with rather a dry, gruff manner'. A contemporary wrote of him: 'There is no stronger character in the British Army than the resolute, almost grimly resolute, absolutely independent, utterly fearless, steadfast, and always vigorous commander . . . This big-boned, square-jawed, strong-minded and strong-headed man was born a soldier . . . of the very best English type.' Buller's frosty exterior concealed a capable mind and a genuine concern for his men, a key ingredient for a popular commander. His career had not been quite as spectacular as Wood's, but impressive none the less. The scion of an old Devon family, he left Eton (having already been expelled from Harrow) to join the 60th Rifles and first saw action in the Second China War of 1860, though he later refused to wear the campaign medal on the grounds that the war was unjustified. Such moral qualms, unusual in a soldier, were not evident during the Zulu War. By then, presumably, ambition had replaced sensibility. His career had taken off with his assignment to Wolseley's Red River Expedition in 1870. Wolseley had met him earlier in China, but only in Canada did he come to appreciate Buller's singular combination of thoroughness and determination. From that point on Buller became a member of Wolseley's famous 'Ring'. Having passed through Staff College, he served as Wolseley's chief of intelligence during the Ashanti campaign. They would work together many times in the future.

But it was as a commander of irregular horse in South Africa that Buller found his true métier. He was a bold and indefatigable rider, leading from the front and by example, inspiring his men with the sheer force of his personality. He would never ask his troopers – hard-bitten men from the fringes of Cape society – to do anything he was not prepared to do himself. They, in turn, would have followed him anywhere. Yet Buller, like Wood, had his faults. His temper was extremely short, particularly with war correspondents: he threatened to horsewhip one on the Gold Coast and threw another out of a mess-tent after he had admitted reading personal mail. Of more relevance to his skill as a military commander was his unwillingness to delegate, preferring to see everything for himself. This was fine for a troop officer, even a regimental commander, but not for a general, who needed to retain a detached overview. The problem did not arise in Zululand because Buller was not senior enough to merit an independent command. Only at the very end of his career – during the Second Boer War – would this fatal flaw in his military make-up have serious consequences for the men who served under him.*

At the early stage of the invasion planning, Buller and the Frontier Light Horse were assigned to No. 5 Column in northern Transvaal, commanded by Colonel Hugh Rowlands, VC. A Welshman from Carnarvonshire, Rowlands had won his Victoria Cross at the Crimean battle of Inkerman by rescuing the wounded colonel of another regiment. Such boldness was singularly lacking in Rowlands's half-hearted attempt to suppress Sekhukhune's Pedi rebellion in the autumn of 1878. So disgusted was Buller with his superior's lack of drive – describing him in a letter to Wood as 'quite useless' – that he made up his mind to decamp at the first opportunity. It was a wise decision, because by January 1879 Rowlands's column had been earmarked to act on the defensive. With Frere's ultimatum about to expire and no sign of a transfer, Buller took matters into his own hands by marching his horsemen south to join Wood's column. Wood welcomed him with open arms, not least because he had so few mounted troops. As for deserting Rowlands, he 'never heard anything further about the serious step he had taken'.

Wood's column had arrived in Utrecht, the heart of the Disputed Territories, in early October. The ostensible reason was to protect the German and Boer settlers in the Luneberg area from further acts of aggression by Mbilini and his Zulu allies. The longer-term

* Notably during the early stages of the Boer War of 1899–1902 when, as commander-in-chief of British Forces, his indecisive and unimaginative generalship contributed to a string of military defeats.

plan, of course, was to prepare for the invasion of Zululand. Bereft of horsemen until Buller joined him, Wood made strenuous efforts to recruit the local Boers. Their initial response was encouraging: at a meeting in Utrecht on 4 December they pledged their support. Many of the older burghers had campaigned against the Zulus; some had survived the Great Trek and even fought at Blood River. They had good reason to support a war against their mortal enemies. But the announcement of the findings of the Boundary Commission, a week later, changed everything. Outraged that the Zulus had been granted nominal sovereignty over the Disputed Territories, most of the Boers withdrew their offer to assist Wood – all except Piet Uys, a leading Utrecht burgher, and forty of his followers.* Uys's father and fifteen-year-old brother had been killed by Dingane's warriors in February 1838. He, like most of his compatriots, had little time for the British and was determined to win back Transvaal's independence; he just hated the Zulus more.

At Chelmsford's request, Wood crossed the Blood River into Zululand on 6 January 1879, four days before the ultimatum was due to expire. He was just seventy-five miles from oNdini, the shortest distance facing the three columns, and so not in any particular hurry. But Chelmsford was both anxious to protect his open left flank and keen for Wood to begin the pacification of the mountainous country to the east of Utrecht, controlled by the abaQulusi tribe,† which was fiercely loyal to the Zulu king. Further to the north-east was the kraal of Mbilini kaMswati, the Swazi prince who had fled his homeland after a succession dispute in 1865. In an attempt to expand his own power-base, Cetshwayo had allowed Mbilini to settle in the Ntombe Valley, close to the Swazi border and the German settlement of Luneberg. The plan was for Mbilini to provide a bulwark against further Swazi and Boer encroachment. He had done just that, raiding cattle from black and white alike, and forging close links with the abaQulusi,

---

* Including four of his sons.

† The abaQulusi were descended from members of one of Shaka's regiments which had been transplanted to the thinly populated area to establish royal control. They were ruled over by izinduna appointed by the king.

who had allowed him to build a second kraal on the slopes of the Hlobane Mountain. Mbilini was unlikely to submit to the British without a fight.

Despite these potential problems Wood was not expected to face the toughest opposition and had just over 2,000 troops under his command: 1,500 redcoats of the 1/13th and 90th Light Infantry (the latter his old corps); 300 African auxiliaries known as 'Wood's Irregulars'; 100 artillerymen and four 7-pounder guns from 11/7th Battery, Royal Artillery; and 200 irregular cavalry, mainly Buller's FLH and Uys's burghers. To transport his stores he had ninety-seven ox-wagons and about 1,700 oxen. Having established his base on Bemba's Kop, east of the Blood River, Wood was ordered to sit tight while Pearson made up ground in the south. Buller and his horsemen occupied themselves by rounding up cattle. Of the 2,500 head that had been captured by 11 January, 2,000 were the property of the abaQulusi, and a significant proportion of those belonged to Cetshwayo. Wood offered to give them back in return for abaQulusi neutrality. But Sikhobobo, the senior abaQulusi induna, refused the offer: he knew Cetshwayo regarded armed resistance to the invader as more important than a few hundred head of cattle.

Wood realized that it would be dangerous to advance with his left flank unsecured. So he took the opportunity afforded by the slow progress of the other two columns to turn his attention towards the abaQulusi strongholds on the Zungwini and Hlobane mountains to the north-east. On 19 January, as a preliminary, he moved his camp to Thinta's Kraal on the White Mfolozi, where he received the submission of the local chief. A day later, while on reconnaissance, Buller and his horsemen discovered about fifty abaQulusi in a kraal at the foot of Zungwini and, in the ensuing skirmish, a dozen were killed at a cost of one FLH trooper injured by an assegai thrown by a wounded Zulu. On hearing from one of Piet Uys's scouts that a much larger force of Zulus was camped on top of the hill, Buller led his men up a 'difficult stony cattle track' and 'found the report was quite true, as the rocky ridges were lined with Kafirs'. He recorded:

I endeavoured to cross the upper plateau . . . but the hill was too strongly
held for us to force it. With the view of ascertaining the full strength of
the enemy, who were coming down to attack us in three columns, I
seized a small stony koppie and commenced an engagement with the
centre column. Our fire soon drove them to cover with a loss of about
eight dead (seen, and a good many more reported), but meanwhile we
were completely outflanked on our right by some 300 Kafirs, who crept
round among the stones and kraantzes of the ridge, and our left by some
400 men, who boldly moved in tolerable order across the open ground
about a mile off.

In danger of being surrounded by the 'horns of the buffalo', Buller
beat a hasty retreat. As he did so, another FLH trooper was
wounded, two more were hit by spent rifle-balls and a burgher's
horse was shot. Zulus followed the retreating horsemen all the way
to the White Mfolozi River, and about a hundred crossed over at
the drift to continue the pursuit. The first Wood heard about the
skirmish was a note he received from Buller at about 7 p.m., 'saying
that he had been engaged for some hours on the Zunquin mountain
with several hundred of the [abaQulusi] tribe, who were pressing
him back, and, as he was writing at sunset, had crossed in small
numbers to the right bank' of the river. Wood was 'considerably'
alarmed by the news because he had just sent seventy empty
ox-wagons back to his supply depot at Balte Spruit and was worried
that the Zulus might intercept them. He need not have worried,
because Buller, since sending his note, had turned on the small
force of Zulus that had crossed the river and forced them to
withdraw to their mountain stronghold.

Realizing that more troops were needed to clear Zungwini,
Wood set out after dark on 21 January with the bulk of his column,★
leaving just two companies to guard the stores and wagons at
Thinta's Kraal. As day broke on the 22nd – about the same time
that Chelmsford was marching out of the camp at Isandlwana –
Wood took the 90th Light Infantry, two guns and the mounted

★ The 90th Light Infantry, two guns and all his horsemen.

troops up the steep western slope of Zungwini. Their appearance on the summit took the abaQulusi by surprise, and by late afternoon they had driven more than a thousand warriors down on to the Ityenka Nek that led to the neighbouring peak of Hlobane. Arriving at the eastern end of Zungwini, they could see up to 4,000 warriors on the northern slopes of Hlobane, mostly abaQulusi but with some of Mbilini's followers as well. Their work done, Wood's men rejoined the 13th Light Infantry at the foot of Zungwini, where they bivouacked for the night. But as Wood and his staff sat round their campfire that evening, they heard the distant boom of cannon-fire from the direction of Isandlwana, fifty miles to the south. On being asked the probable cause, Wood said that he feared guns fired after dark 'indicated' an 'unfavourable situation'. He was not wrong.

In the early hours of 24 January, Wood's combined force marched towards Hlobane with the intention of clearing it of the Zulus that had been spotted on the 22nd. As his men advanced, they came under fire from warriors hidden in rocks under the south-western summit of the mountain. Leaving the 90th Light Infantry and two guns to follow the wagon track with the baggage, Wood moved to the right to engage the warriors with the 13th Light Infantry, Piet Uys's burghers and the other two guns. Wood was not impressed with the fighting spirit of the Boers. He recalled:

It was necessary for Piet and myself to ride in front to induce his men to go on to cover the advance of the guns. When we reached the rocks from whence the fire had come, it was clear we could not hope to get the guns down, so, after driving back a few Zulus who were in broken ground, I turned northwards, and went to a hill under which I had ordered the 90th to halt with the wagons and outspan. When I got there the 90th . . . was three-quarters of a mile in front, advancing rapidly in line, without any supports, against some 4000 Zulus. I looked up the ravine . . . and was concerned to see about 200 Zulus coming down it towards the 90th's Ammunition carts, which had been left with some bugler boys, who had no firearms.

At this critical moment, he was 'accosted' by an African horseman who had just ridden forty-eight miles from Utrecht with a message from Captain Gardner, 'recounting the disaster of Isandhlwana'. It would later emerge that Gardner, having reached Helpmakaar on the 22nd, had found it impossible to induce anyone – white or black – to carry news of the defeat to Wood, whom, he feared, might be attacked next. Eventually a Commissariat conductor agreed to show him the road to Utrecht – though he would not accompany him – and Gardner set off in darkness. By the time he reached Utrecht it was light and his mount was exhausted. Fortunately he 'managed to get a man with a fresh horse to gallop on with a note'. Written at Helpmakaar on the 22nd, it explained how the camp at Isandlwana had been attacked at noon after Chelmsford had ridden out with the bulk of the column 'after a reported enemy'. The note added: 'The Zulu attack succeeded, the Camp is sacked, 2 guns lost, & very many lives. A party of about 50 of those who escaped have made a laager at Helpmakaar, & are holding it expecting hourly to be attacked. I sent two messages to the General, who it is thought returned & was engaged at dusk this evening.'

Wood at once informed Buller 'in one sentence' of the disaster and then sent him and his men up the ravine to 'drive back' the advancing Zulus. Wood himself galloped over to the 90th Light Infantry to remonstrate with its commanding officer for advancing without orders. Fortunately the Zulus in front chose not to fight. 'The young soldiers were very steady,' recalled Wood, 'and expended less than two rounds of ammunition per man; but the Zulus fled from the sight of the advancing line, and went ten paces to one covered by our men. The Frontier Light Horse and the Dutchmen pursued them until they climbed the mountain.' Two hours later, with his position secure, Wood ordered the column to fall in, and, 'against the advice' of some of his senior officers, read to the men the note he had received.

The destruction of part – if not all – of the centre column had ruined the original invasion plan. With his right flank now exposed, Wood was in grave danger and had little option but to withdraw closer to the border. His problem was what to do with the supplies he had stockpiled at Thinta's Kraal. He did not want to abandon any, but had at least seventy loads for which he had no wagons. He solved the problem by inducing Piet Uys and his men – 'themselves wonderful drivers of oxen' – to increase their wagonloads from 1,000 to 8,000 lbs. Travelling at a snail's pace they had got as far as Venter's Drift when on 28 January a note arrived from Chelmsford. Written at Rorke's Drift on the 27th, it gave Wood a 'brief account of the disaster' and told him he had a 'free hand to go anywhere or adopt any measures' he might think best. It ended: 'You must now be prepared to have the whole of the Zulu Army on your hands any day . . . No. 3 Column, when re-equipped, is to subordinate its movements to your column.'

Wood replied on 31 January that he had established his new camp on Khambula Hill, close to the Nqaba-ka-Hawana Mountain, which he 'anticipated being able to hold even against the whole of the Zulu Army'. As Chelmsford did not wish him to 'incur risk by advancing', he added, he would not move 'unless it became necessary to do so in order to save Natal'. His new position was a good one, lying as it did between Utrecht and the abaQulusi strongholds. It consisted of a narrow, open ridge that fell away steeply to the south but more gently to the north, where several miles of open veldt provided little or no cover to an attacker. Wood, however, could not relax. 'I never slept more than two or three hours at a time,' he remembered, 'going round the sentries for the next three months at least twice every night. We shifted camp five times.'

All the while Wood took every precaution to guard against a surprise attack. Since invading Zululand he had regularly sent African scouts twenty miles in front of his main force, as well as mounted patrols six miles out. 'My spies informed me of impending attacks,' he recalled, 'which were predicted for each new and full moon, which periods are held by the Zulus to be auspicious. Mounted men were stationed 6 miles in front by day, and two companies beyond our cattle at grass.' At night, because it often rained, he allowed his outlying picquets to pitch tents 200 yards beyond the main laager. A further 100 yards out were smaller eight-man picquets, six sleeping under blanket shelters while the other two kept a lookout. Wood added: 'Beyond on the paths most convenient for the enemy's approach, under a British officer, were small parties of Zulus,★ whose marvellous hearing by night, and sight by day, enhanced the value of our precautions.'

While his infantry remained within the limits of the camp, Wood's horsemen continued to harry the nearby abaQulusi. On 1 February they even mounted a successful attack on the tribe's old military kraal, situated thirty miles from Khambula at the far end of the Hlobane Range. 'The Kafirs in it fled in all directions,' reported Buller. 'We took 270 head of cattle and entirely destroyed the kraal, which contained about 250 huts. About six Kafirs were killed. We had, I am happy to say, no casualties.' An infantry officer at Khambula could not hide his jealousy in a letter to his sister. 'We find it very dull here doing nothing,' he wrote. 'The Frontier Light Horse under Col. Buller has all the fun; they continually go out and make raids generally succeeding in capturing cattle; yesterday afternoon they brought in nearly 500. I have been made president of the Prize Committee. I have had to turn my hand to a good many odd things since I have been in the service but never expected to find myself a seller of cattle.'

According to a member of the Mdlalose tribe who lived in north-western Zululand, 'the Qulusi [were] utterly demoralized by the defeat and heavy losses inflicted on it by Colonel Wood's Column'. He added: 'They were scattered and unwilling to come together again, asking to be allowed to place their women and cattle in places of safety.' Mbilini would have begged to differ. During the night of 10/11 February he, a local chief called Manyanyoba and a large force of abaQulusi attacked white farms in the Luneberg area, butchering the African labourers who had been left in temporary charge. At the Reverend Wagner's mission station,

---

★ These border Zulus, recruited at Luneberg in November 1878, were attached to the British battalions, six per company. 'Their powers of hearing were extraordinary,' wrote Wood. 'They could see farther than we could with field glasses' (Wood, II, 34–5n).

reported the officer in charge of the Luneberg laager, 'They burnt down three of the Christian natives' houses, killed two men, six women, and burnt seven children alive.' A further forty-four Africans – mostly women and children – were murdered in various kraals before the war party finally made off with 'several hundred' cattle and 'thousands of sheep and goats'.

Wood's response was to send Buller and a combined force of horsemen and African auxiliaries to raid Manyanyoba's kraal in the Ntombe Valley. At a cost of two dead auxiliaries, they killed thirty-four Zulus and recaptured much of the booty taken from the white farms: 375 oxen and 254 goats. But no fresh invasion of Zululand would take place until the arrival of reinforcements from England and the replacement of the transport lost at Isandlwana. In the meantime the indecisive guerrilla war in the north would continue.

The last of the three British invasion forces was No. 1 Column in the south, under Colonel Charles Pearson of the Buffs. Born in 1834, Pearson had not seen action since the Crimean War and was an unemployed colonel on half-pay when he was selected as one of the special service officers to travel out to South Africa in late 1878. Owing to his seniority he had been given command of the largest column with the furthest distance to cover. His first objective, having crossed the Lower Drift of the Thukela, was to establish a base at the mission station of Eshowe thirty miles to the north. From there he would be in a position to coordinate his movements towards Ulundi – over seventy miles of difficult, broken terrain – with the other columns further north.

Pearson's command included two British infantry battalions: eight companies of his own corps, the 2/3rd Regiment ('The Buffs'), which had been in Africa since 1877; and six companies of the recently arrived 99th Regiment. These redcoats were supplemented by a Naval Brigade of 290 sailors from the warships HMS *Shah* and *Active*, complete with two 24-pounder rocket tubes and a Gatling machine-gun that had yet to be fired in battle by British troops. Additional firepower was provided by two

7-pounder cannon and a rocket trough, the balance of the 11/7th
Battery of Royal Artillery that was serving with Wood's column.
He also had a company of Royal Engineers, a squadron of Imperial
Mounted Infantry and elements of five corps of volunteer cavalry,
including the Natal Hussars and the Victoria Mounted Rifles.
Auxiliary troops were present in the form of two battalions of
NNC – the 1/2nd and 2/2nd – and a company of Natal Native
Pioneers. A total of 2,500 white troops and 1,700 Africans: 4,200
in all. Drivers and camp followers brought the grand total to well
over 5,000 men.

During the morning of 12 January, Pearson's vanguard was
ferried across the Lower Drift. As at Rorke's Drift, the crossing was
uncontested, though Zulu scouts were clearly visible in the distance.
Six days later, by which time supplies had been stockpiled and a
fort* built on the Zulu bank, the march north into hostile territory
began. But only half Pearson's column set out on the 18th: he did
not have enough oxen to pull all his wagons and so decided to
forge ahead to Eshowe with just fifty wagons and most of his best
troops. The rest would follow a day later, accompanied by a further
eighty wagons.

By 21 January, hampered by rain-softened ground and three
difficult river crossings, Pearson and his forward column had
covered only fifteen miles. He had earlier received intelligence from
Bernard Fynney, the border agent, that Cetshwayo had dispatched a
single regiment to oppose his column. This was partially true: the
uMxhapho ibutho – 2,600 warriors in their mid thirties – and a
further 900 men of the izinGulube and uDlambedlu regiments had
been detached from the main army on 17 January and sent south
under Chief Godide. But since arriving on the 20th at Hlalangubo,
the royal kraal north of Eshowe, Godide had been joined by a
variety of local levies who had increased his total strength to over
6,000.

Pearson was informed by spies on the 21st that a Zulu impi was
at kwaGingindlovu, another royal kraal five miles to the east of his

* Fort Tenedos.

line of advance. Not wishing to deviate – and demonstrating at the same time a woeful underestimation of his enemy – he sent just two companies of the Buffs to investigate. It was fortunate for them that Godide decided not to stop at kwaGingindlovu after all, but instead moved towards the British camp with the intention of making a night attack. His warriors were in position, waiting for the word, when Godide lost his nerve. The sound of sentries calling to each other had convinced him that the British were prepared for an attack. So he headed for the north bank of the Nyezane River, where the hilly, bush-covered ground provided an ideal site for an ambush.

The British awoke on 22 January to the ominous sight of flattened grass all round the camp. But instead of drawing the obvious conclusion, and waiting until his rear column had joined him, Pearson decided to continue his march with the intention of reaching Eshowe by nightfall. A staff officer★ wrote:

By 7.30 a.m. the advance-guard had reached the Neyezane river (two miles) and crossed over. Thick bush grew all round here; but the cavalry having reconnoitred and seen nothing, vedettes were placed around, and a knoll was selected to breakfast on . . . The wagons had just begun to park when a party of the Native Contingent sent to reconnoitre were fired upon. The firing came from the bush near the river, but the main body [of Zulus] was seen to be coming over the hills on our left to surround us.

The Zulu trap had been prematurely sprung by a patrol of the 1/2nd NNC. According to one eyewitness, the NNC fled, leaving their officers behind them. In fact they had been ordered to retreat by Captain Hart, their regimental staff officer, who recalled:

I saw at once that we had almost fallen into a trap, and I instantly gave the order 'Retire'. At the same moment the Zulus poured down the hill by hundreds at the top of their speed, with a tremendous shout, while

★ Believed to have been Captain McGregor, the brigade major.

others above kept up the fire over the heads of those descending the hill... It was not until the close of the general engagement which followed that I found that one of the lieutenants, two sergeants, and two corporals were killed in the kloof [ravine], evidently with assegais.

A Naval Brigade officer, looking after the wagons in the centre of the column, recorded his reaction to the sound of firing:

I immediately pushed forward, when I found the advance guard hotly engaged. The staff, Lloyd's guns, some of the Buffs, and the bluejackets occupied a low knoll to the right of the road; in front of them was a high hill overlooking our position, in possession of the Zulus. The mounted men were on a plain to our right, and the road was completely commanded by the enemy, who were concealed over the ridge of the hill, and kept up a heavy fire. When I arrived both of our companies were engaged on the left of the knoll; the Zulus annoyed us very much from a kraal further to the left, but a couple of rockets dislodged them and the Native Contingent took it. The Zulus advancing on our left, the bluejackets were ordered there, and being very exposed moving up the road, four of our men were wounded. Driving the enemy along the road, and being supported by two companies of the Buffs under Colonel Parnell, we charged up the hill, when the Zulus took to flight.

All but one warrior, who stood 'leaning forward' with his left hand on his knee, seemingly unconcerned, as Captain Hart galloped towards him. 'I could see glistening on his head the black ring that signifies in Zululand the married man,' recalled Captain Hart. 'He was now only a hundred yards' distant, and in a few moments I should use my revolver, but just then he dropped quickly on one knee, took very deliberate aim at me for a couple of seconds, and fired. He seemed scarcely to believe he could have missed his prize, for he waited to take one eager look at me, as his smoke cleared away, and then seeing me still coming on, he bolted away and disappeared.'

Another naval officer, Midshipman Lewis Coker, had the honour of commanding the first Gatling gun to be used in combat by

British troops.* He wrote: 'On arriving at the foot of the hill where the Head Quarters were I was ordered by Colonel Pearson to bring the gun up and place it opposite a hill, where some natives had taken up a position. I immediately opened fire on them, they retiring into the bush I ceased firing having expended about 300 rounds, and stationed my men to try and pick off a few natives who were annoying us considerably.'

By now the men of the rear column had arrived on the battlefield – but the victory was already as good as won. It was about 9.30 a.m., according to Pearson, when the Zulus 'fled in all directions, both from our front and left, and before the skirmishers on the right'. The most determined Zulu attacks were by the chest, which had appeared at the head of the central spur, and the left horn, which had tried to outflank the right of the British position. The right horn, by contrast, had made only a half-hearted attempt to occupy the spur on Pearson's left. Chief Zimema of the uMxhapho, the regiment that bore the brunt of the fighting, recalled:

As we advanced we had our rifles under our arms and had our assegais in our right hands ready to throw them, but they were not much good . . . We never got nearer than 50 paces to the English, and although we tried to climb over our fallen brothers we could not get very far ahead because the white men were firing heavily close to the ground into our front ranks . . . The battle was so fierce that we had to wipe the blood and brains of the killed and wounded from our heads, faces, arms, legs and shields after the fighting.

The courage and discipline of the Zulus had impressed many of the British. 'I never thought niggers would make such a stand,' wrote Colour-Sergeant Burnett of the 99th. 'They came on with an utter disregard of danger.' But it cost them about 400 lives, many of them 'burnt and scorched up by the shells'. One officer who inspected the ground after the battle 'found dead Zulus in heaps of

* Though one had accompanied Wolseley's Ashanti Expedition of 1873/4 without being fired.

eight or nine, and in one place counted as many as twenty-five'. The British had just twelve killed and seventeen wounded (two mortally), though both Pearson and another officer had horses shot under them. All their preconceptions about the relative ease of the campaign seemed to have been confirmed.

A Zulu informant later reported that Cetshwayo was 'very angry' with Chief Godide and the izinGulube and uDlambedlu regiments 'for not taking a more active part in the fight'. He added: 'It is said they merely looked on, and took no part at all.' Godide did, however, manage to regroup his beaten force and place it across the probable British route of advance to oNdini. But it would not be required to fight again for some time.

Having buried his dead, Pearson pushed on towards Eshowe, bivouacking for the night on a ridge three miles from the battlefield. He reached the Norwegian mission station at ten the following morning and immediately began to entrench it. The plan, according to a member of his staff, was 'to leave our surplus stores here with a small garrison, and move on to [oNdini] in a few days'. The same staff officer left the following description of the post and the destruction that was wrought on it by the arrival of the column:

Ekowe . . . is built on the summit of a high range of hills overlooking the sea, and a wide extent of beautiful hill and dale, deep ravines, and thick bush. Far away northward were rugged precipitous mountains . . . over which, or round which, we were told our future path lay. The station consisted of a church, school and parsonage, and a little distance off were a few more houses – these were all built of brick with thatched roofs. Round them all were gardens, orange-groves, plantations, blue-gum trees, etc. . . Those groves and plantations were, I need hardly say, very speedily cut down to make way for the fire of the white man . . . How calm, how peaceful, it all looked when we marched in that bright morning; now soon to be converted into as hideous a spot as there was in Zululand!

It was not an ideal location for a fort: three sides were commanded by rising ground within easy rifle range; the fourth consisted of a bush-covered ravine that provided ideal cover for any party of attacking Zulus. About 1,400 yards to the south-east was a high, rocky conical hill with thick bush on its far side. 'Up this hill,' wrote the staff officer, 'the Zulus used often to creep at night and fire on the vedettes in the morning as they were being posted, and observe what was going on inside the fort. Fortunately for us they never discovered they could fire *into* the fort from this hill, or from the other high ground surrounding us.' The reason the fort was sited here – when other positions in the vicinity were better suited for defence – was chiefly because the 'water-supply was good' and the church and two of the buildings 'would be useful as a hospital and storehouses'.

But it was not long before news of a setback to No. 3 Column began to filter through: first that 'Durnford had met with a reverse' but that Chelmsford 'had a complete success over the forces opposed to Durnford'; then that Durnford had been killed. 'We naturally supposed,' wrote Colonel Forestier Walker, Pearson's chief of staff, 'that the reverse might cause some delay in our advance.' Finally, at noon on 28 January, a galloper arrived with a telegram from Chelmsford 'countermanding all previous orders'. It had been telegraphed to Fort Pearson from Pietermaritzburg, and brought on by rider. While not going into details, it left Pearson in no doubt that a major disaster had occurred. 'You must be prepared,' it stated, 'to have the whole Zulu force down upon you.' A staff officer recalled:

It was left to Colonel Pearson to decide whether he thought himself strong enough to hold the fort or not: in the latter case, he would march down at once to the [Thukela]. No particulars of the defeat were sent; and it was not till the 7th February that we fully learnt of the disaster that had befallen our comrades at Isandhlwana. A council of war immediately assembled; and it was decided, by a small minority, to hold the fort at all costs. All the cavalry, however, with the two battalions Native Contingent, were to go down at once, as we had not sufficient corn for the horses of the former; and the latter there was no room for in the fort, had we even been able to feed them.

It was in a state of considerable anxiety, not to mention vulnerability, that the remaining 1,339 whites and 355 blacks – many of the latter non-combatants – entered the entrenchment on 30 January. 'Tents were discarded, and the men and officers slept under the wagons, some seventy of which had been placed round the inside of the parapet, and where required, as traverses.' The fort was roughly oblong in shape, with its east and west sides extending for 300 yards, and its north and south sides 120 and 180 yards respectively. The church had been converted into a hospital; the schoolroom and parsonage into storehouses. All other buildings had been demolished to clear the field of fire. For security reasons only white soldiers were allowed in the entrenchment by day; the Natal Pioneers and African drivers were admitted after 'Retreat'. All Africans, in addition, had to wear a blue patch of cloth to distinguish them from Zulu spies. 'They found some difficulty about this,' wrote a staff officer, 'as some had not even a shirt to sew it on to, but tied it with a string round their necks.'

The garrison had 'stores sufficient, as then calculated, to last only three weeks'. One thousand of the 3,000 transport oxen and twenty-eight of the sixty mules were sent back to the Lower Drift on 30 January by different routes. None made it through: about half the oxen and all the mules were intercepted by Zulus; the rest were driven back to the entrenchment. The so-called siege of Eshowe had begun and would last much longer than any of the garrison thought possible.

10. The Cover-up

Relieved as Lord Chelmsford was to find the post at Rorke's Drift still intact on 23 January, he knew that its gallant defence was scant consolation for the earlier bloodbath at Isandlwana. He had left no specific orders for the camp's defence and had made, he knew now, a string of unforgivable errors: he had failed to locate the main Zulu impi; had been been duped by the enemy into splitting his force; and had ignored repeated messages that the camp was under threat. Even as he walked over the corpse-strewn ground at Rorke's Drift, he must have assumed that his recall was inevitable – that his career was over.

But help was at hand from an unlikely source: Major Francis Clery, Glyn's principal staff officer. A charming and talented forty-year-old Irishman, Clery was a noted military theoretician who had lectured on tactics at Sandhurst and written a book on the subject. He had also served for a time as Chelmsford's DAQMG* at Aldershot. Yet he had no practical experience of war by the time he arrived in South Africa as a special service officer in 1878. Posted to No. 4 Column as Wood's principal staff officer, he had expected to fight the Zulu campaign in that capacity. But in December 1878 Chelmsford decided that Glyn needed a 'good staff officer' and 'absolutely no one available'. So he ordered Clery to transfer to No. 3 Column, much to his and Wood's irritation.

It was during a conversation with Chelmsford at Rorke's Drift on 23 January that Clery let slip a vital piece of information: that either Pulleine or Durnford – or both – had disobeyed the written orders he had issued on his own initiative before leaving Isandlwana camp the previous day. Clery later gave an account of

* Deputy assistant quartermaster-general (a medium-grade staff post).

this conversation – and the sudden change in Chelmsford's mood – in a letter to a senior Horse Guards official. He wrote:

The General had not the very smallest apprehension about the camp being attacked, and danger of that kind never dawned – nor did he feel after the first shock of the thing that anyone was to blame for not thinking of such a thing, though he was perfectly alive to the heavy consequences that might arise to himself, for neither he nor Colonel Glyn knew that I had issued the orders. And when on the morning after Isandlwana, after our return to Rorke's Drift, he had gathered the facts that the troops were taken out of camp to attack the Zulus, he only remarked: 'How unfortunate!' But when I pointed out to him that this was directly contrary to the written orders I had left for the defence of the camp, he scarcely seemed able for an instant to realize that I had left these orders, and then said: 'I cannot tell you what a relief it is to me to hear this.'

Chelmsford could hardly believe his luck. But more was on the way with Colonel Crealock's insistence that he had ordered Durnford to 'take command' of the camp at Isandlwana on the 22nd. If this was true, Durnford was the man responsible for disobeying the orders that Clery had left for Pulleine because, as senior officer, he would have inherited those orders. We now know that Crealock was lying: Durnford had simply been told to march to the camp 'with all the force you have with you'. But with Durnford dead and the order lost with him, it was inevitable that Crealock would be believed. His motives are not hard to fathom: as Chelmsford's senior staff officer in Zululand, he would have to take a share of the responsibility if his chief was blamed for Isandlwana. It would not only be Chelmsford's career that was over. 'Lord C.'s staff did every thing in their power to shelter him as it was in their own interest to do,' wrote George Mansel of the NMP. 'I really believe, if justice had been done, the whole lot should have been tried for cowardice & shot.' Was Chelmsford himself part of the conspiracy to scapegoat Durnford? Possibly. But there is no direct evidence, and it is just as likely that he simply grasped the proffered lifeline with the same gratitude that he had Clery's.

Chelmsford's early letters from Rorke's Drift were mercifully free of the exculpations and accusations – specific or implied – that would pepper his later correspondence (possibly because they were written before he had spoken to either Clery or Crealock). On 23 January, for example, he told Frere that No. 3 Column had 'maintained a terrible disaster' with the loss of its camp at Isandlwana. He added: 'The camp had been defended with the utmost gallantry, but the soldiers had been beaten by much heavier numbers.' The officers and men at Rorke's Drift, on the other hand, had 'made a most gallant and effectual resistance'.

But Chelmsford's tone would soon change. Anxious to confer with Sir Bartle Frere – and doubtless eager to get away from the aimless despondency into which the shocked survivors of No. 3 Column had fallen – he left Rorke's Drift with his staff on 24 January and, having spent a night at Helpmakaar, reached Pietermaritzburg on the 26th. The following day he wrote a long letter to Colonel Stanley, secretary of state for War, implying but not stating that Durnford was responsible for the disaster. He wrote:

Lieut. Colonel Pulleine, 1/24th Regt, was left in charge of the camp, and received strict instructions that he was left there to defend it. Shortly before the arrival of Lieut. Col. Durnford in camp with his 450 natives, information had reached . . . Pulleine from the left picquet that a number of Zulus had been seen on that flank. On receiving this information . . . Durnford asked . . . Pulleine to give him two companies of British infantry, in order that he might move up the heights on the left and attack them . . . Pulleine at once stated that his orders were to defend the camp, and that without a positive order he could not allow the companies to move . . . Durnford then took his 450 natives up the heights and went so far as I can learn 5 miles from camp, when he found himself in front of a very large army of Zulus . . . Had the force in question but taken up a defensive position in the camp itself, and utilized there the material for a hasty entrenchment which lay near at hand, I feel absolutely confident that the whole Zulu army would not have been able to dislodge them.

The effect of the disaster, said Chelmsford, had been to cause a 'great alarm' throughout Natal, particularly among the Native Contingent, which had begun to desert. As a result, he concluded, 'the Natal Native allies are no longer to be depended upon, and additional British reinforcements must be sent out if the operations against the Zulus are to be carried to a successful issue'.

Frere took his lead from Chelmsford. Having spoken to him on the 26th, Frere told the duke of Cambridge that the general, 'though greatly worn by all he has gone through', was 'well in health' and a few days' rest would 'see him right'. He added:

He feels the calamity the more because he is naturally averse, pending the result of the inquiry he has ordered, to express any opinion as to who, of the poor fellows who are gone, was to be blamed for the undoubted neglect of orders which led to the disaster. It will probably never be known how such a large body of the enemy got so close, without being seen & their force earlier reported. Nor why the main column with the general were not apprized & recalled earlier in the day. But from all I can learn there was ample time after the enemy were discovered to park the wagons & the detaching of the companies of the 24th more than a mile from the camp instead of concentrating them at the camp, was objected to by Lt. Col. Pulleine, when Lt. Col. Durnford took command.

This was vintage Chelmsford – getting others to state what he could only imply: that Durnford was to blame for the loss of the camp. Frere had also – however inadvertently – touched on Chelmsford's own errors by mentioning the lack of adequate reconnaissance and his failure to return sooner to the camp. The Court of Inquiry, referred to by Frere, had been convened by Chelmsford at Help-makaar on 24 January. It consisted of three members: Colonel Fairfax Hassard of the Royal Engineers (the president) and Lieutenant-Colonels Francis Law and Arthur Harness of the Royal Artillery. Harness, of course, was the man whose attempt to return to Isandlwana during 22 January had been countermanded by Chelmsford. He was therefore in a position to provide some very incriminating evidence against his chief. What better way to silence him than by appointing him to the court; that way he could not testify. The other two officers were suitably unenergetic and not likely to inquire too deeply into the cause of the disaster. Of the president, Clery wrote disparagingly: 'He built a fort at Helpmakaar and shut himself in it, and strongly recommended everybody else to do the same.' Chelmsford himself had earlier described Law as 'not over-fond of work'.

As double insurance, Chelmsford limited the scope of the inquiry to the 'loss of the camp on the 22nd January'. Nor was the court expected to give an opinion or reach a conclusion. 'It was assembled,' wrote Harness, 'solely for the purpose of assisting the General Commanding in forming an opinion.' Eight witnesses made statements at Helpmakaar on 27 January but were not cross-examined: Colonel Glyn, Major Clery, Captains Gardner, Essex and Nourse, and Lieutenants Cochrane and Smith-Dorrien. More detailed written statements were later provided by Essex, Gardner, Crealock and Curling, and added to the court proceedings. The whole was submitted to the secretary of state for War on 8 February with an explanatory note from Chelmsford: 'The Court has very properly abstained from giving an opinion, and I myself refrain also from making any observation or from drawing any conclusions from the evidence therein recorded. I regret very much that more evidence has not been taken.'

Quite what the point of the Court of Inquiry was is not clear. It certainly was not an attempt to discover the cause of the disaster at Isandlwana. If it had been, many more witnesses would have had to be called and cross-examined, including Harness and Chelmsford himself. Instead the officers that did give evidence were only too happy to finger Durnford and, to a lesser extent, Pulleine. Crealock, for example, repeated the canard that he had ordered Durnford to 'take command' of the camp. It is unlikely that the witnesses were subject to any direct pressure from Chelmsford or his staff; but all would have known that their future prospects in South Africa depended upon not falling out with the commander-in-chief.

But just to make sure that the authorities in England drew the correct conclusions, Chelmsford added a helpful memorandum

from Colonel Bellairs, his deputy adjutant-general. Dated
5 February, it stated:

From the statements made before the Court of Inquiry it may be clearly
gathered that the cause of the reverse sustained at Isandhlwana was that
Lt. Colonel Durnford, as senior officer, overruled the orders which Lt.
Colonel Pulleine had received to defend the camp and directed that the
troops should be moved into the open, in support of a portion of the
Native Contingent which he had brought up and which was engaging
with the enemy. Had Lt. Colonel Pulleine not been interfered with and
been allowed to carry out his distinct orders given him to defend the
camp, it cannot be doubted that a different result would have been
obtained.

Chelmsford gave his own assessment of the biased Court of Inquiry
in a confidential memorandum. It stated:

I consider that there never was a position where a small force could have
made a better defensive stand. Assuming that it was thought desirable to
occupy the whole front of Isandhlwana hill, 300 yards in length; this
would have given 4 rifles per running yard to the fighting line. What
force of Zulus could have successfully assaulted a front of battle so
defended? The ammunition was abundant; the soldiers were good steady
shots; and every one before the disaster, felt confident that they could
defeat any numbers that came against them. Had the tents been lowered
as was invariably done afterwards by pulling out the tent-poles, they
would also have formed an entanglement at a convenient distance from
the position to be defended . . . The ground was too rocky to throw up
even a shelter trench, but the waggons which were ready inspanned *at
10am* (vide Lt Cochrane's evidence) could if thought necessary have been
formed into a laager.

Yet neither procedure, he added, was 'absolutely necessary' because
each yard of ground would have been defended by four rifles.
Furthermore a shelter trench was of 'no avail against a rush of
Zulus' and a wagon laager 'was never intended to be used as a

redoubt, but as a protection for the oxen'. Chelmsford was anxious, of course, to defend himself from the charge of leaving the camp unprepared. But the Horse Guards – as we shall see – would not be so easily convinced.

Fortunately Chelmsford had another string to his bow: the successful defence at Rorke's Drift. By emphasizing the heroism and importance of that action, there was every chance he could diminish the political impact of Isandlwana – and possibly save his own skin. In his letter to Colonel Stanley of 27 January, he described the action as 'the most gallant resistance I have ever heard of against the determined attack of some 3000 Zulus'. However, his estimate of the number of defenders – '60 of the 2/24th under Lieutenant Bromhead and a few volunteers and departmental officers, the whole under Lieut. Chard' – was a little on the low side.

Within days of the battle Chelmsford was urging the speedy completion of Chard's official report, because he was 'anxious to send that gleam of sunshine home as soon as possible'. It had, in fact, been written on 25 January but did not reach Pietermaritzburg until 4 February, by which time Chelmsford had left for a tour of Durban and the Lower Thukela. A remarkably fluent and detailed account of the defence, it made special mention of the following men: Lieutenant Bromhead 'and the splendid behaviour of his company'; Surgeon Reynolds 'in his constant attention to the wounded under fire'; Acting Assistant Commissary Dalton 'to whose energy much of our defences were due, and who was severely wounded while gallantly assisting in the defence'; Assistant Commissary Dunne; Acting Storekeeper Byrne (killed); Colour-Sergeant Bourne; Sergeants Williams (wounded dangerously since dead) and Windridge; Corporal Schiess; and Privates Williams, W. Jones, R. Jones, Hook, Roy and McMahon.

The most recent and detailed book on the battle – *Rorke's Drift* by Adrian Greaves – queries whether Chard was the author of this report. 'Remarkably,' writes Greaves, 'amidst the incessant heavy downpours of rain, the mire and chaos, and within two days of the battle, Chard ostensibly managed to obtain a sufficient supply of clean undamaged paper in order to prepare and submit a perfectly sequential report of the battle that was carefully composed, neatly written and complete in extraordinary detail . . . Yet there is no known record of any participant in the battle having assisted Chard with his report . . . For an officer with a reputation for slothfulness . . . the result is a truly masterful and perceptive account of the battle.' Greaves suspects that Major Clery was the author: 'Clery was a confidant of Chelmsford and an experienced report writer.'

Greaves may well be right. No sooner had Chelmsford read the report than he forwarded it on to the War Office with a suitably overblown endorsement:

The defeat of the Zulus, at this post, and the very heavy loss suffered by them, has, to a great extent, neutralized the effect of the disaster, and no doubt saved Natal from a serious invasion. The cool determined courage displayed by the garrison is beyond all praise, and will, I feel sure, receive ample recognition.

He had, he added, taken the liberty of publishing the report in Natal as 'the lesson taught by this defence is most valuable'. The real reason, of course, was to distract from his own responsibility for Isandlwana. What better way to do that than to exaggerate the importance of Rorke's Drift by pointing out that it had saved Natal from invasion – which it had not – and by hinting that not a few Victoria Crosses should be awarded to its defenders? The question was: to whom? Chard's report had singled out fifteen men. But even for Chelmsford that was too many. Bromhead made matters simpler when he finally submitted his own report to his battalion CO, Colonel Degacher, on 15 February. Much shorter than Chard's, it briefly outlined the feats of the six men of his company who had 'especially distinguished themselves' during the battle in or near the hospital: Corporal William Allen and Privates John Williams, Henry Hook, Frederick Hitch, and William and Robert Jones.

As with Chard's earlier report, Greaves believes Bromhead's account was also written by Clery. 'Only two other letters are known to have been written by Bromhead' at this time, writes

Greaves, 'and it can be clearly seen that the style and syntax in the official Bromhead Report differs considerably from that used in the two letters'. The report certainly reads more fluently than Bromhead's other letters – to his sister and a fellow officer – and if Clery was not its author, then he probably polished it up before sending it off to Chelmsford. He hinted as much in a letter written in May 1879:

I was about a month with [Bromhead] at Rorke's Drift, and the height of his enjoyment seemed to be to sit all day on a stone on the ground smoking a most uninviting looking pipe. The only thing that seemed equal to moving him in any way was any allusion to the defence of Rorke's Drift. This used to have a sort of electrical effect upon him, for up he would jump and off he would go, and not a word could be got out of him. When I told him he should send me an official report of the affair it seemed to have a most distressing effect on him. I used to find him hiding away in corners with a friend helping him to complete this account, and the only thing that afterwards helped to lessen the compassion I felt for all this, was my own labour when perusing his composition – to understand what it was all about.

The finished report was signed by Bromhead and submitted, via Degacher, to Colonel Glyn, who had been left in charge at Rorke's Drift. He sent it to Chelmsford, who added the names of Bromhead and Chard as two others worthy of consideration for the award of a Victoria Cross. This was highly irregular. Any such recommendation should have come from the column commander, Glyn. Yet Glyn had made no comment; nor had Colonel Degacher, Bromhead's commanding officer, in his official dispatch on Rorke's Drift. Instead Degacher had recounted the feats of the six men that Bromhead thought worthy of distinction, adding in a note to a private correspondent: 'Does this not deserve a V.C.?' But no mention was made of Bromhead. The reality is that Degacher had a low opinion of Bromhead and did not consider, from everything he had heard of the fight, that he deserved a VC. Yet he regarded some reward as necessary and, shortly after returning to Rorke's

Drift, he took Lieutenant George Banister aside and told him: 'I promised you the [post of] Instructor of Musketry and it is still yours as I never go back on my word, but I should like to do something for Bromhead, and it is about the only thing he is fit for, so would you let him have it, and take instead the Adjutancy.'

Banister replied that he 'did not care for the Adjutancy and had always looked forward to the other thing' but, under the circumstances, 'would not for worlds stand in Bromhead's light'. So the deal was done. But if Degacher had known that Bromhead would receive both a double jump in promotion and a Victoria Cross for his part in the defence of Rorke's Drift, he might not have been so generous. The ordinary soldiers, however, were resigned to the officers receiving most of the credit. 'I daresay the old fool in command will make a great fuss over the two officers commanding our company in keeping the Zulus back,' wrote one of the defenders to his brother. 'But with the private soldiers what will he get? Nothing, only he may get the praise of the public.' The writer underestimated Chelmsford's need for heroes. All six men singled out by Bromhead and Degacher would receive Victoria Crosses, as would the two officers. 'We have at once given the Victoria Cross to the officers & soldiers at Rorke's Drift who you recommended,' wrote the duke of Cambridge to Chelmsford on 10 April, 'and in addition Lts. Chard & Bromhead have been promoted & have at once received Bt Majorities.'

Word of the disaster reached the War Office in London in the early hours of 11 February 1879. It arrived in the form of a telegram from Chelmsford to Colonel Stanley, giving brief details of the defeat and its possible cause. 'It would seem,' wrote Chelmsford, 'that the troops were enticed away from the camp as the action took place about one mile and a quarter outside it.' He added: 'A panic is spreading over the Colony which is difficult to allay. Additional reinforcements must be sent out.' He asked for 'at least' three infantry battalions, two cavalry regiments and a company of Royal Engineers.

The Cabinet, which met in emergency session at two that

21. The ponts at Rorke's Drift

22. *Defence of Rorke's Drift* by Alphonse de Neuville. Many defenders are identifiable: (*right to left*), Lieutenant Chard (in white breeches with rifle), Corporal Allen (handing Chard a cartridge), Corporal Schiess (wearing a bandolier and stabbing a Zulu at the barricade), Padre 'Ammunition' Smith (handing out packets of bullets), Acting Assistant Commissary Dalton (sitting in foreground), Surgeon Reynolds (attending to Dalton), Lieutenant Bromhead (pointing to right), Private Hitch (behind Bromhead), Private Hook (giving Private Connolly a piggyback) and Assistant Commissary Dunne (far left, moving a biscuit box)

23. Lieutenant Gonville Bromhead, commanding B Company, 2/24th Regiment

24. Lieutenant John Chard, RE, the senior officer at Rorke's Drift

A VOTE OF THANKS.

F.-M. Punch. "LIEUTENANTS CHARD AND BROMHEAD, IN THE NAME OF YOUR COUNTRY I THANK YOU AND ALL THE DEFENDERS OF RORKE'S DRIFT. YOU HAVE SAVED NOT ONLY A COLONY, BUT THE CREDIT OF OLD ENGLAND!!"

25. *A Vote of Thanks, Punch* cartoon of 22 March 1879, congratulating the defenders of Rorke's Drift for saving Natal from invasion and redeeming Britain's honour. In truth the battle was little more than a border skirmish

26. Prince Dabulamanzi (*centre*), half-brother of King Cetshwayo, who commanded the Zulu forces at Rorke's Drift. Dabulamanzi and his followers hold a variety of firearms: shotguns, hunting rifles and even outdated Tower muskets

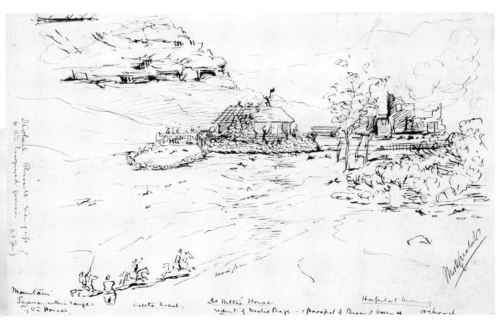

27. Pen and ink sketch by Crealock of the vanguard of Chelmsford's column arriving at Rorke's Drift during the morning of 23 January 1879

THE ILLUSTRATED LONDON NEWS

REGISTERED AT THE GENERAL POST-OFFICE FOR TRANSMISSION ABROAD.

No. 2082.—VOL. LXXIV. SATURDAY, MAY 10, 1879. WITH SUPPLEMENT } SIXPENCE. By Post, 6½d.

28. The Ntombe River massacre, 12 March 1879, when a company of the 80th Regiment was destroyed during a surprise night attack on its laager

29. Three watercolours by Crealock (*clockwise, from below*): one of Wood's Swazi irregulars; Lieutenant-Colonel Redvers Buller, 'a man of iron nerve and extraordinary courage'; a mounted Colonel Evelyn Wood, VC, commanding No. 4 Column

one of Wood's Irregulars

30. Piet Uys (*centre*, with white beard) flanked by his sons. The most prominent Boer to fight on the British side, Uys was killed at Hlobane on 28 March 1879, trying to save one of his sons

31. Pen and ink sketch by Crealock of Khambula Fort

32. A typical Zulu kraal near Fort Pearson

33. Major J. F. Owen (*centre*) of the 10/7th Battery, RA, with one of his two
Gatling guns

34. *The Battle of Gingindlovu*, 2 April 1879, by W. H. Durand

35. *Signalling to Ekowe by Heliograph*, a watercolour by Crealock

afternoon, agreed to send almost double the number of troops requested by Chelmsford: six infantry battalions, two cavalry regiments, two artillery batteries, a company of Royal Engineers and 300,000 rounds of ammunition. It had been advised by the Horse Guards that such numbers were 'necessary not only to fight Ketchwayo but to crush him quickly and effectively'. The public's thirst for revenge and the government's need to restore Britain's prestige were neatly summed up by the *Illustrated London News*:

[The Zulus] are to be defeated; their tyrant is to be deposed; their nation is to be disarmed; their country, for a time at least, must be subdued and held under British rule, though it be only for the safety of our adjacent provinces. But there is no right-minded and honourable man, with a soul of loyalty or patriotism and chivalry in him, who can think fit to hate the Zulus, as a nation, for having inflicted one temporary defeat upon our army in the defence of their own land, and under the command of their hereditary ruler.

As for apportioning blame for the disaster, the government's official line was to wait for more information. In a letter to Queen Victoria that day, Colonel Stanley expressed a hope 'that opinions will not be hastily formed as to the reverse being caused by errors on the part of Lord Chelmsford'. He added: 'No doubt there will be an outcry, on the part of the public, but there are no grounds at present for recalling or superseding him.' But the prime minister, in particular, was incandescent with rage: not only had the war been started without the government's sanction, but it had begun with a humiliating defeat. 'Had a very distressed letter from Ld Beaconsfield,' recorded the queen in her journal, 'in which he says: "It has been a very agitating day, with all this terrible news from South Africa, which to Ld. Beaconsfield's mind, is very unintelligible . . . This sad news has come, when by indefatigable efforts, everything was beginning to look bright. It will change everything, reduce our continental influence, & embarrass our resources."'

The truth is that Britain was still at diplomatic loggerheads with Russia and did not need any further drain on its military or financial resources. The recent war in Afghanistan may have gone well, but Russia had yet to fulfil the terms imposed upon her by the Congress of Berlin: in particular the evacuation of her troops from Bulgaria. 'The last thing that Disraeli needed,' wrote his biographer Robert Blake, 'was a remote campaign which would draw troops away from Europe and threaten his ability to threaten Russia.' So prostrated was Disraeli by the news from South Africa that he languished in a mood of alternating depression and fury for several weeks. But he had little doubt who was responsible. 'It is to be hoped that [Lord Chelmsford] may be equal to the occasion,' he wrote to the queen on 11 February, 'but it is impossible not to feel that this disaster has occurred to the Headquarters Column, which he himself was commanding.'

The queen was of a different opinion. The daughter of a soldier – her father, the duke of Kent, had risen to the rank of general – she had always maintained a keen interest in the achievements and welfare of her troops. When it became clear that British troops were suffering in the Crimea, for example, she had personally superintended the committees of ladies who organized relief for the wounded and eagerly seconded the efforts of Florence Nightingale. She also visited crippled soldiers in hospital (and would do so again after the Zulu War) and had instituted the gallantry medal for all ranks that bore her name.* Her late husband, Prince Albert, was also fascinated by the army. So impressed was the duke of Wellington with Albert's martial abilities that he recommended him as his successor as commander-in-chief. Albert knew, however, that it would never do for a royal consort to hold such an important post. But he had kept up his interest in military affairs: designing uniforms,† encouraging reform, reorganizing the command structure during the Crimean War and even advising the government

---

* *The Times* was not impressed with Albert's design: 'Never did we see such a dull, heavy, tasteless affair . . . There is a cross, and a lion, and a scroll worked up into the most shapeless mass that size admits of' (Weintraub, *Albert*, 325).
† Including the Albert-pattern shako – a tall, peaked cavalry helmet – which was described by *Punch* as a 'cross between a muff, a coal-scuttle, and a slop-pail' (Weintraub, *Albert*, 153).

on strategy. After his untimely death in 1861, aged just forty-two, the heartbroken queen had for a number of years taken only a passing interest in the affairs of state. But gradually her sense of isolation diminished and she began to exercise once again, in Walter Bagehot's words, the 'three great rights' of a British monarch: to be consulted, to encourage and to warn.

By the mid 1870s, though technically above politics, she favoured the domestic conservatism and foreign imperialism of the Tory Party. She got on particularly well with Disraeli, the prime minister, raising him to the peerage as the earl of Beaconsfield in 1876, and allowing him the signal privileges of writing to her in the first person (an honour he wisely reserved for special occasions) and sitting in her presence. He responded with letters of wit, affection and not a little unctuousness. When she inquired after his health, he replied that the best physician 'was the condescending sympathy, of a beloved Sovereign whose Kindness is always as graceful as it is gracious'.

Events in South Africa, however, were about to test this bond of mutual admiration. The queen was at Balmoral Castle when word reached her of the disaster at Isandlwana. She was horrified at the 'fearful' loss of British life and suffered from a headache for the rest of the day. 'How this could happen we cannot yet imagine,' she confided to her journal, 'but fear Col. Durnford was enticed away.' Her private secretary, Major-General Sir Henry Ponsonby, was of a similar opinion. 'I think it will turn out that Col. Durnford was left in charge of the Camp and ought never to have left it,' he wrote to his wife. 'Why he was enticed out we may never know, but I think the blame is his – and not the fault of Chelmsford or the others.' Clearly the Royal Household had been influenced by Chelmsford's telegram, and the queen's sympathy for her former aide-de-camp was evident in a message she instructed Stanley to send at once to South Africa. The queen wanted Chelmsford to know that she 'sympathises most sincerely with him in the dreadful loss which has deprived her of so many gallant officers and men', and that she 'places entire confidence in him and in her troops to maintain our honour and our good name'. At the same time she asked Hicks Beach to send a similar telegram to Frere, expressing her 'deep feeling at the terrible calamity' and her 'implicit confidence' in him. This both ministers did without consulting the Cabinet, much to their colleagues' irritation. The queen would later face severe criticism in Parliament and in the press for expressing her confidence in Chelmsford and Frere before the true cause of the disaster was known. She had, in effect, pre-empted any government attempt to recall either man.

The general inclination at the Horse Guards, however, was to point the finger at Chelmsford. A memorandum of 11 February, signed by three of the most senior army officers,★ stated: 'The force of so-called cavalry at Lord Chelmsford's disposition was too small & not sufficiently trained to act properly as a reconnoitring screen and consequently the commander in chief was ignorant of the position and number of the Zulu forces.' An Intelligence Department memorandum of the same day was even more critical of the commander. 'He does not seem to have fortified the Camp at Isandlana. He did not keep up proper communication with his Camp. He was led away by the Zulus who decoyed him from the Camp. In the meanwhile the Zulus collected in thousands under the hills near the Camp . . . Why were not scouts sent to explore?' It was a question Chelmsford would find hard to answer.

The duke of Cambridge was as shocked and distressed by the news as the rest of his staff. But until Chelmsford's official report had been received, he was prepared to withhold judgement. On 13 February he wrote Chelmsford a sympathetic note, informing him that reinforcements would sail from Britain within a fortnight and that they would be accompanied by three major-generals: Henry Crealock,† Sir Frederick Marshall and Edward Newdigate. 'They are placed at your disposal,' he wrote, 'and whilst giving them the commands for which their rank & abilities entitle them, I hope that you will so arrange as to interfere as little as possible

★ Major-General Sir Charles Ellice, Adjutant-General; Major-General Sir Daniel Lysons, quartermaster-general; Major-General Sir A. Horsford, military secretary.

† Lieutenant-Colonel John Crealock's elder brother.

with the very able & distinguished officers at present at the head of your respective columns.' Soon a fourth officer, Major-General the Honourable Henry Clifford, VC, was added to the list of reinforcements. Though the senior of the four, and an 'officer of great knowledge and experience in former Cape Wars', Clifford was given the thankless, though necessary, task of reorganizing Chelmsford's lines of communications. Crealock would be Chelmsford's deputy in the field.

In Parliament, meanwhile, Disraeli was struggling to put a brave face on the terrible news from South Africa. 'It is a military disaster – a terrible military disaster – but I think we may say it is no more,' he told the House of Lords on 13 February. 'It is not a military defeat arising from the failing energies or resources of the country. It is from accidental and, at this moment, not clearly understood circumstances that the calamity has arisen . . . It would, I think, be desirable that no one should hazard an opinion as to the causes of the disaster until we receive those official and authentic accounts which are, of course, now on their way.' But there was a silver lining – Rorke's Drift – and it provided Disraeli with the same crumb of comfort that it had Chelmsford. 'We must not forget,' he added, 'the exhibition of heroic valour by those who have been spared. At this moment, I am sure, the recollection of those 80 men, who, for 12 hours in a forlorn hope, kept at bay 4,000 of the enemy, and ultimately repulsed them, will prove that the stamina and valour of the English soldiery have not diminished.' Disraeli went on to say that the reinforcements being sent were 'in numbers much beyond what had been applied for' and that better news was anticipated. None of this, he added, would necessarily weaken other areas of British foreign policy, because Russia was gradually carrying out the terms of the Treaty of Berlin and affairs in Afghanistan were in a satisfactory state.

In private Disraeli was much less sanguine. He informed his confidante Lady Chesterfield that the 'terrible disaster has shaken me to the centre, and what increases the grief is that I have not only to endure it, but to sustain others and to keep a bold front before an unscrupulous enemy'. He did not specify which enemy but he could have been referring to either the Russians or the Liberals.

Ordinary Britons were also reeling under the blow to their country's military prestige. They had only learnt that a war was being fought at the beginning of February. A week or so later came the news of Isandlwana. How, they asked over countless breakfast tables, could a modern British Army be defeated by spear-wielding savages (which is how they would have seen the Zulus)? The press was similarly perplexed. 'No such disaster as that at Isandula ought to have been possible with a disciplined force,' opined the *Illustrated London News*. No comparable setback to British arms had occurred since Sir Henry Lawrence's defeat at Chinhut during the Indian Mutiny of 1857–8. Before that you had to go back to General Elphinstone's catastrophic retreat from Kabul in 1842. It was only natural that a traumatized nation would seek out heroes – and villains.

The first detailed accounts of the fighting appeared in the *Daily News* on 25 February. But it was not until the receipt of Chelmsford's official dispatch on 1 March that an accurate assessment of the battle was possible. The queen was not at all satisfied, noting that the dispatch 'does not give the reasons for what occurred'. Nor was the duke of Cambridge happy with Chelmsford's account, telling the queen that it was 'neither good nor clear, & the whole thing inexplicable'. The duke confided to Sir Bartle Frere that Chelmsford's dispatches 'have left us in much perplexity as to what actually occurred & how it all happened'. This was 'most unfortunate', he added, because the 'public interest' was 'very great' and yet it was not happy with the dispatch because 'so many points are omitted or left in doubt'. These points – seven in all – were brought to Chelmsford's attention by an extraordinarily blunt letter from General Ellice, the adjutant-general, on 6 March. The duke wanted to know, he wrote, the answers to the following questions:

(1) How did it happen that Rorke's Drift 'was not put into a state of defence previous to your Lordship's advance to Isandlwana Hill?'

(2) Why was the camp at Isandlwana 'not put into some state of defence by "leaguing" or otherwise'?

(3) Why were orders not given to Pulleine 'to place the camp itself in a state of defence' when Chelmsford departed on 22 January?

(4) 'What steps were taken on the 20th and 21st to reconnoitre and thoroughly search the country on your flank.' ('It seems difficult to understand,' added Ellice, 'how a large Zulu army could have moved itself to the north, and within striking distance of your camp, without some evidence of its proximity having been afforded.')

(5) 'When you heard at 9 a.m. on the 22nd that firing was going on to the left front of the camp, did you make any endeavour to communicate with the camp by sending a detachment of cavalry into it?'

(6) 'Did you at any time after this, and before Commandant Lonsdale reported to you that the camp was in the hands of the enemy, receive any reports, native or otherwise, which led you to suppose that an action was going on near the camp, and, if so, what steps did you take?'

(7) 'When you directed Colonel Glyn to move out on the morning of the 22nd, did that officer make any arrangements for reserve ammunition and a day's supply of rations accompanying this force?'

The duke had no doubt, added Ellice, that Chelmsford would be 'able to give the most satisfactory information' on these points.

Meanwhile the pressure on Disraeli to replace Chelmsford was intensifying. On 12 March he told the queen that, 'with the exception' of Sir Michael Hicks Beach, 'his whole Cabinet had wanted to yield to the clamours of the Press, & Clubs' for Chelmsford's recall. Only after 'great difficulty' had he 'carried the day'. Two days later, having received the latest dispatches from the Cape, Colonel Stanley complained to the queen: 'Lord Chelmsford has added little or nothing to the information which had previously reached us, & it is perhaps to be regretted that he has refrained from any comment upon the Court of Enquiry.' That evening the

Liberal MP Edward Jenkins demanded Chelmsford's sacking on the grounds that when 'any General suffers such a defeat as . . . Isandula, there is a *prima facie* case of incompetency against him'. Chelmsford was vigorously defended by, among others, Sir Stafford Northcote – the chancellor of the exchequer – and Jenkins's motion was withdrawn. But the following day the proceedings of the Isandlwana Court of Inquiry were published in the Supplement to the *London Gazette*, prompting one Liberal peer to insinuate that 'the officers composing the Court might be prejudiced and the result unsatisfactory'. Once again a minister was forced to defend Chelmsford.

But it was not only Chelmsford's job that was under threat: the press, many MPs and several Cabinet members were also clamouring for Sir Bartle Frere's head. Lord Salisbury, the Indian secretary, later told his nephew Arthur Balfour: 'Bartle Frere should have been recalled as soon as the news of the ultimatum reached England. We should then have escaped in appearance, as well as in reality, the responsibility of the Zulu War. So thought the majority of the Cabinet, so thought Dizzy himself.' But Hicks Beach had successfully defended his unruly subordinate then – and he repeated the feat at the emergency Cabinet meeting of 11 February, when Salisbury again recommended Frere's recall. By mid March, however, Hicks Beach felt compelled to inform Frere that his situation was extremely precarious. 'Had all gone successfully,' he wrote, 'comparatively few would have blamed you.' As it was, Sir Charles Dilke, the Radical MP, was about to introduce a motion of no confidence in Frere, and the Tory members 'could hardly be prevailed upon to vote a direct negative to it'. Yet Hicks Beach still hoped to win an amended vote. He added:

Now I come to my colleagues. Many of them are much biased against your policy by the influence for evil . . . which our difficulties in Zululand have had *against* us in Egypt & at Constantinople, in both of which places matters are just now very precarious. But all feel very much as I did when writing to you my private letter of Dec 25th . . . They do not think you ought to have taken the step of making on Cetywayo those important demands as to the disbandment of the army, the resident, and the performance of his promises of better government, without first obtaining our sanction to it . . . But for the support of the Prime Minister . . . I should have had to choose between resigning, and consenting to supersede or recall you. I attach the greatest importance to your continuance in South Africa.

Hicks Beach also pointed out that, contrary to Frere's recent recommendation, the Cabinet was strongly opposed to the annexation of any part of Zululand. Instead they wanted Frere, 'now that it must be all military work in Zululand, and the Transvaal Boers can hardly (I suppose) be dealt with until the Zulu war is over, to return as soon as possible to Cape Town and guide your Ministers towards Confederation'. The key part of this letter is Hicks Beach's cynical admission that a short successful war would have caused Frere's disobedience to be forgiven. But it had been neither, and Frere would have to take the consequences.

On 18 March the queen herself was attacked when 'most impertinent remarks' were made in both Houses of Parliament about the message of condolence and encouragement that she had sent to Lord Chelmsford after hearing the news of Isandlwana. 'But,' noted the queen approvingly, 'they were stiffly and decidedly answered', especially by Disraeli. The explanation he gave in the House of Lords was that there was 'nothing in what has occurred but what is regular and Constitutional'. The queen had simply been expressing her sympathy with Chelmsford's predicament in the hope of sustaining her troops 'in trials of no common character'. In private, however, Disraeli was furious that Stanley had passed on the queen's message without consulting his Cabinet colleagues, because it made it appear that the government was endorsing Chelmsford before the true cause of the disaster was known.

On 23 March, with debates on South Africa looming in both Houses, Disraeli told the queen that he would 'do what he could to support' Frere and Chelmsford, 'but the feeling was strong against them'. As it happened, the motions of no confidence in Frere were comfortably defeated: by ninety-five votes in the Lords on 25 March and by sixty votes in the Commons two days later. In both cases the split was essentially on party lines. The queen was off Cherbourg in the Royal Yacht when she received this welcome news. Her private secretary, Sir Henry Ponsonby, summed up the feeling of most of those MPs who had voted for Frere. 'I do not understand any one to have said Frere was incapable,' he wrote, 'but that he had unnecessarily plunged us into a war. If so the evil is done. To punish him for that by withdrawing him would be to punish ourselves, for it is against Abraham Lincoln's dictum that it is unwise to swap horses while crossing a stream.'

A similar argument was being used to retain Chelmsford. But just when it seemed that the heat was being taken out of the anti-Chelmsford campaign, the British press got hold of an ambiguous letter that the general had sent to Stanley at his lowest ebb. Written at Durban on 9 February, it stated that 'future contingencies' made it desirable for an officer of major-general rank to be sent out to South Africa 'without delay'. Chelmsford added: 'In June last I mentioned privately to [the duke of Cambridge] that the strain of prolonged anxiety & exertion, physical & mental was even then telling on me – What I felt then, I feel still more now . . . Frere concurs in this representation, & pointed out to me that the officer selected, should be fitted to succeed him in his position of High Commissioner.' Despite Chelmsford's postscript that it was his 'earnest desire' to carry on his duties, the obvious implication was that a successor needed to be in place before his health broke down completely.

Part of the problem, of course, was psychological. Buller later told Ponsonby that Isandlwana 'utterly destroyed' Chelmsford. Buller added: '[He] never recovered his nerve after it and seems to have lost his energy. The first thing he did after the disaster was to gallop back with all his Staff to the other end of Natal – an act which alarmed the troops he had left behind and caused a panic in the Colony.' There is no doubt that Chelmsford suffered from severe mood swings in the weeks after the defeat. On 27 January, for example, he told the duke of Cambridge that he was 'inclined to view everything "au noir"' and was in 'daily dread of hearing that some misfortune' had befallen the other columns. The following day he was more upbeat in a letter to Wood:

I have had a long talk with Sir B. Frere this morning . . . It is fortunate there is one with so cool a head and so stout a heart at the head of affairs at this present juncture. He is of the opinion that the Transvaal and the Swazies must be left to look after themselves and that you should draw down nearer to Rorke's Drift column and work hereafter in connection with that column, when it comes to be reorganized, but of course independently . . . If we establish ourselves in good positions . . . we ought to be able to bring the Zulus down upon us again when thoroughly prepared to receive them.

But by 3 February the depression had returned. 'I am fairly puzzled when I contemplate our future operations,' he wrote to Wood. 'I wish I saw my way with honor out of this beastly country, and had you as my travelling companion. Best love to Buller. You two will have to pull me out of the mire.' It was in this state of virtual nervous collapse that Chelmsford requested a possible successor. Of course the press interpreted Chelmsford's letter – when it got hold of a copy in late March – as one of resignation. If not, it was certainly preparing the ground for resignation. But by March Chelmsford's spirits had improved and his superiors saw no reason for a change. A Horse Guards' memorandum, written in response to the demands for his recall, stated:

His Royal Highness has perfect confidence in Lord Chelmsford's ability . . . He has now acquired from experience a perfect knowledge of the country in which he will have to operate, & of the enemy with whom he must contend. He knows the troops & is known by them. The whole thread of operations & all the arrangements necessary to carry them out are in his hands. The period of the year most favourable for military operations has just commenced. Any change in the command at this time & under such circumstances would be most prejudicial and could only be justified by the existence of an obvious incapacity on the part of the officer holding it. That Lord Chelmsford under-rated the battle power of the Zulu Army & the ability of its leaders is now clear – but he did so in common with almost every civilian and soldier in the Cape Colony.

The extent to which Rorke's Drift softened the blow of Isandlwana – and made it easier for the government to retain Frere and Chelmsford – should not be underestimated. Chard's report finally reached London in early March and was published to universal acclaim, with the press full of the heroism and fortitude of the defenders. Nor was the government slow to make political capital: Northcote repeated in the House of Commons Chelmsford's erroneous claim that the 'memorable defence of Rorke's Drift' had saved Natal from invasion. The queen was among the first to offer her congratulations. 'I have received Her Majesty's Commands to express to you her admiration of the gallantry of all who took part in that brilliant defence,' wrote Stanley to Chelmsford on 20 March. 'The fertility of resource displayed in improvising defences and the cool and determined courage by which they were guarded and maintained have been especially remarked by her Majesty and will worthily take a prominent place in the annals of the British Army.' Whether the queen would have been quite so fulsome in her implied praise of Chard and Bromhead if she had known the full story – particularly the part played by Dalton – is another matter. Certainly many in South Africa were astonished when the news of the first eight Victoria Crosses filtered through. Major Clery wrote to a friend:

Reputations are being made and lost here in almost comical fashion, from the highest downwards. At the risk of being looked on as very ill-natured and scandalous, I will have a little gossip with you on the subject. Well, Chard and Bromhead to begin with; both are almost typical in their separate corps of what could be termed the very dull class. Bromhead is a great favourite in his regiment and a capital fellow at everything except soldiering. So little was he held to be qualified in this way from unconquerable indolence that he had to be reported confidentially as hopeless. This is confidential as I was told it by his CO [Colonel Degacher]. Of Chard there is very little to say except that he too is a very good fellow – but very uninteresting. The fact is that until the accounts came out from England, nobody had thought of the Rorke's Drift affair except as one in which the private soldiers of the 24th behaved so well. For as a matter of fact they all stayed there to defend the place for there was nowhere else to go, and in it they fought most determinedly.

Lieutenant Curling, the survivor of Isandlwana, was no less perplexed. 'It is very amusing to read the accounts of Chard and Bromhead,' he wrote home on 28 April. 'They are about the most common-place men in the British Army. Chard is a most insignificant man in appearance and is only about 5 feet 2 or 3 in height. Bromhead is a stupid old fellow, as deaf as a post. Is it not curious how some men are forced into notoriety?'

Other officers were more generous. A captain in the 1st Dragoon Guards, who dined with Chard in May 1879, recorded: 'I never met a nicer humbler fellow than Chard, he never boasted; or mentioned the Zulus, or Zululand except when asked . . . He is nice looking, very quiet and unpretending . . . I asked Chard a great deal about Rorke's Drift, and he told me without any fuss, or making out he had done anything.' The same officer wrote about Bromhead a couple of months later: 'He is a *particularly nice*, humble fellow too.'

But Sir Garnet Wolseley was not impressed by either officer. 'A more uninteresting or more stupid-looking fellow I never saw,' he confided to his journal after presenting Chard with his Victoria Cross on 16 July. 'Wood tells me he is a most useless officer, fit for nothing. I hear in this camp also that the man who worked hardest in the defence of Rorke's Drift Post was the Commissariat officer who has not been rewarded at all.' Captain Walter Jones, RE, had a similarly poor opinion of his former subordinate. 'He is a most amiable fellow and a loss to the Mess, but as a Company officer, he is hopelessly slow and slack. I shall get on much better without him, and with Porter as my senior Sub. Chard makes me angry, with such a start as he got, he stuck to the Company doing nothing. In his place, I should have gone up and asked Lord Chelmsford for an appointment, he must have got it and if not, he could have gone home soon after Rorke's Drift at the height of his popularity and done splendidly at home. I advised him, but he placidly smokes his pipe and does nothing. Few men get such opportunities.'

On 11 September, having pinned the Victoria Cross on Bromhead, Wolseley remarked caustically: 'I have now given away these decorations to both the officers who took part in the defence of Rorke's Drift, and two duller, more stupid, more uninteresting even or less like Gentlemen it has not been my luck to meet for a long time.' A famously brave officer who never won the VC – possibly because his most suicidal act of bravery took place in Burma in 1853 before the institution of the award – Wolseley may have felt more than a tinge of envy. Yet he also knew, from having spoken to officers in South Africa, that Dalton was the real hero of the defence and that, but for him, Chard and Bromhead might have abandoned the post. His informants were almost certainly Evelyn Wood and Redvers Buller. Reporting a conversation with the pair at Balmoral in September 1879, the queen's private secretary informed his wife:

They spoke to me about Rorke's Drift. The defence was brilliant and stubborn. But the puzzle to them was – who was the man who organised it – for it showed genius and quickness neither of which was apparently the qualification of Chard. A dull heavy man who seemed scarcely even able to do his regular work. One day Wood sent him to clear some ground and when he arrived later found nothing done and Chard asleep. Another day he was sent to find a ford & make it passable. Fearing his man and that a halt might be inconvenient to the Army, Wood rode forward. Found Chard quite helpless – he didn't seem to take in clearly what a ford was – and had done nothing. Wood ordered his man to do it. Yet Chard's despatch was a good one . . . Bromhead was fearless but hopelessly stupid. They could understand Chard & Bromhead bravely resisting to the death – but that they should have actively ordered any defence was impossible. They both believe this was done by a Commissary named Dalton.

It was partly thanks to the lobbying of officers like Wood, Buller and Wolseley that Dalton eventually received his just deserts. But even before the first eight awards were announced in the *London Gazette* of 2 May 1879, many people in Britain and South Africa were asking why only Chard and members of the 2/24th had been singled out for praise. 'In your Cartoon, of March 22,' an anonymous officer wrote to *Punch*, 'you, as worthy head of the Army, thank Lieutenants Chard and Bromhead for their heroic defence of Rorke's Drift. In the background are seen some men of the 24th Regiment, and scattered about are quantities of Commissariat Supplies. Cannot you find some corner for a memorial to the only officer who was killed that night while gallantly doing his duty, Assistant-Commissary Byrne? Should you ignore the only officer "severely wounded", to whom all were indebted for his advice and skill in turning his supplies of flour and biscuits into parapets – Assistant-Commissary Dalton? Or the young officer who gained the admiration of all by erecting the last defence under a heavy fire, Assistant-Commissary Dunne? Or Surgeon Reynolds, who only laid on one side his rifle to attend to the wounded?'

Reynolds's case was taken up by, amongst others, an MP called Dr Ward, who asked Colonel Stanley in the House of Commons on 8 May why he had been overlooked. The War secretary's defensive reply was that Reynolds had been rewarded with promotion to surgeon-major and it was premature for him to consider further honours. But honoured he was – and rightly so – on 17 June, when it was announced that he would also receive the Victoria Cross. That still left Dalton and Dunne – and numerous others – and an intensive campaign in Parliament and the press resulted in the duke of Cambridge referring the case to Chard for his opinion. His reply, surprisingly, was not particularly supportive, and had it not been for the tireless lobbying of Sir Edward Strickland, the commissary general, there the matter might have rested. Finally, on 18 October, Cambridge made his decision. 'We are giving the VC very freely I think,' he wrote, 'but probably Mr Dalton had as good a claim as the others who have got the Cross for Rorke's Drift Defence. I don't think there is a case for Mr. Dunne.' Dalton finally received his award at Fort Napier on 16 January 1880, almost a year after the battle and long after the press interest had died away.

But there was still one more Victoria Cross to be awarded for Rorke's Drift: to Corporal Christian Schiess of the 2/3rd NNC. Schiess had performed prodigious deeds during the defence of the inner line – particularly his fearless sortie over the barricade – and the Natal authorities finally managed to persuade the War Office to acknowledge this in November 1879. On 3 February 1880 he became only the fourth non-Briton* to be decorated with the VC.

A total of eleven Victoria Crosses were awarded for the defence of Rorke's Drift, more than for any other single action. One hundred and twenty-two men had survived the fight, meaning one survivor in eleven was a recipient. By contrast, only one VC was awarded for the Battle of Britain and only one for D-Day. Some historians have suggested that the Rorke's Drift awards were deliberately staggered over many months 'to maximize public appreciation' and deflect attention from a drawn-out and costly war. If so, it was because of political rather than military pressure. Cambridge was extremely reluctant to yield to the incessant demand for more VCs. And he was not the only one to query the number of awards. 'It must be confessed,' wrote the editor of the *Broad Arrow* on 23 August 1879, even before the final two awards had been made, 'that the military authorities in Pall Mall have shown lavish prodigality in the distribution of the Victoria Cross, which would probably startle their contemporaries in Berlin.† We say there is a chance of the Victoria Cross being cheapened by a too friendly eagerness in Pall Mall to recognize acts of equivocal valour.'

He had a point. The two senior officers – Chard and Bromhead – had committed no particular acts of outstanding bravery. If they had done, these would, no doubt, have been mentioned in their joint citation. Instead it read: 'The Lieutenant-General commanding the troops reports that, had it not been for the fine example and behaviour of these two officers under the most trying circumstances, the defence of Rorke's Drift post would not

---

* The first was a German-born cavalryman, Sergeant-Major Charles Wooden, who won his VC during the Charge of the Light Brigade in 1854.

† The Germans were notorious for handing out Iron Crosses with the rations.

have been conducted with that intelligence and tenacity which so essentially characterized it.'

This is not to deny that Chard and Bromhead did well after Dalton had persuaded them to remain at their post. They did. But whether they did more than their duty as officers is another matter. Did they, for example, deserve the Victoria Cross more than Dunne, Bourne and Smith? All 139 defenders at Rorke's Drift were, in a sense, heroes: but most because they had to be rather than because they chose to be. This is probably what Sir Garnet Wolseley meant by his biting journal entry of 19 March 1880: 'It is monstrous making heroes of those . . . who, shut up in buildings at Roorke's [*sic*] Drift, could not bolt & fought like rats for their lives, which they could not otherwise save.'

Chard and Bromhead were not, however, the only equivocal 'heroes' of the fighting on 22 January. The story of the gallant but doomed attempt by Lieutenants Melvill and Coghill to save their Queen's Colour had got back to Rorke's Drift within days of the battle. 'This gave special interest to our patrol work in the direction of the Fugitive's Drift,' recalled Captain Harford of the 3rd NNC, 'and I made it my business to accompany any patrol every day and keep an eye on the state of the river, which kept in flood for a long time at that time of the year.' Eventually the water level dropped and it became possible to see the debris on the river bed: saddles, bridles, stirrups, helmets, clothing and boots — but no sign of the lost Colour. At first Colonel Glyn was not prepared to risk sending a party to search for it. But a chat with the forceful Major Black changed his mind. On 3 February a mounted patrol — including Black, Harford and Higginson — reached the spot where the fugitives had crossed but found nothing. Just to the right of the steep path 'by which, it was said, the fugitives had made their way', however, they stumbled upon the bodies of Melvill and Coghill. 'Both were lying on their backs about a yard from each other,' wrote Harford, 'Melvill at right angles to the path and Coghill parallel to it, a little above Melvill and with his head up-hill. Both had been assegaied, but otherwise their bodies had been left untouched.' Thinking they might have the Colour on them, Black

unbuttoned their tunics. Nothing. But they did find Melvill's gold
watch in the waist-pocket of his breeches. It had stopped at 2.10,
presumably the time he had entered the river. Coghill had no
personal effects on him, but 'his bad knee was still bandaged up'.
Having covered the bodies with rocks, the patrol rode back to
Rorke's Drift.

A day later the search party returned. Harford had the job of
inspecting the middle of the river bed and, just beyond the 'corner
of a delta formed by the river', he found the Colour case and knew
the Colour must be near. Then he noticed a pole sticking out of
the water and told the man nearest to him to wade in and get it.
'On lifting it out he brought up the Colour still adhering to it,'
remembered Harford, 'and on getting out of the water handed the
standard to me, and as he did so the gold-embroidered centre scroll
dropped out, the silk having more or less rotted from the long
immersion in water.' But the Colour had been found and, a day
or two later, it was presented to the remnants of the 1/24th at
Helpmakaar amidst scenes of great emotion.

No one was more delighted than Colonel Glyn, the former
commander of the 1/24th, who later sent Chelmsford a long and
not especially accurate report of his officers' attempt to save the
Colour. He ended it by praising the 'noble and heroic conduct of
Lt. Adjutant Melville [sic], who did not hesitate to encumber himself
with the Color of the Regiment, in his resolve to save it, at a time
when the camp was in the hands of the enemy, and its gallant
defenders killed to the last man in its defence, and when there
appeared but little prospect that [he could] save even his own life'.
He also mentioned 'the equally noble and gallant conduct of Lt.
Coghill, who did not hesitate for an instant to return, unsolicited,
and ride again into the river, under a heavy fire of the enemy, to
the assistance of his friend; though at the time he was wholly
incapacitated from walking and but too well aware that any accident
that might separate him from his horse must be fatal to him'. Their
deaths, in trying to save the Queen's Colour of their regiment,
'could not have been more noble'.

So too thought the queen, who spoke to Disraeli of the 'very touching account of the recovery of the Colours, & the finding of the bodies of the 2 poor young officers . . . both leaving widows'. The story was published in the *Graphic* on 15 March, alongside an elegiac poem by J. E. Carpenter entitled 'The Saving of the Colours'. It was one of the three events – along with the last stand at Isandlwana and the defence of Rorke's Drift – that the public could not get enough of during the nervous early months of the war. Impresarios, artists and composers were all alert to the prevailing mood. By April, for example, Hamilton's Amphitheatre in Holborn was charging from sixpence to three shillings to view pictures praising these events, 'pictorially and vividly conveyed by authentic sources'.

The earliest oil painting of the defence of Rorke's Drift was completed by W. H. Dugan in May 1879 and viewed by Colonel Stanley, who commended the artist for tackling the subject before any proper detail was known. Other pictures followed. In April the eminent French battle artist Alphonse de Neuville was commissioned by the Fine Art Society of New Bond Street to paint Rorke's Drift. De Neuville also painted a glamorized picture of Coghill and Melvill cutting their way through a horde of attacking Zulus; unfortunately Melvill is depicted with the Regimental and not the Queen's Colour.

So moved was the queen by the story of Melvill and Coghill's gallantry that she authorized the insertion of a notice in the *London Gazette* of 2 May to the effect that both officers would have been awarded the Victoria Cross if they had lived. This so-called 'Memorandum Procedure' was first used during the Indian Mutiny and repeated in only five other cases – including Melvill's and Coghill's – during the nineteenth century. The families of all six were given retrospective medals in 1907, five years after Edward VII had sanctioned the award of posthumous VCs. The question is: did Melvill and Coghill deserve them? Even Chelmsford, who had the most to gain by the creation of heroes, was not sure. He wrote:

It is most probable that Melvill lost his life endeavouring to save Coghill rather than vice versa. He [Coghill] could hardly walk and any exertion such as walking or riding would have been likely to render him almost helpless. He could not have assisted, therefore, in saving the colours of the 1st 24th and as I have already said I fear he was a drag on poor Melvill . . . I feel sure that Melvill left camp with the colours under orders received . . . In being ordered to leave, however, he no doubt was given the best chance of saving his life which must have been lost had he remained in camp. His ride was not more daring than that of those who escaped. The question, therefore, remains had he succeeded in saving the colours and his own life, would he have been considered to deserve the Victoria Cross?

Sir Garnet Wolseley was even less sympathetic. 'I am sorry that both of these officers were not killed with their men at Isandhlana instead of where they were,' he noted in his journal after visiting their graves. 'I don't like the idea of officers escaping on horseback when their men on foot are killed.' The following March he added: 'Heroes have been made of men like Mellville [*sic*] and Coghill who, taking advantage of their having horses, bolted from the scene of the action to save their lives . . . It is monstrous making heroes of those who saved or attempted to save their lives by bolting.' That may be going a little too far in Coghill's case. He had, after all, put his life at risk by going back for Melvill. But if that was enough to earn him a VC, then Barker and Smith-Dorrien should also each have received one.

In the weeks following Lord Chelmsford's departure the morale at Rorke's Drift plummeted. Packed into the strong entrenchment that Colonel Glyn had built around the destroyed mission house, tormented by the horrors they had witnessed and constantly on guard against a fresh Zulu attack, few managed to get much sleep. The garrison also had to put up with the stench of rotting corpses, clouds of flies that 'cling and stick to you like leeches' and extreme weather that could swing from violent rainstorms to blistering heat. It was all too much for Private Henry Moses of the 2/24th, who wrote home, 'I wish I was back in England again, for I should never leave.'

A lack of space meant the warriors of the NNC were not even afforded the relative safety of the fort. Still angry at their treatment in Zululand (when they had been left without food for almost two days), fearful for the safety of their families in Natal and no longer confident that the British would win the war, this was the final indignity. During the morning of 24 January they laid down their rifles and deserted en masse. 'I am now left without any natives,' Glyn informed Chelmsford. 'What is to be done with Lonsdale and his Europeans?'

In the short term the white officers and NCOs were brought into the entrenchment and given the north-east corner to hold. But their presence simply added to the overcrowding, and before long the rain had turned the interior of the fort into a quagmire. 'In this state of filth we lived and ate and slept for more than two months,' recalled Captain Harford, 'no-one being in possession of anything other than a blanket and the clothes that he stood up in. An exception was made, however, with B Company, who had made such a gallant defence, and they were housed in the attic of Rorke's house with a tarpaulin thrown over the rafters (from which the thatch had been removed) to shelter them from the wet, a well deserved honour. However, even they had their troubles in trying to keep dry, as the tarpaulin often bagged in between the rafters with a collection of water which had to be ejected.' Little wonder that scores of men fell ill with fever and dysentery, including Chard and another survivor of the defence called Private J. Williams. Chard eventually recovered in Ladysmith;* Williams died on 5 February.

Even Glyn and his staff had to make the best of the appalling conditions. Major Clery wrote home:

We have lost everything we had . . . tent, clothing, cooking things, everything in fact – so that when we got anything to eat, we had nothing to cook it in, and when we got something to drink we had nothing to drink it out of. My present abode consists of a tarpaulin held up by some

---

* Though some Natal newspapers mistakenly reported his death.

sticks and this I share with Col. Glyn and the other staff officers. We have a little straw to lie on, but this is the rainy season and as the rain here comes down in torrents our straw gets very soaky at times. The ground is too hard for lying on, so one wakes in the morning very tender about one's bones.

Glyn could have relieved the overcrowding by allowing makeshift tents to be pitched outside the fort. But he refused, according to Harford, because he feared a fresh Zulu attack. So convinced was Glyn that this would happen that 'no-one but the officers and NCOs of the Contingent were allowed outside the Fort'. As Harford and his fellow officers were mounted, it fell to their lot 'to perform all the reconnoitring and patrolling work, and at dawn every morning while the garrison stood to arms we issued out to scour the surrounding country for a mile or two'.

Glyn seems to have suffered a nervous breakdown in the wake of Isandlwana. 'Poor Col. Glyn is naturally much broken by the destruction of his regiment,' wrote Captain Hallam Parr on 24 January. Though Chelmsford had been in operational command, Glyn still felt responsible for the disaster to his column. Moreover he had lost in Nevill Coghill not only his favourite officer but a man he had come to regard as the son he never had. His spirits were temporarily raised in early February by the finding of Coghill's and Melvill's bodies and the missing Colour. But they had sunk again by the time one officer wrote at the end of the month: 'Colonel Glyn (our chief) does nothing and is effete.'

A contributory factor was Chelmsford's attempt to blame Glyn for the 3rd Column's failure to comply with his own *Field Force Regulations* of November 1878, which stated that all camps in enemy territory 'should be partially entrenched on all sides'. In a memorandum to Glyn of 20 February, he wrote disingenuously:

I have no desire whatever to shift any of the responsibility which properly belongs to me on to the shoulders of the officer commanding No. 3 Column. At the same time I am anxious to make it clear that, by accompanying No. 3 Column, I did not accept the responsibility for the numerous details which necessarily have to be considered by an officer commanding a Column in the field . . . As regards outposts, patrolling and the ordinary precautions for the safety of the camp, I consider that for all these arrangements Colonel Glyn was solely responsible and had I interfered in such matters it would have been tantamount to my taking direct command of the Column; a position which I deprecated from the very first.

And yet, according to a private letter from Major Clery, Chelmsford took charge of the column from the start and became involved in every minute operational detail. Glyn was reduced to 'posting the guards, etc.' and was 'scarcely ever seen or heard of'. Clery was well aware that Glyn was being set up. 'It dawned upon some honest mind of the headquarter staff,' he wrote sarcastically in the same letter, 'that as Colonel Glyn was in orders to "command the 3rd Column", perhaps some part of the odium of that business could be transferred from the general's shoulders to his.' But Glyn was not about to play the fall guy. When asked by Crealock to account for his interpretation of orders relating to the camp at Isandlwana, he remarked: 'Odd the general asking me to tell him about what he knows more about than I do.' More specifically he pointed out that a wagon laager for oxen – as demanded by paragraph 18 of *Field Force Regulations* – was not formed at Isandlwana on 21 January because, 'in accordance' with Chelmsford's own instructions, 'half the wagons of the force were under orders to off load their contents next morning & proceed back to Rorke's Drift to bring up more supplies'.

He also refuted Chelmsford's assertion – included in the memorandum of 20 February – that he was bound to protest if 'at any time' he disagreed with the general's movement of troops. 'I was certainly not aware,' Glyn replied on 26 February, 'that my position called on me or entitled me to do this.' He was, however, prepared to accept that he was at all times 'fully responsible for the numerous details which have to be considered by an officer commanding a column in the field'. In particular he was 'solely responsible' for 'outposts and the ordinary precautions for the safety of the camp'.

This was enough to mollify Chelmsford. On 4 March Bellairs wrote to Glyn, expressing Chelmsford's satisfaction that 'his views of the relations which existed between' them as commander-in-chief and commander of No. 3 Column 'are so much in accord with your own'. And there the matter ended. Inspector George Mansel of the NMP later claimed that Chelmsford ceased to pursue the matter because Major Clery 'had kept a written order to Glyn from Ld. C.' that, when produced, 'immediately exonerated Glyn & turned the tables on Ld. C.' Mansel added: 'No doubt Glyn would have been sacrificed if it had not been for Cleary [*sic*], & then to save himself Lord C. turned on Col. D[urnford] knowing that he could not defend himself. I am certain that Ld. C. was put up to this by Crealock. No doubt Glyn & Cleary cd. have done much to show up Ld. C., but I suppose they obeyed some hints to hold their tongues.'

Another reason why Chelmsford was happy to let the matter drop was because the initial response at home to the news of Isandlwana was much more supportive than he could have expected. On 7 March he wrote to Cambridge: 'I cannot tell you with what feelings of pride and gratitude I received the gracious messages from Her Majesty and from your Royal Highness saying that confidence in me as a commander was unshaken.' He must have assumed that Durnford and not he had been blamed for the disaster. Not until the arrival of Ellice's memorandum in early April would he be disabused of this notion. But in early March the outlook appeared brighter than it had for some time. Wood and Pearson were still holding out at Khambula and Eshowe respectively, though the latter was running short of supplies. Large numbers of reinforcements were on their way from Britain, and the Zulus seemed to have little appetite for more fighting. Native reports were 'unanimous in declaring', Chelmsford told Cambridge, 'that the Zulu nation has suffered such severe losses that they are very unwilling to assemble again for fighting'. Not that he believed such reports. 'They will fight again,' he wrote, 'and fight well.'

What Chelmsford told Wood – but not Cambridge – was that messengers had already been received from Cetshwayo, 'asking for peace and saying that our fighting against each other has been quite a mistake!' He added: 'I hope to be able to give him his answer next week by sending a column forward to Ekowe. Sir B. Frere is not prepared to approve of any reply but that of unconditional surrender and general disarmament, coupled with the conditions already laid down.' The reality is that neither Frere nor Chelmsford could afford a negotiated peace: it would both end Frere's dream of confederation and prevent Chelmsford from redeeming his tattered military reputation. Disraeli's government was more ambivalent: it desperately needed to restore Britain's prestige in the eyes of the world, but not at the expense of a costly drawn-out war that would tie its hands in other areas of foreign policy. Hicks Beach would make this point clear to Frere in a series of dispatches: first, in March, forbidding the annexation of Zululand; then, on 10 April, 'desiring that the war should be brought to a conclusion at the earliest moment consistent with the safety of the Colony and the honour of our arms'. But these dispatches would take a month to arrive, and, in the meantime, Frere and Chelmsford were not going to give the home authorities any excuse to cease hostilities.

11. Yet More Disasters

Just when things were beginning to look up for Chelmsford, news reached him of a fresh disaster in the north. Since losing Buller's horsemen in January, the task of Colonel Rowlands's No. 5 Column had been to guard the roads and garrison the Boer towns in northern Transvaal. This was partly to protect them from hostile Zulus but also to overawe the more volatile Boers, who wanted to take advantage of the war in Zululand by rebelling against British rule. The settlements most vulnerable to Zulu attack, however, were in the Disputed Territories, particularly the German village of Luneberg which was within striking distance of Mbilini's and Manyanyoba's kraals in the Ntombe Valley. The threat these chiefs posed was highlighted by their vicious night attack of 10/11 February on white farms in the Luneberg area. The owners, fortunately for them, had gone into laager at Luneberg at the beginning of the war, leaving their black workers exposed to the Zulu onslaught. To prevent a repeat, British troops were ordered to garrison Luneberg and four companies of the 80th Regiment, under Major Charles Tucker,* arrived on 15 February.

Of all the British battalions in South Africa, the 80th had the longest experience of the Zulu frontier. Three hundred of its men had been stationed in Newcastle as early as May 1876, and the rest of the battalion moved to Natal from the Cape a year later. In December 1877 it was garrisoned at Utrecht and later fought in the unsuccessful campaign against Sekhukhune. By January 1879 four of its companies were at Derby on the Transvaal border, and it was from there that they marched to Luneberg. Though not far from Wood's entrenchment at Khambula, and now technically

---

* Later General Sir Charles Tucker.

under his orders, the British garrison at Luneberg continued to use Rowlands's old supply line from Lydenburg via Derby.

In late February a convoy of eighteen wagons – loaded with ammunition, flour and mealies – left Lydenburg to resupply the new garrison. The first part of the journey was relatively safe and no escort was needed. But from the border of Transvaal proper the route was less secure, particularly the drift over the Ntombe River, which was just a few miles from Mbilini's stronghold. So on 1 March Tucker sent a company to escort the convoy from Derby. The convoy's progress was hampered, however, by incessant rain which swelled the rivers and softened the ground. By 5 March, with eight miles still to cover, the convoy was 'broken down at various intervals'. Tucker, fearing an attack by Mbilini, sent a messenger with orders for the company commander to get into Luneberg that night 'at any cost'. Unfortunately the officer took the message literally, abandoning the wagons and reaching the laager with his company at 10 p.m. The escort had managed to get six wagons as far as the Ntombe River, just four miles from Luneberg; but the lead wagon had stuck in the drift, trapping the others behind. A further six wagons with ammunition were three miles further away, trapped on the far side of the Little Ntombe.

The following day Tucker sent a party to recover the ammunition wagons. By now the fifty-yard-wide Ntombe, which at most times of the year was less than a foot deep, had burst its banks, making the drift unusable. So the party spent the day unloading the trapped wagon and pulling it clear. By nightfall they were back at Luneberg. 'The next morning,' remembered Tucker, 'I sent off Captain Moriarty with a hundred men and a wagon loaded with beams and barrels to make a raft, and ordered him to get the ammunition wagons out of their difficulties and bring them on to the other bank of the Intombi and laager them with the wagons already there and wait until the river went down.'

Captain David Moriarty, forty-two, was an experienced officer who had fought against Sekhukhune and served for three years on the Zulu border. He ably carried out his instructions, and by the evening of the 9th, despite torrential rain, had concentrated all the

wagons on the far side of the Ntombe. But the river was still far
too deep to ford, and he and his men were forced to sit it out and
hope the Zulus did not intervene. Tucker rode over during a break
in the weather on 11 March and found Moriarty's command split
into two: thirty-five men encamped on the Luneberg side of the
river; the remaining seventy on the opposite bank with the wagon
laager. Tucker crossed over on the raft to inspect the laager and
was not impressed with the inverted 'V' that Moriarty had constructed, its open base supposedly protected by the river. This was
partly because the water level had dropped a couple of feet, leaving
the two arms of the 'V' several yards short of the river; and partly
because the poles of the wagons were not 'run under one another
or outside the wagon in front', as Tucker had always laagered, but
were 'tied to the back of the wagon in front'. Mealie bags had been
placed up against the poles, but this still left a low gap between the
wagons of two to three feet high that would provide no 'protection
whatever in the event of the Zulus attacking in numbers'. The two
ammunition wagons, containing 90,000 rounds, had been placed
inside the laager and after dark were surrounded by the 250 oxen.
In the event of a night attack Tucker did not see how anyone
'could possibly get to them'. He was aware, however, of Moriarty's
difficulties: 'He was short of oxen, and in the fearful weather he
had experienced it was almost impossible for the men to have
placed them properly, and when they made the laager the water
was up to its base.' It was, in any case, too late in the day to alter
Moriarty's arrangements. So Tucker returned to Luneberg, telling
Moriarty to follow on as soon as he could.

Moriarty's subaltern, Lieutenant Henry Harward, had arrived
with Tucker and spent most of the day searching for lost cattle. He
returned exhausted at dusk and, for a time, fell asleep in Moriarty's
tent, which had been pitched outside the laager at the apex of the
'V'. But he was soon woken by Moriarty and told to take command
of the detachment on the far bank. Moriarty's insistence saved his
life if not his reputation. That night the usual two sentries were
posted on either side of Moriarty's tent, about twenty yards from
the laager. But their vision was restricted to about fifty yards because

of a slight rise to their front. The single sentry on the far side of the river was on higher ground and, if the night had not been wet and misty, he would have had a panoramic view of the laager beneath him.

At around 3.30 a.m. a single shot was fired not far from the camp. The alarm was given and the men turned out on both banks. But Moriarty decided it was nothing and, having told the sentries to keep a good look out, allowed the men to return to their beds. An hour and a half later, as the mist was beginning to clear, the sentry on the opposite bank saw to his horror a huge mass of Zulus advancing silently on the laager, their front extended across the whole valley. 'He at once fired his rifle and gave the alarm,' recorded Tucker. 'The sentries on the other side did the same. Of course the men were up in a moment, some men sleeping under the wagons and some in the tents; but before the men were in their positions the Zulus had fired a volley, thrown down their guns . . . and were around the wagons and on top of them, and even inside with the cattle, almost instantly. So quickly did they come, there was really no defence on the part of our men; it was simply each man fighting for his life, and in a very few minutes all was over, our men being simply slaughtered.'

Moriarty dashed out of his tent with a revolver in his hand and shot three warriors before an assegai was driven into his back. He managed to stagger towards the laager and was trying to climb over a disselboom* when he was shot. Falling to his knees, he cried: 'I am done; fire away, boys.' But few of his men had the opportunity to fight back and most, like him, were assegaied as they tumbled half asleep from their tents. The survivors fled towards the river, closely pursued by Zulus, as the detachment on the far bank tried to give covering fire. Colour-Sergeant Anthony Booth, Harward's deputy, recalled:

I saw the kaffirs on the opposite side of the river, they were then crowding on the tents and wagons. We at once opened fire, and kept the fire up

* Pole at the front of a wagon to which oxen were attached.

for about ten minutes or ¼ of an hour; the kaffirs were then in the river, in great numbers coming towards us, and at the same time assegaiing the men from the other side who were attempting to cross; about 200 Zulus came to our side of the river, and as we saw no more of our men crossing the river, we commenced firing and retiring, having received the order from Mr Harward.

Booth was too discreet to mention in his official report that no sooner had Harward given this order than he grabbed the nearest horse, not his own, and galloped off, leaving his men and a handful of naked survivors from the far bank to withdraw as best they could on foot. For three miles this small group of forty or so men was pursued by Zulus. Every time the Zulus got close, Booth and a rearguard of the bolder spirits stopped and fired a volley, causing their pursuers to disperse. Four men made the mistake of splitting from this group and were all killed. Booth and the rest made it to Raby's Farm, about two miles from Luneberg, where the Zulus finally gave up the chase. Booth's inspired leadership was later rewarded with the Victoria Cross. 'Had it not been for the coolness displayed by this NCO,' read his citation, 'not one man would have escaped.'

Harward's craven conduct could not have been more of a contrast. On reaching the laager at Luneberg, he made straight for Tucker's tent and shouted: 'Major! Major!' Tucker recalled: 'I was up in an instant, and there, at my tent door on his knees, the picture of death, was Harward. He gasped out, "The Camp is in the hands of the enemy; they are all slaughtered, and I have galloped in for my life." He then fell on to my bed in a dead faint.' Tucker revived him with some water and, on hearing his story, ordered all the available horses to be saddled and left instructions for a further 150 men to follow on foot. About a mile from the river Tucker and his horsemen could see 'dense masses of Zulus' leaving the scene. He wrote:

As we approached the Intombi Drift a fearful and horrible sight presented itself, and the stillness of the spot was awful; there were our men lying all about the place, some naked and some only half clad. On the opposite side of the drift . . . all the bodies were full of assegai wounds and nearly all were disembowelled . . . Nearly everything had been broken or torn to pieces, the tents being in shreds and the ammunition boxes torn to atoms, the mealies and flour thrown all about the place. They had killed all the dogs save one, and that we found with an assegai wound right through its neck . . . I shouted at the top of my voice so that any wounded man might know we were at hand. Instantly out of the earth came one of our men and two Kaffirs.

The white soldier had had an extraordinary escape. Throwing himself into the water, though he could not swim, he was carried downstream until he managed to grab hold of the far bank and haul himself out. As he lay on the bank trying to recover, he was attacked by a Zulu wielding an assegai. But he was able to catch hold of the blade, break the shaft and stab the Zulu with his own spear. With more Zulus about, he slipped back into the water and covered his head with grass. He and two African drivers emerged from their hiding places on hearing Tucker's cry.

Moriarty's naked body was found face down just inside the laager. 'He wasn't disembowelled,' recorded Tucker. 'He was a big fine man with quite white hair, and seems to have been known, for we have since heard from a woman that has come in from Manyanyoba that the white captain himself killed three of Manyanyoba's sons.' His body and that of a Dr Cobbin were brought into Luneberg for burial. The rest of the dead – sixty soldiers of the 80th, two white wagon conductors and fifteen black voorloopers – were buried in a long trench.

Tucker estimated the number of attacking Zulus at 'not less than 4,000'. In fact fewer than a thousand were involved, including followers of Mbilini and Manyanyoba, some abaQulusi and even a few members of the royal amabutho who had fought at Isandlwana. They returned to their mountain strongholds with the spoils, leaving thirty dead on the ground.

The cause of the disaster was a combination of bad luck – atrocious weather delaying the recovery of the wagons and weakening the

laager's defences – and inadequate precautions. More sentries
should have been posted further out, and the laager itself was
poorly sited and constructed. For these errors Moriarty was chiefly
responsible. But with Moriarty dead, someone else had to take the
blame and the obvious scapegoat was Harward. 'The moment
Harward saw the Zulus coming across the river,' wrote his commanding officer, 'he saddled up the horse of another man and
galloped out of the camp.' Harward did his best to excuse his
desertion. 'I endeavoured to rally my men,' he reported, 'but
they were much scattered, and finding re-formation impossible, I
mounted my horse and galloped into Luneberg at utmost speed,
and reported all that had taken place.' Colour-Sergeant Booth saw
it differently in a letter to his wife: 'Lieutenant Harward saddled his
horse and galloped away leaving us to do the best we could.'

Having read the reports, the duke of Cambridge thought Tucker
was partly to blame. 'Surely,' he wrote to Chelmsford in mid April,
'there must have been great carelessness in the manner in which
this small detachment was left out so long & so short a distance from
the station of Luneberg . . . without being properly supported.' But
his greatest criticism was reserved for Harward, describing his report
as 'a very *shady account* of his own proceedings in *riding away* to
Luneberg at *full speed* and leaving his men to their fate, when he
thought all was lost'. He should, in the duke's opinion, 'have stuck
to them' and sent someone else to raise the alarm.

There were marked similarities between Harward's conduct and
that of Major Spalding at Rorke's Drift, the only difference being
that Spalding did not abandon his men while an enemy attack was
actually in progress. Cambridge was all for Chelmsford making an
example of Harward. But no action was taken until early the
following year, by which time Wolseley had replaced Chelmsford.
Wolseley had a reputation as a strict disciplinarian, and Harward's
abandonment of his men was, in his opinion, an all too common
feature of the Zulu War that deserved punishment. So Harward
was brought back to South Africa and court-martialled for two
main offences: failing to take adequate security precautions and
deserting his men. The first charge was clearly Moriarty's responsi-

bility (not least because Harward had only reached the laager the day before the disaster) and would never have stuck. The court also accepted Harward's defence that, by the time he galloped off, the situation was so bad that he could no longer exercise his authority. He was acquitted on both counts. But Wolseley took the unusual step of refusing to confirm the verdict:

Had I released this officer without making any remarks upon the verdict in question, it would have been a tacit acknowledgement that I concurred in what appears to me to be a monstrous theory, viz., that a regimental officer who is the only officer present with a party of soldiers actually and seriously engaged with the enemy, can, under any pretext whatever, be justified in deserting them, and by so doing, abandoning them to their fate. The more helpless the position in which an officer finds his men, the more it is his bounden duty to stay and share their fortune, whether for good or ill.

It was in the context of the Harward case that Wolseley condemned the hero worship of Lieutenants Coghill and Melvill as 'monstrous'. They had failed to save their lives by 'bolting'; Harward had succeeded and Wolseley was not about to let him get away with it. Though he was freed and returned to duty, his career was over and he resigned his commission in May 1880.

The impact of the Ntombe massacre, a relatively minor affair, was more psychological than practical. 'It is difficult to convey to those at a distance,' wrote Sir Bartle Frere to the duke of Cambridge, 'an idea of how serious are the moral effects of such misfortune.' Frere was particularly concerned about the impact it would have on Chelmsford. He 'seems to have recovered from all he went through in that terrible last week of January', noted Frere, 'but he is far too heavily worked' and his health was still a cause of 'great anxiety'. He need not have worried. The first reinforcements had begun to arrive, and Chelmsford had his thoughts fixed firmly on the relief of Eshowe, an operation he was planning to lead himself at the end of the month. Pearson's decision to remain at Eshowe rather than withdrawing to the Lower Tugela had had, Chelmsford told Cambridge on 16 March, 'a very good effect amongst the natives, who say that as we are still in Zululand we have not been defeated'. Chelmsford had also received the excellent news that Prince Hamu,★ Cetshwayo's eldest brother, who lived north of the Black Mfolozi River, had gone over to Colonel Wood with all his followers (many of whom had fought at Isandlwana). Chelmsford considered it to be a 'very important event' that would, he hoped, 'spread doubt and distrust in Zululand'. In the hope that he could capitalize on this breakthrough, and also remove some of the pressure from the expedition to relieve Eshowe, Chelmsford gave Wood carte blanche to attempt any offensive operations that he thought 'fit to undertake'. An earlier letter of 17 March had been more specific: 'If you are in a position to make any forward movement about the 27th [March], so that the news of it may reach the neighbourhood of Eshowe about the 29th, I think it might have a good effect.'

Wood's response was immediate. On 28 March, soon after receiving Chelmsford's second letter, he launched a two-pronged attack on the abaQulusi stronghold on Hlobane Mountain. It was an extremely risky operation: not only did Wood not know the exact number of defenders (the estimates ranged from 1,000 to 4,000) but he also had little detailed knowledge of the terrain on the top. At 1,500 feet, the mountain was not particularly high, but it was 'strongly protected by krantzes and terraces, huge masses of boulders and scrub, intersected with stone walls, backed up by caves and fissures in the mountain itself, accessible only by footpaths from the plains below'. It also had two plateaus – an upper and a lower – linked by a terrifyingly steep and rocky path. The eastern plateau was the highest and biggest: about two miles long and a mile and a half wide, its gently undulating grassland strewn with rocks and

---

★ Hamu had commanded a wing of Cetshwayo's victorious army at the Battle of Ndondakusuka in 1856. Before the war he had voted in favour of handing over Sihayo's sons and was regarded by Cetshwayo with considerable and justifiable suspicion. Even by the standards of the Zulu royal family he was a huge man: over six feet tall and almost twenty stone.

boulders. Below it, 700 feet above the plain, lay the smaller western plateau, just a mile long and half a mile wide. A less suitable ground for cavalry is difficult to imagine.

The plan was for Colonel Buller to ascend the eastern end of the mountain with 400 horsemen and a battalion of Wood's Irregulars, while Lieutenant-Colonel Cecil Russell – recently arrived with his squadron of Imperial Mounted Infantry – took 200 cavalry and the other battalion of Wood's Irregulars as far up the western end of the upper plateau as he could 'without incurring severe loss'. Buller's force, which would attack 'at all hazards', was the hammer, Russell's the anvil. 'It is not intended that the western reconnaissance should force the position against strong resistance,' read Wood's order, 'though it will of course advance when it is learnt that the summit has been gained by the eastern force, or sooner if not strongly opposed.' Wood, however, was 'not very sanguine of success'. He warned Chelmsford on the 27th: 'We do not know how steep the Eastern end may be, but I think we ought to make a stir here, to divert attention from you, although, as you see by our last reports, it is asserted that you have only Coast tribes against you, and that all Cetywayo's people are coming here.'

Wood's intelligence, as ever, would prove to be correct. In response to requests for assistance from the hard-pressed abaQulusi – and disillusioned by the frosty British response to his peace overtures – Cetshwayo had remobilized his army at oNdini on 22 March with the intention of sending the bulk of it against Wood at Khambula. This army of 20,000 strong – mainly composed of regiments that had fought at Isandlwana and Rorke's Drift – set off from oNdini on the 24th. It was nominally commanded by Chief Mnyamana of the Buthelezi, Cetshwayo's chief minister and the second most powerful man in the kingdom; but tactical control was still in the hands of the victorious Chief Ntshingwayo, with the aggressive Chief Zibhebhu as his deputy. By extraordinary coincidence – not to mention bad luck for the British – the army was due to liaise with abaQulusi irregulars in the vicinity of Hlobane on 28 March, the day that Wood was planning to launch his attack on the mountain.

Given that Wood had advance intelligence that a large Zulu army was on its way, and that he knew little about the position he was about to attack, his operation against Hlobane smacks more than a little of recklessness. But he was determined, come hell or high water, to help Chelmsford and had complete confidence in Buller's fighting capacity, if not in Russell's.* He had also taken the precaution of keeping back his slow-moving and therefore vulnerable infantry, and of ordering both Buller and Russell to post scouts to 'watch the country to the southward' for signs of Cetshwayo's army.

What made this ambitious operation possible was the recent addition to his command of various units of cavalry: from the demoralized and inactive No. 3 Column had been sent the unpopular Lieutenant-Colonel Cecil Russell with his squadron of Imperial Mounted Infantry and the Edendale Troop of the Natal Native Horse; Commandant Friedrich Schermbrucker and 110 men of the Kaffrarian Rifles, now horsed, had been transferred from the Luneberg garrison; Baker's Horse, 150-strong, had arrived from the eastern Cape; and two units of volunteer cavalry – Commandant Pieter Raaf's Transvaal Rangers and Colonel Frederick Weatherley's Border Horse, 200 men in all – had come from Rowland's column. Weatherley was one of those larger-than-life characters that frequently appeared on the fringes of Empire in the Victorian period. Born in Canada in the 1820s, he had, like Captain Louis Nolan of Light Brigade infamy, served with a crack Austrian cavalry regiment before gaining a commission in the British Army. Some accounts state that he charged with Nolan at Balaklava, but in truth he joined the 4th Light Dragoons after that famous disaster. He did, however, fight with the 6th Dragoons in the Indian Mutiny, where he met and befriended Bartle Frere. His fellow officers were not admirers, one describing him as a patronizing name-dropper and married to a 'flashy' woman who – à la Mrs Duberly† – accompanied her

---

* Believing Russell to be incompetent, Wood had already asked Chelmsford to transfer him but without success.
† Fanny Duberly, the wife of the paymaster of the 8th Hussars, who joined her husband in the Crimea.

husband on campaign 'carrying a revolver, riding like a man and laying about the natives with a riding crop'. He later left the 6th Dragoons under something of a cloud, and in 1877, having lived for a time in Brighton, emigrated to South Africa with his wife and two sons, and bought land near Lydenburg. It was after his flighty wife – to no one's great surprise – left him for a confidence trickster that he raised the Border Horse for service in Zululand. Most of its fifty-four recruits came from the English settler community of the Transvaal and included two of his sons, one a boy of just fourteen.

For the attack on Hlobane, Weatherley's Border Horse was assigned to the main 700-man force under Buller. It also included 158 men of the Frontier Light Horse (under Captain Robert Barton), eighty of Baker's Horse, seventy Transvaal Rangers, Piet Uys and thirty-two of his burghers, the 2nd Battalion of Wood's Irregulars (many of them powerfully built Swazis) and a Royal Artillery rocket battery: a total of 396 horsemen, nine artillerymen and 300 black auxiliaries. Russell had fewer horsemen but more auxiliaries: 206 and 440 respectively.

Because he had the furthest to go, Buller set off from Khambula at 8 a.m. on 27 March and pretended to set up camp well to the south of Hlobane by lighting campfires. It was a ruse to make the Zulus on the mountain think he was about to strike deeper into Zululand, as he had so many times before: but no sooner had darkness fallen than his men were on the move to a bivouac six miles south-east of Hlobane. It was during this move that Buller lost contact with Weatherley's Border Horse. One of Weatherley's officers would later claim that they never received the order to march. Whatever the truth, the result was that Weatherley and his men arrived late for the battle, with tragic consequences.

Russell's force left Khambula at one in the afternoon and, having covered about fifteen miles, bivouacked five miles to the west of the mountain. Wood and his staff joined them, as it was getting dark and, before turning in, the column commander had a long talk with two men familiar with the layout of Hlobane: Piet Uys, who had stayed behind to talk to him, and Captain Charlie Potter of Wood's Irregulars. Wood recalled:

I asked whether, should we have the bad luck after taking the mountain to see Cetewayo's army advancing, we could get down on the North side, and Mr Potter assured me that we could, by leading our horses. Piet Uys was confident that Colonel Buller would get up, without serious loss, and we agreed that, except in the probable contingency of the Zulu main army coming in sight, our operation ought to be a success; then Piet turned to me, said, 'Kurnall, if you are killed I will take care of your children, and if I am killed you do the same for mine.'

Wood agreed.

Buller and his men – less Weatherley's Border Horse, which was still missing – set off from their bivouac at three in the morning of the 28th, and soon reached the narrow rocky path that led up the eastern side of Hlobane. A morning mist concealed their movement and, though they had to lead their horses up the last part of an increasingly steep ascent, they had almost reached the summit when they were fired on by abaQulusi sentries in rocks just below the crest. Buller ordered his most reliable troops, the FLH, to clear the rocks, and as they did so two officers – Lieutenant George Williams and Lieutenant Baron von Steitencron* – and a trooper were shot and killed. Wood's Irregulars were also brought forward and, according to their commander, Major William Knox-Leet, 'swarmed up the hill with praiseworthy courage and rapidity'. Within minutes the Zulu defenders were streaming back across the plateau, and the eastern summit was in Buller's hands. But his first sight of the mountain top was a shock. 'I was horrified at the size of the place,' he wrote later, 'and its unpracticability. A careful inspection showed me there were only 3 ways off the top.' These were: the one he had come up by; a second path to the north-east that led down to the Ityenka Nek;† and a route down the north-western corner – later dubbed the 'Devil's Pass' – to the lower plateau. 'Both of the latter were,' in Buller's

---

* An Austrian-born mercenary who had served as adjutant to Field Marshal von Benedek during the Austro-Prussian War of 1866.
† A saddle of land that linked Hlobane to the next mountain.

opinion, 'paths such as no man in cold blood would try to get a horse down.'

The western path, however, was by far the most dangerous of the three. Buller described it:

On each side of the path was krantz (i.e. precipice) about 120 feet high. The side precipices were formed of masses of rectangular boulders (if there are such things) piled one over the other, in awful confusion, but perpendicularly. At the corner three rocks assumed a certain amount of regularity, and offered a series of insecure footholds as narrow ledges straight down the precipice and about 8 to 12 feet wide. At the bottom of this path (if path it could be called) was the lower plateau from which there was another descent of some 800 yards. Almost as steep but less dangerous, as the rocks were filled in with soil and grass covered.

But there was no time to worry about that at the time. Instead he got on with the task of securing the upper plateau and seizing as many abaQulusi oxen as he could find. He wrote:

The natives who occupied [the plateau] disappeared into the rocks and caves of the side krantzes. These the 2nd Battalion Wood's Irregulars, worked through splendidly, collecting many cattle. To assist them, I placed men all round the edge of the plateau to fire into the rocks below, and I then proceeded to the western edge, beneath which I found Lieutenant-Colonel Russell with a few of his men, the rest being about one mile off, having apparently just ascended the lower Hlobana mountain.

Russell had left his bivouac at 4 a.m. and reached the foot of the western end of the mountain at dawn. By 6.30 a.m. his vanguard of black auxiliaries had made it on to the lower plateau. When Russell himself arrived soon after, he was informed by Lieutenant Cecil Williams, commanding Hamu's warriors, that 'Buller's force was already in possession of the upper plateau, and that he and others could be seen upon it.' Russell remembered:

I at once moved with a small party of the first formed men to try to communicate with Colonel Buller, while the rear of my column was still coming up the hill. I was fired at and my escort returned the fire. I heard Colonel Buller shout 'Bring your men up to fire,' or words to that effect. I sent back to bring up the rest of the force which quickly arrived. In the meantime it had been pointed out that there were large quantities of cattle on the sides of the Hlobana Hill, within easy reach, I therefore directed Commandant White's battalion to go and collect the cattle on the south side of the Nek, and Oham's people those on the north side of the Nek. The Mounted Infantry, Basutos, and Schermbrucker's Corps were ready to cover them with fire. Commandant White brought back a considerable number of cattle to the plateau, but Oham's people drove what they found in a westerly direction, towards the Zunguin. I did not see them again during the day. Captain Browne, M.I., had been directed to cross the Nek, and to get to the top of the plateau, to find out, if possible, if assistance was required from me by Colonel Buller, and generally what was the situation. Everything appeared to be nearly quiet and the whole object of the reconnaissance to be gained.

Contrary to his orders, however, Russell made no serious attempt to get his force up on to the western end of the upper plateau. This was chiefly because he considered the precipitous rocky path that connected the two plateaus as impractical for cavalry. And so it was. But that should not have prevented him from sending either dismounted soldiers or his black auxiliaries – or both – up the path. Browne and twenty of his IMI had, after all, made it up safely. Instead Russell dispersed his force in search of cattle.

Wood had set off that morning even earlier than Russell. Accompanied by his three staff officers, a tiny escort of eight mounted infantrymen and seven mounted Zulus (under Prince Mthonga kaMpande, Cetshwayo's half-brother and rival), Wood intended to exercise a loose overall command by following Buller up the eastern ascent. He and his principal staff officer, Captain the Honourable Ronald Campbell, the second son of the earl of Cawdor, were silent as they rode towards the mountain's sinister outline. But the two younger staff officers – Lieutenant Henry

Lysons, the son of the quartermaster-general, and Llewellyn Lloyd, Wood's interpreter – chattered as gaily as if riding out in England. One of them asked Wood if he was worried they might not reach the top. 'Oh no,' replied Wood, 'we shall get up.'

'Then of what are you thinking?'

'Well,' answered Wood gloomily, 'which one of you will be writing to my wife tonight, or about which of you young men I shall be writing to parents or wife.'

A little further on Wood met Colonel Weatherley and his detachment of Border Horse heading in the opposite direction. Having listened to Weatherley's lame explanation that he had lost his way the previous night, Wood told him to move 'to the sound of the firing, which was now audible on the North-East face of the mountain, where we could just discern the rear of Colonel Buller's column mounting the summit'. But no sooner did the Border Horse come under fire from rocks to their right than they stopped and took cover. An indignant Wood rode past them with his staff and escort and, followed by just six of the Irregulars, continued his ascent. But the ground was now so steep and rugged that they were forced to dismount, all but Wood leaving their horses in a disused stone kraal on a narrow ledge. A 'bad walker', he chose to lead his horse. Less than a hundred yards from the summit the group came under 'well-directed fire' from the front and both flanks, 'the enemy being concealed behind huge boulders of rock'. The bulk of the Border Horse, 200 yards further back, opened up in response, causing Mr Lloyd to remark: 'I am glad of that, for it will make the Zulus shoot badly.'

Moments later a Zulu popped up from behind a rock fifty yards away and shot Lloyd in the back. 'I am hit!' he exclaimed.

'Badly?' asked Wood.

'Yes, very badly; my back's broken!' Wood tried to lift him but found his weight too much. So Campbell took over and carried him back to the stone kraal, where the escort was now sheltering. Wood kept climbing but had only gone a few yards higher when his horse was shot and killed, knocking him down as it fell. Assuring his worried comrades that he was unhurt, he scrambled down to the kraal, where he found Lloyd dying. He tried to pour a little of Lysons's brandy down his throat 'but his teeth were already set'.

Wood now told Campbell to order Weatherley to clear the cave from which his horse had been shot. 'He received the order three times,' recalled Wood, 'but would not leave the cover where he was sheltering.' In disgust Campbell shouted: 'Damn him! He's a coward. I'll turn them out,' and ran forward. Lysons asked if he could go as well and Wood replied: 'Yes! Forward the Personal Escort.' But of the eight men who made up the escort, all of whom were 'disengaged', only four answered the call. These six reached the entrance to the cave without injury, but, on going in, Campbell was shot at point-blank range, the gun being so close that his head was 'half blown off & death was instantaneous'.* Without hesitating, Lysons and a Private Edmund Fowler leapt over his body and fired into the cave, killing one Zulu and forcing another to leave by a separate entrance.†

Within the space of a few minutes Wood had lost two of his best officers and closest friends. Campbell's death was a particularly heavy blow, Wood later telling his widow that he had loved him like a son. To honour his two comrades Wood insisted on burying them then and there, at a spot a little further down the mountain that was clear of rocks. Wood also asked his bugler, Walkinshaw, to retrieve from his dead horse's saddle-bag the prayer-book that Campbell had lent him. That Wood was prepared to risk the life of his favourite bugler for the sake of a prayer-book is an indication of how shattered he was by Campbell's death. The drawn-out and dangerous ordeal of digging the graves with nothing more effective than assegais is additional proof, if any is needed, that Wood had temporarily lost his sense of priority. Even with the approach of several hundred Zulus from the Ityenka Nek he refused to halt the work, insisting instead on the graves being lengthened so that the bodies could lie flat. Only when he was satisfied with the fit did he begin to read an abridged

---

* Wood later claimed that had Campbell lived he would have recommended him for a VC (Emery, 177).
† Both were awarded the VC.

form of the Burial Service from Campbell's prayer-book. Fortunately some of Buller's men, seeing Wood in trouble, had by now opened fire on the advancing Zulus, forcing them to seek cover. It was at this point that a sheepish Weatherley, perhaps hoping to make up for the earlier timidity of his men, asked for and was given permission to move down the hill 'to regain Colonel Buller's track', which had been lost during the fighting. 'He had lost only 6 men dead, and 7 wounded,' sneered Wood, though that was a quarter of his total. Wood himself decided to skirt round the base of the mountain and 'see how the other column had fared'.

Buller meanwhile – having collected more than 2,000 cattle and 'finding the Zulus were becoming every minute more difficult to prevent from mustering on the upper plateau' – had given orders for his scattered detachments to meet at the eastern end of the mountain. 'On arrival there,' he wrote, 'I found that the Zulus had been largely reinforced, and were pressing us hard, and that, owing to the great size of the mountain, and the great difficulty of the path by which we had to retire, there was every possibility of the enemy being able to assemble at one end out of fire, then rush upon us as we retired. I accordingly sent Captain Barton down the hill with 30 men to bury Lieutenant Williams at once and return to camp direct.'

Bobby Barton was a great favourite of Buller. A special service officer on detachment from the Coldstream Guards, he had been living cheek by jowl with Buller since the previous July and had recently taken over the day-to-day running of the FLH. Buller regarded him as a 'dear good honest, loveable creature' in whom he had yet to find 'anything to reprobate, but each day something new to like'. Imagine Buller's feelings when, shortly after dispatching Barton, his scouts drew his attention to activity in the valley to the south: marching in five great columns were the 20,000 men of the main Zulu Army. Mehlokazulu, one of the heroes of Isandlwana, was with them and recalled:

The English forces went up the mountain and did not see us; we came round the mountain . . . a great many were killed on the top; they were killed by the people on the mountain. We did not go up the mountain, but the men whom the English forces had attacked followed them up. They had beaten the Qulusi, and succeeded in getting all the cattle of the whole neighbourhood which were there, and would have taken away the whole had we not rescued them.

Mehlokazulu was referring to the column of regiments – including the iNgobamakhosi, uKhandempemvu and uMcijo – that was detached from the main army to assist the abaQulusi in cutting off the British retreat down the east side of the mountain. Buller described the hopelessness of his situation in a letter to his aunt: 'We were 30 miles from camp. Our horses had been under saddle since 3 a.m. It was then 10 and they had had nothing to eat really since the previous morning. I saw that we had not a chance of getting back the way we had come so I at once sent 2 men after Barton telling him to return by the right of the mountain. Alas for the use of careless words! By rights I meant the north side. Poor Barton, going down the [mountain] with his back to it, understood that he was to turn to his right and so went to the left or S. side on which was the Zulu impi.'

On the way down Barton and his men bumped into Weatherley's Border Horse coming the other way. Barton explained that, with a large Zulu impi on its way, he had orders to push round the southern side of Hlobane. Weatherley decided to join him. As the seventy or so horsemen reached the corner of the mountain and began to ride west they were confronted with the chilling sight of a huge Zulu column racing towards them. With little hope of getting past them, they turned back and, under a heavy crossfire, headed for the Ityenka Nek. Chased by the uKhandempemvu and uMcijo, and with the abaQulusi streaming down from the mountain to cut them off, the terrified horsemen headed for the centre of the nek. Captain Dennison of the Border Horse, one of the few survivors, remembered the ground beyond the nek was 'extremely steep with a succession of precipitous ledges'. Some troopers simply tumbled to their deaths; others were assegaied as they struggled to get down. Sitshitshili, a mounted officer of the uMcijo Regiment, followed several men and killed them. As he approached another victim, the man turned his carbine round and shot himself. It was during this terrifying descent that Weatherley and his fourteen-year-old son were killed.

About twenty-five men made it over the nek, including Barton, Dennison and a Lieutenant Poole, who had lost his horse. Dennison claimed that they tried to make a stand, 'but finding the enemy outflanking us we had to race for our lives across country in the direction of Makatee's Kop'. Many were killed during the pursuit, including Barton and Poole. Their fate remained a mystery for fourteen months after the battle until Wood heard the details from Sitshitshili. Barton had taken up Poole behind him but their combined weight was too much for his exhausted horse and Sitshitshili easily caught them. They dismounted and separated, but Sitshitshili quickly overhauled Poole and shot him. He then went after Barton, who stopped, pointed his revolver and pulled the trigger. Nothing. It had misfired. The Zulu's response was to lay down his weapons and make signs for Barton to surrender.* As Barton lifted his hat in acknowledgement, he was shot and wounded by another warrior. 'I could not let anyone else kill him,' recalled Sitshitshili, 'so I ran up and assegaied him.'†

Wood was on his way round the base of the mountain when Prince Mthonga, whom he had sent out to the ridge on his left flank, indicated by signs that a large impi was approaching. 'Cantering up,' recalled Wood, 'I had a good view of the Force, which was marching in 5 columns, with the flanks advanced, and a dense Centre – the normal Zulu attack formation.' It was 10.30 a.m. Wood at once dispatched Lysons to Russell with the following order: 'There is a large army coming this way from the South. Get into position on the Zunguin Nek.' Wood's intention was for Russell to take up a defensive position on the nek of land between the lower plateau of Hlobane and the Zungwini Mountain, from

---

* 'Did you really want to spare him?' asked Wood. 'Yes,' replied Sitshitshili. 'Cetewayo had ordered us to bring one or two Indunas down to Ulundi, and I had already killed seven men' (Wood, II, 55n).

† At Wood's request, Sitshitshili located both bodies and helped to bury them.

where he could cover Buller's retreat. But Russell interpreted the order to mean a saddle of land to the west of Zungwini between it and Khambula. What possible good he hoped to do there, when he knew that Buller was exposed on Hlobane, he never did explain. In his report Wood rejected Russell's excuses and came perilously close to accusing him of cowardice:

Colonel Russell reports that he moved from the Inhlobana to Zunguin's Neck, but this is incorrect. On the contrary, he went away six miles to the western corner of the range, and for which Wood's Irregulars . . . and [Hamu's] men were making, driving the abandoned cattle. Colonel Russell ordered all the captured cattle to be abandoned and made off very rapidly under the western end of the range. He thus uncovered the retreat of Oham's people, about 80 of whom were killed by Zulus running down from the Inhlobana.

Wood's criticism was minor compared to the fury that was vented upon Russell by the men he abandoned on Hlobane, particularly Buller and Russell's own deputy, Lieutenant Browne.

Having spotted the advancing Zulu Army, Buller knew that his only hope of escape was down the 'Devil's Pass' to the lower plateau, where he 'supposed Russell was'. From there he could 'get back to camp easily by the E. of Zunguin if we could avoid the Zulu army, and tolerably easily by the N. or W. of Zunguin if we could not'. He therefore gave orders for his force to withdraw to the west side of the mountain, but as it did so it was pursued by hundreds of abaQulusi, who had appeared as if by magic from rocks and caves. Protected by a rearguard of the FLH, however, Buller and most of his men reached the pass only to discover that 'Russell was gone' and the retreat was 'uncovered'. Russell had even abandoned his deputy, Lieutenant Browne, who was waiting for orders at the top of the pass. But this was no time for recriminations. Those would come later.

Major Knox-Leet, commanding the 2nd Wood's Irregulars, was among the first to attempt the fearsome descent. He remembered 'an almost perpendicular krantz composed of extremely irregular boulders and stones and very narrow. With so many men and horses to go down the operation at any time would have been an extremely difficult one, but with the enemy pressing on it appeared almost impossible.'

For a time, with Lieutenant Browne and the rearguard holding the abaQulusi back, the operation went relatively well, and many made it to the bottom in one piece, though a number had lost their horses. Buller wrote: 'We had to get down the frightful path under a constant & ever increasing fire, but we should have done tolerably & safely I believe had not my stupid rearguard ceased firing, mistaking Zulus for friends. In a moment the Zulus were among us in the rocks. How I got down I shall never know.'

Captain Cecil D'Arcy of the Frontier Light Horse was halfway down when a rock 'the size of a small piano' struck his horse on the rear leg, 'cutting it right off'. As he struggled to release its saddle he heard a scream. 'I looked up,' he recorded, 'and saw the Zulus right in among the white men, stabbing horses and men. I made a jump and got down somehow or other, and ran as hard as I could with seventy rounds of ball cartridge, a carbine, revolver, field-glass, and heavy boots.' D'Arcy's subaltern, Lieutenant Arthur Blaine, was in the middle of the mêlée: 'We could not hit them even with our carbines, for we were too jammed up. The officers could not use their swords. A lot of us got down, and then we rallied our fellows and made a stand for a time.'

Thanks to Buller, the FLH did indeed make a stand; but for a time it was touch and go. 'When I got to the bottom there was a sort of panic,' recalled Buller. 'Most of the men were dismounted & for a moment I feared a catastrophe but they soon rallied.' Seventeen men were killed during the descent, including Piet Uys.★ He had got down safely, but, seeing his son in trouble, he went to assist him and was assegaied in the back. 'He was my guide, counsellor & friend,' wrote Buller, 'his loss is a most serious one to

★ Wood kept his promise to Uys by recommending that 36,000 acres of government land be set aside for his nine children. The award was eventually authorized by the Colonial Office after pressure from both Frere and the queen.

all South Africa & irreparable to me. He really was the finest man morally speaking I have ever met.'

With Buller and the FLH acting as rearguard, most of the survivors were able to cross the lower plateau and descend to the plain by the same steep krantz that Russell had used. The exceptions were three officers who chose a more direct route over the north face: Major Knox-Leet, mounted on an artillery pack-horse, one of his subalterns called Lieutenant Duncombe and Lieutenant Metcalfe Smith of the FLH, who was on foot. They had only got down a short way when a crowd of Zulus appeared at the crest, spotted them and began the pursuit with 'loud shouts'. Knox-Leet recalled: 'The side of the hill was extremely steep, and very irregular, with large boulders in all directions, and when we had got about half way we found we had taken the wrong direction and were over a precipice.' Their only option was to retrace their steps in the hope of re-finding the path, which they managed to do with the Zulus almost upon them. With his horse done in, Duncombe dismounted and tried to escape on foot, turning three times to shoot Zulus who were within fifteen yards of him. But eventually he was overtaken and killed. Metcalfe Smith would have gone the same way if Knox-Leet had not urged him to grab on to his horse's pack-saddle. Even then he was unable to keep up, forcing Knox-Leet to stop and haul him up behind him. 'My horse at this time was almost exhausted,' remembered Knox-Leet, 'and the ground even rougher and steeper than higher up, and the Zulus . . . were all but on us.' Other Zulus could be seen running up the valley below them in an attempt to cut them off from the rest of Buller's force, which was just beginning to emerge to their left. There seemed to be no hope. But with a final effort Knox-Leet's horse reached the valley floor ahead of the Zulus and cantered off to safety. 'Had it not been for Major Leet,' wrote Metcalfe Smith, 'nothing could have saved me, and I owe him the deepest gratitude, which I shall feel as long as I live.' Knox-Leet's selfless action was doubly commendable in that he, like Coghill, had injured his knee a few days earlier and would almost certainly have been killed if he had been separated from his horse.

The ordeal for the survivors of Buller's column was far from over. Still in close pursuit were abaQulusi irregulars, and, with only about half the horsemen still mounted, progress was slow. Buller personally rescued at least three men from certain death by galloping back and taking them up behind him. One of them was Captain D'Arcy, who had himself committed a selfless act of bravery by giving his replacement horse to a wounded FLH trooper. Buller was awarded a VC and thought that D'Arcy should have been. The latter eventually won one in a subsequent engagement.

Only when Buller and his men reached Russell's position on the saddle beyond Zungwini were they truly safe; which is more than could be said for Russell when he came face to face with a furious Buller. Russell tried to defend himself by saying he had been given no orders to wait for him. 'Perhaps not,' replied Buller, 'but you had no orders to abandon me. I trust I may not go out with you again.' The following day, Russell sought Buller out and admitted: 'You are quite right. My metier is not South African fighting.' Buller told Wood that he was 'damned' if he would 'ever serve again in a joint operation with Russell'. Wood paid little attention to the threat until it was repeated by Lieutenant Browne. None of them would go so far as to label Russell a coward; rather, he was incompetent and 'unable to act in emergencies'. Wood put it this way in a letter to Chelmsford: 'There is no want of personal courage on Colonel Russell's part, but I firmly believe his presence here in command is detrimental to the Public Interest.' He recommended that Russell be given the non-combat role of commanding a remount depot. Chelmsford – who had his own reservations about Russell – was quick to sanction the move.

Wood and his tiny escort remained on Zungwini Mountain until 7 p.m., 'hoping to cover the retreat of any more of our men who might come up'. Buller finally appeared and, seeing Wood, uttered a heartfelt 'Thank God!' His greatest fear was that Wood had been cut off at the eastern end of the mountain. 'I never knew until that day,' wrote Wood, 'the depth of regard which Buller felt for me.' Buller's work, however, was not yet done. At 9 p.m., having returned to Khambula camp, he received word that some survivors were coming in from the direction of Potter's Store, which lay to the north-east. Buller was exhausted, mentally and physically, and had hardly slept for two days; it was dark, pouring with rain and the country was swarming with hostile Zulus. Yet he never hesitated. Hoping against hope that one of the survivors was Barton, he saddled his horse and left at once, leading spare horses behind him. A little later he returned with Dennison and the six survivors of the Border Horse.

Wood later told the queen that it was 'wonderful' what Buller 'had done on that terrible day'. Chelmsford, having visited the site of the battle in May, was beside himself with admiration. 'With any other leader,' he wrote to the duke of Cambridge, 'the enormous steepness of the ascent & the other physical difficulties would have been sufficient to prevent an attack by mounted men; but Lt. Col. Buller is a man of iron nerve & extraordinary courage, and is able to lead those under him where others would fail. How he escaped being killed himself I cannot understand, as he was, I believe, the very last man in the retreat and must have had any number of Zulus all around him.' Chelmsford was in no doubt that Buller deserved the Victoria Cross, commenting that 'he has no doubt won it already several times, but no one was able to speak of it but himself'.

But for Buller the battle was 'a defeat – not of Wood but of himself', and he 'thought perhaps he was to blame in some way'. He was being far too hard on himself and generous to Wood. He had done everything that could have been expected of him that day and more. If anyone was to blame, Wood was: both for launching an attack against an unknown position and at a time when he knew the Zulu Army was approaching. But bad luck also played a part. Wood's intelligence was that the Zulu Army had left oNdini on the 26th. The likelihood of it reaching Hlobane in two days was, Lloyd had estimated, 'a hundred to one against'. What he did not know was that it had actually left oNdini two days earlier, giving it plenty of time to cover the ground. Fortunately for Wood, Chelmsford was happy to accept a share of the blame. 'I am quite sure,' he wrote to Cambridge, 'that General Wood would never have allowed the attack to be made had I not asked him to make a diversion in favour of the column moving forward to relieve Ekowe.'

Buller's casualties at Hlobane were ten officers and eighty men killed out of a total European force of 404. Both Wood and Russell also lost two officers. The latter pair, Captain Potter and Lieutenant Williams, were killed with over a hundred of their black levies as they tried to return with the captured cattle. Once again the Zulus had taken no prisoners, despite Cetshwayo's demand that officers be brought in for interrogation.

12. The Tide Turns

Hlobane did have one positive outcome for the British: by diverting the main Zulu Army from its original line of march, it delayed the attack on Khambula camp by at least a day, giving Wood time to fine-tune his already formidable defences. The keystone to his position was an elongated earthwork redoubt he had built on a narrow ridge of tableland to the front of the camp. In it were two of his guns; the other four were in the open between the redoubt and the main wagon laager, which was twenty yards lower and 300 yards to its rear. Unlike Moriarty's laager, which had more holes than a sieve, this one was a veritable fortress: the wagon wheels were chained together, each wagon pole lashed to the wagon in front, and a rampart of earth had been used to seal off the gaps between the wheels. A mealie-bag wall with firing embrasures along the outside buckrail completed this near impregnable structure.

A short way below and to the right of the redoubt was a smaller wagon laager in which the column's 2,000 cattle were kept. Its right flank, and that of the main laager, rested upon a rocky ravine that provided a potential attacker with a good deal of cover. The slope to the left of the camp was much gentler and offered a far better field of fire. Before leaving for Hlobane, Wood had ordered the construction of a wooden palisade between the redoubt and the south end of the cattle laager, 'to stop a rush from the ravine on to the fort'. To those who 'objected that the Zulus would charge and knock it down by the weight of their bodies', he replied 'it would cause a delay of several minutes, during which 300 or 400 rifles, at 250 yards range, ought to make an additional barricade of human bodies'. Wood had, in addition, ordered range markers to be set up at varying distances from the camp.

Despite the losses suffered at Hlobane, and the desertion during the night of 28 March of Piet Uys's burghers and most of the black levies, Wood still had a garrison of 2,086 officers and men. Its backbone was provided by the Martini-Henrys of two British infantry battalions: the 90th Light Infantry (711 men) and 1/13th Light Infantry (527 men). In support he had the carbines of 669 cavalrymen (including seventy-four black troopers of the NNH) and the varied firearms of fifty-eight of Wood's Irregulars. There were also eleven Royal Engineers and 110 artillerymen of the 11/7th Battery with their six 7-pounders. Most of these men were defending the main laager; smaller garrisons manned the redoubt and the cattle laager.

At dawn on the 29th the mist was so thick that visibility around the camp was reduced to a hundred yards. Wood was asked if, under the circumstances, the wood-cutting party of two companies should be sent out as usual. After some thought he said yes: it was always possible the Zulus would not attack that day and his men would certainly 'fight better' in a day or two with cooked food inside them. So he accepted the risk, but ordered two subalterns to be ready to recall the companies at a moment's notice.

He also sent Commandant Raaf with twenty of his Transvaal Rangers to scout the edge of the Zungwini Plateau. At around 10 a.m. the mist lifted and Raaf reported that the Zulu Army was cooking breakfast in its bivouac a few miles south of the mountain, along the headwaters of the White Mfolozi. Wood used the time to strengthen the wooden palisade between the redoubt and the cattle laager. At 11 a.m. Raaf sent word that the Zulu Army was advancing. Wood now recalled the wood-cutting parties and had the oxen driven into their laager. He also had reserve ammunition boxes opened and placed behind the firing line. On being asked whether the infantry should 'hurry their dinners', Wood replied: 'No, there is plenty of time.' So well drilled were the men of his column that they could strike their tents and be at their posts within seventy seconds of hearing the 'Alert'.

Before long the five huge columns of the Zulu Army were clearly visible from the camp, advancing from the south-east. Wood's greatest fear was that they would bypass Khambula and head for the relatively undefended town of Utrecht. To his great relief, however, the columns halted at a distance of about four miles, probably to allow the war doctors to make their final minis-trations and to give the commanders the chance to discuss their plans. An hour later the army resumed its advance in the distinctive 'horns of the buffalo' formation: the left horn – the uMcijo, uMbon-ambi, uNokhenke and uKhandempemvu regiments – advanced up the valley to the south of the camp; the chest – made up of the uThulwana, iNdlondlo, uDloko, uDududu, iSangqu, iMbube and iNdluyengwe regiments – climbed the eastern end of the Khambula Ridge; and the right horn – the iNgobamakhosi and uVe – marched round to the north.

The exact intention of the Zulu commanders on that day is still a matter of debate. Cetshwayo later claimed that, having learnt the lesson of Rorke's Drift, he gave Mnyamana strict orders not to attack the camp. Instead he was 'to advance on Khambula, encamp close by, harass the camp by attacking the horses and cattle when out at pasture, and worry the garrison in every possible way, so as to force Wood to come out and fight in the open'. And yet the success of the Zulus at Hlobane had 'greatly elated' the younger warriors, who 'thought if they attacked the camp the next day they would obtain an easy victory'. Despite this, Mnyamana's intention was to 'stand by his original plans' and he 'gave orders accordingly'. Only when an insubordinate regiment – the iNgobamakhosi – attacked prema-turely did he decide to attack 'with the whole of his army'.

The iNgobamakhosi had been goaded into making this prema-ture assault by Buller, who rode out with the Mounted Infantry, the freshest of the cavalry, and fired into the flank of the Zulu right horn. Buller wrote: 'They did not stand our attack as I pressed home, and the advance of their right column, about 2,000 strong, turned & charged us. I need not tell you that the 80 or 90 men I had got on their horses pretty quick, & we scampered back to camp holding a running fight with them as we went.'

For some it was a close run thing. The sight and sound of the charging Zulus caused several of the horses to bolt, stranding a number of riders. One man was killed, and Colonel Russell cer-tainly would have been if Lieutenant Browne, his disgruntled deputy, had not gone back to help him mount with the Zulus just yards away.* On the iNgobamakhosi charged, until, at a range of 300 yards, they were stopped in their tracks by rifle-fire from the main laager and the north face of the redoubt. The four 7-pounders on the nek completed the rout with round after round of shrapnel. 'We thought the Zulu army was not far off,' recalled their junior induna Mehlokazulu, 'but it appears that at this time the main body had not yet got up . . . The horsemen galloped back as fast as they could to camp; we followed and discovered ourselves close to camp, into which we made the greatest possible efforts to enter. The English fired their cannon and rockets . . . We, when the Zulu army did come up, were lying prostrate, we were beaten.'

From his position behind the wooden palisade, Wood saw 'a fine tall Chief' of the iNgobamakhosi hit in the leg as he ran well ahead of his men. 'Two men endeavoured to help him back as he limped on one foot,' wrote Wood. 'One was immediately shot, but was replaced by another, and eventually all three were killed.' A warrior of the uMxhapho remembered: 'Everyone in the iNgobamakhosi lay down as the safest, for the bullets from the white men were like hail falling about us. It was fearful, no one could face them without being struck . . . I found myself near a large white stone† placed there by the white people; behind this I got, and remained there.' Buller's sortie had been far more successful than he could have hoped. 'It was evident it upset their plans,' he wrote, 'for during the whole day that corner of the camp remained unsurrounded.'

The iNgobamakhosi assault did, however, set off a chain-reaction thanks to the ferocious rivalry between the different Zulu regiments. A warrior of the uThulwana recalled:

The izinduna [commanders] . . . watched the fight from a hill. When we got near the camp some horsemen came out to meet us. Then the

---

* For saving the life of a man he had no wish to serve under, Browne was awarded a VC.
† Almost certainly a range marker.

iNgobamakhosi rushed after them; they retreated, and the iNgobamakhosi said they would attack, and actually advanced the main body of the
impi. Then the uMcijo on the other side rushed on, too – there was a
rivalry between the uMcijo and the iNgobamakhosi as to whom should
be first in the camp, so they both go on ahead, and by the time we came
up to attack in front they were exhausted and almost beaten.

The first attack had gone in at 1.45 p.m. Half an hour later, by
which time the iNgobamakhosi had gone to ground, the left horn
and chest charged the main laager and cattle kraal respectively. By
using the cover provided by the steep ravine, the uMcijo were able
to get within a hundred yards of the main laager before bursting
into the open. But they were cut down by rapid rifle fire from the
companies of the 1/13th Light Infantry, who were guarding the
main laager's southern flank. The chest too was driven back by a
storm of fire. Now the Zulus changed tactics, sending about forty
riflemen with captured Martini-Henrys into a patch of mealies that
had grown up among the rubbish heaps to the rear of the main
laager. From there they were able to fire into a company of the
1/13th that was holding the right rear of the cattle kraal, causing
a number of casualties and prompting Wood to withdraw them
closer to the fort. One 1/13th man was shot in the leg as he belatedly fell back. Instinctively Wood ran out to help him but was
stopped by Captain Maude, Campbell's replacement, who shouted:
'Really it isn't your place to pick up single men.' Maude went
out instead with Lieutenants Lysons and Smith, of the 90th, and
brought him in, but not before Smith had been hit in the arm. By
now the uNokhenke had driven the remaining half-company of
the 13th out of the cattle kraal, enabling Zulu snipers to fire
from its barricades into the unprotected artillerymen on the nek.
Lieutenant Frederick Slade, commanding the rear section of guns,
wrote home:

I was now left alone on the neck & the enemy with Martini Henry rifles
(captured on the 22nd January) made it *very* hot for me & I never expected
to leave that neck alive. In less time than it takes me to write this, my

No. 2 . . . was shot right through the body. My dear old horse Saracen was shot . . . But my men stood at their guns like bricks . . . On came the Zulus in 1000s and by 3.30 p.m. they had actually driven our infantry out of and occupied the cattle laager which was only 40 yards from my guns. I fired round after round of case into them, hitting oxen & Zulus alike, & a merry hail of bullets were pouring into us. [Captain Alan] Gardner was shot through the thigh . . . I shot the man who wounded Gardner with my revolver, so you may imagine how close they were.

As the battle reached its crisis point, Wood spotted large numbers of uMbonambi gathering in the ravine to the south of the main laager, their leaders trying to encourage them to charge. To pre-empt the attack he ordered two companies of the 90th to 'double over the slope down to the ravine with fixed bayonets, and to fall back at once when they had driven the Zulus below the crest'. He could see, as he waited for his orders to be carried out, a Zulu chief waving a red flag in an attempt to induce his men to come out of the ravine. Wood took aim with a borrowed carbine, the sight at 250 yards. But the heat of the barrel made him fire before he was ready, with the muzzle still at the chief's feet. The bullet, however, struck the chief in the stomach, knocking him over backwards. Two more indunas picked up the flag in turn, and both were shot by Wood aiming deliberately low.

The two companies of the 90th, meanwhile, had filed out of a gap in the main laager and, led by Major Hackett and Captain Woodgate, charged towards the ravine. 'At first the advance was successful,' recorded Woodgate, 'a large number of men giving way before the two companies and retiring from the crest down the slope. But coming under a heavy and well-directed cross-fire from other quarters, the two companies were ordered to retire, having lost two officers (Major Hackett and Lieutenant Bright) and about 25 men killed and wounded.' The shots had come from both the rubbish heaps and the cattle kraal, one bullet hitting Hackett in the temple and costing him the sight in both eyes.

At around the same time, Buller broke up an assault by the uMcijo of the left horn with another bayonet charge from the main laager, this time by a company of the 1/13th. Fearing further attacks, Wood rushed over to the main laager and was met by Buller, who asked him 'cheerily' why he had come. 'Because I think you are just going to have a rough and tumble,' replied Wood. But he had underestimated the disruption the two bayonet charges had caused the Zulu left. The pressure from the chest was also beginning to slacken. Thinking the Zulus were 'about to retreat', an officer came up to Lieutenant Slade and proposed a 'rush to retake the cattle laager'. Slade agreed: 'Sword in hand we went in at the double, I managing to run up one of my guns by hand. And a right royal reception we gave them. The 1/13th charged on our flanks, but after a few minutes we had to retire & we only got the guns back just in time, as the Zulus had lined the wagons & were assegaiing our men.'

The main Zulu effort, however, had fizzled out and the bodies of hundreds of warriors littered the ground around the British positions. More attacks came in, including one by the iNgobamak-hosi at around 4.30 p.m., but they were uncoordinated and not pressed with any vigour. Finally, at about 5.15, Wood ordered Slade and two companies of the 1/13th to clear the cattle laager, and this time they were successful. He, meanwhile, led another company to the edge of the ravine, 'where they did great execution with the bayonet amongst the Undi Regiment, who were now falling back'. All across the field the Zulus were retiring. It was time to release the horsemen. 'We were up & at them,' wrote Buller. 'Had it not been dark their loss would have been very heavy, still I cannot think that the killed & wounded in the pursuit was less than 300 at the least.' Captain Cecil D'Arcy and his troop of FLH, having narrowly survived the flight from Hlobane, were in a vengeful mood: '[We] followed them for eight miles, butcher-ing the brutes all over the place. I told the men, "No quarter, boys, and remember yesterday" . . . On the line where I followed them there were 157 dead bodies counted next day.' According to Chelmsford, who visited the battlefield in early May, the death toll would have been much greater if the horsemen had not been 'unable from physical fatigue to make as much of the pursuit as they might otherwise have done'. If just two regular cavalry regiments had been present, he told the duke of Cambridge, 'the war would now be over, as the Zulus were too tired to get away fast'.

A further 785 Zulu bodies were found in the vicinity of the camp and buried in mass graves. Amongst them were a great many izinduna who, according to Cetshwayo, had 'exposed themselves a great deal, attempting to lead on their men'. The British also recovered 'large numbers' of assegais and 325 firearms, including fourteen Martini-Henrys – marked 24th or 80th Regiment – and one Snider Carbine; the rest were obsolete weapons such as Tower muskets and Enfield rifles.

British losses were, as at Nyezane, comparatively light: eighteen men killed, and eight officers and fifty-seven men wounded (though three officers and seven men would later die of their wounds). The total Zulu dead may have been as high as 2,000. A month after the battle, British patrols were still coming across corpses on the line of the Zulu retreat. And, if a Private John Snook of the 90th is to be believed, the garrison at Khambula added to the death toll with an atrocity every bit as bad as the one at Rorke's Drift. 'On March 30th, about eight miles from camp,' he wrote to the landlord of his local, the Royal Oak in Tiverton, 'we found about 500 wounded, most of them mortally, and begging us for mercy's sake not to kill them; but they got no chance after what they had done to our comrades at Isandhlwana.'

Snook's letter caused a furore in England when it found its way into the *North Devon Herald*. The Aborigines' Protection Society at once protested to the War Office, which, in turn, questioned Wood. His denial was emphatic: 'The whole of the infantry were employed all day on the 30th, except when at divine service, in burying the 785 dead Zulus close to camp . . . I believe no Zulus have been killed by white men except in action, and, as I rewarded Wood's Irregulars for every live Zulu brought in, I had many saved.' Either Wood was lying, Snook was, or he had got the date wrong and was actually referring to the Zulus 'butchered' by the mounted men on the 29th. What is not in doubt, however, is that few Zulus were given any quarter after the battle. Should we be surprised? Not especially. British troops have generally responded to their opponents' atrocities with the Old Testament mentality of 'an eye for an eye'. The Indian mutiny being a case in point. This is not to say that the Zulus deserved everything they got. The widespread destruction of Zulu kraals during the war, for example, was inexcusable. But if an army takes no prisoners, and mutilates its victims' corpses into the bargain, it can hardly be surprised when its foe follows suit.

Wood later commended the steadiness of his troops, noting with satisfaction that each man had fired an average of thirty-three rounds during the four-hour battle. 'Though that evening,' he wrote, 'I heard that some of them had thought the possibility of resisting such overwhelming numbers of brave savages, 13 or 14 to one man, was more than doubtful. I had no doubt, and lost all sense of personal danger, except momentarily, when, as on five occasions, a plank of the hoarding on which I lent was struck [by a bullet].'

Despite Mnyamana's best efforts, most of the Zulu regiments broke up after Khambula and dispersed to their homes. Only a small fraction of the army accompanied Mnyamana back to oNdini to face Cetshwayo's wrath. 'The King was very angry when we went back,' remembered a warrior of the uThulwana who had also fought at Rorke's Drift. 'He said we were born warriors, and yet allowed ourselves to be defeated in every battle, and soon the English would come and take him.' His greatest fury was reserved for Mnyamana, his former favourite, who had ignored his instructions not to attack the camp. In his eyes Mnyamana had allowed the flower of Zulu manhood to perish in an unnecessary battle. But what was done was done.

Cetshwayo must have known after Khambula that victory in the field was no longer possible, and that even a negotiated peace was probably beyond his grasp. The fighting spirit of his soldiers – so high after Isandlwana – had been sapped by the sickening slaughter of three successive battles, two of them comprehensive defeats. Never again would his warriors show the same dash and disregard for their safety as they had at Isandlwana and Khambula; never again would the British risk a battle in the open without overwhelming firepower. It was no longer a question of if the British would win the war, but when.

On the same day that Wood won his signal victory in the north, Chelmsford set out from the Lower Drift of the Thukela to relieve Eshowe. He was not taking any chances: his force was by far the most powerful to enter Zululand and contained the equivalent of almost four infantry battalions: the whole of the 57th, 3/60th and 91st; and a total of seven companies from two more, the 3rd and 99th. It had, in addition, detachments from the Naval Brigade, two 9-pounder guns, four 24-pounder rocket tubes, two Gatlings, a mounted contingent and two battalions of NNC. In all, there were 3,390 white troops and 2,280 black auxiliaries. With the majority of Cetshwayo's warriors busy in the north, the Zulu army opposed to him would have a numerical advantage of only around three to one. Given the devastating effect of British firepower, this was never going to be enough.

Chelmsford also had the invaluable services of the 'white *induna*', John Dunn. For a time, hoping to remain neutral, Dunn had refused all Chelmsford's offers of employment. But the British government's response to Isandlwana – the immediate dispatch of thousands of reinforcements – had convinced him that the Zulus could not win or even 'draw' the war and that his only hope of regaining his lands was at the head of a British army. His initial concession to Chelmsford, at the end of February, was to supply him with information about Zulu troop movements from his spies in southern Zululand. By the time Chelmsford marched on Eshowe, Dunn had accepted the official position of chief of intelligence and was accompanied by 244 retainers. Dunn's reports were extremely useful. One in particular, by an induna called Magumbi, not only gave a remarkably accurate estimate of the total Zulu force south of the Mhlathuze River – 15,000 – but also where its various components were located. The report concluded: 'The whole nation is ordered out, even the sick; but . . . the orders which come from the king are so frequent and contradictory that a state of much confusion prevails.'

Determined to take advantage of the apparent disarray of the Zulu forces in the south, Chelmsford ordered the relief force to march as soon as enough reinforcements were in place. He had decided, he informed Colonel Stanley on 25 March, not to follow in Pearson's footsteps but instead to take the parallel coastal route because it went through 'an easy open country for ¾ of the distance, whereas by the other line the road runs through bush country the whole way'. The troops would march without tents and would bivouac in the open with only a blanket and waterproof sheet as cover. But this saving of weight was more than offset by Chelmsford's decision to carry one month's provisions for the new Eshowe garrison (of 1,000 Europeans and 300 black auxiliaries) and ten days' supply for his own column. More than a hundred ox-wagons and forty-four carts were needed to convey these supplies, slowing the advance of the column to a maximum of eleven miles a day. He ended his letter to Stanley in typically equivocal fashion: 'A force moving . . . with ox transport through a difficult country is heavily hampered, if attacked determinedly by large numbers, and whilst feeling every confidence in the ability, courage and determination of those under my command I trust that should our efforts fall short of what is no doubt expected of us, that circumstances may be duly taken into consideration.'

Chelmsford's unnecessary – but in some ways understandable – caution was reflected in a memorandum he issued to his troops before departure. Among other things he insisted that: each wagon and cart was to be supplied with easily accessible ammunition boxes with screwdrivers attached; all regimental reserve boxes, on the other hand, were to have the 'screw of the lid taken out'; each battalion was to take along 'its proper proportion of entrenching tools'; at night the force would construct a square wagon laager 'with a shelter trench round it', with the European troops bivouacking between the trench and the laager, and the auxiliaries, horses and cattle inside the laager itself; at night outlying sentries would be placed up to half a mile from each face of the laager; and the daily march would begin only after the scouts had reported that no sizeable enemy force was in the vicinity.

The advance began at 6 a.m. on the 29th and, having covered about ten miles, the column formed a wagon laager on the right bank of the Nyoni River. The following day it reached the amaTigulu River after a slightly shorter march. There was still no sign of the enemy, but reports kept coming in from the border agents that 'bodies of Zulus had been seen moving in an Easterly direction from the Indulinda range' to the west of Eshowe. Concluding from this that he would not reach Eshowe without a fight, Chelmsford remained at the amaTigulu during 31 March to give his wagon train the chance to close up. Each wagon required a double-team of oxen – thirty-two as opposed to sixteen – to get it across the deeper than usual drift, and by the end of the day the laager had been reformed just one and a half miles beyond the river. That same day Chelmsford's scouts reported 'small bodies of Zulus in the vicinity of the Amatakulu bush' to his front, while Captain Barrow branched off to the right with part of his mounted contingent and burnt a number of kraals, including one belonging to Makwendu kaMpande, yet another of Cetshwayo's half-brothers.

On 1 April the column made a leisurely march to the Gingindlovu Stream, close to the military kraal where Chief Godide had planned to camp during Pearson's initial invasion in January. There it constructed its nightly laager on a slight knoll with a good view of Eshowe, just fifteen miles away. For the first five of these miles the road wound its way through swampy, 'bushy and very difficult' country; the last nine were a 'steady ascent' with long grass and undulating ground making it ideal for an ambush. Understandably apprehensive about what lay ahead, Chelmsford was almost relieved when Dunn told him a large Zulu force would probably attack them the following morning. Dunn had gleaned this intelligence by riding the mile down to the Nyezane River at dusk, swimming across and witnessing with his own eyes a huge Zulu bivouac in the hills to the north. Confirmation came in the form of signals from Eshowe that a big enemy force was on the march towards the Nyezane.

The British position, as a result, was made particularly strong. Inside the wagon laager, 130 yards square, were placed the 2,000

oxen, 300 horses and 2,280 black troops. The ground between the
laager and shelter trench, a distance of about twenty yards, was
garrisoned by the 3,390 white troops and defended on each corner
by a rocket tube and either a 9-pounder or a Gatling. At midnight,
just to be sure, Chelmsford ordered the shelter trench to be strengthened. There had not been enough time, however, to cut down
the thick bush and grass that came to within a hundred yards of the
trench. That night the air was thick with tension and, had the
garrison not been expecting an attack, an incessant downpour
would still have made sleep very difficult. A false alarm only added
to the garrison's misery. 'I passed a very wretched night,' recorded
Guy Dawnay, an old Africa hand who had been attached to the 5th
NNC, 'as in the confusion of the alarm all one's things – that is my
waterproof sheet – had got trodden in the mud . . . I slept wet
through in a slough of mud and surrounded by Kafirs.'

At 4 a.m. on 2 April the troops stood to arms. A heavy mist made
the early morning gloom even more impenetrable than usual. At
about 5.45, half an hour before dawn, the mounted scouts reported
large numbers of Zulus advancing on the square. 'No preparation
was necessary,' wrote Chelmsford, 'and no orders had to be given
beyond the saddling up of the horses of the Officers of the Staff:
the troops were already at their posts and the cattle had not been
let out to graze.' Within fifteen minutes the attack began on the
north face of the entrenchment, which was being held by the
3/60th Rifles.

The attacking Zulu army was a hotch-potch of local irregulars,
coastal regiments and detachments from some of the principal royal
amabutho, including the iNgobamakhosi, uMcijo, uNokhenke,
uMbonambi and iNdluyengwe. It numbered around 12,000 men
and was commanded by Somopho kaZikhala, one of the king's
trusted advisers. Amongst his numerous influential deputies were
Prince Dabulamanzi, the defeated general at Rorke's Drift, whose
homestead lay to the west of Eshowe, Mavumengwana, joint commander at Isandlwana, and Sigcwelegcwele, senior induna of the
iNgobamakhosi. The bulk of the army spent the night of 1 April
in the hills to the north of the Nyezane; the balance, including

most of the irregulars, were camped away to the west of the laager. According to the newspaper correspondent Charles ('Noggs') Norris-Newman, who spoke to Zulu prisoners after the battle, the main impi had only just arrived, did not have time to 'send out scouts' and was 'ignorant' of the British strength. Furthermore there had been a 'difference of opinion' amongst the commanders as to whether an attack should be made that evening; eventually Dabulamanzi had persuaded Somopho and the others to adopt the 'plan of having food and a night's rest before attacking'. A staff officer at Eshowe heard a slightly different version. 'It was the Zulu intention,' he wrote later, 'to have attacked the fort that day, and to have smoked us out with burning faggots, but they could not resist the temptation of first annihilating the relieving column, which they took to be smaller than it really was.'

The two Zulu forces, advancing from separate directions, came in sight of the British at almost exactly the same time: 6 a.m. Captain Hart of the NNC remembered one of his men saying 'Impi' as he pointed towards the Nyezane: 'I looked there and saw what might have been easily mistaken for a streak of bush, bordering a stream and disappearing back into the distance miles away. But it was not a bush; a few instants of observation showed that it was in motion: it was a stream of black men rapidly approaching our position from our left front; it was a Zulu army!' Having crossed the river at two drifts a mile apart, these warriors rapidly formed into the traditional chest and left horn, the former advancing on the north face and the latter on its north-eastern corner. At the same time the right horn emerged from the bush to the north of Misi Hill and, dividing itself into two, headed for the western and southern faces of the entrenchment. The reserve, or loins, was with the commanders in the hills north of the Nyezane.

The Gatlings and rocket tubes on the corners of the north face opened up first and, when the Zulus had approached to within 500 yards, the Martini-Henrys of the infantry joined in. Captain Hart could not but admire the skill with which the Zulus advanced through this storm of fire:

No whites ever did, or ever could skirmish in the magnificent perfection of the Zulus. Unencumbered by much clothing, in the prime of life and as brave as it was possible for any men to be, they bounded forward towards us from all sides, rushing from cover to cover, gliding like snakes through the grass, and turning to account every bush, every mound, every particularly high patch of grass between us and them, and firing upon us, always from concealment. If total concealment were possible, we should not have seen a Zulu till he reached our trench, but it was not possible.

A private of the 3/60th on the north face recorded: 'Soon the Zulus got within 300 yards of our laager, they having crept up under cover afforded by the long grass, clumps of trees and bushes. It was here our fire caused them to fall in heaps. Notwithstanding this they came on and made a most determined attempt on the right front corner, and although we had been pouring into them showers of lead and iron for about twenty minutes, yet some actually got within twenty yards of our trenches.' The private was particularly impressed with the behaviour under fire of Chelmsford and the other senior officers.

Colonel Northey of the 60th Rifles was hit early in the engagement. Although seriously wounded in the shoulder, he still continued to give encouraging words to his men. He died four days after to the regret of all ranks . . . During the action Lord Chelmsford was on foot and going round the laager encouraging the men and directing the fire; and he complimented the 60th Rifles on our behaviour. Our Commanding Officer, Colonel W. Leigh Pemberton, who was acting Brigadier, was going about coolly smoking a fine smelling cigar. The Staff were principally mounted and had their horses either shot or wounded under them. Colonel Crealock was slightly wounded in the left arm.

A very different account of the performance of the young and inexperienced recruits of the 3/60th at the outset of the battle was given by one of their officers:

Our men were awfully frightened and nervous at first, could not even speak and shivered from funk, so we – the officers – had enough to do to keep the men cool . . . I myself did not quite like the first few shots as they whizzed over our heads; but found I had such a lot to do to keep the men in order and telling them when to shoot, that I did not mind a bit.

Once checked on the north face, the attack rolled round to the west, where Lieutenant George Johnson of the 99th Regiment was killed. At the same time a far more serious and determined assault was made by the right horn on the south face. Standing behind the 91st Highlanders in the shelter trench was Guy Dawnay with his trusty carbine:

We kept up a heavy fire at every black figure we saw, but they crawled through the grass, and dodged behind bushes, shooting at us all the time, and soon every bush in front of us held and hid two or three Zulus. I had heard more bullets whizzing past us in the first five minutes than in any other quarter of an hour of our fight . . . It was a great mistake not having cleared all the bits of bush in front of us, as they afforded splendid covers. No Zulu, though, could live under our fire . . . Our sights came down from 500, 400, 300, 200, to 100 yards; but no Zulu got nearer to the shelter trench than thirty-one yards. We found afterwards that they had made the heaviest attack on our front, because they fancied it was only held by the Native Contingent.

The mounted force had already left the laager to clear the remaining Zulus from the north face. Now Chelmsford ordered it to gallop down the east face and take the Zulu right horn in the flank. At almost the same time, as the Zulu attack on the south face began to waver, Dawnay and his NNC were unleashed:

All the other officers had to go back inside the laager and saddle up, and so, as I made up my mind to go on foot, I had a lot of men to myself. On reaching the ridge not thirty yards in front of us, we found a great lot of Zulus in the hollow; but they only stayed to fire one volley, and then 'balekile'd'; the volley dropping three men. We ran as hard as we could, had to cross a swampy bit of grass, which gave me the worst stitch I ever had, fired at them again as they collected on the next hill and pulled up to shoot at us, and then followed on, the Zulus now running for their lives. I tried in vain to stop them assegaing the wounded, but it was perfectly impossible in the heat of the pursuit, as the Zulus, however badly wounded, always turned round with their assegais when we neared them.

At the moment that the NNC left the laager, Captain Barrow and the mounted infantry 'drew swords and charged' the retreating Zulus, 'who were in large numbers, but utterly demoralized'. Barrow recalled:

The actual number of men killed with the sword were probably few, but the moral effect on the retreating Zulus as the swordsmen closed in on them was very great. In most cases they threw themselves down and shewed no fight, and were assegaid by the Natal Native Contingent who were following up. A few Zulus showed fight and assegaid one or two horses, but the majority did not do so . . . The half squadron then rallied and followed up again to a distance of about 1¼ miles from camp, when it was at last checked by a spruit. I have no hesitation in saying that had a regiment of English cavalry been on the field on this occasion scarcely a Zulu would have escaped to Umisi Hill.

In a little over an hour the Zulu attack had been utterly routed. Chelmsford estimated their losses at around 1,000 men: 471 bodies were found that day within 1,000 yards of the entrenchment and buried; a further 200 were found in the days to come; and the rest either died of their wounds or were killed by long-range artillery fire. British casualties were a paltry two officers and eleven men killed and four officers and forty-four men wounded. Lieutenant Milne, Chelmsford's naval ADC, was one of many officers who rode round the laager after breakfast to inspect the column's handi-work. 'A Zulu is hideous in death,' he wrote to his father, 'his whole expression is satanical & many were so badly hit about the head that it made them still more hideous. But they are plucky fellows and a brave enemy.'

The rest of the day was spent burying the dead and moving the site of the laager. On receiving a congratulatory heliograph message from Eshowe, Chelmsford flashed back that the garrison would be relieved the following day. He had decided to abandon the post, he added, because the road was too difficult for transport; instead it would be moved to Gingindlovu and 'all future operations would be conducted on the coast road'. Early on 3 April, leaving behind a reduced garrison, Chelmsford set off on the last leg to Eshowe with fifty-eight carts full of provisions. Slowed by fifteen miles of difficult swampy tracks, the last eight up a steep ascent, the vanguard did not reach the fort until after dusk. They were comfortably beaten by a solitary horseman, wearing an officer's coat and a sword, who came in sight of the ramparts at around 5 p.m. One of Pearsons's staff wrote:

Who is he? A special messenger from Lord Chelmsford, with important dispatches? Our doubts were soon dissolved by the arrival of the horseman, who, dismounting, proved to be Mr N[orris] N[ewman] of the 'Standard'. 'First in Ekowe!' he exclaimed, with a self-satisfied air, 'proud to shake hands with an Ekoweian.' We were all very gratified at his condescension and asked the 'news'. A second horseman appeared . . . his horse much blown. 'Who is he?' we asked. 'That is the gentleman of the "Argus" newspaper.' They had had a race who should be first in Ekowe, the 'Standard' winning by five minutes. I fear they did not meet with that warm and hospitable welcome which they expected, for there seemed some difficulty getting a dinner for themselves and horses . . . We had barely sufficient food to satisfy our own enormous appetites.

A more enthusiastic welcome was given to Captain Barrow and his mounted contingent when they arrived at 6 p.m. A full ten weeks had elapsed since Barrow and his men had left the fort, and the handshakings and congratulations were long and heartfelt. But the loudest cheer of all was reserved for the arrival of Chelmsford and the infantry at 8 p.m. Pearson had gone out with a column to meet them, and the two generals rode in side by side. 'All was excitement,' remembered a private of the 3/60th, 'and the shouts and cheers of congratulations on all sides were very affecting . . . The ramparts were manned and three cheers were heartily given when the General and Staff arrived, and great excitement was shown when the 91st Regiment came in with their pipes playing.'

Next morning, as Pearson and his men began the long march back to the Lower Thukela, Chelmsford led a mounted raiding party towards Prince Dabulamanzi's kraal at Ntumeni Hill, seven miles to the west of Eshowe. Accompanying the party was Charles Fripp, a special artist for the *Graphic* newspaper:

There were mounted infantry in their red coats and tanned helmets, volunteers clad in serviceable cord clothing and slouch felt hats, native irregulars similarly clad, but besides rifle and banderole, having their assegais in a sheath bound to the saddle, and wearing no boots rode with their big toe only in the stirrup; and were mounted on small but strong African horses. The country through which we passed was down-like, covered with long African grass, dense bush growing in large patches in the valleys and hollows . . . After some hard riding we sighted some more irregular horsemen leading a Zulu prisoner with a rein round his neck between them; and following, we shortly afterwards joined a small party of horsemen, one of whom was a thickset man clad in the ordinary cord clothing of Englishmen in South Africa. He wore a short beard, and clear grey eyes looked out from under the broad brim of his felt hat: this person was John Dunn, known as Cetywayo's 'white man', and he sat in his saddle, rifle butt on thigh, quietly speaking to the prisoner, a young Zulu fellow of fine physique and steady fearless bearing.

In the distance Fripp could see the mounted troops setting fire to Dabulamanzi's hut and stockade. The prince is said to have been among a group of forty or so Zulus who were watching the destruction from a nearby hill. Chelmsford and his staff were busy observing the hill, from which appeared 'little puffs of smoke, followed by distant reports and the whistle of bullets overhead'. Fripp recalled: 'Being at a long range (over one thousand yards), this fire was unanswered except by Dunn, who lay on his back and fired a few shots in return. Dabulamanzi was a first-class rifle-shot, and it was suggested that he and Dunn were having a match.' Neither was to record a hit.

The following day Chelmsford withdrew to Gingindlovu, where a new laager was formed on the 6th. Three days later, buoyed by his victory, he was back in Durban. His intention, he told the duke of Cambridge in a letter of 11 April, was to entrust future operations in the coastal region to the recently arrived Major-General Crealock. Crealock's task was to establish a strong permanent post along the coastal road between the Thukela and Mhlathuze rivers. Chelmsford had divided his enlarged force into two: the 1st Division under Crealock; and the 2nd Division, which would operate in the north, under Major-General Edward Newdigate. Both would eventually converge on oNdini in a simplified version of his original plan of campaign, with Chelmsford accompanying Newdigate's force. As a reward for all his good work, Wood kept his independent command, but it had been renamed the Flying Column and would operate in conjunction with Newdigate's division. Sir Frederick Marshall, another reinforcement general, had been given command of the Cavalry Brigade (attached to Newdigate's division) and Henry Clifford put in charge of the 'Base of Operations', where, said Chelmsford, he had 'already done much to systematize the work here'.

Chelmsford did have one gripe: Sir Henry Bulwer's refusal to allow Natal blacks to undertake raids into Zululand during the operation to relieve Eshowe. 'I felt,' wrote Chelmsford, 'that I might possibly have to encounter the full strength of the Zulu army and I was anxious to create a diversion in its favour by simultaneously raiding from one end of the line to the other.' And yet Bulwer positively forbade any such cooperation. 'I consider that the action of Sir Henry Bulwer is quite indefensible,' he added, '& if persevered in must completely prevent my making any use of the large numbers of Natal Natives who are now in arms along the Border . . . Sir H. Bulwer from my first arrival in Natal has thrown every obstacle in my way whilst at the same time he has endeavoured by long memoranda, minutes & dispatches to make it appear that he has given me all the assistance I have asked for.' Buoyed by the recent victories of Khambula and Gingindlovu, Chelmsford felt confident that the authorities in Britain would back him and not Bulwer. As it turned out, his breach with Bulwer provided Disraeli's government with an excuse to replace him.

It did not help that the duke of Cambridge was rapidly losing faith in Chelmsford's abilities as a general. This was partly because of his growing conviction that Chelmsford, and not Durnford, had been chiefly responsible for Isandlwana; and partly because of a series of critical letters from the newly arrived Clifford. On 17 April, for example, Clifford related a conversation he had had with Phil Robinson, the war correspondent of the *Daily Telegraph* who had accompanied the Eshowe relief force. 'He said,' wrote Clifford, 'that Lord C. was entirely in the hands of his Military Secretary, Crealock, who being a snob . . . had turned every officer & civilian against himself & Ld. C. That no one could get a word with him without Crealock being there. That he and [Colonel] Bellairs were not on speaking terms . . . That Lord C. had a very small & imperfect General Staff.' In the war correspondent's opinion, Chelmsford's strange conduct was because he was 'mad', because he was 'governed by Crealock & kept in ignorance of all going on about him', or because 'he wished to be recalled or killed'. Clifford suspected the second reason and went on to describe his first meeting with Chelmsford after the latter had returned from Eshowe:

I told him . . . that it was the opinion of a large portion of the military & civilian world that great mistakes had been made, that the usual precautions & rules of war had been disregarded & I pointed out to him in full what the military faults attributed to him were . . . I told him he must to a certain extent concentrate his forces; do away with at any rate some of his small columns & attack by fewer roads . . . I concluded by saying that [his critics] said that he was entirely led by Crealock & was shut out by him from the world & did not know his own positions & the faults found with him . . . He took it *most kindly* & in some things allowed I was right. But I could see at once what a little world he has lived in, how little he has understood his position & what has been going on in the world.

It had, said Clifford, been his suggestion to concentrate the troops into two main bodies: the 1st Division and 2nd Division (with Cavalry Brigade attached). He had managed to get round Chelmsford's chief objection – that it would take away Wood's independent command – by renaming his force 'Wood's Flying Column'. This, apparently, had 'delighted' Chelmsford 'wonderfully'. And yet there was still much to be done. The Commissariat had been unable to give him a return 'showing where their officers were employed', and he had asked each department 'to put down on a map' where their stores, magazines and depots were. As for Chelmsford's future plan of campaign, Clifford had felt compelled to advise a slow advance in force as opposed to a 'rapid one cut off from its advance depots & lines of communication with no connections between the divisions'. He added: 'I may be wrong but I should never forgive myself if I allowed him to cross the frontier & enter in the war again without telling him what appeared to me false moves.'

In a subsequent letter from Pietermaritzburg on 21 April, Clifford attacked the wastefulness and incompetence of the Commissariat: 'I fear the cost of the war will be *something awful*. I try all I can now to check expenditure, but with no one to do so from the first it is most difficult. I think there should be some check over the expenditure by the Commissariat Department. I am much disappointed with Strickland, he has no idea of organization & it appears to me that the expenditure in his department is lavish, everything is carried through by money which is expended at a fearful rate.' The point was hammered home in early May when Clifford quoted from a subordinate:

Butler writes . . . today from Durban: 'I believe the abuses of the Transport System to be so great that it would require a court of inquiry permanently sitting to deal with them. The Commissariat are now paying 3/- a cwt from Botha's Hill to P.M. Burg . . . The man who has the contract will make £20,000 out of the British Government. It is a *shameful & shameless scene of extravagance*. I believe that had you been here five months ago you would have saved government more than a million of money . . . The Commissariat have avoided *a total break down* by *awful* expenditure of public money.

No amount of money, however, could compensate for the organiz-ational chaos of the Commissariat and the difficulty of procuring transport for the second invasion. Chelmsford admitted as much in a letter to Cambridge of 24 April. 'The difficulties of our transport arrangements seem to increase rather than to diminish, and I am afraid considerable delay in our advance must necessarily ensue. The drivers and leaders of our ox transport are all natives, and cannot be adequately replaced by Europeans, even if they could be procured.' Six days later he informed the duke that Strickland had warned of a complete breakdown in transport unless the Natal government provided African drivers. 'The fact is,' he wrote, 'that [Bulwer] as supreme chief has the will and the power to order out natives for the purpose. But the government machinery is so faulty that his orders are carried out with great difficulty, and when the natives come out under his orders there appears to be no power to prevent them deserting or any means of punishing them for doing so.'

13. Sir Garnet Wolseley

The queen was holidaying at Baveno, Lake Maggiore, when the 'unfavourable news' of Wood's defeat at Hlobane reached her on 8 April. On top of the disaster on the Ntombe and the recent death of Prince Waldemar, her daughter Vicky's youngest son, it was enough to plunge her into the depths of despair. But gladder tidings were on the way: first the news of Khambula and then word that Eshowe had been relieved by Chelmsford after a convincing victory at Gingindlovu. 'Such a great thing,' noted Victoria in her journal on 22 April.

Disraeli was not quite so upbeat, informing the queen in a letter of 24 April that there was 'still much in the state of S. Africa which must occasion anxiety'. The lifting of the siege of Eshowe was indeed a great relief, he wrote, but 'disaster still haunts us in that country'. Although 'veiled by the subsequent repulse' of the attack on his camp, it could not be 'concealed that Colonel Wood has experienced a great misfortune' at Hlobane. Four days later, by which time the queen had returned to England, the prime minister was in much better spirits during an audience at Windsor Castle. 'The news from the Cape had made him terribly anxious,' recorded the queen, 'but he is much easier in his mind now.' Part of the reason was the favourable reception given to Sir Stafford Northcote's Budget statement by the House of Commons earlier in the month. In it he had expressed his hope that a Budget surplus of £1.9m would be enough to pay the expenses of the Zulu War and that no new taxes would be required. This did, however, depend upon the war being brought to a 'speedy close', an eventuality that had become more likely since the twin victories of Khambula and Gingindlovu. Disraeli was also feeling more upbeat about other areas of foreign policy: Yakub Khan, Sher Ali's son and successor as amir of Afghanistan, was about to conclude a favourable treaty with the British;

Russia was on the verge of ending months of sabre-rattling by finally evacuating all Ottoman territory; and Disraeli was optimistic that the recent crisis in Egypt, where the Khedive had sacked his British and French finance ministers, would be 'got over'.

Disraeli did not believe, however, that Chelmsford was the right man for the job in Zululand. On 12 April he told the prince of Wales, a fervent supporter of both Frere and Chelmsford, that there seemed to be a 'want of energy' in South Africa which was 'most deplorable'. He added: 'A general of genius might put all right but, I fear, he does not exist, or is locked up at Cyprus.' He was referring, of course, to Sir Garnet Wolseley, who had been serving as high commissioner of Cyprus since the island was ceded to Britain by the Congress of Berlin in 1878. Fortunately Wolseley was due back in London on 21 May, ostensibly to sit on a Board of General Officers that had been convened to investigate the short service system, but actually because Disraeli and Stanley wanted him to be available in case a replacement for Chelmsford was needed. First, however, the powerful support for Chelmsford in royal circles would need to be weakened; and his recent success at Gingindlovu did not make this any easier.

But an unexpected bonus for the government was the steady weakening of support for Chelmsford at the Horse Guards. The general had responded to the duke of Cambridge's demand for more information on Isandlwana in early April, the letter reaching London a month later. His responses to the seven queries were as follows:

(1) He had not put Rorke's Drift into a 'state of defence' prior to advancing on Isandlwana because the 'labour of getting troops & supplies across the Buffalo River and of making the roads passable for wheeled transport' had occupied 'nearly the entire strength of No. 3 Column' during that period. The troops at Isandlwana were, in any case, covering 'the ford on the Buffalo'.

(2) He had not laagered at Isandlwana because the wagons 'were under orders to return to Rorke's Drift on the 22nd January in order to bring up more supplies'.

(3) Distinct orders *were* left by Glyn regarding the defence of the camp and therefore Chelmsford had not bothered to send any fresh instructions to Durnford when he was ordered up from Rorke's Drift.

(4) A small patrol of IMI 'did make a long patrol in the direction from which the enemy eventually advanced but failed to discover more than a few Zulus who were evidently scouts'.

(5) He had responded to the message that 'firing was going on to the left front of the camp' at 9 a.m. on the 22nd by sending his ADC up a hill from which the camp 'could be plainly seen with a telescope'. With no sign of any enemy near the camp and 'no further report or request for assistance being received from the officer commanding the camp' he felt he had 'a right to assume it was a false alarm'.

(6) He received 'no report whatever previous to Commandant Lonsdale reporting that the camp was in the hands of the enemy' that led him to 'suppose that an action was going on near the camp'.

(7) The troops marched out of camp with one day's ration and, so he thought, 'their *regimental* reserve ammunition of 30 rounds', though he had referred the matter to Colonel Glyn for confirmation.

Unfortunately for Chelmsford, Cambridge was far from happy with these explanations – and rightly so. Most were half-truths and obfuscations, and some – like the claim that he had received no warning that the camp was in danger after the original message from Pulleine – close to a downright lie. There was, for example, the note that Pulleine had sent at noon on the 22nd, saying that he could not move the camp because of 'heavy firing to the left'. Chelmsford denied ever receiving this message, but he was certainly given others that he had ignored. He made no mention of these; nor of the fact that he countermanded Colonel Harness's attempt to return to Isandlwana in the early afternoon of the 22nd.

In the light of his misgivings about Chelmsford's conduct at Isandlwana, Cambridge had little confidence in the general's new plan of operations. He felt, in particular, that the gap between the two invading columns was far too big. 'You have no lateral communication,' he wrote to Chelmsford on 8 May, 'so that one column cannot support the other which I think is a great misfortune. Surely one column would have been better with one base of operations.' He was no more impressed with Chelmsford's decision to cancel a request for mules – which the War Office had bought at the 'great expense of £46,000' – because he had since discovered he could get them at the Cape.

The queen, like her son, was still a staunch supporter of both Chelmsford and Frere. But she was due to leave for Balmoral ('her misty Highland home') on 21 May and would not be best placed to prevent a change in the South African command. Disraeli certainly wanted one. 'The news from the Cape very unsatisfactory,' he informed Lady Chesterfield on 8 May, 'Chelmsford wanting more forces, though he does nothing with the 15,000 men he has. He seems cowed and confused.'

Hicks Beach was also dissatisfied with Chelmsford and Frere for failing to respond to the peace feelers put out by Cetshwayo in March. His dispatches of March and April had made it quite clear, he told Disraeli on 15 May 1879, 'that bona fide overtures for peace should be encouraged'. In Parliament, meanwhile, the issue of the queen's unequivocal support for Frere in the aftermath of Isandlwana had reared its ugly head in an adjourned debate on 14 May. The outraged monarch condemned the debate as 'shameful' and lambasted Sir Stafford Northcote, the leader of the House of Commons, for being 'too apologetic'. But for Disraeli, who had pretty well made up his mind to replace both Frere and Chelmsford, the debate was timely. On 18 May, in his last audience with the queen before she left for Balmoral, he told her that he was 'very anxious about the Cape' and that the 'feeling against Sir Bartle Frere and Lord Chelmsford was very strong'. She, in turn, condemned the critics as 'very wrong', 'strongly protested against anyone being sent out to conclude peace, and said no one ought to be sent to supersede the others, but merely to carry a message and explain the views of Government'.

Disraeli appeared to concur, but was simply biding his time.

On 19 May he prepared the ground for the dual supersession by informing the queen that the Cabinet had received an 'abundance of private information' that showed that the expenditure on transport in South Africa 'was enormous & aggravated by the misunderstanding' that appeared to exist between Chelmsford and Bulwer. Five of his senior ministers – including Stanley and Hicks Beach – were still broadly supportive of Chelmsford, 'but all acknowledged that your Majesty's government were left in a state of great darkness, & that no one seemed clearly to understand what we were aiming at, & what terms would satisfactorily conclude the war'. No final decision had been made, he wrote, but the 'prevalent, not to say unanimous, opinion seemed to be that without superseding either Sir Bartle or Lord Chelmsford a "dictator" shd. be sent out, intimately acquainted with the views & policy of your Majesty's government, who should be able to conclude peace . . . & effect a general settlement'.

The 'dictator' the government had in mind, Sir Garnet Wolseley, duly arrived in London on the day the queen left: 21 May. Next morning he took a hansom cab from his hotel to the Horse Guards in Whitehall and had a 'long talk' with Major-General Sir Charles Ellice, the adjutant-general, who 'said he believed I should be sent at once to the Cape'. Wolseley recorded:

He thought the Govt. was then discussing the question of what was to be done in South Africa and that it would lie between [Field Marshal] Lord Napier [of Magdala] and I, but that he believed one of us would be sent. I quickly said, if that is the case, I am the man, for they will never send old Napier. The subject then turned upon Chelmsford and upon his disastrous campaign. He asked me what I should have done had I been in power at home when the sad news arrived. I said at once, that as soon as I had received Chelmsford's dispatch I would certainly have recalled him, as from his own showing in my opinion he was unfit for such an important command: he then told me that he and others at the Horse Gds. had backed up the Duke in backing up Chelmsford, and he gave me to understand that it was entirely the Horse Guards influences that had saved him from being recalled.

That was not strictly true: the queen had been, and was still, a rock of support for Chelmsford, and even Disraeli did not at first want to supersede him because he was unconvinced that such a measure would shorten the war. But the initial support for Chelmsford at the Horse Guards had been an important factor, and Wolseley himself believed that had he, an outspoken reformer, been in command he would have been shown 'no mercy'. Wolseley wrote: 'I believe most firmly that it was the feeling that if Ld. C. was recalled I should have been sent out to replace him, that saved Chelmsford. It was from no great affection to him that he was spared, but from hatred to me. The Duke thinks I am already too powerful in the Army and he desires to keep me back lest I should ride regularly over Him.'

Wolseley may have been right, because, when the duke at last decided that Chelmsford would have to be superseded, he did everything in his power to replace him with Lord Napier of Magdala, the 68-year-old hero of the Abyssinian campaign. But the Cabinet decided that he was too old and Wolseley should go instead to Natal 'with full civil and military powers'. Wolseley was told this in the 'strictest confidence' by Colonel Stanley after his meeting with Ellice. Stanley, who had come straight from the Cabinet, was keen for Wolseley to leave 'at once, by the next mail if possible, which left London on that day week'. He told Wolseley that he had long had him in mind for the South Africa command and that he had summoned him home from Cyprus for that very reason, though an excuse had been given 'to put men off the real secret'.

Wolseley next went to Downing Street to speak to Disraeli. On being asked for his advice on the situation in Natal, Wolseley said it was 'to make peace as soon as it can possibly be done with honour, as nothing was to be gained' by conducting the war 'in a fashion that would entail a ruinous cost upon the country'. Disraeli replied that he was not satisfied 'with the manner in which things had been conducted in South Africa, and referred in strong terms to the mismanagement of military operations'. He then corrected himself, pointing out that it was 'partly mismanagement & partly ill luck, for ill luck always attends upon mismanagement'. Wolseley thought, but did not say, that the opposite was true in Chelmsford's case: 'for his mismanagement was followed by the most extraordinary good fortune'; had it been otherwise, 'he would not now be alive to tell the tale'. At no time during the interview did Disraeli mention Wolseley's appointment. The only hint was his request for the general to remain in town for a few days. Wolseley took this to mean that he wanted first to obtain the queen's sanction. And so he did. But Disraeli knew that it would not be given willingly and that, in effect, he would have to present her with a fait accompli.

The following day, after yet another Cabinet meeting on the affairs of South Africa, Disraeli broke the news to the queen in Scotland by telegram. 'The Cabinet is of opinion,' he wrote, 'that the Civil & Military Commands should be rearranged . . . Sir Garnet Wolseley to be Your Majesty's High Commissioner & Commander in Chief for Natal, Transvaal & territories adjacent, including Zululand, & to have within that area supreme civil & military authority under your Majesty. Sir Garnet having superior rank the present Commander in Chief will become the second in command.' Frere's authority would henceforth be limited to the Cape and adjacent territories, while Chelmsford, Bulwer and Lanyon would all be superseded by Wolseley, who would enjoy complete authority in the theatre of operations. The telegram ended with a request for the queen to telegraph her response – either approving or demanding more information – as 'time is precious'.

The queen was out driving when this 'startling telegram' arrived at Balmoral and did not receive it until early evening. She was a day short of sixty and had spent the trip in sad contemplation of the previous twelve months when she had lost her 'darling child', Princess Alice, and two grandchildren. The news that the Cabinet was trying to replace Frere and Chelmsford, two men in whom she had complete confidence, with a general of whom she did not approve, was enough to turn her sorrow into rage. Her sharply worded response was the closest she came during her long association with Disraeli to issuing an outright rebuke. She wrote:

If the Cabinet are really of opinion that the proposed arrangement in South Africa is absolutely necessary I will not withhold my *sanction* though I cannot *approve* it. I cannot but feel that such a step will lead to the immediate resignation of both Sir Bartle Frere & Ld. Chelmsford. This I would deeply deplore as it would in my opinion lower this country in the eyes of all Europe as well as encourage our enemies in South Africa. Has the Commander in Chief been consulted? Why is Sir Garnet Wolseley considered the most fit person? He is not likely to be conciliatory.

Disraeli had already, on the 23rd, written a letter that explained in more detail the decision to send Wolseley out to South Africa. The Cabinet had been particularly alarmed, he said, by the latest dispatches, which indicated 'dissensions' between Bulwer and Chelmsford. Then there was 'private information★ that several members of the staff were not on speaking terms' and 'the disheart-ened condition of the troops approaching to demoralization'. To soothe the queen, Disraeli stressed that neither Frere nor Chelms-ford were being recalled. This letter was backed up by one from Colonel Stanley, which accused Chelmsford of not being 'master of the situation'. Stanley added: 'He is vague in his demands, admits his want of knowledge of the Zulu country & apparently is on bad terms with the Colonial Government.'

These two letters arrived at Balmoral on 24 May, the queen's sixtieth birthday. In the absence of a response to her telegram, she fired off a second one, condemning the government's apparent reliance 'on information derived from private sources, a course which I never think desirable especially when I remember the period of the Crimean War'.† Two more days went by without any word from Disraeli. Then, 'not having received any answer, or further explanation', she was 'greatly startled & much annoyed' to be told on the 26th that Wolseley's appointment had been announced in the House of Commons that afternoon.

★ One of the correspondents was undoubtedly General Clifford.
† A conflict in which many soldiers' private letters, highly critical of the conduct of the war, were published in British newspapers.

She immediately sent a telegram of protest to Disraeli, pointing out that while 'anxiously awaiting' an answer to her cipher telegrams, she had received word that an announcement had been made in Parliament 'of all that she so strongly objected to'. What, she demanded to know, did this mean? Earlier that day she had written Disraeli a carefully worded letter in defence of both Frere and Chelmsford:

Whatever fault may have been committed in declaring (perhaps) too hastily war, Sir B. Frere seems to have succeeded by his personal influence in conciliating those important portions of the Colonies, who were considered to be disaffected. To reward his efforts therefore by sending out an officer with the powers proposed instead of encouraging him will be a *public mark* of want of confidence, at a moment of *great difficulty* which will have a most disastrous effect both at home and abroad – & will make it almost impossible for any public man to serve his country if on the *1st* misfortune occurring he is to be thrown over! The case of Lord Chelmsford may perhaps be *less* certain, but he also seems to have been successful of late – and the Queen most *strongly* protests against the use of *private* information . . . It is absolutely necessary to prevent *any* peace being concluded which the Government would disapprove. Send some one out with messages to Sir B. Frere and Lord Chelmsford to explain exactly *what* the Government wish and *what* they *object* to. But do not upset everything which will be the case if an officer, whoever he may be, is sent out with the Powers proposed. The Queen would sanction the proposal submitted *if* her *warnings* are disregarded but she could not *approve* it.

When the queen's telegram of protest arrived, Disraeli feigned surprise and distress. The Cabinet thought, he replied by cipher on the 27th, that she had 'sanctioned, though not approved, the proposal, & therefore, as the House was going to be adjourned for Whitsuntide, they had considered it best to make the announcement, forgetting he had not answered' her telegram. In a letter sent that day he explained, somewhat disingenuously, that a final decision was only taken by the Cabinet on the 26th after a 'long and deep consideration' of both her telegrams. He added:

But the deliberation ended [with] the Cabinet unanimously adhering to their previous decision, & also in urging the appointment of Sir G. Wolseley instead of Lord Napier; among other grounds, on his local experience of the scene of war . . . It was with much difficulty that Lord Beaconsfield secured the arrangement that Sir Bartle Frere should remain as High Commissioner of the Cape Colony & its dependencies . . . No one upheld Lord Chelmsford.

He was, he concluded, 'pained that your Majesty disapproves of the policy of your Majesty's servants, but he is, himself, deeply convinced that the measures in question were necessary'. It was not Disraeli's letter that soothed the queen's ruffled feathers, however, but a 'satisfactory' one from Sir Michael Hicks Beach, which pointed out that Frere himself had stressed the need for a general with both civil and military powers. 'Lord Chelmsford seems not to be up to the mark,' she recorded in her diary after the receipt of both letters on the 28th. 'The demands for every sort of thing are so boundless, the disagreement with others so unsatisfactory, etc.'

The recriminations from the queen would continue for some days: why were her telegrams not responded to? Why was Wolseley chosen ahead of more senior generals? Disraeli and his ministers did their best to placate her. But the decision was taken, and they had got their way. The experience of the previous week had, nevertheless, not been enjoyable for the ailing prime minister. 'We have had a terrible time of it, six Cabinets in eight days,' he wrote to Lady Chesterfield. 'I believe it has never happened before. However, Sir Garnet Wolseley goes to S. Africa and goes tomorrow night, though between ourselves the Horse Guards are furious, the Princes all raging and every mediocrity as jealous as if we had prevented him from conquering the world.'

Wolseley, meanwhile, had received confirmation of his appointment from the prime minister at Downing Street on the 26th. The general recorded: 'Dizzy was very complimentary . . . but all that he said regarding his confidence in me . . . made me feel all the more how curious & uncomfortable it was that he had not come to this present decision three months ago. If he had done so, I could have saved the country I believe an enormous outlay by declaring Martial law & then pressing transport . . . Now I shall reach Natal too late to make any new arrangements if the war is to be finished by the end of August: I shall have to follow in the lines laid down by Chelmsford, lines which I believe to be fundamentally wrong.' Wolseley then had a meeting with Stanley, Hicks Beach and W. H. Smith, the first lord of the Admiralty, at which it was agreed that he would be given an extra battalion of Royal Marines as well as Colonel Sir Pomeroy Colley, then serving as Lord Lytton's private secretary in India, as his chief of staff with the local rank of brigadier. This latter concession much annoyed Cambridge, who suggested Clifford for the post. But Wolseley was adamant and got his way. His greatest fear, however, was that the war would be over by the time he reached South Africa. Or, even worse, that he would fail in the field. 'That the man who is leader of the military movement in favour of reform should be worsted by the Zulus,' he wrote, 'would give the Stand Still party a fresh impetus. They would say, ah, see what reform has led to!' The press, however, was 'extremely complimentary' about his appointment, as was the Liberal Opposition in Parliament.

On 29 May, shortly before his departure, Wolseley received his final instructions from Hicks Beach:

It is the desire of Her Majesty's Government that the present war be brought to an end as soon as this can be done consistently with the honour of our arms and the safety of the British Colonies. There appears some reason to hope that the evidence which has been given of the power of Her Majesty's forces may have disposed the Zulus to submission. And it will be your first duty on arrival . . . to encourage any *bonâ fide* proposals which may afford a reasonable prospect of a satisfactory peace . . . You will carefully bear in mind that the object of Her Majesty's Government is not to add to the extent of the British possessions adjoining Zululand, but to relieve them from the danger to which they have hitherto been exposed . . . The detailed arrangements by which that policy may best be carried into effect can only be properly matured by you after full consideration of the circumstances which may exist on your arrival in Natal.

In other words he had been given complete discretion to negotiate a 'satisfactory peace' – which did not necessarily mean outright victory in the field. The only limits imposed upon him were time – as soon as possible – and a veto on annexation that, in effect, made confederation impossible. Both Frere and Chelmsford's careers, as a result, hung in the balance.

Wolseley took his leave of a bad-tempered Cambridge – 'indignant at the men I had asked for as Special Service Officers' – at his residence, Gloucester House, during the afternoon of 29 May. From there he travelled by cab to Paddington Station, where a 'great crowd of people' had gathered to see him off. 'All the way to Dartmouth, at every station where the train stopped,' he recorded, 'my carriage was besieged by a howling crowd. All very flattering, but it made me think of my position & the difficulties I have before me . . . Popularity is easily obtained, easily lost and should always be taken at its true value.' During the night, Wolseley was joined on the train by 'that madman' Lieutenant-General Sir William Olpherts, VC, who 'interfered seriously' with his sleep. Olpherts wanted to go with him to South Africa, but Wolseley was not so keen. 'He is the bravest of the brave,' he wrote, '& were he only a captain how gladly would I avail myself of his services, but he is one of those who having done admirably in a subordinate position cannot see for himself that the qualities required of by a General need not be possessed by the very best subaltern officer.' After arriving at Dartmouth in the early hours of 30 May, he had 'great difficulty in getting rid of' Olpherts, who wanted to embark with him on the steamer SS *Edinburgh Castle*. Only when the ship's captain barred Olpherts from boarding did he finally desist. At midday on the 30th, with Wolseley and his staff safely on board, the steamer finally got under way for South Africa. But it would not reach Cape Town for more than three weeks,★ and, in the interim, much had happened in Zululand.

★

★ During which time, on 4 June, Wolseley celebrated his forty-sixth birthday.

While Chelmsford's supersession was being settled in London, he was getting on with the task of redeeming his military reputation: a task that required nothing less than the destruction of the main Zulu Army. To achieve this he had, by the beginning of May, no fewer than two regiments of regular cavalry – the 1st (King's) Dragoon Guards and the 17th (Duke of Cambridge's) Lancers – twelve infantry battalions, five artillery batteries (one with Gatlings) and a vast array of supporting troops. Most of the volunteer corps and surviving African levies were still in the field. This gave him a grand total of more than 17,000 men, including 9,000 British infantry and 1,000 British cavalry. To oppose this awesome concentration of modern firepower the Zulus had only 25,000 exhausted and demoralized warriors. Chelmsford could not fail to win an overwhelming victory. Or could he?

Before he made the attempt, however, there was the small matter of burying the British dead at Isandlwana. The failure to give the bodies a decent burial had been the cause of much resentment and controversy since the battle. According to Captain Harford, the whole of the Rorke's Drift garrison had been 'eager to march back to Isandhlwana and bury the dead, but the authorities considered that too great a risk would be run'. By 'authorities' he meant Chelmsford, who, on 14 February, assured Colonel Glyn that the task would be undertaken once reinforcements had arrived. On 3 March, as if true to his word, he asked Glyn to consider how best to 'bury the dead at Isandlwana'. What force would he require? What road would he move down? Yet by 18 March he had changed his mind. 'I am inclined to think,' he wrote to Glyn, 'that the melancholy duty will have to be deferred until we have completed our work in Zululand.' He saw it, in effect, as a distraction that would 'seriously delay the advance of the northern column on its proper line'. But another factor may have influenced his decision: the danger that a full-scale burial party would find incriminating documents, particularly Crealock's order to Durnford of 22 January. By postponing the expedition he would increase the likelihood that such papers were either removed by the Zulus or destroyed by the elements.

Unbeknownst to Chelmsford, Glyn had given the recently promoted Lieutenant-Colonel Wilsone Black of the 2/24th permission to take a small party of horsemen back to Isandlwana on 14 March. It was comprised of thirty-three men, including fourteen officers of the NNC, fourteen men of the NMP and a handful of men from the 24th Regiment. Amongst the NNC officers was Lieutenant John Maxwell, who recorded:

There were bodies about in all directions, but hardly any dead Zulus. The bodies of the men of the 24th, mostly in their shirt sleeves, principally in small groups of 10 to 20, intermixed here and there with the bodies of Volunteers, distinguishable by their uniforms. In one place I noticed the bodies of several Volunteers together. What seemed to affect me most – strange to say – was the sight of six grey Artillery horses (English) lying where they had been assegaied in their harness; also a span of mules inspanned to a light travelling wagon. The dead of men, horses, and oxen, lying about was an affecting sight, and the stench was indescribable and almost suffocating . . . There were quantities of stores knocking about, amongst the rest haversacks, ammunition boots, and Artillery drivers' boots, a pair of which I noticed attached to Capt. Symonds' saddle.

As the party rode back over the saddle, it was fired upon by Zulus in rocks no more than eighty yards away. No one was hit and the party made it back to Rorke's Drift unscathed. Black brought away with him 'several of the general's papers', which were returned to their owner in Durban. Black also reported that almost a hundred wagons were still intact on the battlefield. Chelmsford, however, refused to sanction a large-scale operation to recover them and bury the dead, giving the 'sickening' stench of the corpses as his excuse. Many of the men who made up the garrisons at Helpmakaar and Rorke's Drift were outraged. 'This column ought to have taken some of [the wagons] back long ago,' wrote Captain Jones of the Royal Engineers, 'but we stick, stick, and have no go.'

This all changed in mid May, for two reasons: Chelmsford now had regular cavalry to provide security; and his chronic transport problem meant that the abandoned wagons at Isandlwana could no longer be ignored. At dawn on 21 May – six days after Black had led a second mounted patrol to the battlefield, recovering amongst other things Lieutenant Pope's diary – General Marshall set off from Rorke's Drift with some Natal volunteers, a composite cavalry regiment, five companies of the 2/24th, a battalion of the NNC and two guns. Only the horsemen and some of the black auxiliaries made it as far as the battlefield, arriving at around 9.15 a.m. Accompanying them were two war correspondents: Archibald Forbes of the *Daily News* and Melton Prior of the *Illustrated London News*. Forbes wrote:

No Zulus were seen. Flanking parties covered the hill on each side of the track, along which the head of the column pressed at the trot, with small detachments of Natal Carbineers in front of the Dragoons Guards. Now we were down in the last dip, had crossed the rocky bed of the little stream, and were cantering up the slope that stretched up to the crest on which were the waggons. Already tokens of the combat and bootless flight were apparent. The line of retreat towards Fugitive's Drift . . . lay athwart a rocky slope to our right front, with a precipitous ravine at its base. In the ravine dead men lay thick – mere bones, with toughened, discoloured skin like leather covering them, and clinging tight to them, the flesh all wasted away. Some were almost wholly dismembered, heaps of clammy yellow bones. I forbear to describe the faces, with their blackened features and beards blanched by rain and sun. Every man had been disembowelled. Some were scalped, and others subjected to yet ghastlier mutilation. The clothes had lasted better than the poor bodies they covered, and helped to keep the skeletons together.

All the way up the slope, I traced, by the ghastly token of dead men, the fitful line of flight. Most of the men hereabouts were infantry of the 24th. It was like a long string with knots in it, the string formed of single corpses, the knots of clusters of the dead, where, as it seemed, little groups might have gathered to make a hopeless, gallant stand and die. I came on a gully with a gun limber jammed on its edge, and the horses, their hides scored with assegai stabs, hanging in their harness down the steep face of the ravine. A little further on was a broken and battered ambulance waggon, with its team of mules mouldering in their harness, and around lay the corpses of soldiers, poor helpless wretches, dragged out of an intercepted vehicle, and done to death without a chance of life.

Approaching the crest, Forbes discovered that the 'slaughtered ones lay thick, so that the string became a broad belt'. Many wore the black uniform of the Natal Mounted Police. His colleague Prior was momentarily overcome:

In all the seven campaigns I have been in . . . I have not witnessed a scene more horrible. I have seen the dead and dying on a battle-field by hundreds and thousands; but to come suddenly on the spot where the slaughtered battalion of the 24th Regiment and others were lying at Isandhlwana, was far more appalling. Here I saw not the bodies, but the skeletons, of men whom I had known in life and health, some of whom I had known well, mixed up with the skeletons of oxen and horses, and with waggons thrown on their side, all in the greatest confusion, showing how furious had been the onslaught of the enemy. Scattered over the field of carnage were letters from wives or parents at home to their husbands or sons in the field, & portraits of babies and children sent by mothers to loving fathers – one was signed 'dear darling Dadda'. I could not help the tears coming into my eyes.

According to Forbes, Durnford's body was discovered in a patch of long grass 'near the right flank of the camp', his 'long moustache still clinging to the withered skin of his face'. Forbes added:

Captain ['Offy'] Shepstone recognised him at once, and identified him yet further by rings on the finger and a knife with the name on it in the pocket, which relics were brought away. Durnford had died hard – a central figure of a knot of brave men who had fought it out around their chief to the bitter end. A stalwart Zulu, covered by his shield, lay at the Colonel's feet. Around him, almost in a ring, lay about a dozen dead men, half being Natal Carbineers, riddled by assegai stabs. These gallant fellows were easily identified by their comrades who accompanied the column. Poor Lieutenant Scott was hardly at all decayed. Clearly they had rallied round Durnford in a last despairing attempt to cover the flank of the camp, and had stood fast from choice when they might have essayed to fly for their horses. Close beside the dead, at the picquet line, a gully traverses the ground in front of the camp. About 400 paces beyond this was the ground of the battle before the troops broke from their formation, and on both sides of this gully the dead lie very thickly. In one place nearly fifty of the 24th lie almost touching, as if they had fallen in rallying square. The line of straggling rush back to camp is clearly marked by skeletons all along the front.

What Forbes did not mention, and possibly did not witness, was 'Offy' Shepstone removing a packet of papers from Durnford's coat. This packet almost certainly contained a copy of the hastily composed order that Colonel Crealock had sent during the early hours of 22 January. If such a document had fallen into the hands of Durnford's family or supporters, particularly his sweetheart Fanny Colenso, it would have destroyed Chelmsford's claim that Durnford disobeyed a direct order to 'take command' of the camp at Isandlwana prior to the battle, and that this was the chief reason for the defeat. It was imperative for Chelmsford, therefore, that the order never saw the light of day, and Shepstone, it seems, was part of the conspiracy. Why? Because he despised Durnford's pro-Colenso humanitarian stance on 'native' affairs and had never forgiven him for criticizing the performance of Shepstone's regiment, the Natal Carbineers, at the Bushman's River Pass débâcle. He may also have been currying favour with Chelmsford in the hope of, say, a cushy staff appointment.★ We will never know for certain. But in the light of the deliberate cover-up that Chelmsford and his staff engineered in the aftermath of the battle, it seems logical to assume that they were once again involved. Whatever the case, the order was not made public during Chelmsford's lifetime, despite the fact that Crealock's order book, containing a copy, was found and returned to its owner in June 1879.

★ For more detail on the removal of papers from Durnford's coat, see the Epilogue.

The removal of Durnford's papers took a matter of seconds. He was then wrapped in a piece of canvas, possibly part of a tent, and buried under a cairn of stones, as were the rest of the non-24th dead. But at Colonel Glyn's special request, the bodies of the 24th were left where they lay. He wanted men of their own regiment to bury them and, with the surviving companies of the 1/24th at Helpmakaar, this would not take place until June 1879, almost six months after the battle.

Marshall's men spent several hours at Isandlwana. In that time, recalled the senior captain of the 17th Lancers: 'We fired the kraals all round, drove in the cattle we could find & shot what we couldn't catch.' Forbes spent his time wandering aimlessly through the 'desolate camp, amid the sour odour of stale death'. He wrote:

I chanced on many sad relics – letters from home, photographs, journals, blood-stained books, packs of cards. Lord Chelmsford's copying book, containing an impression of his correspondence with the Horse Guards, was found in one of his portmanteaus, and identified, in a kraal two miles off. Colonel Harness was busily engaged collecting his own belongings. Colonel Glyn found a letter from himself to Lieutenant Melvill, dated the day before the fight. The ground was strewn with brushes, toilet bags, pickle bottles, and unbroken tins of preserved meats and milk. Forges and bellows remained standing ready for the recommencement of work. The waggons in every case had been emptied, and the contents rifled. Bran lay spilt in heaps. Scarcely any arms were found, and no ammunition. There were a few stray bayonets and assegais, rusted with blood. No firearms.

Meanwhile the wagons worth salvaging – thirty-three in total, 'besides a cart or two, and two water carts' – had been hitched up to teams of horses and, at noon, began the return march to Rorke's Drift. 'If we had had more horses,' wrote Guy Dawnay,★ 'we might have perhaps brought out some eight more [wagons]; all the rest would want a deal of mending first. We had buried some of the

★ Dawnay had been attached to General Marshall's staff.

bodies . . . and had brought off some £4,000 worth of wagons, had found the 24th order book made up to January 21 [and] the staff of the colours of the 24th, etc.; in all a good day's work.' The following day the cavalry marched north to Landsman's Drift, from which point Newdigate's 2nd Division, with Chelmsford accompanying it, was about to undertake the second invasion of Zululand.

Chelmsford's loose plan was for his two divisions – Newdigate's in the north and Crealock's in the south – to converge on oNdini. But he appreciated that Crealock's 1st Division had to advance over much more difficult terrain and so allocated it a largely supporting role. 'The objective of the Northern force will be Ulundi [oNdini],' he wrote to Crealock on 12 April, 'and it is to be hoped that the 1st Division will be able to grapple successfully with the difficulties of the [Mhlathuze] river between Undi and St Paul's, and establish eventually an entrenched post and supply depot in the neighbourhood – thus assisting in the general advance against the King's own kraal.'

He had decided that Newdigate's force would cross the Blood River at Koppie Allein and, having linked up with Wood's Flying Column, rejoin the old Rorke's Drift/oNdini road in the vicinity of Babanango Mountain. There were two obvious alternatives: advance along the more northerly route past the Inlazatye Mountain that had originally been assigned to Wood's No. 4 Column; or the even shorter route past Isandlwana. The first was rejected because it would leave most of the Middle Thukela open to a Zulu counterattack; the second because he did not want to demoralize his young and inexperienced reinforcement troops by exposing them to the horrors of the Isandlwana battlefield. Colonel Buller confirmed this when he later told the queen's private secretary that Chelmsford chose the route he did because he had 'an unconquerable horror' of passing Isandlwana again.

Aware that a new British offensive was imminent, and that his depleted army was in no fit state to repel it, King Cetshwayo sent a stream of envoys to sue for peace in the second half of May. One such message was delivered by a local chief called Ndwandwe to Fort Chelmsford, an earthwork that General Crealock had constructed on the Lower Nyezane, on 15 May. From there the message was telegraphed to Chelmsford, who at once consulted Frere in Kimberley. Frere's response was that the terms of the ultimatum of 11 December 1878 were not negotiable. If Cetshwayo still wished to 'treat for peace', wrote Frere, 'he must send indunas of a suitable rank, fully empowered by the Great Council, as well as by himself, to the General's camp; in the meantime the movements of Her Majesty's forces cannot be suspended'. To these impossible terms, Chelmsford added more of his own: the surrender of all the captured Martini-Henry rifles, the two 7-pounder guns, all prisoners taken, 10,000 firearms, and a fine of between 10,000 and 20,000 cattle 'to be paid at once' and not by annual instalments. Frere and Chelmsford, the two men with the most to lose if hostilities were suspended, were doing everything in their power to see the war through to a victorious conclusion.

The long-awaited second invasion finally began on 31 May 1879 when Newdigate's 2nd Division crossed the Blood River into Zululand. The following day – Whit Sunday – began with an early Divine Service. 'But we got no breakfast,' recalled Corporal William Roe of the 58th Regiment, 'and had to march all day with nothing at all to eat, for they had served us out with flour the night before and we had nowhere to cook it.' It was a scorching day and the troops were exhausted by the time they reached their camping ground on the slopes of the Thelezeni Mountain, sixteen miles to the east, in the late afternoon. An hour or two later, by which time darkness was beginning to fall, Chelmsford was writing letters in his tent when a staff officer burst in: the Prince Imperial was missing.

14. The Prince Imperial

An extraordinary sequence of events had brought Prince Louis Napoleon – the 23-year-old former heir to the imperial throne of France – to South Africa to fight for his country's oldest enemy. Born in Paris on 16 March 1856, the first and only son of Emperor Napoleon III and the great-nephew of Napoleon Bonaparte, Louis had spent the first fourteen years of his life as a pampered monarch-in-waiting. But all this changed in 1870, when his father was deposed after a string of French defeats in the early stages of the Franco-Prussian War. Louis was forced to flee to England with his mother, the Empress Eugénie, and, despite a warm welcome from Queen Victoria, who had always had a soft spot for the French imperial family, he found it difficult to adjust to life in exile. His father was released by the Prussians after a brief imprisonment in 1871 and, for a short time, joined Louis and his mother in their rented mansion at Chislehurst in Kent.* But the broken former emperor died during an operation to remove a gallstone in 1873, and thereafter the hopes of the Bonapartists rested upon the slight shoulders of his shy and unprepossessing seventeen-year-old son.

By then, thanks to the intercession of the queen, Louis had entered the Royal Military Academy at Woolwich as a gentleman-cadet. The War Office's only condition: that Louis, a foreign prince, would not be able to take up a commission in the British Army on graduation. One of the prince's closest friends at Woolwich was Lieutenant Arthur Bigge, a gunner officer.† Bigge later told Sir Henry Ponsonby that the prince was a 'clever fellow' who 'devoted himself to any work he had to do'. At the age of twenty he had

---

* Camden House.
† Bigge's battery was part of Wood's column and saw action at the Battle of Khambula.

written a long memorandum on 'the improvements desirable' in artillery. 'Bigge says he may be right or wrong,' wrote Ponsonby, 'but he knows very few artillery officers who at 20 could have written such a paper . . . He was most eager and attentive in any matter he took up. He very seldom talked much of his prospects in France and when he did it was usually in chaff. Still it was evident that he always hoped to return there. Whether he ever believed that he would, Bigge cannot say.'

After three fruitful years at Woolwich, Louis passed out seventh in his class and first in the final examination. He was allowed to lead the passing-out parade in front of the duke of Cambridge and his mother, the guest of honour, who wept when he was singled out for praise in the governor's speech. In memory of his great-uncle, who had started his career as a gunner, Louis announced that had he been able to take up a commission it would have been with the Royal Artillery rather than the more prestigious Royal Engineers, in which corps the first ten graduates were traditionally guaranteed a place. As a special privilege, Louis was allowed to join Bigge's battery of the Royal Horse Artillery for its summer manoeuvres at Aldershot in 1875 and again in 1876. But apart from these happy bouts of part-time soldiering and the occasional visit from French Bonapartists, Louis had to content himself with the life of the idle rich: house parties, gentlemen's clubs, hunting and foreign travel.

Much to his mother's horror he was a frequent companion of the prince of Wales – who was thirteen years his senior – sharing his passion for schoolboy pranks if not for loose women. Despite the many opportunities available to him, there is no evidence that he had affairs. A superb rider, he would sooner have been aboard a horse than a woman. That is not to say he was uninterested in the fairer sex. Court gossip suggested that Louis's determination to serve in South Africa, and his reckless bravery while there, was an attempt to impress Princess Beatrice, the queen's youngest daughter, and make himself more acceptable to the British public. He had known Beatrice since first arriving in the country and there is no doubt that the two of them were close. But his love for Beatrice – if love it was – was of the strictly honourable kind.

An even more powerful motive for seeking active service, however, was the need to live up to the glories of his ancestors,
particularly his great-uncle. Only by proving himself in war would
he show himself to be a true Bonaparte. It explains why he and a
cousin – with his mother's begrudging support – offered their
services to the Austrian Army in the autumn of 1878 when it
seemed that Austria was about to be drawn into the Balkan conflict
between Russia and Turkey. Much to his chagrin, his offer was
not accepted, though he consoled himself in hindsight with the
knowledge that Austria did not come to blows. His appetite for
action, however, was undiminished. 'I am,' he wrote to his friend
Arthur Bigge, 'thirsting to smell powder.'

The opportunity came quicker than he could have imagined. In
the hectic week that followed the arrival of the news from
Isandlwana on 11 February 1879, as reinforcements were being
thrown together, Louis volunteered his services. The initial
response from Colonel Stanley, relayed to Louis by the duke of
Cambridge on 20 February, was not encouraging. The government
was not prepared, he said, to depart from its general rule of refusing
to allow anyone to go on active service except those who were
'called upon to go as a matter of duty to the State'. He nevertheless
appreciated the prince's 'chivalrous motives'. There was, however,
an alternative. On 21 February, in reply to an inquiry from the
duke, Stanley confirmed that he had no objection to the prince
travelling to South Africa as an observer. To facilitate this, Stanley
was prepared to write to Chelmsford, 'an old friend' in the Brigade
of Guards. The duke at once put this option to Louis, who readily
agreed. A slightly concerned queen noted in her journal: 'Heard
from George C. that the Prince Imperial is determined to go.
Difficulties were made as to his actually serving but George suggested his going out on his own hook, specially recommending
him to Sir Bartle Frere . . . The Prince is delighted and expressed a
great wish to serve and show his gratitude to me and the British
nation. He is to start on Thursday.'

In his letter of introduction to Frere, the duke said that Louis
wanted 'to see as much as he can of the coming campaign, in the

capacity of a spectator'. He requested Frere to 'give him any help in your power to enable him to see what he can'. A similar letter was dispatched to Chelmsford. It concluded: 'He is a fine young fellow, full of spirit & pluck; having many old cadet friends in the Artillery, he will doubtless find no difficulty in getting on, & if you can help him in any other way, please do so. My only anxiety on his account, would be that he is too *plucky* and *go-ahead*.' In other words, keep an eye on him. Cambridge was right to issue the warning: Louis had the reputation of a bit of a daredevil whose favourite party trick was vaulting on to a horse. It was a skill that would fail him in Zululand.

Though his mother Eugénie did not want him to go, fearing for his safety, she would not stand in his way and duly thanked the duke for helping her son. But the queen was aware of her true feelings. 'Heard the Prince Imperial had embarked at 4,' she wrote in her journal on 27 February, 'such a trial & separation for the poor Empress!'

On learning that the Prince Imperial had volunteered to go out to South Africa, the British public gave him a rousing send-off, as his tearful mother escorted him on board the troopship SS *Danube* at Southampton docks during the afternoon of the 27th. But one man was not elated when he heard the news: Disraeli. Worried that any favour shown to Louis might offend France's Republican government, he wrote to Salisbury in annoyance: 'I am quite mystified about that little abortion, the Prince Imperial. I thought we had agreed not to sanction his adventure? Instead of that he has royal audiences previous to departure, is reported to be a future staff officer and is attended to the station by Whiskerandos★ himself . . . What am I to say on this? H.M. knows my little sympathy with the Buonapartes.' Salisbury replied: 'I am as puzzled as you are. Every way it seems to me a mistake.' And so it would prove.

Louis, however, could not see beyond the delicious prospect of glory in battle. On 26 March, two days after reaching Cape Town, he wrote to his mother from Government House: 'Tomorrow I

★ Field Marshal Lord Napier of Magdala.

leave for Durban where I am eager to arrive, for a battle is expected.'
He landed at Durban on 1 April, but was too late to take part in
Chelmsford's relief of Gingindlovu, which was already under way.
It was during his stay in Durban, anxiously awaiting Chelmsford's
return, that he bought a replacement for a horse that had died on
the voyage. The new horse was a handsome grey gelding, between
fifteen and sixteen hands, that Louis named 'Tommy'. It was not,
as some have suggested, highly strung and skittish, but placid,
good-tempered and easy to mount.

Chelmsford returned to Durban on 9 April and was met at the
station by Louis and the four reinforcement generals. He at once
took to the young prince and offered him a post as an extra
aide-de-camp. Louis was delighted and told him that it was what
'he himself was anxious for'. On informing the duke of Cambridge,
Chelmsford asked him to assure the empress that he would 'look
after the Prince to the best of my ability' and was sure he would
find him a 'very valuable addition' to his staff. No doubt Chelmsford
thought he could keep an eye on Louis if he was a member of his
staff. But by giving him semi-official military status he had already
gone further than the duke had intended.

The impression Louis made on the other members of the staff
was generally positive. 'The Prince was a charming young fellow,
burning to distinguish himself, a capital rider and swordsman,'
wrote Captain Molyneux. 'But of course, like all high-spirited
young men a little difficult to manage, and I think the fever never
quite left him.' He had caught a slight fever soon after landing
at Durban but was well enough to accompany Chelmsford to
Pietermaritzburg on 17 April. A fall from an unruly horse five days
later, however, meant that he had to remain in bed when the staff
moved on to Ladysmith. He rejoined them on the 27th, having
travelled up in Chelmsford's carriage, and was part of the expedition
in early May to Khambula camp, where he enjoyed an emotional
reunion with Bigge and Lieutenant Frederick Slade, another friend
from Woolwich. At Utrecht, where Chelmsford established his
headquarters on 6 May, Louis met Paul Deléage, the correspondent
of *Le Figaro* who had been sent to cover the Prince Imperial's war

exploits. Deléage, a staunch Republican, had expected to find an
effete dilettante and was pleasantly surprised by the eager, self-
effacing young prince, declaring him 'a Frenchman with all the
qualities of that race'.

A crucial area of staff work prior to and during the invasion of
enemy territory was the survey of possible routes of advance. This
task was ordinarily the responsibility of the Quartermaster-
General's Department but, until now, Chelmsford had got by
without a dedicated staff officer, relying instead on old maps and
scraps of intelligence. General Clifford's promptings had, however,
encouraged him to regularize his staff arrangements and on 8 May
he appointed Lieutenant-Colonel Richard Harrison, RE, a
reinforcement officer, as his assistant quartermaster-general in
charge of surveying. Harrison recalled:

I said I would do my best; but I was well aware of the difficulties that had
to be faced . . . No road reports or military sketches of the country existed.
There was very little information regarding the enemy . . . That same
afternoon an officer, Lieut. Carey, 98th Regiment, was appointed to assist
me in military sketching; and the Prince Imperial was lent me to collect
and compile information in regard to the distribution of troops and
depots.

Lieutenant Jahleel Brenton Carey was an obvious choice to assist
Harrison. Born in July 1847, the son of a Leicestershire vicar, he
had been educated in France before passing out of Sandhurst with
a free commission in 1865. With no money and even less influence,
he chose to join a battalion of the unfashionable West India Regiment, in which he could live in comparative comfort. He served
with it for five years in West Africa, Central America and Jamaica.
But in 1870 it was disbanded, and Carey left on half-pay with few
prospects. He at once volunteered to join the English Ambulance
– a humanitarian organization that was offering medical aid to both
sides during the Franco-Prussian War – and on his return was
offered an exchange into the 81st Regiment. From there he transferred to the 98th Regiment and in 1878 was accepted into the

Staff College. He passed out with 'high testimonials' in time to volunteer for service in Zululand, arriving in late March with a draft of the 94th Regiment. His appointment as Harrison's DAQMG may well have been partly due to his excellent conduct* during the evacuation of the supply ship SS *Clyde*, which went down with vast quantities of stores and ammunition en route from Cape Town to Durban on 3 April. He had also been commended, during the march up-country with drafts of the 1/24th, 'for surveying the route for the troops, and in the selection of camping grounds'. Now he would have to do the same in hostile territory, and Louis, an observer, had been detailed to help him. It helped that Louis was a keen learner and that Carey spoke excellent French. The suggestion that the two became close, however, is not borne out by the evidence. Both took part in a number of reconnaissances prior to the invasion, but only one in each other's company. Nor did they mess together: Louis dining with the general's staff and Carey in Harrison's tent.

Louis left on his first patrol, in company with Harrison and William Drummond, on 13 May. Two days later, having met up with Buller and 170 horsemen at Conference Hill, they rode south past Thelezeni Hill towards the northern edge of the Nqutu Range, where they spied a small band of Zulus on the hill to their front. Lieutenant Charlie Raw was sent ahead with six of his Basutos, and when they reached the summit they discovered that the Zulus had gone. But this did not deter the excitable Louis. 'After galloping about from point to point,' recalled Harrison, 'the Prince espied a Zulu on a distant kopje, and went for him. Off went Lieutenant Raw and the six Basutos after the impatient Prince, and on came Baker's Horse in the wake of the Basutos. The kopje was reached in time for them to see a few scared Zulus making off across country, far down on the plains below.'

Louis had shown, during his first exposure to Zulus, what a liability he would be to those charged with his safety. Nor was it an isolated incident. A trooper of the FLH recalled:

* For which Carey was mentioned in dispatches.

When we were on the move during the day, riding in half-sections, he was a real terror; if any Zulus were seen – and they were usually on the slope of a hill – he would dart out of the rank, his servant behind him, and race sword in hand to get them . . . Twice on that patrol I was ordered – being a light-weight and having a fleet horse – with several others to head him off . . . After a long chase, we would gallop up on either side of him shouting 'Halt!' He would draw rein, smiling sweetly, and say, 'Thank you, thank you!' replace the sword in the sheath, and calmly ride back with us. The wigging he was going to receive from Buller did not appear to trouble him in the least.

Buller was incensed and, once the patrol had returned to Utrecht, told Chelmsford that he would not allow 'the Prince to accompany him again on his reconnaissances, considering it too dangerous, as the Zulus were concealed every where'. Heeding the warning, Chelmsford told Harrison to ensure Louis never 'left the immediate precincts of the camp without a proper escort'. His duties, thereafter, were to be confined to sketching 'the camps occupied by Headquarters, and the roads they traversed when on the march'. The work of sketching in the field would now be the exclusive preserve of Harrison and Carey.

But on 29 May, two days before the second invasion was due to begin, Chelmsford relented by taking Louis with him on a final reconnaissance of the route they would take on 1 June. Their escort consisted of three troops of the 1st Dragoon Guards; a fourth troop was ordered to start an hour earlier 'to see the road was clear, and no chance of the Commander in Chief being surprised'. The patrol was uneventful and, on the ride back, Louis was asked by Captain Molyneux, Chelmsford's ADC, why he had risked his life chasing Zulus on the 15th when the death of a warrior or two would hardly change the course of the campaign. 'You are right, I suppose,' responded Louis, 'but I could not help it. I feel I must do something.' At that moment, hearing a shot from the flank, Louis again drew his sword and galloped off into the gathering gloom.

Molyneux started after him, shouting, 'Prince, I must order you to come back!'

Luckily Louis saw sense and reined in. 'It seems I am never to be without a nurse,' he remarked balefully, adding: 'Oh, forgive me. But don't you think you are a little too phlegmatic?'

Molyneux reminded him of their earlier conversation and Louis laughed, saying he had answered him 'rather neatly'.

Meanwhile Carey and a staff officer called Captain Jones had accompanied the advance troop – forty men of the 1st Dragoon Guards, under Captain Harry Watson, and two black guides – to 'make a rough sketch of the proposed road'. Carey knew Watson well, having passed through Staff College with him the previous year. Once through the gap between the Nceceni and Thelezeni mountains, they rode due south until they came to the edge of the Nqutu Hills and some recently evacuated kraals. 'The ashes of the fire being still hot,' wrote Watson, 'I suppose the beggars had seen us coming up the hill.' They then turned to the north-west and, after recrossing the Tshotshosi River, examined yet more near-deserted kraals, where they spoke to four women who said the men had left the previous day. 'Both Carey and Jones were delighted at having gone so far,' recalled Watson. He then gave the order to feed the horses, but kept a close eye on the neighbouring mealie fields.

'Will you offsaddle?' asked Carey.

'Decidedly not,' replied Watson. 'My horses have got nosebags with a feed of corn, and only half of my troops shall feed at a time, the other half remaining mounted, and when the first half have fed, they can mount whilst the others feed.'

'I see, Watson, you neglect nothing,' said Carey.

'I don't like mealie fields,' came the response, 'for they could conceal a force.'

'You are quite right,' conceded Carey.

No sooner had the horses finished feeding than Captain Herbert Stewart, Marshall's brigade major and another classmate from Staff College, rode up with some other staff officers and informed Watson that Chelmsford would not be joining him. Watson had, said Stewart, 'gone too far' and would not get his troop back 'by nightfall'. Watson admitted his error. Hearing that his regiment 'might not be sent into Zululand at all, but into the Transvaal', he had taken the opportunity to see as much of the enemy's territory as he could. But he had overdone it, and on the way back, just as Stewart had warned, one of his troop horses broke down when he was still twelve miles from camp. Watson elected to remain behind with the stricken horse, as did his sergeant-major, one other trooper and two of the African guides. The rest of the patrol rode on, and Watson and his small party, moving at a 'snail's pace', finally reached the 2nd Division's main camp at Koppie Allein at 9 p.m. He was mightily relieved, but could not help feeling that 'Carey and Jones behaved a little shabbily, for they never waited to see how I was getting on with my dismounted man and sick horse, but hurried on into camp with my advanced guard.' They did not, he supposed, 'fancy a bivouac out'. Sadly, Carey failed to learn anything from this eerily prescient patrol.

Two days later the invasion began, and, by nightfall, the bulk of Newdigate's 2nd Division was camped on the Zulu bank of the Blood River. That evening an impatient Louis asked Harrison if he 'might extend his sketch beyond the camp to be occupied the next day, and make a reconnaissance of the road to be traversed the following day'. Without consulting Chelmsford, Harrison agreed, provided that Louis took his 'usual escort'. He knew that no impi was in the neighbourhood and assumed that cavalry patrols would be roaming 'far in advance of the camp' and therefore the prince would be safe. A little later Carey asked if he might go along to 'verify' his earlier sketches and Harrison agreed. There was, however, no pressing operational reason for such a patrol. Carey had ridden over the same ground twice and the approximate position for the camp on 2 June had already been chosen. Harrison was simply indulging Louis's thirst for adventure. He had not, however, consulted Chelmsford, and by giving Louis permission to ride ahead of the main column he was contravening the general's instructions to keep the prince close to the camp. Before Louis departed, a further safeguard would be disregarded: never to allow the prince to leave camp without a 'proper escort'.

During the morning of 1 June, as the column prepared to march to its next camp on the slopes of Thelezeni Mountain, Carey went to the Cavalry Brigade HQ to collect a mixed escort of Bettington's* and Shepstone's Horse.† In the event, Stewart, the brigade major, ordered up half a dozen men from each corps. But the six Basutos of Shepstone's Horse paraded in the wrong place, and Louis, impatient to be off, insisted on leaving without them. Carey was loath to pull rank on the prince and so left instructions for the Basutos to meet them en route. The patrol, when it left, was composed of just nine men: Louis, Carey, a Zulu guide, Sergeant Willis, Corporal Grubb and Troopers Cochrane, Le Tocq, Abel and Rogers of Bettington's Horse. The troopers took along two spare horses and a white terrier that had attached itself to their mess.

Louis rode out of camp at the head of the patrol, armed with a revolver and sword, and wearing the dark blue undress uniform of the Royal Artillery. Beneath his white cork sun-helmet his hair was closely cropped; a thin moustache contrived, but failed, to make his baby face appear older. He was riding his favourite horse, the tall grey 'Tommy' that he had bought in Durban. A couple of days earlier, noticing that Louis had problems mounting Tommy, Captain Lord William Beresford‡ had asked: 'Is the horse too high for you, sir?'

No, said Louis, but his trousers were 'too tight', making it difficult for him to mount. He was wearing the same trousers on 1 June.

Carey was armed with just a pistol and sporting the type of dark blue patrol jacket favoured by the staff. Yet his bushy moustache and old-fashioned mutton-chop whiskers made him instantly recognizable. Bettington's men were clad in the same buff corduroy jackets and wide-brimmed hats worn by the NNH, and they too carried Martini-Henry carbines.

It was a bright, crisp winter morning, and, after a gentle ride of an hour or so, the party reached the northern slope of Thelezeni Mountain, close to the site chosen for the 2nd Division's camping

---

* Raised after Isandlwana by Captain Claude Bettington, the former adjutant of 2/1st NNC, and mainly composed of white NCOs of the disbanded 3rd NNC.
† Formerly Durnford's NNH, now commanded by Captain 'Offy' Shepstone.
‡ Buller's ADC.

ground, where they were supposed to meet Shepstone's Basutos. As they waited, they were met by Colonel Harrison, who had come forward to lay out the camp. Harrison was disturbed to see no sign of the Basutos, whom he had 'specially ordered to be detailed, because they have a much keener sense of sight and hearing than Europeans, and consequently made better scouts'. His parting words, as he rode off to attend to his own duties, were that they were 'not to go forward without them'. But the prince was having none of it, and, when Carey insisted on waiting for the Basutos, he replied: 'Oh no we are quite strong enough.' Given that Louis had no official military rank and was technically a civilian, Carey was in nominal command of the patrol. Yet he had clearly waived his military superiority in deference to the prince's social standing. To all intents and purposes, therefore, the prince was in control. The Honourable William Drummond, Chelmsford's intelligence chief, put it thus: 'The Prince, who was very fond of soldiering, took the command of the men, Carey allowing him to do so to please him.'

From the site of the Thelezeni camp the patrol continued for seven miles along the spine of a ridge until it came within sight of the Tshotshosi Valley. With the sun now directly overhead and the horses tired from their exertions, Carey suggested offsaddling in the centre of the flat-topped ridge. But Louis said he 'preferred to do so nearer the river and merely ordered the men to loosen their girths'. He and Carey spent the next half an hour sketching from this commanding position, and then led the patrol down into the valley, where, about 300 yards from the river, they came upon a small Zulu kraal with six beehive huts surrounding a stone cattle pen. Once the Zulu guide had checked that the kraal was deserted, Louis gave the order to offsaddle.

The kraal was hemmed in on three sides by thick grass and plantations of mealies that stood six feet high. A hundred yards from its entrance, over mostly open ground, lay a shallow donga with a tiny stream at its centre that emptied out into the Tshotshosi. Carey may not have recognized it, but, according to Captain Watson, who returned there in August, it 'was one of the very kraals we visited' during the patrol of 29 May. 'I cannot imagine,' wrote Watson, 'a worse position for halting, close to the river bed, along which any number of the enemy might have crept, with tall thick grass up to the kraal itself. Anyone could get close up the kraal without being perceived.' Drummond was even more critical: 'They had no business to off saddle their horses at all, 9 miles in the enemy's country, and they selected as dangerous as possible a spot for doing so.' Clearly Carey had learnt nothing from his earlier patrol with Watson; either that or he was so in awe of his royal companion that he dared not gainsay him.

It was now 2.40 p.m., and for the next hour or so the members of the patrol relaxed in the sun while their unsaddled horses grazed near by. Some made coffee with water from the river; Louis dozed against one of the huts. At 3.20 Carey sat down next to him and they discussed the merits of his great-uncle's military campaigns of 1796 and 1800. Then, at around 3.35 p.m., Carey suggested saddling up, as it was getting late. No, said Louis, wait another ten minutes. But only half that time had elapsed when he told Carey to give the order. It took a few minutes to gather the horses and, as they were being saddled, the African guide announced that he had seen a Zulu at the river. There was no panic, but the saddling process became a little more urgent. When they were finished, Carey gave the order 'Mount' and the men began to swing into their saddles. As they did so, a shot rang out from the long grass to the south of the kraal, followed by a fusilade. Carey, one of the first up, 'saw the puffs of smoke, heard the volley fired into us, and saw the Zulus rush forward with a shout'.

It was a party of about forty local Zulus from various royal regiments – including the iNgobamakhosi, uMbonambi and uNokhenke – who had stayed behind to track the British advance. Some of them were relatives of Sobhuza, the owner of the kraal, who had gone into hiding with his family. They had spotted the British descending the hill and, seeing their paltry numbers, decided to attack. It had taken them this long to work their way down a nearby hill, up the bed of the Tshotshosi and into the long grass round the kraal.

On hearing the shots, the horses reared and plunged. Carey's first instinct was to flee towards the donga and he gave his horse its head. He was closely followed by Cochrane and Abel, the first two into their saddles. Halfway to the donga Abel's horse was shot and he was thrown to the ground.

Corporal Grubb and Sergeant Willis were the next to leave the kraal, Willis's feet not yet in the stirrups. As Grubb rode out of the kraal, he saw Rogers trying to escape on foot. Closely pursued by Zulus, Rogers turned and fired. Seconds later he was assegaied in the back. That just left Louis, Le Tocq and the African guide. Le Tocq's horse had shied on hearing the gunshots, almost throwing its rider and causing him to drop his carbine. He got off to recover it but could not remount properly, and made his escape with his stomach resting on his horse's saddle. From this awkward vantage point he could see that Louis had also failed to mount and was running alongside his horse, 'clinging to the stirrup leather or part of the holster'.

On seeing Abel's horse fall ahead of him, Grubb's horse lurched to the right, closely followed by Willis's. Le Tocq now appeared on their left, still lying across his horse, and shouted: 'Put spurs to your horse, boy, the Prince is down.' Grubb looked round and saw Louis 'hanging on to something below his horse' which he took to be a stirrup leather or one of the holsters that hung in front of his saddle. Then he 'dropped and the horse seemed to trample him'. Grubb claimed later that he was about to fire at the prince's pursuers when his horse jumped into the donga and threw him on to its neck, causing him to drop his carbine. Moments later Tommy appeared without his owner.

Carey, Cochrane and Le Tocq all crossed the donga to the front of the kraal; Grubb, Willis and the riderless Tommy a little further to the right. As he scrambled up the far incline, Cochrane looked back and saw Louis running towards the donga with at least fourteen Zulus in close pursuit. Yet he made no attempt to stop and help him; nor did Carey, though he later said he tried and failed to rally the men. According to the Zulus, the fleeing riders did not slow down until they had reached a patch of rocks that was at least half a mile away. Louis was left to his fate.

Having failed to vault into Tommy's saddle, he had managed to cling on to the near-side pistol holster as his horse charged after the others. But, just a few yards from the donga, the stitching between the two holsters gave way and Louis fell heavily to the ground. As he rose, badly winded, he turned to see a group of at least eight Zulus charging towards him. His hand went instinctively to his sword hilt, but there was nothing there: his belt had snapped during the bumpy flight from the kraal and a warrior had already picked up the fallen sword. He drew his revolver instead and fired at the nearest warrior. The bullet missed and the warrior replied with a throwing assegai, which caught Louis in the shoulder. He pulled it out and fired at a second warrior, but missed again and was hit by a second spear. Neither of the wounds was fatal, and Louis still had enough energy to run into the donga before turning to fire two more ineffective shots. A third spear caught him in the thigh and, having tugged it free with his right hand, he was in the process of shifting it to his left when he stumbled in a hole and fell backwards. The Zulus were on him in an instant, a warrior named Xabanga being the first to stab him in the chest. Others followed suit and he was almost certainly dead by the time a spear was driven through his right eye, bursting the eyeball and entering his brain. Abel had been killed by this time – stabbed in the back as he rose from his fall – though Mnukwa, the induna of the small party, had tried to take him alive. The black guide was also dead, intercepted a short distance from the kraal as he tried to escape on foot.

Could Louis and some of the others have been saved if Carey had rallied the escort? Probably not. They had just three carbines and a revolver between them, and Louis was killed within a very short time of the initial ambush. But Carey should at least have tried. Instead he, Cochrane and Le Tocq kept riding hard until they had almost reached the top of the ridge, ignoring the flagging Grubb's signal for them to stop. Only after they had slowed to a walk did Grubb and Willis catch up. It was now that Grubb confirmed that the prince had fallen. Carey, not wanting to believe the inevitable, asked him twice if he was certain. Yes, came the

reply. Then there was nothing for it, said Carey, but to ride back
to camp with the awful news.

Wood's Flying Column, meanwhile, had set up camp near the
Mvunyane River to the north. Buller and members of his staff were
out reconnoitring the road for the next day's march when they saw
five horsemen riding towards them, 'waving their arms about
and shouting'. Recognizing Carey, Buller asked him what had
happened. He could only mumble, in reply, that the Zulu Army
was 'after them'.

'Where is the prince?' snapped Buller.

'I fear he is killed,' said Carey.

To which Buller responded: 'Then you ought to be shot.'

There was 'but one feeling out there', one of those present said
later. 'That Capt. Carey was a "coward", & had ridden away for
his life.'

Buller at once trained his telescope in the direction of the fatal
kraal and 'could only discover 6 Zulus, driving back 3 loose horses
over the hill, in the contrary direction'. The small number of Zulus
made Carey's dereliction of duty even less forgivable in his eyes; as
did the knowledge that, only the day before, he had specifically
warned Carey to avoid that very kraal because he knew it was
'inhabited' by an 'old woman & others' and was 'unsafe'.

Followed by a disconsolate Carey and the surviving troopers,
Buller led the way back to the 2nd Division's camp at Thelezeni.
They arrived after dark and, on the way to Chelmsford's tent,
Carey met Colonel Harrison and gave him the bad news.

An incredulous Harrison asked: 'You don't mean to say you left
the prince?'

'It was no use stopping,' implored Carey. 'He was shot at the
first volley.'

'You ought to have tried, at all events, to bring away the body,'
remarked Harrison.

Much 'overcome' by what Harrison had said, Carey related what
had happened in as much detail as he could remember. 'Immediately
afterwards,' recalled Harrison, 'I went to see Lord Chelmsford, and
asked him to allow me to go at once and look for the Prince. After

what Carey had said I hardly expected to find him alive, but anyhow I thought I might bring home his body. The Chief, however, would not let me go; all he said was, "I don't want to lose you too."'

William Drummond and a number of other officers also volunteered 'to go out to the spot at once and try to find the Prince, dead or alive, but the general would not permit it'. He was 'averse', thought Drummond, 'to risking fresh lives in the dark'. He was also in a state of shock. Just when the campaign was beginning to go his way, this had to happen. The repercussions back home were too awful to contemplate. That evening Major Grenfell saw him 'in his tent with his head on the table in a state of absolute despair'.

Carey, meanwhile, had returned to his tent to write a letter to his wife that reeked of self-pity and not a little self-justification. He wrote:

You know the dreadful news, ere you receive this, by telegram. I am a ruined man, I fear, though . . .I could do nothing else . . . Our camp was bad, but then, I have been so laughed at for taking a squadron with me that I had grown reckless and would have gone with two men. To-morrow we go with the 17th Lancers to find his body. Poor fellow! But it might have been my fate. The bullets tore around us, and with only my revolver what could I do? The men all bolted and now I fear the Prince was shot on the spot as his saddle is torn as if he tried to get up. No doubt they will say I should have remained by him, but I had no idea he was wounded and thought he was after me . . . Annie, what will you think of me! I was such a fool to stop in that camp; I feel it now, though at the time I did not see it . . . Of course all sorts of yarns will get into the papers, and without hearing my tale I shall be blamed, but honestly, between you and me, I can only be blamed for the camp.

The following morning would reveal the prince's fate. General Marshall led the huge search party of two squadrons of the 17th Lancers, one of the 1st Dragoon Guards, a screen of irregular horsemen and Bengough's battalion of NNC. Chelmsford could not bring himself to go and sent his ADC, Captain Molyneux, in his stead. Guided by Carey, the search party left at seven and reached the kraal two hours later. Some of Buller's horsemen were already there. Near to the kraal they had found the bodies of Abel and Rogers, 'both assegaied, & one wounded horse which we afterwards shot'. There was no sign of the African guide. The prince's body was discovered in the donga. Surgeon-Major Scott reported:

It was stripped and laying on its back, and covered with assegai wounds, no bullet wound being found upon it. On close examination of the wounds, the position of the arms, and other indications, we were led to the conclusion that death could only have resulted after a severe struggle. Out of seventeen wounds, all of which were received in front, only five, in all probability, would have resulted in death. The left forearm was wounded in two places, leaving no doubt but that the injuries had been received in self-defence. On his person we found a gold neck chain, to which was attached some medals, and near his body was one blue sock marked 'N', also a pair of spurs, all of which were brought into camp.

The rest of his clothes and possessions had been taken by the Zulus, including his sword, which was later presented to Cetshwayo. Many of the stab marks on his chest were post-mortem and consistent with the Zulu practice of *hlomula*, whereby each warrior marked his participation in the killing of a gallant foe. He had also been eviscerated.

A guard of honour, composed entirely of officers, carried Louis's body on a makeshift stretcher of lances and blankets to a horse-drawn ambulance further up the hill. Then Dawnay and one or two others built a small cairn out of rocks to mark that spot where the prince had fallen. Abel and Rogers were buried a short way off.

The ambulance reached the camp on Thelezeni at 2 p.m., and, three hours later, the whole division was ordered to attend a funeral parade. The troops were formed up on three sides of a hollow square and into its centre processed a guard of artillerymen with reversed carbines, then a gun carriage carrying Louis's body wrapped in the *tricolore* of Republican France, and finally Chelmsford and his staff. Paul Deléage, the distraught correspondent of *Le Figaro*, described the doleful scene:

Around the body, the officers of the Royal Artillery, that is to say, nearly all the comrades of the Prince's studies, and a little farther off, leaning sadly on his cane, with reddened eyes and heavy heart, that unfortunate General who has been spared no misfortunes since the day of his arrival in South Africa, and then a few paces from Lord Chelmsford the officers of the General's staff, the comrades of yesterday . . . And on either side, those two red lines of soldiers, old and young, fixed and motionless, leaning on their rifles, some thinking of their comrades whose blood had already been drunk by the soil of Zululand; others dismayed to see, at their first step upon that wild land, so many high things laid low by the assegai of the Zulu.

The day after the funeral Louis's body began the long journey back to England, and Paul Deléage went with it. 'Poor little fellow,' wrote a lieutenant of the 94th, 'he was awfully cut up & he is going home. He said he dared not send a telegraph to the Empress, but takes back the chain & locket, the pall cover, i.e. the tricolor flag, a lock of his hair & a spur & one of his socks that he found.'

Before the funeral Chelmsford had passed on the melancholy news to Sir Bartle Frere in the form of a brief telegram. He now wrote a more detailed letter of explanation, describing the sequence of coincidences that had cost Louis his life: first, he had not been aware that the prince had been given permission to reconnoitre the ground for the next camp, and had he been he would never have let the prince go with such a small escort; second, the prince had refused to wait for the six Basutos, who 'would have acted as scouts when the Prince off-saddled and would have prevented his being surprised'; thirdly the party 'off-saddled in the only dangerous place along the whole line, where high tamboskie grass and a large mealie field gave every facility for a surprise'; fourth, the prince, when asked to saddle up by Lieutenant Carey, requested another ten minutes which 'made all the difference'; fifth, the prince 'was riding his tallest horse, on to which he had always great difficulty in mounting'. Chelmsford added:

I suppose my enemies in the English Press will make a raid upon me again and endeavour to throw the whole blame upon my shoulders. I have always felt that it was somewhat unfair to saddle me with the responsibility which naturally would be attached to such a charge, but I had to accept it with all the rest. I did my best to prevent the Prince from running undue risks, but unless I had kept him tied to my saddle, I could not ever be sure that he was not doing something foolish and risky.

Chelmsford attached no specific blame, at this stage, to Lieutenant Carey. But the feeling among the soldiers of Newdigate's 2nd Division and Wood's Flying Column – particularly the officers – was universally hostile to Harrison's deputy. 'The indignation in camp is great,' wrote a captain of the 94th Regiment, 'as there is no doubt whatever that if Lieutenant Carey and the Natal Horse had stuck to the Prince, which it was their duty to do, he, poor boy, would now have been alive.' Lieutenant Frederick Slade of the artillery, a friend of the prince since Woolwich, was even more vitriolic in a letter to his mother:

Neither Carey nor his men made the slightest attempt to stand, & in plain words 'they ran away' & left the poor dear little Prince to die fighting on foot single handed. I cannot telegram what we all think of Carey's behaviour, but will tell you what Buller told him to his face yesterday when they met, 'You ought to be shot'. I think I may safely say that *this* is the opinion of every man in the column. To think that a British officer should leave any man, and more the *Prince Imperial* of *France* to fall into the hands of the Zulus without making the slightest attempt to save him, is too disgraceful. I had rather be lying at the bottom of the deepest donga in Zululand than be in Carey's shoes.

The large press corps was hardly more sympathetic to Carey. As Phil Robinson of the *Daily Telegraph* hurried back to Utrecht to telegraph the news to Britain, he met Captain Harry Watson and told him that it was 'a most disgraceful business, and that Carey deserved to be shot'. Watson was not that surprised, never having thought of Carey as particularly brave. 'I suppose he got in a panic,' wrote Watson to his family, 'but it brings awful disgrace on the Service.'

Such was the level of opprobrium directed towards Carey that on 4 June – by which time the 2nd Division had advanced its camp to the Tshotshosi Valley, just a few hundred yards from Sobhuza's kraal – he demanded a Court of Inquiry to clear his name. It met the same day, with General Marshall as president, and considered evidence from Harrison, Carey and the surviving members of the patrol. Its conclusion was that Carey failed in his duty to take charge of the escort and was 'much to blame' for leaving half of it behind. Moreover, said the court, the 'selection of the kraal where the halt was made' showed a 'lamentable want of military prudence' and it deeply regretted 'that no effort was made to rally the escort and show a front to the enemy'. It therefore recommended that Carey be tried by general court martial.

The trial was delayed for a few days because a large force of Zulus had been spotted on high ground to the east of the Ntinini Stream and a battle seemed imminent. But the warriors turned out to be local levies, rather than royal troops, and a minor action by British cavalry on 5 June – during which the adjutant of the 17th Lancers was killed – was the sole consequence. That same day the 2nd Division established a new laager on the Nondweni River and, a day later, a stone earthwork that came to be known as Fort Newdigate was begun near by. It was to be the first in a chain of strongpoints leading back to Koppie Allein.

The troops, however – many of them young and inexperienced – felt far from secure in Fort Newdigate. During the evening of 6 June, a panic by sentries of the 58th on the east of the laager resulted in a 'regular blaze of rifles' as the alarm spread round the camp. 'I felt sure it was all humbug,' wrote Guy Dawnay, 'and managed to make the men on my right cease firing, a bullet from somewhere inside the camp whizzing past my head as I was talking to them. Never saw anything so dangerous, and it was from beginning to end a false alarm.' Seven men were wounded and a number of horses killed before order was restored. Major John Chard was on picquet duty with a party of Royal Engineers and, having survived Rorke's Drift, narrowly escaped being shot by his own side. One regiment had fired more than 1,200 rounds and an artillery battery had used six rounds of canister, a shell reserved for close-range fire, without seeing a single Zulu. Little wonder that Fort Newdigate was henceforth known as 'Fort Funk'.

It was strangely apt – if somewhat unfortunate for the defendant himself – that Carey's court martial should take place at this inauspicious location. Wood's Flying Column had returned to the border for supplies and, as the 2nd Division awaited its return, Chelmsford took the opportunity to hold the trial. It began on 12 June with Colonel Glyn, now commanding a brigade of the 2nd Division, as president and Carey conducting his own defence. The charge was that Carey had 'misbehaved before the enemy' on 1 June when 'in command of an escort in attendance' on the Prince Imperial, 'who was making a reconnaissance'. On the patrol being attacked he had 'galloped away' and did not even attempt 'to rally the said escort, and otherwise defend the said Prince'.

Carey's defence rested on convincing the court that he had not been in command and that nothing could have been done to save Louis. The evidence of the other four survivors was largely supportive as to the first point – the prince had indeed appeared to be in command – but not necessarily the second. Trooper Le Tocq, for example, said that he would have expected help if he had been in the prince's place. 'They might have assisted me by firing and keeping the enemy in check,' he declared. Sergeant Willis seemed to support this view when he said that they could easily have rallied at a distance of 250 yards from the donga and still made good their escape. Cochrane and Grubb, on the other hand, thought that no useful help could have been rendered the prince.

In his closing speech, Carey emphasized the suddenness of the attack and the panic of the horses. 'I acted on the spot for the best,' he said in a voice shaking with emotion, 'and as I thought, for the safety of my party. I deeply regretted the loss of the young Prince and would willingly have changed places with him, but I do not now believe, that any effort of mine could have saved him.'

The prosecuting officer, Captain Brander, responded with a simple yet unanswerable point: 'No word of any witness goes to show that the slightest attempt was made to rally or defend the Prince, whereas all agreed that they galloped away.' The members of the court agreed and, though they privately sympathized with Carey, their official verdict was guilty. All that Glyn could do to lessen the severity of the crime was offer a number of extenuating circumstances, including the observation that Carey 'did not appear to realise' he was the senior officer, and that the escort 'was composed of men not under the same discipline as soldiers'. Chelmsford was also sympathetic, noting in his covering note to the Horse Guards that he had no reason to believe Carey was 'wanting in courage', but rather had 'lost his head, and consequently failed to take the action which the circumstances demanded'.

Pending confirmation, the findings of the court were not made public. But on 19 June it was announced by General Order that Carey would be sent home to England and would 'remain under arrest' until 'the decision of H.M. the Queen consequent on his trial by General Court Martial has been notified'.

That very same afternoon, as he attended the opening of an exhibition at the Grosvenor Gallery, Disraeli was handed a telegram with news of Louis's death. 'This is terrible news,' he exclaimed.

'Yes,' said a fellow MP, 'and I am afraid that the French will accuse our people of having deserted him and left him to his fate.'

'I am not so sure they will be wrong,' Disraeli agreed. 'Well! My conscience is clear. I did all I could to stop his going. But what can you do when you have to deal with two obstinate women?'

That evening at 11 p.m., one of the aforementioned 'obstinate women' was at her writing desk at Balmoral when her faithful servant John Brown brought her the tragic news. 'The young French Prince is killed,' he said quietly. Then a tearful Princess Beatrice came in with the telegram from Lady Frere and, having read it, the queen put her hands to her head and repeated several times: 'No, no, it can't be!'

Her first thought was for Louis's mother. 'Poor dear Empress!' she noted in her journal. 'Her only child, her *all*, gone! I am really in despair . . . The more one thinks of it the worse it becomes. Got to bed very late, it was just dawning! And little sleep did I get.'

Lord Sydney travelled to Chislehurst the following morning to break the news to Eugénie. But she already knew that something was wrong, and, as Sydney entered her room, she had to be supported by her chamberlain and doctor. 'What is it? Tell me!' she cried out in French.

Sydney replied that it was '*très grave*' and finally that it was 'the worst that could be'. Eugénie 'remained motionless at first' and then threw herself into Sydney's arms before collapsing in a chair. She asked to see the telegram, but threw it away before doing so. She read it later and kept repeating: '*Mon pauvre fils, seulement 23 ans!*'★ Her sole consolation was that they had recovered the body and it was on its way home.

The queen, meanwhile, was looking for someone to blame. 'He should never have been sent with so few men on reconnaissance,' she wrote. 'One cannot help feeling it might have been prevented.' So too thought the duke of Cambridge, who deeply regretted his own involvement. He had warned Lord Chelmsford that Louis was '*too plucky* and *go ahead*', he told the queen on 22 June, adding, 'What could I say more. Surely it was a broad hint to him to be on his guard. It was impossible to say to him he was *never* to go into danger, but upon such a hint Lord Chelmsford was in my opinion *most culpable* in allowing him ever to be away from his own Head Quarter Staff.' It was, said the duke, by far the worst incident in a catalogue of horrors and he now agreed with the queen that it was 'time to send out a new Commander'. As for Lieutenant Carey and the others 'who left the Prince to his fate', he would await the results of the inquiry but he did not see 'how any explanation can possibly be made'.

Louis's body was landed at Woolwich on 11 July, having been transferred to an Admiralty yacht from the troopship *Orantes* the

---

★ 'My poor son, only 23 years old!'

day before. His private funeral took place in Chislehurst on the 12th. The queen had wanted a state funeral, but this was vetoed by the government on the grounds that it would be both inappropriate and politically sensitive. 'After all,' wrote Disraeli, 'he was nothing more or less than a pretender to the throne of France supported by a well-organised and very active clique, but representing numerically only a small minority of people.'

The funeral was impressive, none the less, with 40,000 people – British and French – lining the procession route from Camden House to St Mary's Church in Chislehurst, where Louis was eventually laid to rest in a tomb beside his father. While the prince of Wales, Hicks Beach, Stanley, Cambridge and a host of generals followed the coffin,★ the queen went to pay her respects to Eugénie. The curtains were still drawn in the empress's room and the queen could hardly see her. 'She came towards me,' she wrote, 'and sobbed much, and when I put my arms around her, telling her no one felt for her as I did, she gently said, "*Je vous remercie, Madame, pour toutes vos bontés.*"† She asked if Beatrice was there, and kissed her also. Then we left the room.' Later the queen told Disraeli how well the ceremony had gone. 'I hope the French government will be as joyful,' he commented sourly. 'In my mind, nothing could be more injudicious than the whole affair.'

Two days later, the queen received a copy of the 'painful' evidence given to the Court of Inquiry, 'showing how the poor prince was deserted'. She thought it 'incredible that there was not one who remained behind to try and save this precious life.' So too did Colonel Leigh Pemberton of the 60th Rifles, who had travelled back with the body. He feared, he told the queen on the 14th, that the prince's 'own eagerness and anxiety to do something' had led him to be chosen for the fatal patrol; and yet it was 'dreadful' that the prince 'was not defended to the last'.

In late July the queen commissioned Lady Butler, the celebrated war artist and wife of General Sir William Butler, to paint a picture

★ Disraeli excused himself on the ground of illness.
† 'I thank you, Madame, for all your kindness.'

of the Zulu War. Butler wanted to depict the finding of the Prince Imperial's body and, at first, the queen agreed. But Victoria soon changed her mind, out of deference to the empress's sensibilities, and suggested the 'Defence of Rorke's Drift' instead. Butler agreed and in December gave the queen a sneak preview of the almost finished painting. 'It will be splendid & the drawing is most powerful,' wrote the queen. 'The figure of Private Hitch★ is the most finished and wonderfully like. All officers & men are portraits, & everything is painted from descriptions, & just as it was, down to the very smallest detail. She made them put themselves into the very attitudes in which they were. Major Chard is also very like. Major Bromhead is to be painted near him.' She had invited both Chard and Bromhead to Balmoral on their return from South Africa. Chard stayed for two days in October and impressed the queen with his quiet and modest demeanour. But Bromhead had gone fishing in Ireland and did not receive his invite until it was too late. He was not asked again.

★ The Queen had presented Hitch with his Victoria Cross during a visit to Netley Military Hospital on 12 August. 'He is,' she recorded, 'a tall good looking young man, with a very determined expression, but very modest & bears a high character . . . He could not say a word & I fear afterwards fainted' (RA QVJ: 12 August 1879).

15. Ulundi

Sir Garnet Wolseley had mixed feelings as the steamer *Edinburgh Castle* anchored off Cape Town during the evening of 23 June: relief that the three-week voyage was over, but apprehension that he might have arrived too late. As if reading his mind, a fellow passenger shouted to a small boat that came alongside: 'Is the war over?'

No, came the welcome reply, and 'a thrill of pleasure seemed to light up every heart' of the general's party. But the warm glow was quickly replaced with a shudder as the informant told them of the death of the Prince Imperial. 'I thought of his poor Mother & of the party in France who built their hopes upon him,' wrote Wolseley in his journal. 'What a war it has been!'

Word of his appointment – and Frere and Chelmsford's de facto supersession – had reached Cape Town unofficially on the 14th. Wolseley thought the Freres, under the circumstances, were 'doubly anxious to be gracious' and was impressed by the warm welcome they gave him and his staff at Government House on the 23rd. That night Frere and Wolseley sat up late discussing the war, with Frere insisting that history would 'show how right he was & how weak-kneed & cowardly are the present Cabinet'. He was tired, he said, of writing private letters to Hicks Beach and receiving nothing in return. As for the conduct of the war, there seemed to be no 'directing head' with everyone 'acting on his own hook' and no staff arrangements. One report, possibly from Clifford, said that 'Chelmsford has lost all his influence & is care-worn and will be very glad to be relieved'. This was music to Wolseley's ears. 'If he wishes to go home when I arrive,' he wrote in his journal, 'I shall gladly let him do so, & hope he will take his Crealock with him: if he took both brothers I should not be sorry.' But Wolseley had hopelessly underestimated Chelmsford's determination to clear his name.

Chelmsford first heard the crushing news of his supersession on 17 June, as he was about to resume his advance from the Nondweni River. Coming so soon after the death of the Prince Imperial, it must have seemed that the fates had conspired against him, that he would never be given the chance to erase properly the stain of Isandlwana. Then it occurred to him that Wolseley could not hope to reach the front for at least two weeks. If, by then, he had beaten the main Zulu Army and burnt oNdini – or Ulundi, as it was known to the British at the time – then all would not be lost. He decided to press on at all hazards while, at the same time, ignoring any instructions from Wolseley to halt.

The increasingly frantic attempts by Cetshwayo to achieve a negotiated peace were also given short shrift. On 4 June, for example, Chelmsford had sent three messengers back to the Zulu king with his latest conditions for a cessation of hostilities: the restoration of all horses, oxen, arms and ammunition taken during the war; and the surrender of 'one or more' regiments named by Chelmsford; then, and only then, would he discuss the 'final terms of peace'. The preconditions were preposterous and Chelmsford intended them to be so. But Cetshwayo persevered, sending two more messengers to Fort Pearson on the Lower Thukela. They arrived on 25 June and begged the British to halt their advance while negotiations took place. If the march on oNdini continued, they said, Cetshwayo would have no option but to resist, 'as there will be nothing left but to try and push aside a tree that is falling upon him'. Like all the messengers before them they were disregarded.

A day later Wood's Flying Column moved down into the valley of the emaKhosini to destroy abandoned kraals. One of them, esiKlebheni, housed the royal *inkatha*: a coil of rope bound in python skin, handed down by Shaka himself, which was said to embody the unity of the Zulu nation. Its consumption in the flames of esiKlebheni was an ominous warning. But Cetshwayo was unaware of its destruction for some time, and, on 27 June, he made yet another attempt to seek terms. His envoys found Chelmsford in his new camp on the Mthonjaneni Heights, just seventeen miles from oNdini. As well as a letter from the king they brought with them two huge elephant tusks and 150 oxen as a gesture of good faith. The letter was placatory in tone but pointed out that negotiations could not take place while the British kept advancing, burning and plundering kraals as they went. Chelmsford's reply was brief: the advance would continue until all his preconditions had been complied with; but, as Cetshwayo had sent some cattle and stated that the two captured cannon were on their way, he would not cross the White Mfolozi until the evening of the 28th. If all his conditions had not been complied with by then, Cetshwayo would have to 'take the consequences'. The disconsolate messengers left the next day, telling Chelmsford's interpreter that they 'would have to fight now', because it was impossible for Cetshwayo to meet the general's demands.

That same day Chelmsford turned to deal with the other main threat to his hope of a crowning victory: Wolseley. No sooner had Wolseley landed at Cape Town than he was urgently demanding a situation report from his predecessor. But the telegram had to be sent via General Clifford at Pietermaritzburg and did not reach Chelmsford in the field until the 28th. In his long reply that day, Chelmsford said that he planned to leave a strong entrenched post on the Mthonjaneni Ridge with at least 400 infantry and all the spare 'oxen, horses, mules, wagons and impedimenta'. The remainder of the force would move towards oNdini 'without tents, and with ten days' provisions' and would probably be attacked before it crossed the White Mfolozi. Spies had reported that three large enemy columns had left the main military kraal at oNdini that morning and were moving in the direction of the river. His original intention had been for Crealock's column to create a diversion for the two forces advancing from the north. This had not happened – partly because Crealock's advance had been slowed by difficulties with transport and terrain – but he had planned for such a contingency by not relying 'upon any help from the coast column'. As for what he would do after he had destroyed oNdini and the surrounding military kraals, he could not say for certain. But supply problems made it extremely unlikely that he would 'be able to hold on to' the oNdini Valley. It was more likely that he would leave an advanced post and withdraw with the rest of his troops closer to the border. He was writing, he said, 'on the supposition that we shall be unable to inflict such a decisive defeat on the enemy as will oblige Cetewayo to agree to any terms that may be imposed upon him'. He was hopeful, nevertheless, that the 'enemy will stand' and give his troops 'the opportunity they are longing for'.

Wolseley, meanwhile, had left Cape Town for Durban. 'Crealock & Chelmsford are operating on independent lines & are not in communication with one another,' he noted in his journal on 24 June. 'Nothing could be more unpromising or more fraught with danger than the existing condition. Of course a happy stroke of good fortune might possibly end the war at any moment, but I confess I can see no probability of it under present circumstances with a demoralized army the men of which in all ranks are thoroughly sick of the war & have lost all confidence apparently in their leaders.' He had, of course, a low opinion of Chelmsford's professional abilities and had been further prejudiced by Clifford's private correspondence. The morale of the 2nd Division was, it is true, not all that it could have been, and some officers and men were delighted to hear of Wolseley's arrival. 'To hear he was coming out,' wrote Captain Watson in late June, 'was almost as good as a Victory.' But Chelmsford was still broadly popular with his ordinary soldiers.

Wolseley and his staff landed at Durban on 28 June and at once set off by train for Pietermaritzburg, finishing the last half of the journey in a 'four horse trap' in 'danger of our lives'. He had a long conversation with Clifford and recorded:

Crealock with 1st Division has been pottering about for the last two days evidently afraid to advance. He has no dash & judging from his past history is very careful of his own hide & not likely to expose his valuable person to any dangers. He advanced at last to his present position only when he heard of my early arrival. Chelmsford has been pushing on well ahead also since he heard I was likely soon to be on the spot and to supersede him. He has apparently cut himself off from his base in order to prevent my communicating with him. No one knows where he is at the moment, but he & his evil genius, that arch-snob young Crealock, are now doing all they know to do something brilliant before I can join the troops in the field.

On 30 June, with still no response from Chelmsford, Wolseley received a cable from Marshall at Landsman's Drift: 'Position of army nine miles from Ulundi. Newdigate and Wood intrenched quarter of a mile apart. Zulu have been estimated at ten thousand . . . General opinion is not sufficient infantry unless attacked in position.' Wolseley replied:

Flash immediately to Chelmsford the following message from me and get his acknowledgement & receipt of this message: 'Concentrate your force immediately and keep it concentrated. Undertake no serious operation with detached bodies of troops. Acknowledge receipt of this message at once, and flash back your latest news. I am astonished at not hearing daily from you.

Wolseley left Pietermaritzburg for Durban on 1 July, and that afternoon, shortly before boarding a ship to Port Durnford, he finally received Chelmsford's response to his demand for a situation report. It made him even more anxious to get to the front before a disaster ensued. He was taking the coastal route via Port Durnford – an open beach on the coast of Zululand where Crealock had established a landing stage – because he thought it was the quickest. It would also give him the opportunity to select a 'great base on the sea near Crealock's present position', from where he planned to operate with one huge united column. By substituting Chelmsford's slow-moving wagons with up to 10,000 African 'carriers' he hoped to be able to bring the war to a 'speedy termination'.

Unfortunately for Wolseley, heavy winds prevented him from landing at Port Durnford on two consecutive days: 2 and 3 July. He almost made it during the morning of the 3rd, but a tow-rope broke on the cargo boat he had transferred to and it was forced to return to his original ship, HMS *Shah*. Shortly before noon, with the sea 'very bad', he reluctantly asked the captain to return to

Durban so that he could proceed to Port Durnford by land. En route to Durban he wrote to his wife: 'All this puts me out very much, and I am anxious about Chelmsford's column. He has violated every principle of war in his plan of campaign, and has, in fact, courted disaster. As far as this war is concerned, Crealock's column might just as well have been in England.' If Wolseley had managed to land at Port Durnford on 2 July he might – just might – have interfered with Chelmsford's plans for a decisive battle. But it was not to be, and Chelmsford, with time running out, was not to be thwarted.

On 30 June, having built and garrisoned three strong wagon laagers on Mthonjaneni, he led a combined column of some 5,500 men and 200 ox-wagons down into the valley of the White Mfolozi. All were lightly equipped, without kit or tents, and with rations for just ten days. But the thick belt of thorn-brush on the valley floor hampered their progress, and that day they covered just five miles. During the torturous march they were met by yet more peace emissaries with a final letter from the king translated – as the two before had been – by Cornelius Vijn, a young Dutch trader who was living in Zululand when the war broke out. The envoys handed Chelmsford the sword of the dead Prince Imperial and promised the imminent arrival of the two 7-pounders and yet more cattle. What they did not realize, however, was that Vijn had added a codicil of his own to Cetshwayo's letter to the effect that the king and his people, if not the princes and chiefs, still intended to fight. Chelmsford kept up his pretence of being willing to negotiate by offering to accept the 1,000 rifles taken at Isandlwana in lieu of the surrendered regiment. He also extended the deadline to 3 July, as long as his advance to the banks of the White Mfolozi – 'to enable my men to drink' – was not opposed. But this was mere rhetoric. Chelmsford knew that Cetshwayo could not even comply with his preconditions for peace, and he was simply hoping for a safe passage through the dangerous thorn-bush to the south-west of the river. The open Mahlabathini Plain on the far side, however, was ideal for the type of pitched battle that he so desperately sought.

On 1 July, Wood's Flying Column reached the Mfolozi unmolested and at once began to construct a laager on a slight rise about half a mile from the drift. From this vantage point they could see part of the Zulu Army manoeuvring in the plain beyond and, though no collision took place that day, the men of 2nd Division panicked on hearing that the Zulus were approaching the river and laagered on a hill a mile and a half to the rear. Lieutenant James MacSwiney of the 94th recorded:

We set to work with a vengeance, making a shelter trench round the wagons about 3 feet high, and cut down the trees round, so by night we had about 50 yards pretty clear & we laid down with our blankets round us. I had just gone into a sort of sleep when I heard a shot, and we all fell in. The 24th behaved very badly. They had a regular stampede, rushed in without arms right inside the laager. Fortunately nothing came of it, or else we should all have been eaten up as the Zulus call it. In another hour we had another alarm, so it was very jumpy work.

Next morning the 2nd Division moved forward to join the less nervous Flying Column and, by nightfall, the combined force was protected by a double wagon laager and a small stone fort. That day Cetshwayo made a final attempt to come to terms with the British by ordering a herd of royal white oxen to be driven towards the enemy camp as a peace offering. But the young warriors of the uMcijo regiment, guarding the fords, turned the herd back in disgust. There would, they declared, be no surrender while there were still warriors willing to defend the king. Later that day, while addressing his regiments at oNdini, Cetshwayo criticized the uMcijo for their impulsive and unauthorized action. The British were bound to win a pitched battle, he said, and when they did he would be left at their mercy. No, his warriors protested, they would defend him until the last. Cetshwayo knew better, but, sensing his warriors were determined to fight, he gave them the following advice: avoid at all costs an attack on an entrenched position and, if they did manage to defeat the British in the open, they were to halt their pursuit at the river because of the threat from the guns in the double laager.

At daybreak on 3 July, Zulu snipers on the bluff overlooking the drift began shooting at watering-parties and bathers, and even into the laagers themselves. Chelmsford responded at noon – the deadline for Zulu compliance with his preconditions for peace – by firing shells into the dense brush. He also herded the cattle he had been sent by Cetshwayo back across the river: a symbolic end to the truce. An hour later Buller led a mounted attack against the Zulu snipers. As a hundred men of Baker's Horse crossed at the main wagon drift and made straight for the heights, Buller forded the river lower down with 400 riders and wheeled to take the Zulu position in the flank. The pincer movement took the Zulus by surprise and, within minutes, they were streaming back towards oNdini.

Buller followed – keen to reconnoitre the ground for a possible battlefield – and almost blundered into a carefully prepared trap. Waiting ahead in the Mbilane Valley, concealed in long grass, were 4,000 warriors under Chief Zibhebhu, who, with great courage, had ridden out with a small party of horsemen to lure the British on. Fortunately Buller smelt a rat and, just a couple of hundred yards from disaster, ordered his men to halt. The Zulus could wait no longer and, rising from the ground, fired a volley that killed three men and unhorsed a number of others. One man, an NCO of the Mounted Infantry, was lying pinned beneath his dead horse as the huge line of warriors charged forward. Regardless of the risk, Lord William Beresford dismounted, released the man and tried to help him on to his own horse. But the NCO, stunned by his fall and heavily built, refused to cooperate. The pair were saved by Buller's quick thinking. Seeing them in difficulties, he ordered the retreating men of the FLH to turn and fire a volley. This held the Zulus back for long enough to allow Sergeant Edmund O'Toole to dismount and help Beresford. By the time they had got the injured man on to Beresford's horse, the Zulus were just yards away. Beresford killed one with his sword before all three made their escape, O'Toole riding alongside Beresford's horse to keep the half-conscious NCO in the saddle.

A similar act of gallantry was performed by Captain D'Arcy of

A LESSON.

36. *Despise Not Your Enemy,* a *Punch* cartoon of 1879,
underlining the hard lesson the British had to learn in Zululand

37. One of the last photographs of Prince Louis Napoleon (or the Prince Imperial), the 23-year-old former heir to the French throne, taken in Durban in April 1879

38. Pen and ink sketch by the Prince Imperial of a skirmish with Zulus

39. The donga near the Tshotshosi River where the Prince Imperial was killed on 1 June 1879

40. Monochrome watercolour by Melton Prior of Lord Chelmsford and his staff looking towards oNdini from Babanango Mountain

41. A British bivouac on the right bank of the White Mfolozi River, 3 July 1879 (the day before the Battle of Ulundi)

42. The famous oil painting of the Battle of Ulundi from behind British lines by the French artist Adolphe Yvon. The original is almost eight metres long and was intended to be viewed as a curved surface, giving an all-round panorama. Because of the difficulty of photographing such a huge canvas, only the central section is shown above

43. Lord Chelmsford (*centre*, on white horse) and staff inside the British square during the Battle of Ulundi

THE ILLUSTRATED LONDON NEWS,

REGISTERED AT THE GENERAL POST-OFFICE FOR TRANSMISSION ABROAD.

No. 2099.—VOL. LXXV. SATURDAY, SEPTEMBER 6, 1879. WITH WHOLE SHEET SUPPLEMENT SIXPENCE. By Post, 6½d.

44. Captain Lord William Beresford winning the VC near oNdini

45. General Sir Garnet Wolseley, Chelmsford's replacement as British commander in South Africa, who arrived too late to prevent his predecessor from winning the Battle of Ulundi and, effectively, ending the war

46. An anonymous watercolour of the capture of Cetshwayo by Major Marter of the 1st (King's) Dragoon Guards on 28 August 1879

47. Private Frederick Hitch, shortly after receiving his VC from Queen Victoria. 'He is a tall good looking young man,' she recorded, 'with a very determined expression . . . He could not say a word, and I fear afterwards fainted.'

48. Private Henry Hook, VC. Note the scar in the centre of his scalp, made by a Zulu assegai at Rorke's Drift

49. Seven VC winners of the 24th Regiment in Brecon for the unveiling of the Zulu war memorial on 23 January 1898. They are: (*standing, left to right*): ex-Private Robert Jones (Rorke's Drift, committed suicide six months later), Sergeant Henry Hook (Rorke's Drift), ex-Private William Jones (Rorke's Drift); (*sitting:*) ex-Private D. Bell (Andaman Islands), Colonel E. S. Browne (Khambula), ex-Private Frederick Hitch (Rorke's Drift), Lance-Corporal John Williams (Rorke's Drift)

the FLH – the officer saved by Buller at Hlobane – who rode back to help a dismounted trooper. He had just managed to pull the trooper up behind him when the horse reared and threw them both. Though hurt by the fall, and with the Zulus closing in, D'Arcy refused to leave the stunned trooper. He eventually got him back on the horse and, with his last ounce of energy, climbed up beside him and galloped off.★ They and the rest of the mounted force made it safely back to the drift. It had been a close-run thing, but Buller escaped with the loss of just three men. More importantly, he returned to the laager with valuable information about the ground on which Chelmsford planned to give battle.

That night the Zulus advanced close to the river and kept the nervous British troops awake by singing their 'infernal war song'. The journalist Charles Fripp recalled:

With ever increasing shrillness thousands of exultant voices rose and fell in perfect rhythm faintly but clearly upon our ears. It was the war chant of thousands of Zulu warriors, whose sonorous voices were bringing forth songs of devotion to their King through the stillness of the night, swaying their supple bodies and gleaming weapons in fierce unison with their beating feet beneath the same calm moon shining on our silent camp. Louder and louder grew the song, and although miles distant one could hear the higher voices prevail above the resonant roar of the bass; indeed it seemed as if the singers were nearing the drift and some of the men stood quietly to their arms; but after some waiting there seemed no probability of an attack, and . . . we lay down, and lulled by the low confused murmur of the cattle in the laager, again fell asleep.

The troops were silently roused at 4 a.m. and, after a hurried breakfast, were ordered to assemble on the other side of the main drift, which Buller's horsemen, crossing lower down, had earlier secured. The total attacking force was composed of around 4,166 white troops, 958 black auxiliaries, twelve cannon and two Gatling

★ Both Beresford and D'Arcy were awarded VCs. Beresford refused to accept his unless O'Toole was similarly honoured and this was eventually agreed to.

guns. Left behind to guard the fort and laager was a company of Royal Engineers and five companies of the nervy 1/24th Regiment, composed of veterans who had avoided the massacre at Isandlwana and raw recruits from Britain. Some of the old hands regretted the lost opportunity to avenge their fallen comrades; others were glad to be out of a battle whose outcome in their minds was very much in the balance. Even the recently promoted Brigadier-General Wood was prepared to admit later that 'all were not confident how our men would face a horde of Zulus in the open', though he 'could not contemplate the possibility of any man in the Flying Column quailing'.

Once over the river the infantry was formed into a huge hollow square – four ranks deep – with the guns, ammunition and tool carts in the centre. In this formidable, but essentially defensive, formation it began the march to oNdini, screened on all four sides by the cavalry. The high ground between the kwaBulawayo and kwaNodwengu military kraals was reached at about 7.30 a.m. Chelmsford reported: 'Dark clusters of men could be seen in the morning light on the hill tops to our left and left-front. To our right where the largest number of the enemy were believed to be, we could see but little as the mist from the river and the smoke from their camp fires hung heavily over the bush below.'

Leaving the kwaBulawayo kraal to be burnt by his rearguard, Chelmsford moved his square 700 yards beyond kwaNodwengu on to 'high ground uncommanded from any point and with but little cover, beyond long grass, near it'. This was the site that Buller had selected during his reconnaissance the previous day. Away to the left and left front of the square could be seen regiments of the Zulu Army 'in good order and steadily advancing to the attack'. More appeared 'from the thorn country on our right and passed round to [kwaNodwengu] and to our rear, thus completing the circle round us'.

The exact number of Zulus in opposition to Chelmsford's force is much disputed. Cetshwayo later insisted that all his amabutho were represented at the battle and that the army was the same size as that at Isandlwana. It was, on that reckoning, about 20,000 strong, but with a reserve of 5,000 that did not become engaged. Contrary to some reports, Cetshwayo was not in personal command, having left oNdini with his *isiGodlo* during the evening of 3 July for the emLangongwenya kraal of his father, about two miles to the east. When reports arrived the following morning that the British had crossed the White Mfolozi, he moved further east to the kwaMbonambi kraal and stayed there throughout the battle, anxiously awaiting news of the outcome. The Zulu commanders and a number of royal princes – including Ziwedu, Cetshwayo's favourite – watched the battle from nearby Mcungi Hill. The generals included Mnyamana, Ntshingwayo, Zibhebhu and Sihayo among their number.

As the Zulus completed their encirclement, the British cavalry screen on both sides of the square became engaged. 'We set fire to one of the kraals,' wrote Private George Turnham of the 17th Lancers, 'and this seemed to be the signal for the beginning of the fight. No sooner did the Zulus see smoke than they came running out of their cover like a swarm of bees and completely round us. The fire was opened by the Basutos (these men are as brave as lions; they ride small shaggy ponies that can stand any amount of fatigue), our regiment of lancers retiring with them on the infantry.' The front and rear faces of the square wheeled out to let the riders past. Once they were all inside, the square was closed and the battle began in earnest. It was a little before 9 a.m.

Many of the reinforcement troops were awestruck by the disciplined way the Zulu regiments advanced in perfect order with clouds of skirmishers preceding loose lines of companies four deep. But they were about to attack a near impregnable defensive position, its gently sloping ground providing a perfect field of fire and ideal terrain for a cavalry pursuit. 'The fire opened from the artillery at a long range,' recorded Corporal William Roe of the 58th on the rear face, 'and did fearful execution for we could see their heads, legs, and arms flying in the air. In all directions, on they came till they were within range of our rifles, our two front ranks kneeling and our two rear ranks standing . . . And when they reached the range of our rifles, we opened a fearful fire upon them . . . They were falling down in heaps, as though they had been tipped out of carts.'

The Zulus responded with long-range – if generally inaccurate – rifle-fire that caused 'many casualties' in the tightly packed square. But they could not hope to win the battle unless they broke the square, and the most valiant effort to do so was made by the veterans of the iNgobamakhosi, iNdluyengwe, uThulwana and uVe regiments. Moving up a patch of dead ground, they suddenly appeared 130 yards from the right rear corner of the square. 'It was,' wrote Guy Dawnay, who was holding his horse at that corner, 'the only really thick mass I ever saw attacking.' He added:

Our fire didn't check them the least; nearer they came – 100 yards – 80 yards – still rushing on, a thick black mass. Lord Chelmsford came galloping up, telling the 58th and 21st to fire faster; Newdigate pulled out his revolver. The nine-pounder crashed through them again and again; but at that short distance the canister did not burst. Everyone thought it would be hand to hand in another minute, when at 60 yards the mass faltered, wavered, and withered away. The cavalry was told to mount; but as soon as mounted told again to dismount, a body again coming on at our 21st and 94th side of the square.

'It was a fearful sight,' recalled Corporal Roe. 'You could not see many yards in front, for the dense clouds of smoke from our guns. After coming up so close as they did we made up our minds to fight in close quarter with our bayonets, and swords, but the enemy began to shake in front of our fire, and they halted dead for a few seconds, and then turned round and flew for their lives. As soon as our column saw this they all gave three cheers.' It was while he was cheering that a lance-corporal of Roe's regiment was killed by a bullet that passed through his open mouth and out of the back of his head.

Lieutenant MacSwiney's section of the 94th, which was holding part of the rear face, lost seven of its twenty men – two men killed and five wounded – in a matter of minutes. 'A bullet went through one poor fellow's thigh and fell at my foot,' he wrote to his mother. 'They sent 2 companies up who were in reserve to reinforce us if necessary and every moment I thought they would make a dash at us, but we kept up such a fearful fire that I was quite content that no one could advance against us.' Fred Slade, commanding two guns in the centre of the right face alongside the unfurled Colours of the 1/13th, wrote two days later: 'Our fire was so hot & well directed that no troops in the world could have stood up to it & it is marvellous the way in which the Zulus came on, not seeming to care in the least for gun, gatling or rifle.' But on the day of the battle itself he was less complimentary, noting how 'the enemy did not come on half as well as at Kambula'. Wood thought the same, though the front face held by the Flying Column was the least threatened. 'I was rather disgusted that the Zulus made such a feeble attempt,' he wrote to General Horsford a week later. 'An Induna . . . who was wounded at Kambula and surrendered yesterday, said: "Our hearts were broken at Kambula. I did not go within shot of you this time."' Captured later, Mehlokazulu confirmed that the Zulus had received a 'severe lesson' at Khambula 'and did not fight with the same zeal'. Many of the warriors hung back out of range and within half an hour the Zulu attack had foundered. It was now that Chelmsford ordered his cavalry into action.

Guy Dawnay, who was given permission by Newdigate to accompany the 17th Lancers, recalled:

It was a grand moment. We were told to go round to the left by Lord Chelmsford, but on reaching the ridge, found too few Zulus to make it worth our while, and found ourselves exposed to a nasty cross fire from them, and from the big body fronting our face of the square . . . [Colonel Drury] Lowe at once swung round to the left, and went at once at the big body, who kept on running and firing at us. As we neared them they ran . . . but still, though our horses were getting a bit blown, we overtook them, and with a cheer were among them, each troop choosing its own line . . . The first man I reached turned round with shield in left hand and assegais and gun in right, and I found my long heavy Life Guard sword . . . do well. It cut clean half way down the shield, hit something hard, and caught the Zulu on the neck I think; down he went, and the next minute a lance went through him.

Dawnay went on to sabre an induna and knock down another warrior with his horse before reining in with the other riders. They had driven the main body of Zulus into broken ground on the side of a hill that was not suitable for horses. As they retired, the Zulus opened fire, hitting several men and horses, but most returned safely to the square. The 17th Lancers alone accounted for up to 150 Zulus; Buller's irregulars and the Mounted Infantry killed a further 450. This brought the total number of Zulu dead to around 1,500 of the 20,000 men engaged. British casualties were just three officers and ten men killed, and a further one officer and sixty-nine men wounded.

With the Zulu Army routed, Chelmsford advanced the whole force to the banks of the Mbilane stream, where it rested and ate lunch. Buller's cavalry, meanwhile, had been ordered to burn oNdini, and this had prompted a number of mounted officers to vie for the honour of reaching Cetshwayo's capital first. The 'race' was won by Lord William Beresford, and it may have cost another aristocratic competitor, the Honourable William Drummond, his life when he was ambushed en route by a handful of Zulu stragglers and killed. Beresford later told the queen that Drummond had gone off 'in a huff' in the direction of oNdini after the commander of some irregular African horse – probably Cochrane – had rebuked him for trying to prevent his men from firing on wounded Zulus. He seemed to be 'quite off his head' and rode into a party of Zulus, who killed him. His body was found two weeks later, near the river to the left of oNdini, wearing just his boots and spurs. He was, in Buller's opinion, a 'very odd mannered man' and 'half a Zulu' having lived a good deal with them. He died, he thought, on a hare-brained mission to 'try to catch' the king.

Unaware of the death of his intelligence chief, Chelmsford and his staff had ridden over to oNdini to witness its destruction. Guy Dawnay was with them:

We galloped up to Ulundi . . . but it was already blazing on all sides. We made our way into the Tsigodhlo, the king's part, into a maze of small compartments with usually one enormous hut and two or three smaller ones in each fenced-off compartment, and ransacked it all pretty thoroughly, but there was no loot at all, nothing but here and there a spoon, a shield, a string of medlars dried, fat-jars, etc. It was jumpy work staying long there, as the way out was rather intricate and amidst a mass of blazing huts and fences and clouds of smoke ... The kraals are enormous, 500–700 yards across, and with three to eight rows of huts close built.

Corporal Roe watched the conflagration from the Mbilane:

In a very short time the whole of the King's city, Ulundi, was in flames. This was a fearful sight to see. You would think the whole world was on fire when there was a dense mass of flames seven miles in length. There was 4 thousand and 95 kraals burned to the ground. The King's kraal was in the centre of a large circle, this circle was 5 miles round it, and all the kraals are made of sticks and plaited straw, or at least grass, which are in the shape of a bee hive. But the King's kraal was built in the shape of a proper house with a thatched roof.

'It was a grand sight,' wrote Fred Slade, '& we all felt that *at last* the power of the Zulus had been destroyed.' Chelmsford thought so too, and, having returned to the Mbilane at noon, he paraded his men and congratulated them on their 'good conduct' and 'steadiness in firing' during the battle. Two hours later, with the band of the 1/13th playing *Rule Britannia* and *God Save the Queen*, the whole force retraced its steps to the camp on the Mfolozi. Many of the men were laden down with mementoes of the battle: shields, assegais and knobkerries. But other booty was in distinctly short supply, as the Zulus had stripped their kraals before departing. The only really valuable items looted from oNdini were three tusks found in Cetshwayo's house by Beresford, Commandant Baker and Captain Cochrane of the NNH. They took one each.

At 5 p.m. that evening, with Chelmsford's private 'victory' telegram safely stowed in his saddle-bags, the war correspondent Archibald Forbes set off on his epic lone ride back to Landsman's Drift. He was followed three hours later by Guy Dawnay with the 'official' dispatch. After a gruelling ride of twenty-five and a half hours, with only the occasional break to change horses, Dawnay reached Landsman's Drift at 9.45 p.m. on 5 July, only to find that Forbes had beaten him by a couple of hours.

News of the crushing defeat was brought to King Cetshwayo on the day of the battle by lookouts posted in the hills. Determined not to be captured, he at once left kwaMbonambi for the broken country to the east, where he was later joined by Mnyamana and some warriors of the uMcijo. But, fearing the warriors would attract attention, he sent them away. On 6 July he also sent off his eleven-year-old heir Dinuzulu, most of his women and his remaining cattle to seek sanctuary with Chief Zibhebhu in the north-east of the country. He himself, travelling on foot with just a few women and servants, headed for Mnyamana's ekuShumayeleni kraal, where he remained for a month, trying in vain to negotiate with the British.

Chelmsford, meanwhile, had moved most of his force back to the Mthonjaneni Heights on the 5th. They were joined there the following morning by the Flying Column and the wounded. That day Chelmsford wrote Stanley a lengthy dispatch of the battle in which he estimated Zulu numbers to have been as high as 25,000, or more than 'assembled at Kambula'. He concluded:

It appears that Ketshwayo himself arranged the disposition of his forces and that they considered they would have no difficulty in defeating British Troops if they advanced in the open, away from their wagons. I feel I have a right in saying that the results of the Battle of Ulundi, gained by the steadiness of the Infantry, the good practice of the Artillery, and the dash of the Cavalry and Mounted Troops, will be sufficient to dispel this idea from the minds of the Zulu Nation and of every other tribe in South Africa for ever.

He had ignored Wolseley's instruction only to send dispatches via him because, he told Stanley, he was anxious for the account of the battle to 'reach you with as little delay as possible'. He then repeated his request – first made in a letter written on the 5th – for permission to resign his command on the grounds that he had 'done a considerable amount of work' over the previous eighteen months. He hoped, he said, that the request would be 'favourably received'.

Wolseley had reached the tented camp of Fort Pearson during the evening of 5 July to be greeted with the news of Chelmsford's victory in the shape of a telegram from Archibald Forbes at Landsman's Drift. He had half been expecting such news and sent a magnanimous reply via Crealock, congratulating Chelmsford on his victory. He wrote in his journal: 'I think this ought to be the last affair of the war of any consequence. Chelmsford can now return home with a halo of success about him. Cetewayo will now most probably be a fugitive and I can now hope to end the war and make peace leaving him out altogether in the cold.'

On 7 July, having spent a night en route at Fort Napoleon, Wolseley linked up with General Crealock's 1st Division at Port Durnford. He had as little time for Crealock the general as Crealock the man:

He came out to meet us [wrote Wolseley]. Just the same vain swaggering snob he has always been. I believe his manner to his Staff & all about him is most disagreeable & his manner to the men as it always was in the 90th is offensive . . . As far as this war is concerned, this first Divn. might as well have been marching along the Woking & Aldershot road. If he had been eager for the fray he might have brought the enemy to an engagement near the Inyezane or Emlalazi rivers & so had the credit of finishing the war before Chelsmford did so but Crealock is more of the Autumn Manoeuvre General than the fighting leader in the field.

Wolseley met John Dunn the following day and, though he doubted his integrity, accepted that he was a 'power in Zululand' and intended to make as much use of him as possible. His plan, he wrote in his journal on 8 July, was to increase Dunn's powers 'by making him paramount Chief' of the territory that bordered Natal. 'I shall thus secure the civilizing influence of a White man over the district of Zululand nearest to us, and he and his people will be a buffer between us and the barbarous districts of Zululand beyond.'

He considered it 'absolutely necessary for the safety of Natal' to divide Zululand into a number of self-governing districts, with Dunn's the biggest and most important. Exactly how many – and who would govern them – he had not yet decided.

During his stay at Port Durnford, Wolseley received a telegram from Chelmsford written on 6 July. It read:

With your approval I purpose to send back 2d Division to Fort Newdigate with the wounded . . . and to bring up another convoy of supplies should it be required; the Flying Column to proceed to join you via Kwamagwaza and St Pauls, a strong post being left at the former place . . . A hasty evacuation of the country I now occupy seems to me advisable at the present moment, and I await your further instructions before carrying it out.

The telegram had been sent the long way via Landsman's Drift – probably deliberately – and did not reach Wolseley until the 8th. He was horrified that Chelmsford, having won a great victory, was about to abandon the Zulu capital. By return he sent instructions for Chelmsford to leave Wood's Flying Column in the neighbour-hood of Mthonjaneni and proceed himself to St Paul's with the 2nd Division. But the message either went astray or was ignored, because on 9 July Chelmsford replied: 'I hope to reach Saint Paul's with flying column about fourteenth. The 2nd Division marches tomorrow. Unless instructions to the contrary are received from you, it will proceed to Fort Newdigate, and after giving over wounded and sick to an escort from Koppie Allein will encamp in Upoko valley, where grass and water are plentiful.' He had been prevented from leaving Mthonjaneni before then, he added, by severe rainstorms.

Wolseley had already dispatched a messenger with a duplicate of his instructions to leave Wood near oNdini. 'I am anxious to maintain the forward position the troops now occupy as long as I can possibly feed them there,' he noted in his journal on the 9th. 'This is very desirable for political reasons.' But it made no difference. Chelmsford and the Flying Column left for kwaMagwaza on 9 July, and a day later the 2nd Division began the march back to Fort Newdigate.

It was also on 9 July that Chelmsford, irked by the peremptory tone of Wolseley's letters, sent an angry letter of complaint to Colonel Stanley. He had, he said, been informed of his demotion in a most irregular fashion: not through official channels but by a general order issued by Wolseley on his arrival in South Africa. He would have been quite prepared to 'submit and subordinate' his plans to Wolseley's control; but he 'could not accept the inferior command' to which Wolseley had 'considered it within his power to reduce me'. His only option – to 'extricate' himself from 'a false position' – was to resign his command and return to Britain 'with as little delay as possible'. Wolseley was more sympathetic than angry when he got wind of Chelmsford's backbiting. 'He is evidently much put out by being superseded,' he wrote to his wife on the 10th, 'and I have had some trouble in making him answer the helm. Now, however, that he has had some success he ought to be happy, and I hope he means to return home at once. I feel for him with all my heart, for I know how he must have suffered.'

But he was not happy to hear that Wood and Buller, his two protégés, were also hoping to return to Britain after eighteen months of 'constant work'. He was, he noted in his journal on the 13th, 'extremely sorry' to hear the pair were 'pretty well used up & must go home'; not least because he had earmarked the two of them for any 'further operations' that might be necessary in Zululand or the Transvaal, where the Boers were becoming increasingly fractious. To Wood, however, he simply expressed his sorrow and grief that they were 'both seedy' and added that 'a run home' would soon restore their health. 'You and Buller have been the bright spots in this miserable war,' he wrote, 'and all through I have felt proud that I numbered you among my friends, and companions-in-arms.'

Wolseley finally reached St Paul's on 15 July, having left Port Durnford with an escort of 150 horsemen two days earlier. 'As I rode up the very steep hill on which the St Paul's Mission stands,' he wrote, 'Chelmsford and his Staff overtook me . . . I cannot say that my meeting with Chelmsford was a pleasant one. He has persistently ignored my military authority over him, although I have told him I have a Commission giving me command of the Troops in South Africa.' Wolseley had nevertheless tried to make 'every allowance' for Chelmsford knowing that it must be 'unpleasant finding a superior officer sent to supersede him'. Yet at dinner that evening he found Chelmsford in 'good spirits' and 'glad to be going home'.

Wolseley stayed the night with the Flying Column and was told by both Wood and Buller that Chelmsford was 'not fit to be a Corporal'. They were referring, in particular, to his precipitate withdrawal from oNdini. Buller later told Sir Henry Ponsonby that, contrary to reports, supplies were plentiful and that he had offered to stay at oNdini with just 600 men. 'Wood would have stayed with more,' added Buller. 'But it was so obvious that we should have held it, that any exertion should have been made to stay.' So why did Chelmsford retire? asked Ponsonby. 'It was nervousness,' said Buller, 'and dread of what might occur next to diminish what he considered the lustre of the crowning victory. But we were all so sorry and not I alone but many asked him to leave a force. Only fancy how much grander for his own reputation to have welcomed Wolseley at Ulundi.'

The following morning Wolseley inspected the Flying Column and was impressed by what he saw. 'It marched past remarkably well,' he wrote. 'I wish all those old gentlemen who cry out against our present military system could have seen the three Infantry Battalions of which it is composed, the 1/13th L.I., the 80th Regt. & the 90th L.I.; the last named was the youngest lot of fellows, but they are quite fit for work of any sort, and there was only about 1 per cent of sick amongst them.' Under Wood's instructions, the men of the Flying Column had spent the previous night washing out the coffee colour of their belts and pipeclaying them back to their original white. 'When we marched past,' wrote Wood, 'although the clothing was ragged, the men's belts and rifles were as clean as if they had been parading in Hyde Park.'

That day Wolseley made one last attempt to persuade Wood to

stay in South Africa by offering him command of a force to be sent against the still-recalcitrant Chief Sekhukhune of the Pedi. But Wood was determined to go. 'I haven't had an unbroken night's rest for eight months, and am not of the same value as I was last January,' he told Wolseley. He needed at the very least, he said, a fortnight at sea. What about Buller? asked Wolseley. 'He is even more "run down" that I am,' came the reply, 'his legs being covered with suppurating Natal sores.'

So Wolseley bowed to the inevitable and issued the following order of congratulation: 'In notifying the Army in South Africa that Brigadier-General Wood, V.C., C.B., and Lieutenant-Colonel Buller, C.B., are about to leave Zululand for England, Sir Garnet Wolseley desires to place on record his high appreciation of the services they have rendered during the war . . . The success which has attended the operations of the Flying Column is largely due to General Wood's genius for war, to the admirable system he has established in his command, and to the zeal and energy with which his ably conceived plans have been carried out by Colonel Buller.' Wolseley also told Wood that he would recommend him for promotion to major-general, a step in rank that was confirmed soon after Wood's return.

Early on the 17th, Wolseley and Chelmsford rode out of St Paul's with their respective staffs and escorts: Wolseley was bound for his forward camp on the Mhlathuze and Chelmsford for Eshowe, the first leg of his long journey back to Britain. When they parted, further down the road, the niceties were observed but nothing more. Both were relieved that their awkward meeting had finally come to an end.

Wood and Buller left a day later for Pietermaritzburg with an escort of just ten men. As they rode past the serried ranks of the Flying Column, a collective shout of 'God speed you' brought tears to Wood's eyes. 'We had served together, one battalion eight months, and the other for eighteen months. Much of the time had been fraught with anxiety; the good-bye of these men, of whom it was commonly said in South Africa, "I worked their souls out," and whom I had necessarily treated with the sternest discipline, was such that I have never forgotten.' Buller also cried as he took his leave of his beloved Frontier Light Horse.

On reaching Eshowe, Wood received the welcome news that he was to be knighted for his Zulu exploits. Buller's reward, for his reckless bravery at Hlobane, was the coveted VC. The pair joined Chelmsford in Pietermaritzburg for a celebratory dinner given by the leading citizens and the festivities were repeated, complete with congratulatory addresses and gifts of silver plate, in Cape Town. On 27 July all three embarked by steamer for Britain: Chelmsford never returned to South Africa; Wood and Buller did go back at different times, but not with happy results.

16. The Aftermath

The queen was having lunch at her favourite residence, Osborne House on the Isle of Wight, when word of Chelmsford's victory at Ulundi arrived by telegram. 'Thank God!' she wrote. 'It is an immense thing & I trust will finish this terrible war.' She at once sent off a note of congratulation to the superseded general.

Even Disraeli's spirits were lifted by the news that, he informed the queen, 'combined with the long-awaited sunshine fill everyone with sanguine hopes'. The Queen could rest assured, he told her, that no troops would be withdrawn from the 'scene of war' until 'after the gravest deliberation'. Three times it had been his lot to advise 'on the question of peace or war' and three times he had chosen the latter: in Abyssinia, Afghanistan and now Zululand. And in all three cases, he added with extraordinary overstatement, the wars had 'been brief, & complete, & successful'. The war against the Zulus had certainly not been brief; nor would it truly be over until Cetshwayo was caught and the last embers of resistance extinguished. As for Afghanistan, it was about to explode in a fresh orgy of bloodletting. But Disraeli could not know that and it was only natural, after all the pressure he had been under, that he should seek to bask in the glory of Chelmsford's final victory.

The queen's joy, on the other hand, was tempered with sorrow. 'How sad,' she wrote on hearing the news, 'is the thought of the dear young Pce. Imperial's untimely end, so dreadful, so unnecessary. Had he but remained with Ld. Chelmsford, or even Col. Harrison, he might have been in this engagement, probably unharmed, or at least merely wounded! What a pride & joy it would have caused him! He would have returned home proud & happy!' But it was not to be and the queen was determined that Captain Carey,* the man

---

* He had been promoted to captain for previous good conduct on 6 June.

she held responsible for Louis's death, would be suitably punished. Imagine her dismay, therefore, when James O'Dowd, the deputy judge advocate general,* advised her on 26 July that the guilty verdict of the court martial should be overturned on a technicality. She wrote in her journal:

The evidence is much as it was before, but the court martial has been loosely & almost in some instances illegally conducted; there is no evidence that they were sworn; the various important points were not insisted on; the 2 charges of misbehaviour before the enemy, in fact cowardice, & of not returning to try & save the Prince, cannot be proved. The 2nd . . . it seems Capt. Carey could not have done. The 1st, I must say, though it may not be cowardice, & unfortunately not punishable, I consider a great want of feeling & of that chivalry which everyone owes, not only to a Prince, but to any superior, friend, or indeed fellow creature, & the impression left is very painful. He ought to be tried over again, & this I said, without pressing it, as *my* opinion . . . Any way, the man will be branded for life, for neglect of doing what he *ought* clearly to have done, & what so many have done, including an instance of the greatest bravery on the part of Lord William Beresford the day before the battle of Ulundi.

She wrote in a similar vein to her cousin the duke of Cambridge, pointing out that while '*legally* Lieut. Carey has *not* committed a fault *capable* of being punished *as an act of cowardice*', he deserved censure for making no effort to rescue the prince. Cambridge concurred with 'every word of her remarks' and said he was in the process of compiling a memorandum 'of every opinion' that would be promulgated on Carey's return.

Colonel Stanley also agreed with the queen, telling her on 30 July that there was 'no doubt as to Lieutenant Carey's conduct not having been what it ought, & the same with the troopers'. But Carey could not be punished because the court martial had been 'irregularly conducted'. The best thing, the queen decided, would

* The army legal officer who was reviewing the case.

be for Carey to be 'got quietly out of the way, without making a martyr of him'.

Carey finally arrived back in British waters on 20 August when the SS *Jumna*, the troopship that had carried him from Cape Town, anchored in Plymouth Sound. For a time he was kept on board, though journalists were permitted to interview him. Finally, on 22 August, the *Jumna* proceeded the short distance to Spithead and Carey was escorted ashore. He was taken directly to the Portsmouth office of the General Commanding the Southern District, Prince Edward of Saxe-Weimar, who read him a copy of the duke of Cambridge's memorandum. It began by shifting any subsidiary blame from Chelmsford to Colonel Harrison, who had authorized the ill-fated reconnaissance without his superior's permission. 'His orders to Lieutenant Carey were not sufficiently explicit,' read the memo, 'and he failed to impress upon the Prince the duty of deferring to the military orders of the officer who had accompanied him, and the necessity of guiding himself by his advice and experience.' If Harrison had 'displayed more firmness and forethought in his instructions to Lieutenant Carey and the Prince', said Cambridge, 'the train of events would have been averted'. Carey, however, was far from absolved:

Lieutenant Carey from the first formed a wrong conception of his position. He was sent, not only to perform the duties of his staff office, but to provide the military experience which his younger companion had not acquired. If his instructions were defective his professional knowledge might have prompted him as to his duty.

He imagined, but without the slightest foundation for the mistake, that the Prince held a military rank superior to his own, and acting throughout on this strange misconception, he omitted to take for the safety of the party those measures of precaution which his experience had taught him to be essential.

At the moment of attack, defence was impossible, and retreat imperative. What might have been done, and what ought to have been done when the moment of surprise had passed, can only be judged by an eye-witness; but His Royal Highness will say . . . it will ever remain to

him a source of regret that, whether or not an attempt at rescue was
possible, the survivors of the fatal expedition withdrew from the scene of
the disaster without the full assurance that all efforts on their part were
not abandoned until the fate of their comrades had been sealed.

While hard on Harrison and too easy on Chelmsford, the memorandum was a pretty fair assessment of Carey's part in the débâcle.

Having read it in full, Prince Edward gave Carey a copy of the
section referring to him. He then announced that, on the advice
of the judge advocate, the findings of the court martial had not
been confirmed by the queen and that, as a result, Carey was
released from arrest and free to rejoin his regiment. The general
later saw Lieutenant-Colonel Knollys, who was staying with
Carey's family in Portsmouth, and told him that he 'strongly
advised' Carey to 'keep quiet, and not to do anything to encourage a party feeling for or against himself, not only for his
own sake, but for that of the Empress'. Carey was 'distinctly to
understand', he added, 'that his position was that of a man who was
neither condemned nor acquitted – but one whose sentence by
court martial was *not* confirmed'. Knollys said that he would pass
on the message and that he too had 'advised the family to keep
quiet'.

But Carey was too stubborn to listen. He issued a string of
statements to the press in the days following his arrival in Britain
including, on 28 August, the following exculpation: 'As I have
done nothing to be ashamed of, and I desire nothing more than
ample publicity and inquiry into all the facts of the case, a full and
complete account of these proceedings may yet be given forth . . .
These opinions now having been ratified by the voice of my fellow
countrymen I feel that my honour and character as a soldier, and
as an English gentleman, have been vindicated.' Even more ill
judged – not to say downright scurrilous – were the remarks he
made to reporters of the *Daily News* and the *Gaulois*, a French
newspaper, while anchored off Plymouth: in particular, the
assertion that Louis and not he had selected the site for offsaddling.

The empress was understandably outraged by Carey's attempt to blame her son for his own death and refused point-blank his insensitive request for an audience. And, unbeknownst to him, she had a trump card to play: the letter that Carey wrote to his wife after the tragedy, a copy of which had been sent to Eugénie by a former friend of the Careys with the improbable name of Miss Octavia Scotchburn. The queen, who was sent a copy by the empress on 26 August, was in no doubt that the letter incriminated its author. It gave, she noted in her journal, 'a totally different account of the case, to the one he stated at the court martial, & has allowed to be published, showing he knew he was in command, that he told the Prince Imperial the place was safe, & that he hurried away as fast as he could, praying to be saved!' It was, she thought, 'a wretched letter, full of mawkish, sickening cant!'

Sir Henry Ponsonby, her private secretary, saw the letter a little differently. 'They have been copying it here,' he wrote to his wife from Balmoral where he and the queen had arrived on the 27th, 'and condemned it as weak foolish canting and self condemnatory and that if published would ruin him. I have now read it and cannot quite see it so.' He added:

The essence no doubt condemns him for choosing the camping spot. 'I shall get wigged for the position I took up, but trust for nothing more ... I certainly told the Prince I considered the kraal safe and I did so.' 'Poor fellow, it might have been my fate. The bullets tore around us and with only my revolver what could I do. The men all bolted and now I fear the Prince was shot on the spot. No doubt they will say I should have remained by him but I had no idea he was wounded and thought he was after me.' These are the chief points bearing on the question. If Carey accused the Pce. of choosing the ground then perhaps he might be met with his retort. But I don't think that he individually ever has. The papers have and his friends who made him a hero have. But I don't think he has. The burden of his song has not changed. 'I could not have saved him.' I feel convinced that if this letter were published it would (except in condemning him for choosing the spot – for which he was not tried) raise the feeling in his favour.

Ponsonby was wrong. Carey had claimed on a number of occasions – in his official report of 1 June, in his evidence to the court martial and in his comments to journalists – that Louis had selected the site. The queen knew this, having read the trial transcript, and was all for extracts of the letter being sent to *The Times*. But Eugénie was more circumspect and, instead, got her elderly chamberlain, the duc de Bassano, to ask Carey to explain the discrepancy between the letter and the quotes that appeared in the *Gaulois* and the *Daily News*. Presumably, said Bassano, the quotes were inaccurate and he called upon Carey to contradict them and so 'remove the stain so unjustly cast on the memory of the Prince'.

A copy of Carey's reply was sent to Balmoral. 'It is,' Ponsonby told his wife, 'a history of the whole affair.'

Accepting responsibility for the choice of the camping spot which he says he did not at first choose – but when the Prince observed that it was better than the one on the top of the hill because of the water – he assented and considers himself responsible for it. His answers to his interviewers are correct but perhaps imperfectly understood and he deeply regrets he ever had anything to say to them at all! They declare it to be a long rigmarole and so it is – with many contradictory statements. But we could not expect the man to admit himself directly a liar. He reconciles his apparently conflicting statements and not altogether unsuccessfully. For instance he alludes to the great difficulty of insisting or giving unasked for advice – when he was not in command – to the Prince Imperial, because of his high social position (this is the key of the question from this point of view). Like all Princes he assumed superior airs and authority as usual.

Nevertheless, said Ponsonby, the empress now had the means to clear her son if she wished to because Carey had given her permission to publish his letter. 'But if she is satisfied – and prefers to let the matter drop I believe that would be best.' Eugénie had come to the same conclusion and, via one of her ladies, told Carey by letter that she did not think he had satisfactorily answered Bassano's queries and therefore it would serve no useful purpose to continue the correspondence. Carey replied, nevertheless, asking what else he could do? He was 'not guilty', he insisted, and 'no Carey' had ever appealed for mercy. The empress did not respond.

In South Africa, meanwhile, Colonel Harrison was 'very much put out' by the criticism of him in the duke of Cambridge's memorandum. Wolseley sympathized. 'I think this is very unfair,' he wrote, '& is merely a repetition of what was done regarding the Isandhlana disaster where the blame was thrown upon Durnford, the real object in both instances being to screen Chelmsford.' As for Carey, he did not see how any officer could ever again associate with him: 'Technically in the eye of quibbling lawyers the proceedings may not have been strictly regular, but the fact that he was tried by a court of officers & found guilty of cowardice remains . . . He had therefore better leave the service & obtain a subscription from those who worked so hard in his favour, to enable him to start in some line of life more congenial with his cowardly heart. The greengrocer or the undertaker calling might perhaps suit him.'

But Carey, convinced that he had done nothing wrong, chose the worst possible course: to rejoin his regiment, the 98th, at Malta in late 1879. Despite being ostracized by his fellow officers, he soldiered on for three more years and was released from his torment only by a fatal illness. He died of peritonitis while on garrison duty at Karachi, India, on 22 February 1883.

Lord Chelmsford's victory at Ulundi may have broken the back of the regular Zulu Army, but there was still much for his successor to do to pacify the country. On reaching his camp on the Mhlathuze River on 17 July, Sir Garnet Wolseley was told by John Dunn that Chelmsford's 'precipitate retreat from Ulundi' and the withdrawal of his troops from Mthonjaneni a few days later 'had had a very bad effect on the country'. Cetshwayo, Dunn explained, was 'plucking up heart in consequence' and had already collected with Zibhebhu's assistance 'some 3,000 or 4,000 armed men around him'. This was a gross exaggeration. Zibhebhu still had, it is true, a large number of his Mandlakazi warriors in the field. Cetshwayo himself was at Chief Mnyamana's kraal, beyond the Black Mfolozi, with only a modest personal retinue.

But Wolseley knew that his vision of a divided Zululand was impossible while Cetshwayo was still at large. The country could 'never settle down', and the chiefs who had already surrendered would not dare to remain in Zululand, as they knew they would be 'eaten up' by Cetshwayo as soon as the British left. 'I feel there is nothing for it,' wrote Wolseley on the 17th, 'but to return with a force to Ulundi and dictate terms to everyone from thence. Cetewayo must either be killed or taken prisoner or driven from Zululand before this war is considered over.' Yet Wolseley did not expect any more serious fighting and, with one eye on the political benefits, began to break up Chelmsford's huge army by sending a number of regiments home. 'I shall thus,' he wrote, 'get rid of useless Generals and reduce expenditure.' Henceforth he would use small mobile columns and the support of the Swazis★ and friendly Zulus, particularly those loyal to Prince Hamu, to snuff out the remaining pockets of resistance.

Before moving north, however, he was determined to complete the submission of the coastal chiefs, and almost all of them responded to his call for a meeting near the destroyed emaNgweni kraal on 19 July. Some of the most senior – including Prince Dabulamanzi and Chief Gawozi of the Mpungose – had already surrendered. Most of the rest were only too happy to agree to Wolseley's relatively easy terms: the surrender of all arms and royal cattle. His only other condition was an acceptance that the Zulu kingdom was no more. It would, he told his audience, be divided into 'four or five Districts' and he would name the chiefs who would 'exercise independent & sovereign power' in those districts when he reached oNdini. Zululand was to be kept for the Zulus. His listeners, in response, 'expressed themselves highly pleased by what they had heard'. No Zulu victor would have been so generous.

Wolseley then turned his attention to the north, where hardly any of the great chiefs had yet sued for peace. He put this down to Cetshwayo's presence and prayed that 'some amiable assassin would

---

★ Who had at last agreed, now that the power of the Zulus was broken, to cross the Phongolo River like vultures falling upon a carcase.

kill him'. In the meantime, not really expecting that to happen, he called a meeting of the northern chiefs near the destroyed capital of oNdini for 10 August. They would be offered, he let it be known, the same terms that had been accepted by the coastal chiefs, and any who refused to attend would be treated as enemies and punished accordingly.

On 7 August, en route to oNdini, Wolseley met a delegation from the king led by the influential Chief Mavumengwana. He handed Wolseley a letter from Cetshwayo that said he had 'never killed any white men' who came into his country, was 'very sorry the war was ever made' and was 'very anxious for peace'. He was about to send in as many cattle as he could collect and hoped to be 'left alone in the country which his father gave him'. Wolseley's response was brief: if Cetshwayo surrendered, his life would be 'spared' and he would be 'well treated'. He would promise nothing more.

Later that day Wolseley was given an even more recent message from Cetshwayo by John Dunn. The king was prepared to surrender, it said, if the British agreed to give him a kraal in Zululand where he could live as a 'private individual'. This was unacceptable, Dunn told Wolseley, because as soon as British troops had left Cetshwayo 'would simply begin his old game of intrigue until he had again established his power over the country'. On a more optimistic note, Dunn said he was sure all the great chiefs would surrender at oNdini on the 10th.

He was wrong. But one man did arrive at Wolseley's camp that day: Cornelius Vijn, the Dutch trader who had been kept by Cetshwayo since the beginning of the war. He came with a message from the king, whom, he said, he had left at a kraal five miles beyond the Black Mfolozi the day before. Cetshwayo's new terms as related by Vijn were optimistic in the extreme: he wanted to remain king of Zululand. This could never happen, replied Wolseley. The terms on offer were the same as those given to Mavumengwana: his life and nothing more. Then he would not surrender, said Vijn. Seemingly at an impasse, Wolseley tried bribery. 'If you will take a party of Cavalry to the kraal where the King is so that he may be captured I will give you £200.'

Vijn – still smarting from the fact that Zibhebhu had robbed him of everything, even his gun – agreed at once. He left the following day, but not before telling Dunn, while under the influence of drink, that Cetshwayo had promised 'to make him a great man & give him plenty of cattle' if he could persuade Wolseley to let Cetshwayo remain as king. While Wolseley waited for news of Cetshwayo's capture, he was delighted to hear that a cavalry patrol had located the barrels of the two missing 7-pounders in a nearby donga; of the gun carriages there was no sign.

The following day Vijn returned empty handed. Cetshwayo had moved to another kraal, ten miles further away, but in Vijn's opinion could still be caught. Wolseley at once dispatched Barrow's Horse and a troop of the 1st Dragoon Guards to make the attempt. On 14 August Barrow reported that he had reached the kraal where Vijn had left the king, but it was empty. Apparently Cetshwayo had been warned of their approach and departed the day before. Wolseley told Barrow to 'hunt up every nook' by dividing his force into groups of twenty riders. 'We ought to catch him soon dead or alive,' noted Wolseley, '& I trust we may be able to do so within a week, for all my chances of settling matters satisfactorily depends upon it.'

That was not strictly true because, even without Cetshwayo's capture, the outlook in the north was beginning to brighten. On 14 August five of the most important northern chiefs – including Mnyamana, Cetshwayo's former chief minister, and Ntshingwayo, the commander at Isandlwana – had arrived at Wolseley's camp with 150 lesser chiefs and 600 head of royal cattle. But they brought no arms and Wolseley told them that he could not accept their surrender until they had: the five major chiefs were kept as hostages while their followers went back to collect their weapons. Two days later Prince Ziwedu, Cetshwayo's favourite brother, came in and was also detained. By 20 August, however, Cetshwayo was still at large and Wolseley's patience wearing thin. Henceforth, he announced, any kraals that gave refuge to the king would be destroyed and their cattle confiscated.

As he fretted near oNdini, Wolseley fell increasingly under the spell of the extraordinary John Dunn. He had, he confided to his journal, never met a man who was more of a puzzle to him. He added:

[Dunn] has never been in England & most of his life he has passed in Zululand without any English or civilized society, and yet in his manner he is in every way the Gentleman. He is quiet, self-possessed and respectful without any servility whatever, and his voice is soft and pleasant. He is much more of the English Gentleman than any of the self-opinionated & stuck up people who profess to be 'our leading citizens' in Natal . . . He leads a curious solitary life, but he says he enjoys it thoroughly, being in every way his own King . . . He has as many wives & concubines as he wishes to keep & he has a clan about him who are all ready to obey his slightest nod. He pays periodical visits to Natal & has his books letters & newspapers sent to him regularly. I wish I dared make him King of Zululand, for he [would] make an admirable ruler; however I am giving him the largest District in the country, an arrangement that I believe will be the small end of the wedge [of civilization] inserted into it.

More great chiefs submitted in late August: notably Mgojana, the Ndwandwe chief, on the 23rd and Zibhebhu three days later. Mehlokazulu was also brought into Wolseley's camp as a prisoner on the 26th. Only Cetshwayo and some chiefs in the far north – including the redoubtable Manyonyoba and Mahubulwana, the principal induna of the abaQulusi★ – were still on the loose. But not for long. By threatening Chief Mnyamana that he 'should have nothing' if he did not cooperate, Wolseley forced him to betray his former master. Mnyamana at once sent instructions to his adherents to deliver up the king and on 28 August he was duly captured by a British patrol. The location was the remote kraal of one of Mnyamana's subchiefs, Mkhosana, deep in the Ngome Forest. Two mounted British patrols, using intelligence from informants, were involved in the operation: one under Captain Lord Gifford and the

---

★ Mbilini, the 'Hyena of the Phongolo', had been mortally wounded during a skirmish with British horsemen on 4 April.

other led by Major Marter of the 1st Dragoon Guards. Marter got his man but only after Gifford, having located Cetshwayo's hiding place first, delayed moving in until it was dark. Marter preferred not to 'take any risks' and at once approached the rear of the kraal, which was surrounded on three sides by 'nearly precipitous rocks' and 'dense undergrowth, and creepers'. It was a wise decision, thought Captain Watson, because had Marter 'advanced by the open side', the alarm would have been given and Cetshwayo would probably have escaped deeper into the forest.

Instead Cetshwayo was taken completely by surprise, as Marter's men, having left behind their scabbards and anything else that might give them away, silently led their horses down a steep cliff before surrounding the kraal. 'They knew him instinctively by his gallant bearing,' wrote Watson, who spoke to those involved. 'They say he is one of the best looking Zulus they have seen, that he walked like Caesar. He could not understand being ordered about, and when told he must leave the kraal, or it would be burnt over his head, he could not make it out. He never hurried himself, walked at *his own* pace, and was perfectly cool and collected. He expressed his astonishment at being captured.'

Wolseley had just finished breakfast on 29 August when an officer hurried up, saluted and said, 'They've caught him, sir.'

It was a huge weight off his mind: not only because the weather was threatening to break and he was reluctant to keep troops in central Zululand during the rains, but also because he was urgently needed in the Transvaal, where trouble was brewing. 'Thank God it is now all over,' he wrote in his journal that night. 'I have telegraphed Frere to pass the Bill enabling me to send him to Robin [*sic*] Island.'

Eight servants and as many women – some of them wives – had been captured with Cetshwayo. The king and the women were mounted on mules and by mid morning of the 29th had reached the east bank of the Black Mfolozi, opposite a small British camp. They crossed on foot, escorted by dragoons, riflemen and NNC, and were received in the camp by a royal guard of the 3/60th Rifles. Cetshwayo was led to a specially built platform, where he was offered refreshments. 'Although he did not eat much,' recorded a private of the 3/60th, 'I noticed he relished his Kaffir beer, which was carried in a large earthen vessel on the head of No. 2 wife, number 1 carrying his drinking mug.'

Cetshwayo finally arrived at Wolseley's camp near oNdini during the morning of 31 August. He had walked most of the way from the Black Mfolozi because his fat legs were too chafed to allow him to ride comfortably. Wolseley had sent an ambulance cart to collect him but the king could not stand the jolting and preferred to walk. The only time he betrayed any emotion was when he caught sight of the blackened ruins of his capital. Otherwise he maintained an impressively regal bearing and those who saw him enter the camp said he 'walked as if he was the Conqueror'. Even Wolseley was forced to concede that Cetshwayo had a 'very wise countenance' and was 'quite the King in his bearing and deportment'.

Wolseley knew that any interview with Cetshwayo would be awkward and so asked John Shepstone, who spoke Zulu, to conduct it instead. Shepstone told the ex-king that, as he had broken his coronation promises, his kingdom would be divided among his leading chiefs. Cetshwayo's response was to beg to be allowed to remain in Zululand. His people had forced on the war, not him, he said in desperation. He claimed never to have been told the terms of Sir Henry Bulwer's ultimatum and 'a series of other lies'. When Shepstone would not budge, Cetshwayo broke down in tears. He knew he was to be sent into exile, he said, and would rather die. Shepstone replied that his eventual destination was a secret and he would be told on the way. He then introduced Cetshwayo to Captain Ruscombe Poole, RA, who would be responsible for his person.

A couple of hours later, surrounded by a strong mounted escort, Cetshwayo and his women set off in an ambulance wagon on the first leg of a journey that would take them by land and sea to exile in the Flagstaff Bastion of Cape Town's seventeenth-century castle. 'He is very fat,' commented Wolseley, 'but as he is tall he carries it off.' He thought, but could not be certain, that as Cetshwayo was carted away he was wearing round his considerable midriff 'a coloured tablecloth'. It was hardly a fitting outfit for the once feared king of the Zulus.

Cetshwayo's capture had an immediate effect on those still fighting. Mahubulwana submitted on behalf of the abaQulusi on 1 September; Manyonyoba followed suit three weeks later. On the same day that Mahubulwana came in, Wolseley announced the details of his settlement of Zululand to a huge audience of assembled chiefs. The country would be divided into thirteen independent chiefdoms, subject only to arbitration by a British resident. Wolseley had been heavily influenced in his choice of chiefs by John Dunn, who was himself given the biggest and most strategically important of the thirteen districts, stretching from the coast to the Middle Thukela. The other key border districts were, not surprisingly, given to chiefs who had actively assisted the British during the war: Chief Hlubi of the Tlokwa, whose Basutos had fought as irregular horse, was granted the district west of the Thukela and Buffalo junction, including the former lands of Sihayo and the two Matshanas; and Prince Hamu was rewarded for his early defection with the important north-west region. Wolseley, moreover, ceded the entire former Disputed Territory between the Phongolo and Bivane rivers (including the Ntombe Valley and Luneberg) to the Transvaal.

The remaining border districts were given to Sekethwayo of the Mdlalose, a former isikhulu and one of the first chiefs to submit; Mgojana of the Ndwandwe, the tribe that had been paramount in the region in the pre-Shaka period; Zibhebhu of the Mandlakazi, who, though he stayed loyal to Cetshwayo almost to the last, had long been semi-autonomous in his north-eastern domain; and Somkhele, a powerful chief whose grandfather was an induna of the Mthethwa paramountcy.

Other prominent chiefs to benefit were Mdlanlela of the Mthethwa, the other great pre-Shakan tribe; Mfanawendlela, a former isikhulu and chief of the Zungu; and Ntshingwayo, the victor of Isandlwana, who was given the district turned down by Chief Mnyamana of the Buthelezi. The reason Mnyamana gave for his refusal was that he did not want to give up tribal lands to the north of the Black Mfolozi, which now formed part of Prince Hamu's district. It is also possible that he was trying to curry favour with Hamu, who, he assumed, might one day become king. Whatever the reason, it was a choice he would live to regret.

Wolseley's settlement was based primarily on strategic consider-ations: how to ensure the security of the neighbouring British territories and prevent a resurgence of royal power. To this end all the border and coastal districts were given to chiefs who had aided the British during the war, shown themselves to be semi-autonomous of the royal house or capitulated early enough to have gained a measure of British trust (and Zulu mistrust). Many of the chiefs in the interior, on the other hand, were either nonentities or likely to remain under the influence of their more reliable neigh-bours. It was a policy that owed much to the British school of Indian defence – of which Brigadier-General Sir Pomeroy Colley,★ Wolseley's chief of staff, was a noted advocate – whereby friendly border rulers were overseen by British residents. But in South Africa, as in India, the theory did not always work in practice.

No sooner had British troops left Zululand than tensions began to surface between Wolseley's placemen and supporters of the former regime – in particular, between Chief Zibhebhu and the uSuthu tribesmen who occupied the southern part of his district. The disagreements came to a head over the custody of Dinuzulu, Cetshwayo's eleven-year-old heir, who had been sent to Zibhebhu with twenty women of the royal household for safekeeping after the Battle of Ulundi. Dinuzulu eventually managed to escape, with the help of Mnyamana, and took refuge with his uncle Ndabuko, an uSuthu chief, who refused Zibhebhu's requests to return him. Zibhebhu responded with punitive raids.

When Cetshwayo heard about his son's difficulties, he redoubled his efforts to be repatriated. In April 1881 he was moved from Cape Town Castle to a farm called Oude Molen on the Cape Flats, where his nearest neighbour was Langilabele, the exiled Hlubi

★ Colley was on detachment from his post in India as private secretary to the viceroy, Lord Lytton.

chief. While at Oude Molen he sent letters to anyone he thought might help: politicians and officials in the Cape, Natal and Britain; former adversaries like Sir Evelyn Wood and even Queen Victoria herself. Disraeli's Tory government had fallen in April 1880 – partly as a result of the political fall-out from the Zulu and Afghan wars – and been replaced by W. E. Gladstone's Liberal administration, which took a softer line on imperial issues. It had, for example, decided not to send more troops to avenge Major-General Sir Pomeroy Colley's* defeats in the Boer rebellion of 1880–81, otherwise known as the Transvaal (or First Anglo-Boer) War. Instead Major-General Sir Evelyn Wood, who had returned to South Africa to take command of British forces, was instructed to conclude a humiliating peace whereby Transvaal regained much of its independence. It was the only war lost by the British during the whole of the Victorian period, and its outcome delayed confederation for more than a generation. Sir Bartle Frere, his policy already in tatters, had been recalled by the new Liberal government in the summer of 1880. He died four years later at the age of sixty-nine.

With confederation no longer a possibility and the Transvaal border the responsibility of the Boers, the Colonial Office saw less need to keep Zululand weak and divided. Wolseley's policy of divide and rule had, in any case, not prevented infighting between the rival factions. By the summer of 1881, for example, Zibhebhu had driven the uSuthu leaders from their homes in the Vuna Valley within his chiefdom. A few months later Prince Hamu defeated the royalist abaQulusi on the right bank of the Bivane River.

It was partly in response to this escalating violence that Gladstone's government agreed to Cetshwayo's request in the summer of 1881 to be allowed to visit Britain to plead his case in person. He hoped to be able to persuade the British authorities that only his presence in Zululand could prevent a full-scale civil war. After various delays he finally reached Britain on the steamer *Arab* on 5 August 1882. He was greeted in London by large and enthusiastic

* Colley himself had been killed during the last of the defeats, Majuba Hill, on 27 February 1881.

crowds, eager to see for themselves the monarch of a nation of warriors that had, for a time, bested the British Empire. On 14 August he was granted the honour of a brief audience with Queen Victoria in the drawing room at Osborne. He took with him three chiefs – including Mkhosana, his long-standing companion – and was accompanied by John Dunn and his minder Henrique Shepstone, son of Sir Theophilus. The queen recorded:

Cetewayo is a very fine man . . . He is tall, immensely broad, and stout, with a good-humoured countenance, and an intelligent face. Unfortunately he appeared in a hideous black frock coat and trousers, but still wearing the ring round his head, denoting that he was a married man. His companions were very black, but quite different to the ordinary negro. I said, through Shepstone, that I was glad to see him here, and that I recognised in him a great warrior, who had fought against us, but rejoiced we were now friends. He answered much the same, gesticulating a good deal as he spoke, mentioned having seen my picture, and said he was glad to see me in person. I asked about his voyage, and what he had seen, and then named my three daughters, at which he said 'Ah!' After further commonplace observations, the interview terminated.

It had lasted just fifteen minutes. As Cetshwayo and his chiefs left the room, they gave Victoria the Zulu royal salute by raising their right hands and shouting, '*Bayete!*' They then had lunch alone before leaving in a open carriage. As they drove away, Cetshwayo caught sight of the queen and stood up in salute. He remained standing until they were out of sight.

Far more important to his future, however, were the three interviews he had with Lord Kimberley, Hicks Beach's successor as colonial secretary. He was delighted to hear from Kimberley that he would, after all, be restored to his kingdom. There was just one catch: it would not be the same size as his pre-1879 kingdom, or even as big as Wolseley's thirteen districts. Instead his authority would be confined to the central portion of his former kingdom. It would, moreover, be hemmed in to the south and west by the Reserve Territory, made up of the former districts of Dunn and

Hlubi, which would be run by officials recruited from Natal; and to the north by the expanded chiefdom of Zibhebhu – the only one of Wolseley's thirteen chiefs to retain his independence – who would, it was hoped, act as a counterbalance to royal ambitions.

The arrangement was a disaster. Within two months of his muted return to Zululand in January 1883, Cetshwayo's uSuthu supporters were at war with Zibhebhu. It did not go well: the invading uSuthu Army was destroyed by Zibhebhu's numerically inferior force in the Msebe Valley, and on 21 July, near the rebuilt capital of oNdini, Cetshwayo's remaining troops were routed by a combined force of Zibhebhu and Hamu's warriors. More than fifty Zulu chiefs were killed – including Ntshingwayo, the victor of Isandlwana – most because they were too old and fat to escape. For Cetshwayo it was the second time in four years that he had been forced to flee his burning capital. This time he went west and, though wounded in the pursuit, eventually managed to escape to the Reserve Territory. He was given a house near the site of his father's kwaGqikazi kraal and there, during the afternoon of 8 February 1884, he is said to have died of a heart attack. His supporters insisted he was poisoned by Zibhebhu's agents, and they may well be right because Mnyamana narrowly survived a similar attempt on his life at around this time.

Cetshwayo's son and successor, King Dinuzulu, got his revenge on Zibhebhu on 5 June 1884 when his uSuthu warriors, with the help of mounted Boers, defeated the Mandlakazi at the Battle of Tshasheni. But by agreeing to the Boers' exorbitant demands for more than a million hectares of land, enough to establish the New Republic, and a protectorate over the rest of Zululand, Dinuzulu fell foul of the British, who had no intention of allowing Boer influence to extend to the sea. In October 1886, Lord Salisbury's Tory administration agreed to recognize the new Boer state on condition that it dropped its suzerainty over the Zulus. Less than a year later the Colonial Office responded to Natal's promptings by annexing what remained of Zululand to the British Crown. And so, eight years too late, the British government finally assumed responsibility for its victory in 1879, during which time Zululand had been ravaged by famine and civil war, and two thirds of its territory lost to the hated Boers.

. Dinuzulu led a bold but ultimately doomed rebellion against British rule in 1888–9 and was exiled with two of his uncles on the mid-Atlantic island of St Helena. Only after Zululand was finally absorbed by Natal in December 1897 was Dinuzulu allowed to return. But he could do nothing to prevent the extension of Natal's 'native system' to Zululand, whereby two fifths of the land was parcelled out to white farmers and the rest kept as Zulu 'reserves'. Shepstonism had triumphed at last.

The Zulus are still counting the cost of the 1879 war. Chief Mangosuthu Buthelezi* is convinced that, had it not been for British aggression, Zululand would have remained an independent state like Lesotho and Swaziland. Recent attempts to win back Zulu sovereignty – led by Buthelezi's Inkatha Freedom Party – have been the cause of much bloodshed in post-apartheid South Africa. But the Zulu sense of national consciousness, pride and unity is currently undergoing something of a revival. Buthelezi has served as a government minister, and the role of the Zulu monarchy in the province of KwaZulu/Natal is recognized and protected by the South African constitution. The Zulus were conquered in 1879 but not, it seems, defeated.

---

* The direct descendant of Chief Mnyamana of the Buthelezi on his father's side and King Cetshwayo on his mother's.

Epilogue
'I trust I may never serve under him again'

On 2 September 1879 a 'tall, very thin' and 'much worn' man was brought into Queen Victoria's presence in the drawing room at Balmoral. It was Lord Chelmsford, the former commander-in-chief of British forces in South Africa, who a week earlier had arrived back in Britain from Zululand. As the queen had not seen him since he succeeded to his title, he 'kissed hands' before expressing 'great gratitude' for the confidence she had shown him. He then kneeled to receive from Victoria the Knight Grand Cross of the Order of the Bath (GCB).★ 'He is singularly pleasing & gentlemanlike,' noted the queen in her journal.

Next day, after lunch, Chelmsford presented the queen with a large Zulu shield. 'This one,' she recorded, 'white with a little black, belonged to the regiment of unmarried men & was taken out of the King's Shield House, in his Kraal, at Ulundi . . . Had a great deal of conversation about many things, including Ulundi, and the reason of the retreat after it, for which Lord Chelmsford has been blamed. He said it was because there were not enough provisions, and that if he had detached only a small portion of troops to follow the King, they might have been beaten, and Cetewayo would have claimed the victory, thereby entirely doing away with the effect of the victory at Ulundi.'

They spoke again after dinner on the 4th and at tea a day later. The queen recorded:

With regard to [Isandlwana] Ld. Chelmsford said no doubt poor Col. Durnford had disobeyed orders, in leaving the camp as he did; & poor

---

★ The honour had been recommended by the duke of Cambridge and sanctioned by the Cabinet. Both had reservations about Chelmsford's performance during the war but felt that the victory at Ulundi deserved some recognition.

Col. Pulleine had also done wrong, though for some time he refused to come, only going to the assistance of Col. Durnford when the Zulus had almost already got there. Ld. Chelmsford knew nothing, Col. Durnford never having sent any message to say he was in danger . . . I could not attempt to repeat all [he] said . . . but this much is clear to *me*: viz. that it was not *his* fault, but that of *others*, that this surprise at [Isandlwana took place]. He said: 'I cannot attack dead men,' but I hope he will be able to prove how unjust people have been towards him . . . I told Ld. Chelmsford he had been blamed by many, & even by the Government, for commencing the war without sufficient cause. He replied that he believed it to have been quite inevitable; that if we had not made war when we did, we should have been attacked & possibly overpowered. He never believed the Zulus were so strong, & thought they had a force of 20,000 men, whereas it was 60,000, but it had been impossible to obtain correct information on this point.

Most of what Chelmsford told the queen during these conversations was, in effect, a pack of lies. Durnford did not disobey orders to 'take command' of the camp at Isandlwana because no orders were ever issued. Chelmsford almost certainly knew this, because Crealock's order book, containing a copy of the actual order to Durnford, had been recovered from the battlefield in May and returned to its owner. As for implying that he knew nothing about the seriousness of the attack on the camp, that too was a lie. Durnford himself had not sent a 'message to say he was in danger', but many others had and some of these messages had filtered through to Chelmsford during the morning of 22 January. The war was certainly not inevitable – though the British government had given Frere every indication that they wanted the Zulu question dealt with sooner or later – and the Zulu strength was never as great as 60,000. But the queen – always susceptible to a handsome man with good breeding – wanted to believe Chelmsford and that was half the battle won. Ponsonby, perspicacious as ever, was not quite so easily convinced. 'Every one must like him,' he wrote to his wife on 7 September, 'for he is so quiet and easy to get on with and so free from swagger or bitterness against any one . . . But all these things do not make a General. I don't feel satisfied. There is always some one who has not served him properly.'

Even the queen was forced to see a different side to Chelmsford when Wood and Buller arrived at Balmoral on 9 September. Having knighted one and pinned the Victoria Cross on the other, she joined them for dinner and was particularly taken with Wood. 'Sir Evelyn,' she noted, 'is wonderfully lively & hardly ceases talking, which no doubt comes from his deafness & inability to hear any general conversation . . . Col. Buller . . . though naturally averse to talking, told me much that was very interesting.'

But it was only when the queen pressed a reluctant Wood to speak his mind during a private audience on 10 September that a true picture began to emerge. 'Lord Chelmsford is the kindest & most loveable of men,' said Wood, 'but he is *not* hard enough for a soldier.' Asked to explain, Wood said that Chelmsford, though 'as brave as a lion', was 'nervous about responsibility' and 'was *alarmed* to send out patrols or to reconnoitre'. He had, as a result, 'lost men' unnecessarily. The following day, having spoken to Wood and Buller together, she recorded:

[Buller] thinks there were not above 35,000 Zulus. Ld. Chelmsford said 60,000 . . . Another gt. mistake was the splitting up of the Army with so many different detachments thereby endangering them, & crippling their action. Sir E. Wood was always urging on Ld. Chelmsford to fight the Zulus in the open, whereas he was always afraid of this, & I gathered from Sir E. Wood he wd. not have fought the battle of Ulundi had it not been for his urging it on him, & the success was unbounded. The men who had become demoralized & panic-stricken by inaction behaved admirably.

Buller was even more frank in a conversation with the queen's private secretary. 'As we walked Buller's heart opened to me in confidence,' wrote Ponsonby.

Chelmsford would do nothing but potter over details. Wood forced him on. Even at Ulundi it was all that Wood could do to make him advance to the place where the fight took place. Once in action Chelmsford was cool and ready. But in movements hesitating and nervous. He was so personally popular, both with officers and men, that 'we were determined to pull him through and we did'.

It was a pity, said Ponsonby, that Chelmsford had been compelled to retire from Ulundi from 'want of provisions'. Not true, replied Buller: 'We had ample provisions – that is to say if he had not sent them away – and we could have got them up quickly.' Both he and Wood had offered to remain at oNdini, but Chelmsford had refused out of fear that his victory might be tarnished by a subsequent reverse. Buller summed up his military opinion of his former commander when he told Ponsonby: 'I hope I may often meet Chelmsford again as a friend but I trust I may never serve under him again as a General.'

Despite being privy to this inside view of the war, the queen retained her affection and respect for Chelmsford, and did everything in her power to secure him official recognition for his services during the war. She believed that his victory at Ulundi had wiped out the stain of Isandlwana and, since his return, had been pressing the prime minister to accord him the honour of an official invitation to his country residence, Hughenden Manor in Buckinghamshire. But Disraeli was violently opposed to such a gesture. An 'official interview' would not be possible, he told the queen in a remarkably forthright letter of 30 August, because he had 'virtually recalled Lord Chelmsford from his command' for reasons that he considered to be 'peremptory'. Writing in the third person, he added:

He mixes up Lord Chelmsford, in no small degree with the policy of the unhappily precipitated Zulu war, the evil consequences of which to this country have been incalculable. Had it not taken place, your Majesty would be Dictatress of Europe

[He] charges Lord Chelmsford with having invaded Zululand 'avec un cœur léger';★ with no adequate knowledge of the country he was

★ 'with a light heart'.

attacking, & no precaution or preparation. A dreadful disaster occurred
in consequence, & then Lord Chelmsford became panic-struck; appealed
to yr. Majesty's government frantically for reinforcements, & found
himself at the head of 20,000 of your Majesty's troops, in order to reduce
a country not larger than Yorkshire . . . [And] had he not been furtively
apprised by telegraph that he was about to be superseded, Lord Chelmsford would probably never have advanced to Ulundi. His retreat from
that post was his last & crowning mistake.

The queen thought that Disraeli was being far too hard on Chelmsford and that he deserved a chance to reply to the criticisms that
had been heaped upon him by the press and Opposition MPs since
Isandlwana. '*He* has obtained the decisive victory at Ulundi which
has paralysed Cetewayo,' she wrote. All his successor, Wolseley,
had done, on the other hand, was to 'send home the troops and
some of the best officers'. She could not deny that Chelmsford had
made mistakes, but she could not '*bear* injustice or want of generosity towards those who have unbounded difficulties to contend
with'. Disraeli, however, would not budge, and the most he was
prepared to grant Chelmsford was a formal interview in Downing
Street. This took place on 7 October and was, inevitably, an
awkward occasion, though neither participant left a written record.
Moreover, Disraeli had, in the interim, underlined the snub to
Chelmsford by inviting Wood to Hughenden, albeit at the queen's
request. To Wood, one of the few genuine heroes of the Zulu
War, Disraeli was charm itself and later told the queen that he was
'delighted' with the general's visit.

Whether the queen would have remained so loyal towards
Chelmsford if she had been aware of the confidential memorandum
on Isandlwana that had been sent to him by Sir Charles Ellice,
adjutant-general, on 11 August 1879 is another matter. It read:

Having very carefully considered the evidence taken before the Court of
Inquiry on the Isandlana disaster; the supplementary evidence afterwards
sent home, and the answers transmitted by your Lordship to certain
questions . . . [the duke of Cambridge] has come to the conclusion that

the primary cause of the misfortune, and that which led to all the others, was the under estimate formed of the offensive fighting power of the Zulu army. This was not unnatural . . .

The idea of a well disciplined native Force advancing firmly on, and closing rapidly in the open with British battalions armed with the breechloader and supported by Rifled guns was not duly realised.

In fact such confidence in the superiority of the breechloader in British hands was felt that your Lordship did not hesitate to base your plan of campaign upon the power of three isolated columns . . . Such a division of force was justifiable only on the belief that each of these columns was able to support alone, the impact of the whole Zulu power.

To this belief in the crushing effect of our weapons, and the small probability of the enemy venturing upon a flank attack in the open, is evidently due the immediate causes of the defeat at Isandlana.

Ellice then listed the causes:

1. The advance from Rorke's Drift without any persistent effort being made to put this, the immediate base of our operations in Zululand, in a proper state of defence before it commenced.
2. The non-preparation on the 21st January, either by the formation of a laager formed out of the wagons not told off to return to Rorke's Drift for supplies on the following day, or by the construction of a small redoubt, of any means of defence for the Troops in Camp in case of attack.
3. Your Lordship moving out of Camp on the morning of the 22nd with a battalion of Infantry, four guns, and the mounted infantry to attack the enemy some ten miles off, whilst it was in this defenceless state, even though you had ordered up Colonel Durnford's Native Contingent to reinforce it.
4. The not thoroughly searching, with horsemen, the country to the North-East of the Camp, when the enemy was known to be in force ten miles to the East on the Ulundi Road.
5. The evident discredit attached from the first, by those at Head Quarters, to the idea of a really serious attack being made upon the Camp when thus left.

6. The dissemination, in two directions, of the one regular battalion which remained in Camp on the attack being actually delivered, when the only chance of safety consisted in the immediate construction of a small laager, or in massing the troops in square, with a supply of ammunition in the centre, ready to break through one or other of the Zulu encircling wings.

The preamble and points one to five were all direct criticisms of Chelmsford; only point six was a criticism of Pulleine and, to a lesser extent, Durnford.

The queen might have been equally disturbed if she had known the true story behind the discovery of Durnford's body at Isandlwana on 21 May 1879. The colonel had been posthumously accused by Chelmsford and his staff of disobeying an order to 'take command' of the camp on the day of the battle. The order in question, therefore, should still have been on his person. Yet 'Offy' Shepstone always denied finding papers on Durnford's body, telling Fanny Colenso that had he discovered any 'they would have gone down to you with the knife & rings'. He would admit only to finding his brother George's papers, 'which may have given rise to the idea'.

But a very different version of events would emerge from other witnesses. At the time of the expedition to Isandlwana, Fanny Colenso was staying at Pietermaritzburg with Shepstone's wife, Helen. Soon after receiving Durnford's personal effects, which she sent on to his brother in England, Fanny met 'Offy' in person. 'I was rather struck,' she wrote later, 'by the warm manner in which he spoke of Col. Durnford and of his own extreme satisfaction at having been the man to find, & show respect to, the body of such a hero. For I was well aware that Mr Shepstone had never felt warmly towards Colonel Durnford during the latter's life time, since the volunteers were condemned and Colonel Durnford highly commended by the Court of Inquiry upon the Bushman's River Pass Affair in 1873.'

The *Natal Witness* had published a telegram on 27 May 1879 that stated that 'after the papers and maps found on Durnford's person had been removed, a pile of stones was heaped over the body'.

When shown this passage by Fanny, Shepstone said it was a 'mistake'. There were, he added, 'no papers of any kind, and could not have been because there was no coat'. Fanny believed him and made no further inquiries at that time. Meanwhile in England, Durnford's brother Edward, also a colonel in the British Army, heard about the papers from a separate source. Veterinary Surgeon Longhurst of the 1st Dragoon Guards had written to his family in England on 22 May, describing Durnford's burial and the fact that a letter had been taken from his body. So Edward Durnford asked Fanny to make further inquiries. She had left for England by the time the 1st Dragoon Guards returned to Pietermaritzburg, but a family friend received confirmation from Longhurst that the story was true. Soon after this meeting the regiment sailed for India and, for a time, Longhurst clammed up. Twice Edward Durnford wrote for more information and twice he received no reply. But a third attempt through Longhurst's commanding officer, Colonel Marter, had the desired effect. Longhurst sent back a full account of what he had seen on 21 May 1879, including the assertion that he 'saw him, Capt. Shepstone, distinctly take' from Durnford's body 'two finger rings & a pocket knife' and 'also a packet of letters from his coat pocket'.

Fanny was 'exceedingly puzzled' by the reference to a coat. Not only Shepstone but members of Chelmsford's staff had always insisted that the body was found coatless. So she asked Edward Durnford to double-check. Longhurst's response was emphatic: 'I believe that I was the first officer to recognize your brother's body ... and I am confident that he then had on a blue coat.' Other members of his regiment, he said, remembered seeing Durnford's body and that 'he wore a coat'. A separate witness, who disinterred Durnford's body in October 1879 for reburial in Pietermaritzburg, confirmed that he was wearing a coat. When Fanny challenged 'Offy' Shepstone about Longhurst's claim that he had seen him removing papers from the body, Shepstone replied, 'Capt. Longhurst's statement as regards papers is a *deliberate untruth*. I took no papers of any kind from Col. Durnford's body, nor were any taken from him, in my presence.'

Shepstone was almost certainly lying. His motives for taking incriminating papers from Durnford's body are obvious: he had never forgiven Durnford for criticizing the conduct of his regiment, the Natal Carbineers, in the Bushman's River Pass incident; and he may well have been trying to curry favour with Lord Chelmsford, the man who had the most to lose if the true text of Colonel Crealock's order to Durnford ever came to light. Chelmsford was still, at that stage, commander of British forces in South Africa, and Shepstone may have been seeking a plum staff appointment. If so, he was to be disappointed and, in a final irony, served the remainder of the campaign as commandant of Durnford's old corps, the Natal Native Horse. This might explain his cryptical remark to Fanny Colenso in the spring of 1881: 'Lord Chelmsford has not stood by me, and I don't see why I should stand by him any longer.'

Fortunately for Chelmsford, Shepstone quickly came to his senses and decided not to expand on this claim. Instead he tried to cover his tracks by removing from the file of the *Natal Witness* the issue for 27 May 1879, which included the incriminating telegram. The editor of the *Witness*, Mr Statham, later told Fanny that Shepstone borrowed the file in late 1882, explaining that 'he wished to look up some points connected with the Zulu war'. When Fanny checked the file she found that both the issue for 27 May and the Supplement for 7 June, in which the text of the telegram was repeated, had been removed, 'apparently with a knife'.

Yet Fanny continued her hunt for the 'truth', enlisting as supporters such influential figures as Colonels R. Hawthorn and Charles Luard, successive commandants of the Royal Engineers in Natal. Eventually, to put an end to the speculation, Shepstone agreed in April 1886 to appear before a Court of Inquiry. Its remit, however, was limited to whether papers had or had not been found on Durnford's body. Lieutenant-General Henry Torrens, then acting high commissioner and commander of British troops in South Africa, was aware of the potential danger to Chelmsford's reputation and wrote to Luard, who had convened the inquiry: 'I have taken measures to limit proceedings and to prevent, I trust, the possibility of other names, distinguished or otherwise, being dragged into it.'

In the event the court found in favour of Shepstone. While his witnesses confirmed his story, those produced by Luard were less than convincing (with Fanny suspecting the powerful Shepstone family of foul play). In addition, many of Luard's best witnesses were unable to get leave from the army or civil service to attend the inquiry. Torrens forced Luard to write a letter of apology to Shepstone, and then wrote a note of his own to Chelmsford: '— tells me that you are gratified at the action I have taken in this wretched charge against Theophilus Shepstone, in which an attempt has been made to involve you.' Fanny died of tuberculosis on 26 April 1887 but went to her grave convinced that Shepstone was part of a conspiracy to transfer the blame for the defeat at Isandlwana from Chelmsford to Durnford. She may well have been right.

Certain documents supportive of Durnford had already come to light. In June 1885, in response to an advertisement in the *Natal Witness* for papers connected to Durnford, a Pietermaritzburg businessman called F. Pearse sent the following letter to the editor:

I write to inform you that I have in my possession a document which was picked up on the field of Isandhlwana by my brother A. Pearse, late trooper in the Natal Carbineers. It appears to be the instructions issued by Lord Chelmsford to the late Colonel on taking the field. I have written to my brother to ascertain whether he is willing to part with it.

Trooper Pearse, it later emerged, had found Durnford's portmanteau and took from it a packet of papers. He must have agreed to hand them over because they were later sent to the editor of the *Witness* and eventually found their way into the Royal Engineers' Museum at Chatham. They included a copy of the instructions that Chelmsford issued to his column commanders on 23 December 1878 and the penultimate order to Durnford, signed by Major Spalding and sent on 19 January 1879. The instructions are telling, because the suggested defensive formation in the event of a Zulu attack was very similar to the one formed at Isandlwana. But the order is even more important, because it makes clear Chelmsford's intention that Durnford's No. 2 Column should operate in conjunction with, rather than as part of, Glyn's No. 3 Column. In the absence of a direct order on the 22nd, therefore, there was no reason for Durnford to assume that Chelmsford wished him to take command of the camp at Isandlwana.

Far more significant, however, was the discovery of Colonel Crealock's order book – containing a copy of his crucial order to Durnford during the early hours of 22 January 1879 – by Colonel Black when he returned to the battlefield for the third time, in June 1879, to bury the soldiers of the 24th. Black gave the order book to Crealock, who, for obvious reasons, kept its existence quiet – until 15 July 1886, that is, when he responded to an inquiry from a Major Jekyll at the War Office by stating the exact wording of the order. There was no request for Durnford to 'take command' of the camp, as Crealock had claimed after the battle; he was simply instructed 'to march to this Camp at once with all the force you have with you'. Jekyll's reply, on 17 July 1886, thanked Crealock on behalf of a General Nicholson, who had requested the information. The general, added Jekyll, had asked the question 'simply for his private information & in no way for official use'. These letters were not made public at the time.

Chelmsford's military reputation remained, therefore, largely intact during his lifetime. His claim, in a speech in the House of Lords on 19 August 1880, that Durnford's disobeyal of orders had caused the loss of the camp, was never properly refuted. And yet Crealock, and almost certainly Chelmsford, had been in possession of the correct version of the order for over a year. They must have assumed that it would not see the light of day – and they were right. Despite his supersession by Wolseley, Chelmsford basked in the glory of his one-sided victories at Gingindlovu and oNdini. The queen, taken in by his duplicitous explanation of the disaster at Isandlwana, showered him with honours. As well as awarding him a GCB, she made him Gold Stick at Court and, partly to prolong his military career, governor of the Tower of London. He was also promoted to full general, though he never received another active command. He died in 1905, at the age of seventy-eight, playing billiards in his club.

Even before they knew the full story, however, senior officials at the War Office were questioning Chelmsford and Crealock's version of events. A confidential and undated War Office memorandum – possibly written by Ellice in August 1879 – stated:

Col. Durnford was commanding an independent column, and received his orders direct from the General. The Column commanded by Col. Glyn was at Isandhlwana, and on the force marching out Col. Pulleine recd. orders to take command during Col. Glyn's absence. It could never have been intended and doubtless never was intended to put an officer in command of another column over Col. P.'s head for a portion of a day. Col. D's move up to join the General, 'cooperate' is the General's own word, was entirely in accord with his previous orders. Doubtless finding himself Senior Officer on the spot when the action had already commenced he, according to the custom of the service, took command, but this was at too late a period to remedy the fatal errors of position selected before his arrival.

So Durnford was cleared in private; but never officially, never in public. Never, that is, until the Durnford papers finally came to light in the 1960s.*

What of the other 'heroes' who survived the war? Sadly, as is often the case, the ordinary soldiers were quickly forgotten. Of the seven non-officers who won VCs at Rorke's Drift, three fared particularly badly. Corporal Christian Schiess, having recovered from his wound, worked for a time in the telegraph office in Durban. But

---

* F. W. D. Jackson was the first historian to examine the Durnford Papers at the Royal Engineers' Museum in Chatham in 1963. They had been deposited there at an unrecorded date by an unrecorded person. Some of the documents, however, were too fragile to be inspected. Jackson had to wait until 1989 to read all of the Durnford Papers. He did so with Julian Whybra, and they published their findings the following year in the journal *Soldiers of the Queen*.

by 1884 he was out of work and destitute. In the hope of a fresh start he accepted a free passage to England on HMS *Serapis*; tragically he died en route and was buried at sea.

Private Robert Jones, one of the 'hospital four', left the army in 1888 and worked intermittently as an agricultural labourer. Unable to provide for his family, he shot himself in the back garden of his home in Peterchurch, Herefordshire, in 1898. He was buried in the local graveyard, but, because it was thought he had committed suicide,★ his gravestone faces in the opposite direction to the other plots.

Jones's namesake and the man who fought by his side, Private William Jones, was invalided out of the army with chronic rheumatism in 1880 and failed to find regular employment. He was reduced to re-enacting the defence of Rorke's Drift in theatres and even appeared in Buffalo Bill's Wild West Show when it toured Britain in the 1880s. But penury forced him to pawn his VC, and, by 1912, recurring nightmares about Zulus had unhinged his mind. He died the following year and was buried in a public grave.

Corporal William Allen never properly recovered from his wound, though he served for a time as sergeant-instructor of musketry in the 4th Volunteer Battalion of the South Wales Borderers. He died of influenza in March 1890.

Private Frederick Hitch was also discharged on account of the serious injuries he received at Rorke's Drift. He joined the Corps of Commissionaires but had his VC stolen off the front of his coat in 1901. It was never recovered, though King Edward VII authorized a replacement in 1908. Hitch later became a cab driver and died at home in Chiswick during a taxi strike in 1913.

Private Henry Hook returned home in 1880 to learn that his wife, believing him dead, had sold his property and remarried. He moved to London and worked for many years as the cloakroom attendant in the Reading Room of the British Library. He died of tuberculosis in Gloucester in 1904.

★ His family still dispute the suicide verdict, arguing that the gun had a hair trigger and the shooting was an accident.

Private John Williams outlived all his fellow VC-winners. Discharged from the army reserve in 1893, he worked for many years as a civilian in the regimental depot at Brecon, finally retiring in 1920. He died in Cwmbran in 1932 at the age of seventy-five.

Of the four officers who received VCs for Rorke's Drift, James Reynolds lived the longest. Promoted to surgeon-major, he was present at the Battle of Ulundi and eventually died, aged eighty-eight, in 1932.

Gonville Bromhead did not fare so well. The queen obviously forgave him for not accepting her invitation to Balmoral – though he was never invited again – because she later sent him a signed photograph of herself. But, true to form, he failed to take professional advantage of his fame and did not rise above the rank of major. He never married and saw out the remainder of his army career in South Asia, serving in Burma in the late 1880s and finally succumbing to enteric fever at Allahabad, India, in 1891. He was just forty-five.

John Chard also remained a bachelor, though his career was marginally more successful than Bromhead's. He had just been promoted to full colonel when he died of cancer of the mouth, having earlier had his tongue removed, in 1897. The queen remained a devotee to the end, inquiring after his health and later sending a wreath of laurel leaves with a handwritten card: 'A mark of admiration and regard for a brave soldier'.

The premature and unremarked death of James Dalton, the real hero of Rorke's Drift, could not have been more of a contrast. In December 1879, having just recovered from his wounds, he was promoted to assistant commissary and put out to grass on half-pay. With his army career effectively over, he sailed for England in early 1880 and quickly faded into obscurity. He later returned to South Africa as a civilian and staked a claim in the newly discovered gold fields of the Witwatersrand. But his 'Little Bess' mine failed to prosper, and he died of a sudden illness in a Port Elizabeth hotel in 1887. Mourners were in short supply.

Bibliography

Primary Sources, Unpublished

Official Documents

THE NATIONAL ARCHIVES (TNA), KEW
Colonial Office (CO): 48; 179
War Office (WO): 30; 32; 33; 34

Private Papers

DEVON RECORD OFFICE, EXETER
Buller Papers: Correspondence and Papers of Sir Redvers Buller

FAMILY PAPERS (FP)
Denis Barker, 'The Last Colonial', unpublished biography of his grand-father W. W. Barker

GLOUCESTERSHIRE RECORD OFFICE (GRO)
Hicks Beach Papers: Correspondence and Papers of Sir Michael Hicks Beach (later Viscount St Aldwyn)

KILLIE CAMPBELL AFRICANA LIBRARY (KCAL), DURBAN, SOUTH AFRICA
Maxwell Papers: Lieutenant J. Maxwell, 'Reminiscences of the Zulu War'
Newmarch Papers: Papers of T. E. Newmarch
Watkins Papers: Reverend Owen Watkins, 'Fought for the Great White Queen: Edendale'
Watson Papers: The Papers of Captain Harry Watson, 1st KDG

Wood Papers: Correspondence and Papers of Sir Evelyn Wood

Wolseley Papers: Papers of Sir Garnet Wolseley

KWAZULU-NATAL ARCHIVES (KZN), PIETERMARITZBURG, SOUTH AFRICA

Colenso Papers

Shepstone Papers: Papers of Sir Theophilus Shepstone (SP)

Wood Papers: Sir Evelyn Wood Collection

THE NATIONAL ARCHIVES (TNA), KEW

Buller Papers: The Papers of General Sir Redvers Buller

Wolseley Papers: The Papers of Field Marshal Lord Wolseley

Wolseley Journal: Sir Garnet Wolseley's South African Journal, 1879–80

NATIONAL ARMY MUSUEM (NAM), LONDON

1st Chard Report: Official Report of Lieutenant John R. M. Chard, 25 Jan. 1879

Chelmsford Papers: Papers of General Lord Chelmsford

Clark Letter: Letter from Captain Stanley Clark to 'Min', 22 May 1879

Fynney Pamphlet: F. B. Fynney, 'Pamphlet on the Zulu Army', 6610–45

Goatham Letters: Letters of Private Ashley Goatham

Hamer Letters: Letters of James Hamer to his father

MacSwiney Papers: The Papers of Captain James MacSwiney, 94th Regiment

Ransley Papers: W. G. Ransley, 3/60th Rifles, 'On Service'

Roe Diary: The Diary of Corporal William Roe, 58th Regiment

Slade Letters: Letters of Captain F. G. Slade, RA

Stafford Statement: Statement by Walter H. Stafford on the Battle of Isandlwana given in 1939

Turnham Letters: Letters of Private George Turnham, 17th Lancers

ROYAL ARCHIVES (RA), WINDSOR CASTLE

Victorian Archive: RA VIC

Victorian Additional Archive: RA VIC/Add

Ponsonby Letters: The Letters of Sir Henry Ponsonby

Cambridge Correspondence: The Military Correspondence of HRH
  Field-Marshal the duke of Cambridge
Queen Victoria's Journal: RA QVJ

ROYAL ENGINEERS' MUSEUM (REM), CHATHAM
Durnford Papers

SOUTH WALES BORDERERS' MUSEUM (SWB), ROYAL REGIMENT
OF WALES, BRECON

Banister Letters: Letters of Lieutenant George Stanhope Banister to his
  father
Brickhill Report: Copy of a Report by J. F. Brickhill of Lord Chelmsford's
  Field Force
Clery Letters: Letters of Major C. F. Clery
Coghill Diary: Diary of Lieutenant Nevill Coghill, VC
England Letters: Two letters from E. L. England, 13th LI, to his sister,
  dated 11 Feb. and 10 June 1879
Glyn Letters: Letters of Colonel R. T. Glyn, Lieutenant-General Lord
  Chelmsford and General Sir A. J. Cunynghame
Head Letter: Letter from 'Bob Head', 2/24th, to his brother (F. Williams),
  Rorke's Drift, no date
Higginson Letter: Lieutenant W. Higginson to Lord Chelmsford, 17
  Feb. 1879
Mainwaring Letter: Brigadier-General H. G. Mainwaring to the Editor
  of the *Morning Post*, c. 1921
Morris Letters: Letters from Private G. Morris to his parents, 5 Nov. 1878
  to 16 Dec. 1879
Pulleine Message: Message from Lieutenant-Colonel H. B. Pulleine to
  Lord Chelmsford, 22 Jan. 1879
Symons Account: Captain Penn Symons, 'Account of the Battle of
  Isandhlwana'

Primary Sources, Published

Published Documents, Diaries, Letters and Memoirs

Colenso, Frances, *My Chief and I* (Pietermaritzburg, 1994, but originally published in London in 1880 under the pseudonym Atherton Wylde)

Colenso Letters: Rees, Wyn (ed.), *Colenso Letters from Natal* (Pietermartitzburg, 1958)

Curling Letters: Greaves, Adrian, and Best, Brian (eds.), *The Curling Letters of the Zulu War* (Barnsley, 2001)

Dawnay Journal: Private Journal of Guy C. Dawnay (privately printed, 1886)

Disraeli Letters: Zetland, Marquess of (ed.), *The Letters of Disraeli to Lady Bradford and Lady Chesterfield*, 2 vols. (London, 1929)

Emery, Frank (ed.), *The Red Soldier: Letters from the Zulu War* (London, 1977)

Hallam Parr, Captain H. A., *A Sketch of the Kafir and Zulu Wars* (London, 1880)

Hamilton-Browne, Colonel G., *A Lost Legionary in South Africa* (London, 1912)

Hansard, 3rd Series, 1830–91

Harford Journal: Child, Daphne (ed.), *The Zulu War Journal of Colonel Henry Harford, CB* (Pietermaritzburg, 1978)

Harrison, General Sir R., *Recollections of a Life in the British Army* (London, 1908)

Laband, John (ed.), *Lord Chelmsford's Zululand Campaign 1878–1879* (Stroud, 1994)

Martineau, John, *The Life and Correspondence of Sir Bartle Frere*, 2 vols. (London, 1895)

Mitford, B. *Through the Zulu Country: Its Battlefields and Its People* (London, 1883)

Molyneux, Major-General W. C. F., *Campaigning in South Africa and Egypt* (London, 1896)

Mossop, G. *Running the Gauntlet* (London, 1937)

Norris-Newman, C. L., *In Zululand with the British throughout the War of 1879* (London, 1880)

Smith-Dorrien, General Sir Horace, *Memories of Forty-Eight Years' Service* (London, 1925)

Victoria Letters: Buckle, George Earle (ed.), *The Letters of Queen Victoria: A Selection from Her Majesty's Correspondence and Journal between the years 1862 and 1885*, 3 vols. (London, 1926–8)

Wolseley Journal: Preston, Adrian (ed.), *The South African Journal of Sir Garnet Wolseley 1879–1880* (Cape Town, 1973)

Wood, Sir Evelyn, *From Midshipman to Field Marshal*, 2 vols. (London, 1906)

Newspapers and Journals

Blackwood's Edinburgh Magazine
Brecon County Times
Broad Arrow
Cambrian
Cape Times
Chums
Daily News (London)
Fraser's Magazine
Graphic
Illustrated London News
Listener
London Gazette
Morning Post
Natalia
Natal Mercury
North Devon Herald
Royal Magazine
Strand
The Times
Western Mail

Secondary Sources

Articles and Chapters

Emery, Frank, 'Soldiers' Letters from the Zulu War', *Natalia*, no. 8, Dec. 1978, 54–60

Fripp, Charles E., 'Reminiscences of the Zulu War', *Pall Mall Magazine*, vol. 20, 1900, 547–62

Jackson, F. W. D., and Whybra, Julian, 'Isandhlwana and the Durnford Papers', *Soldiers of the Queen*, issue 60, Mar. 1990, 18–31

McGregor, Major ['One who was there'], 'The Zulu War with Colonel Pearson at Ekowe', *Blackwood's Edinburgh Magazine*, no. 765, July 1879, vol. 126, 1–29

Muziwentu, 'A Zulu Boy's Recollections of the Zulu War', *Natalia*, no. 8, Dec. 1978, 8–20

Nairne, Captain S. N. McLeod, 'The Death of the Prince Imperial', *Journal of the Royal United Services Institute*, vol. 79, Feb. 1934, no. 513, 750–51

Wood, Walter, 'An Account by Private Alfred Henry Hook, 2/24th Regiment', *Royal Magazine*, Feb. 1905

Books

Beckett, Ian, *Isandlwana* (London, 2003)

Blake, Robert, *Disraeli* (London, 1966; 1969 edition)

Cope, Richard, *Ploughshare of War: The Origins of the Anglo-Zulu War of 1879* (Scottsville, 1999)

Droogleever, R. W. F., *The Road to Isandlwana: Colonel Anthony Durnford in Natal and Zululand 1873–1879* (London, 1992)

Farwell, Byron, *Queen Victoria's Little Wars* (London, 1973)

Featherstone, Donald, *Weapons and Equipment of the Victorian Soldier* (Poole, 1978)

Gillings, Ken, *Battles of KwaZulu-Natal* (Durban, 2000)

Greaves, Adrian, *Isandlwana* (London, 2001)

— *Rorke's Drift* (London, 2002)

— and Rattray, David, *David Rattray's Guidebook to the Anglo-Zulu War Battlefields* (Barnsley, 2003)

Guy, J., *The Destruction of the Zulu Kingdom* (London, 1979)

Harrington, Peter, *British Artists and War* (London, 1993)

Hattersley, Alan F., *Carbineer: The History of the Royal Natal Carbineers* (Aldershot, 1950)

Haythornthwaite, Philip J., *The Colonial Wars Sourcebook* (London, 1995; 1997 edition)

Holme, Norman, *The Noble 24th: Biographical Records of the 24th Regiment in the Zulu War and the South African Campaigns 1877 to 1879* (London, 1999)

Holmes, Richard (ed.), *The Oxford Companion to Military History* (Oxford, 2001)

Jerrold, Walter, *Sir Redvers H. Buller, VC* (London, 1900)

Johnson, Barry C., *The Life of Henry Hook, VC* (London, 1986)

Knight, Ian, *The Zulus* (London, 1989)

— *'By the Orders of the Great White Queen'* (London, 1992)

— *The Anatomy of the Zulu Army* (London, 1995)

— *With His Face to the Foe* (Staplehurst, 2001)

— *The National Army Museum Book of the Zulu War* (London, 2003)

Kuhn, William M., *Henry and Mary Ponsonby: Life at the Court of Queen Victoria* (London, 2002)

Laband, John, *Fight Us in the Open: The Anglo-Zulu War through Zulu Eyes* (Pietermaritzburg, 1985)

— *The Battle of Ulundi* (Pietermaritzburg, 1988)

— *The Rise and Fall of the Zulu Nation* (London, 1997)

— and Mathews, Jeff, *Isandlwana* (Pietermaritzburg, 1992)

Lock, Ron, *Blood on the Painted Mountain: Zulu Victory and Defeat, Hlobane and Kambula, 1879* (London, 1995)

— and Quantill, Peter, *Zulu Victory: The Epic of Isandlwana and the Cover-up* (London, 2002)

Longford, Elizabeth, *Wellington*, 2 vols. (London, 1969 and 1972)

Maxwell, Leigh, *The Ashanti Ring: Sir Garnet Wolseley's Campaigns 1870–1882* (London, 1985)

Morris, Donald, *The Washing of the Spears: The Rise and Fall of the Great Zulu Nation* (London, 1966)

Porch, Douglas, *Wars of Empire* (London, 2000)

Ritter, E. A., *Shaka Zulu* (London, 1957)

Roberts, Andrew, *Salisbury: Victorian Titan* (London, 1999)

Robinson, Commander C. N. (ed.), *Celebrities of the British Army* (London, 1900)

Stalker, J., *The Natal Carbineers* (Pietermaritzburg, 1912)

Strachan, Hew, *Wellington's Legacy: The Reform of the British Army 1830– 1854* (Manchester, 1984)

— *Military Lives* (Oxford, 2002)

The Register of the Victoria Cross (Cheltenham, 1997)

Webb, C. de B., and Wright, J. B., *A Zulu King Speaks* (Pietermaritzburg, 1978)

Weintraub, Stanley, *Albert: Uncrowned King* (London, 1997, this edition, 1998)

— *Victoria* (London, 1987)

Yorke, Edmund, *Rorke's Drift 1879* (Stroud, 2001)

Young, John, *They Fell Like Stones: Battles and Casualties of the Zulu War, 1879* (London, 1991)

Documentaries

'Zulu – The True Story', *Timewatch*, BBC2, 24 Oct. 2003

Notes

Abbreviations

Cope	Richard Cope, *Ploughshare of War: The Origins of the Anglo-Zulu War of 1879* (Scottsville, 1999)
Curling Letters	Adrian Greaves and Brian Best (eds.), *The Curling Letters of the Zulu War* (Barnsley, 2001)
Droogleever	R. W. F. Droogleever, *The Road to Isandlwana: Colonel Anthony Durnford in Natal and Zululand 1873–1879* (1992)
Emery	Frank Emery (ed.), *The Red Soldier: Letters from the Zulu War* (London, 1977)
Greaves	Adrian Greaves, *Rorke's Drift* (London, 2002)
Holme	Norman Holme, *The Noble 24th: Biographical Records of the 24th Regiment in the Zulu War and the South African Campaigns 1877 to 1879* (London, 1999)
Jackson & Whybra	F. W. D. Jackson and Julian Whybra, 'Isandhlwana and the Durnford Papers', *Soldiers of the Queen*, issue 60, Mar. 1990, 18–31
Knight	Ian Knight, *The National Army Museum Book of the Zulu War* (London, 2003)
Laband	John Laband (ed.), *Lord Chelmsford's Zululand Campaign 1878–1879* (Stroud, 1994)
Martineau	John Martineau, *The Life and Correspondence of Sir Bartle Frere*, 2 vols. (London, 1895)
Morris	Donald R. Morris, *The Washing of the Spears* (London, 1966)
VC Register	*The Register of the Victoria Cross* (Cheltenham, 1997)
Wolseley Journal	Adrian Preston (ed.), *The South African Journal of Sir Garnet Wolseley, 1879–1880* (Cape Town, 1973)

Wood   Sir Evelyn Wood, *From Midshipman to Field Marshal*,
                        2 vols. (London, 1906)
Zulu Victory   Ron Lock and Peter Quantill, *Zulu Victory: The Epic
                        of Isandlwana and the Cover-up* (London, 2002)

Prologue

1   '*a most useless officer*' . . . '*stupid-looking*': *Wolseley Journal*, 16 July 1879,
    57.
1   '*The party of R.E*': Greaves, 99.
2   '*the enemy moving*' . . . '*dash at the Ponts*': 2nd Chard Report,
    21 Feb. 1880, in Holme, 270.
3   '*You will be in charge*': ibid., 272.
3   *Less than fifteen* . . . '*at all costs*': 1st Chard Report, 25 Jan. 1879, NAM,
    6309-115.
3   *orders were given* . . . *work to continue*: Wood, 'An Account by Private
    Alfred Henry Hook, 2/24th Regiment', *Royal Magazine*, Feb. 1905.
4   '*How many are there?*': Hitch Account, in Holme, 284.
4   *The spellbound redcoats* . . . *south wall*: Bourne Account, ibid., 279.
4   '*Here they come!*': Interview with Roger Lane, Sergeant Gallagher's
    great-grandson, 'Zulu – The True Story', *Timewatch*, BBC2, 24 Oct.
    2003.

Chapter One: The Zulus

5   '*the most politically sophisticated*': Laband, *Rise and Fall*, 11.
10 '*What is the matter?*': ibid., xiv.
12 '*heaped like pumpkins*': Morris, 149.
16 '*walking repository of Zulu lore*': Laband, *Rise and Fall*, 138.
19 *relations would continue on the 'same footing*': Shepstone Report, in Cope,
    35.
20 '*Cetywayo is a man of considerable ability*': ibid., 36–7.

Chapter Two: Confederation

22 '*being improved*': Blake, *Disraeli*, 535.

22 '*I plight my troth*': *Victoria Letters*, II, 322.

23 '*I greatly doubt*': Carnarvon Minute, 20 June 1874, TNA, CO 179/114.

23 placed '*much confidence*': Carnarvon to Pine, 7 Nov. 1874, in Cope, 38.

24 *host of military reforms*: The so-called 'Cardwell reforms' included: the abolition of the purchase system for commissions; the rationalization of army departments; and the subordination of the commander-in-chief to his political master, the secretary of state for War.

24 '*The Queen . . . naturally leans*': *Wolseley Journal*, 23 May 1879, 28.

24 *What was needed . . . common law*: Cope, 46–7.

24 '*objection that we are too weak*': Wolseley to Carnarvon, 12 June 1875, in ibid., 48.

24–5 *The solution proposed . . . need for direct rule* : Cope, 80–83.

26 '*The Transvaal . . . must be ours*': Carnarvon to Frere, 12 Dec. 1876, in Cope, 102.

26 '*the resources of the Transvaal*': Report by Francis Oats, 12 Nov. 1876, ibid.

26 '*with a secret dispatch*': Carnarvon to Disraeli, 20 Sept. 1876, ibid., 105.

27 '*origin, nature and circumstances*': Cope, 122.

29 '*quarrelsome and* mutinous' . . . '*Impatience of control*': Roberts, *Salisbury*, 225.

29 the '*present state of things*' . . . '*in Europe*': Frere to Shepstone, 28 Oct. 1877, in Cope, 149.

29 *Shepstone . . . the king*: Shepstone to Frere, 23 Nov. 1877, ibid.

30 '*We have always been*' . . . '*honest work*': Frere to Shepstone, 17 July 1877, ibid., 149–50.

30 '*taking Cetywayo and his Zulus*': Carnarvon to Bulwer, 5 Aug. 1879, ibid., 150.

30 '*H.M. Govt. are rather nervous*': Sir Robert Herbert to Shepstone, 7 June 1877, ibid., 151.

30 '*must & ought to come eventually*': Carnarvon Minute, 5 June 1877, TNA, CO 179/123.

31 '*the most incontrovertible*': Shepstone to Carnarvon, 2 Jan. 1878, in Cope, 171.

32 '*I am fully satisfied*': Quoted in ibid., 180.

32 '*Cetywayo is the secret hope*': Shepstone to Carnarvon, 11 Dec. 1877, KZN, SP 68.

32 '*You make no reference*': KZN, SP 27.

33 '*Nobody seems to think*': Minute by W. R. Malcolm, 28 Mar. 1878, TNA, CO 179/126.

33 *aggressive measures*: They included making public the request for a £6m vote of credit to fund a war with Russia and sending British warships through the Dardanelles to protect Constantinople.

33 '*Hicks Beach . . . is the only man*': Roberts, *Salisbury*, 225.

34 '*utterly taken*' . . . '*break in the clouds*': Frere to Carnarvon, 17 Feb. 1878, in Martineau, II, 219.

34 '*They came on in four divisions*': ibid., 213.

34–5 '*I presume that the presence*': Hicks Beach Papers, GRO, D2455/ PCC/22.

35 '*should always be retrospective*': Martineau, I, 272.

36 '*mine of wealth*': Quoted in Cope, 201.

36 '*You must be master*': Frere to Hicks Beach, 10 Aug. 1878, Hicks Beach Papers, GRO, D2455/PCC/1/16.

36 '*reign of barbarism*': Quoted in Cope, 202.

36 '*make the best of it*': Frere to Shepstone, 7 Oct. 1878, KZN, SP 33.

36 '*giving the shells*': Minute by Edward Fairfield, 10 Mar. 1879, TNA, CO 48/489.

37 *Even Frere . . . new constitution*: Frere to Hicks Beach, 10 Aug. 1878, Hicks Beach Papers, GRO, D2455/PCC/1/16.

38 *lacking in* '*flair, intuition*': Laband, xxv.

39 '*The newspapers will . . . give you*': Frere to Hicks Beach, 30 Apr. 1878, Hicks Beach Papers, GRO, D2455/PCC/1/5.

39 *He justified the move . . . precautions*: Frere to Hicks Beach, 16 July 1878, Hicks Beach Papers, GRO, D2455/PCC/1/12.

39–40 '*The Zulus have been very kind*': Thesiger to Shepstone, 8 July 1878, in Laband, 3.

40 '*If we are to have a fight*': ibid., 21 July 1878, in Laband, 5.

Chapter Three: The Road to War

41 '*It is possible*': Thesiger to the surveyor-general, 12 Aug. 1878, in Cope, 223.

41 '*fully determined*' . . . '*least anxious*': *Wolseley Journal*, 48.

41 '*the most ordinary measures*': Thesiger to Frere, 11 Aug. 1878, GRO, D2455/PCC/1/18b.

41 '*Invasion of Zululand*' . . . '*attack or defence*': Laband, 6.

41–2 *a similar memorandum* . . . *staff work*: ibid., 9–11.

42 '*in readiness to follow*' . . . '*keep the peace*': Frere to Hicks Beach, 10 Sept. 1878, Hicks Beach Papers, GRO, D2455/PCC/1/22.

42 *Thesiger needed his* '*support*' . . . *him present*: ibid., 20 Aug. 1878, Hicks Beach Papers, GRO, D2455/PCC/1/18a.

42 '*The people here are slumbering*': ibid., 30 Sept. 1878, Hicks Beach Papers, GRO, D2455/PCC/1/24.

42–3 *an invasion of Natal* . . . *with a rifle*: Thesiger to Stanley, 28 Sept. 1878, in Laband, 12–16.

43 '*no way of settling*' . . . '*never be safe*': Hicks Beach Papers, GRO, D2455/PCC/1/26.

44 '*to make the drift passable*': Minute by colonial secretary, 9 Oct. 1878, in Cope, 224.

44 '*seized & assaulted*': Frere to Hicks Beach, 7 Oct. 1878, Hicks Beach Papers, GRO, D2455/PCC/1/24.

44 '*not to be wondered at*': Quoted in Cope, 225.

44–5 '*a feeler and of great significance*' . . . *for his arrest*: ibid.

45 '*not accidents, but acts*': Frere to Hicks Beach, 19 Jan. 1879, Hicks Beach Papers, GRO, D2455/PCC/2/4.

45 '*I hear of troops arriving*': Cetshwayo to Bulwer, 16 Sept. 1878, in Cope, 222.

45 *considered the terms* . . . *far too harsh*: Disraeli's government resented, in particular, the creation of a pro-Russian big Bulgaria and Russian gains in Asia minor at Turkey's expense. If ratified, the treaty would have deprived Turkey of most of its European empire and forced it to pay Russia a huge indemnity.

46 '*When V-Roys*': Quoted in Blake, *Disraeli*, 662.

46 '*millstones round our neck*': ibid., 665.

46 '*If anything annoys me*': *Disraeli Letters*, II, 189.

47 '*considerable exception*': Hicks Beach to Frere, 10 Oct. 1878, Hicks Beach Papers, GRO, D2455/PCC/22.

47 '*did not want reinforcements*' . . . '*to send them*': Hicks Beach Papers, GRO/D2455/PCC/13.

48 '*We decided to send out*': ibid.

48 *On 1 November* . . . '*successful termination*': Hicks Beach to Disraeli, 3 Nov. 1878, ibid.

48 '*The Government are not prepared*': Hicks Beach Papers, GRO, D2455/PCC/22.

49 *But, as Hicks Beach told Frere...* '*keep out of war*': ibid.

49 '*I can quite understand*': ibid.

49–50 '*I am inclined to think*': Chelmsford to Wood, 23 Nov. 1878, Wood Papers, KZN, A598/II/2/9.

50–51 '*local, defensive reasons*' . . . '*be peaceful*': Cope, 235.

51 '*Even the most blind optimists*': Hicks Beach Papers, GRO, D2455/PCC/1/29.

51–3 *A long, rambling* . . . *not be allowed to continue*: 'Message (No. II) from his Excellency the Lieutenant Governor of Natal to Cetywayo, King of the Zulus', RA VIC/033/37.

53 '*That's, I fear, the worst thing*': Colenso to Chesson, 23 May 1880, in Cope, 238.

53 *Bulwer later confirmed* . . . *not been attacked*: *Wolseley Journal*, 30 June 1879, 48.

53 *But in a letter* . . . '*more than necessary*': Cope, 238–9.

54 '*Have the Zulus complained?*': Quoted in Morris, 292.

54 *When Shepstone finished* . . . *Shepstone refused*: Cope, 241–2.

55 *The messenger returned* . . . *unless provoked*: Frere Memorandum, 24 Dec. 1878, Chelmsford Papers, NAM, 6807-386-8-4.

55 '*it will be impossible*': Cope, 243.

55 '*quite changed his tone*': Frere to Hicks Beach, 6 Jan. 1879, RA VIC/033/41.

56 '*ornaments and badges*': ibid.

56 *'any delay'*: Laband, 52.

56 *'further inforcement'*: Telegram from Frere to Hicks Beach, 6 Jan 1879, RA VIC/033/40.

56 not to *'push on too far'* . . . *had elapsed*: Chelmsford to Wood, 4 Jan. 1879, Wood Papers, KZN, A598/II/2/2.

56 *Fynney received word*: Cope, 244.

57 *'It seems to contain'*: Hicks Beach Papers, GRO, D2455/PCC/22.

57 *'further communications'*: ibid., D2455, PCC/1/31.

57 *'I hope that Chelmsford's plans'*: ibid., PCC/1/32.

57 *'When I first came'*: ibid., PCC/22.

58 *It was followed on 13 January*: Frere to Hicks Beach, 6 Jan. 1879, RA VIC/033/41.

58 *'short and successful'*: Hicks Beach to Disraeli, 13 Jan. 1879, Hicks Beach Papers, GRO, D2455/PCC/13.

Chapter Four: Preparing for War

59–60 *Fynney's report . . . political affiliation*: F. B. Fynney, 'Pamphlet on the Zulu Army', NAM, 6610-45.

60 *'In conducting operations'*: Knight, 32–3.

60–61 *His initial plan . . . African auxiliaries*: Thesiger to Stanley, 14 Sept. 1878, in Laband, 9–11.

61 *'intelligence, abilities, zeal'*: Droogleever, 15–16.

62 *'They sang a war song'*: ibid., 36.

63 *'Everyone was too tired'*: Trooper H. Bucknal, in ibid., 43.

63–4 *Despite falling badly . . . hanging by his side*: Droogleever, 43–53.

64 *The operation had been a fiasco . . . others died*: Fanny Colenso to Mr Sanderson, 3 July 1879, Colenso Papers, KZN, A204/8.

64 *'two or three shots'*: Droogleever, 67.

64 *'extenuating circumstances'*: ibid., 71.

65 *'to ensure safety'*: ibid., 167.

66 *The role of the NNC . . . Zulu assault*: Jackson & Whybra, 20.

66 *'full of ardour'*: Droogleever, 185.

66 *'old friends'*: ibid.

67 '*At first . . . the General promised him*': Fanny Colenso to Mr Sanderson, 21 July 1879, Colenso Papers, KZN, A204/8.

67 '*I shall have some 3000 men*': Droogleever, 175.

69 *According to Inspector . . . 'resign our commissions*': George Mansel to Fanny Colenso, 25 Mar. 1882, Colenso Papers, KZN, A204/6.

70 '*Oh, Sir,' said the colour-sergeant . . . 'not a gentleman*': Colonel W. K. Stuart, in Haythornthwaite, *The Colonial Wars Sourcebook*, 30.

71 '*Now we want men*': Cambridge to the queen, 18 May 1879, RA VIC E24/72.

71 '*these poor young fellows*': RA QVJ: 9 Sept. 1879.

72 '*old, steady shots*': Frere to Carnarvon, 17 Feb. 1878, in Martineau, II, 213.

72 '*In the British Army*': Symons Account, SWB, 6/A/3, 8.

72 '*scum of the earth*': Longford, *Wellington*, I, 321.

72 '*It was not uncommon*' . . . '*and affection*': Surgeon-General William Munro, in Haythornthwaite, *The Colonial Wars Sourcebook*, 31.

72 '*For it's Tommy this*': Quoted in ibid., 32.

73 '*We might as well pretend*': Strachan, *Wellington's Legacy*, 81.

73 '*They are very strict*': Private James Cook, 2/24th, *Brecon County Times*, 24 May 1879.

73 '*There was a large plank*': Watson Papers, KCAL, KCM 4275, 20–21.

73–4 *Infantry uniforms . . . company wagon*: Featherstone, *Weapons and Equipment*, 116–17.

75 *two-inch brass screw*: And not 'nine stout screws', as suggested by one historian (Morris, 300).

76 '*rather a queer dwarfed appearance*': Curling Letters, 22.

77 '*He had not a very good manner*': Sir H. Ponsonby to his wife, 11 Sept. 1879, RA VIC/Add A36/18.

77 '*that arch-snob*' . . . '*evil genius*': Wolseley Journal, 28 June 1879, 46.

77 '*governed by Crealock*': Major-General Clifford to Cambridge, 17 Apr. 1879, RA VIC/Add E/1/8633.

77 '*he had confidence*': Laband, xxix.

78 '*did all his work*': Ponsonby to his wife, 11 Sept. 1879, op. cit.

78 *more than 27,000 oxen . . . and carts*: Morris, 319.

80 '*Our movements*' . . . '*speedy close*': Cambridge Correspondence, RA VIC/Add E/1/8503.

80 '*I suppose we will give*': Private G. Morris to his mother, 28 Dec. 1878, SWB, ZC 2/1/10, L1953.33.

80 '*I can tell*': Private A. Goatham to his parents, 18 Dec. 1878, NAM, 8311-73.

80 '*I think we shall lose*': Sergeant John Lines, Oct. 1878, in Emery, 'Soldiers' Letters from the Zulu War', *Natalia*, no. 8, Dec. 1978, 56.

80–81 '*We are longing*' . . . '*Our ultimatum has been sent*': Curling to his mother, 21 Nov. and 11 Dec. 1878, *Curling Letters*, 80, 82.

81 '*The Zulus are ready to fight*': Emery, op. cit., 37.

81 '*We all thought*': Lieutenant G. S. Banister to his father, 27 Jan. 1879, SWB, 6/A/6, 1985.67.

Chapter Five: Invasion

82 *a grand total*: Symons Account, SWB, 6/A/3, 2.

82 *1,891 European and 2,400 African troops*: The breakdown of troops was: N Battery, 5th Brigade, Royal Artillery – 5 officers and 126 NCOs and men; 1/24th Regiment – 16 officers and 375 NCOs and men; 2/24th Regiment – 23 officers and 748 NCOs and men; Natal Mounted Police – 4 officers and 128 troopers; Natal Carbineers – 10 officers and 90 NCOs and troopers; 1st Sqn, Imperial Mounted Infantry – 4 officers and 107 NCOs and men; Newcastle Mounted Rifles – 32 men; Buffalo Border Guard – 20 men; Army Hospital Corps – 11 NCOs and men; Natal Native Contingent – 68 European officers, 124 European NCOs and 2,400 Africans.

83–4 *They talked for three hours . . . spend the night*: Wood, II, 29.

84 '*That he should take command*': Clery to Colonel G. Harman, DAG Ireland, 17 Feb. 1879, SWB, ZC 2/3, L1964.47.

85 '*skirmished or rather clambered*': Chelmsford to Frere, 12 Jan. 1879, in Laband, 60.

85 '*picturesquely situated*': Symons Account, op. cit., 3.

85 *killing '9 or 10 of the enemy*': Chelmsford to Frere, 12 Jan. 1879, in Laband, 61.

85–6 '*I am in great hopes*' . . . '*complying with the demand*': ibid.

86 *Chelmsford told Wood*: Wood Papers, KZN, A598/II/2/2.

86 *Irritated by the delay* . . . *No. 1 Column*: Droogleever, 175.

86 *But he had second thoughts* . . . *the border*: Chelmsford to Durnford, 1 Jan. 1879, in ibid., 182.

86–7 *A week later* . . . *occupied Eshowe*: ibid., 185–6.

87 '*I saw a change*': Captain Dymes, 1/1st NNC, quoted in ibid., 191.

87 '*Unless you carry out*': Chelmsford to Durnford, 14 Jan. 1879, in Laband, 68.

88 *On 15 January Durnford* . . . *at Kranskop*: Droogleever, 92.

88–9 *On 16 January Chelmsford* . . . '*moving further north*': Wood Papers, KZN, A598/II/2/2.

89 '*shelter*' *in the Mangeni Hills* . . . '*upon them*': Quoted in *Zulu Victory*, 75–6.

90 '*very steep, stocky eminence*': Symons Account, op. cit., 4–5.

91 *The site for the camp* . . . *to Chelmsford himself*: *Zulu Victory*, 132–3.

92 '*Tell the police officer*': ibid., 134.

92 '*Well, sir* . . . *if you are nervous*': ibid.

92 *He later claimed* . . . '*for use as a laager*': Chelmsford's draft reply to the duke of Cambridge's queries, no date, NAM, 6807-386-8-56.

92 '*No. 3 column moves tomorrow*': Laband, 73.

92–3 *A separate order* . . . *cross by the 22nd*: Droogleever, 194.

93 '*At 1 pm I started*': Chelmsford to Frere, 21 Jan. 1879, in Laband, 74.

94 *But on the way back* . . . *next two days*: Coghill Diary, SWB, 6/A/2, d.1966.68.

94 '*The camp was pitched*': Symons Account, op. cit., 5.

94 '*My troops*': Laband, *Fight Us in the Open*, 5.

95 '*We had scarcely*': ibid., 6.

95 '*Cetshwayo came out*' . . . '*buy guns*': ibid., 6–7.

95 '*Cetshwayo hoped to be able*' . . . '*across the sea*': ibid., 9.

96 '*I have not gone over the seas*' . . . '*take us first*': Supplement to the *Natal Mercury*, 22 Jan. 1929.

96 '*You are to go against*': Statement of a Zulu deserter, Supplement to the *London Gazette*, 21 Mar. 1879.

97 '*If you come near*': Supplement to the *Natal Mercury*, 22 Jan. 1929.

97 '*I told Ntsingwayo*' . . . '*thought best*': Cetshwayo to Sir Hercules Robinson, 29 Mar. 1881, in Webb and Wright, *A Zulu King Speaks*, 54–8.

98 *'parallel to and in sight of '* . . . *'to our left'*: Statement of a Zulu deserter, op. cit.

98 *'The officers of the different'*: Cetshwayo to Sir Hercules Robinson, 29 Mar. 1881, op. cit.

99 *'more thoroughly'* . . . *'left in the country'*: Chelmsford to Frere, 21 Jan. 1879, in Laband, 75.

99 *'On his way home'*: Coghill Diary, SWB, 6/A/2, d.1966.68.

99 *'Cetshwayo had sent an impi'* . . . *'not arrived'*: Account by Lieutenant Milne, RN, TNA, WO 33/34, S6333.

99–100 *'Zulus were in force'* . . . *'whether it was defended'*: Crealock Journal, 21 Jan. 1879, RA VIC 033/44.

100 *'These officers brought'*: Glyn to the DAG, 6 Feb. 1879, SWB, 1983.13.

100 *'to attack if and when'*: Account by Lieutenant Milne, RN, op. cit.

100 *'The instructions to both these commanders'* . . . *'messed up in'*: Clery to Harman, 17 Feb. 1879, op. cit.

101 *'counted fourteen Zulu horsemen'* . . . *'the fact'*: Account by Lieutenant Milne, RN, op. cit.

101 *'to reconnoitre there'*: Crealock Journal, 22 Jan. 1879, op. cit.

101 *'for some unaccountable reason'* . . . *'day's work'*: Brigadier-General H. G. Mainwaring to the editor of the *Morning Post, c.* 1921, SWB, ZC 2/3/14, 1957.60, 8–9.

101–2 *'without instructions'* . . . *'attack or not'*: Clery's Report, no dates, WO 33/34, S6333.

102 *When Chelmsford was asked* . . . *late in the day*: Crealock Journal, 21 Jan. 1879, op. cit.

102 *'covered pretty well with thorns'* . . . *company of NNC*: Lieutenant J. Maxwell, 'Reminiscences of the Zulu War', KCAL, F968.3 Max, 1.

102 *his men had captured*: Hamilton-Browne, *Lost Legionary*, 118.

102–3 *'We now started'*: Maxwell, 'Reminiscences', op. cit., 1.

103 *'horses in rings'*: ibid.

103 *'There was some grumbling'*: *Harford Journal*, 25–6.

104 *'About 2 a.m. I awoke'*: Maxwell, 'Reminiscences', op. cit., 1–2.

104 *'not a man would have escaped'*: Trooper W. Clarke, in *Zulu Victory*, 146.

104–5 *Major Clery was sleeping* . . . *'but you do it'*: Clery to Harman, 17 Feb. 1879, op. cit.

105 '*Move up to Sandhlwana*': Lieutenant-Colonel Crealock's Statement to the Court of Inquiry, no date, Supplement to the *London Gazette*, 15 Mar. 1879.

105 '[*I*] *was told to order Durnford*': Crealock Journal, 22 Jan. 1879, op. cit.

106 '*You are to march to this camp*': Droogleever, 198.

106 '*as soon as he could see*': Crealock's Statement to the Court of Inquiry, op. cit.

106 '*It ought to have been*': Smith-Dorrien, *Memories*, 10.

106–7 '*As I did not want to give any warning*' . . . '*keep the Camp*': Clery to Harman, 17 Feb. 1879, op. cit.

108 '*nobody from the General downwards*': ibid.

108 move in '*small detached bodies*': Information received from Umtegolalo, a Zulu wounded at Rorke's Drift, on 23 Jan. 1879 by W. Drummond, Supplement to the *London Gazette*, 15 Mar. 1879.

109 '*videttes of the English force*': Statement of a Zulu deserter, op. cit.

109 '*That day the moon had waned*': Laband, *Fight Us in the Open*, 13.

109 *Most of the Zulu sources agree*: Umtegolalo, op. cit.

109 '*my chiefs were again consulting*': Laband, *Fight Us in the Open*, 13.

Chapter Six: '*There is nothing to be done*'

110–11 '*I at once ordered*' . . . '*mounted corps*': Chelmsford to Stanley, 27 Jan. 1879, NAM, 6807-386-8-30.

111 '*We marched 12 miles*': Symons Account, SWB, 6/A/8.

111 Chelmsford '*was from the first*': Clery to Colonel G. Harman, DAG Ireland, 17 Feb. 1829, SWB, ZC 2/3, L1964.47.

111 '*Staff Officer*': SWB, ZC 2/3/12, M1982.82.

112 '*He returned it to me*': Clery to Harman, 17 Feb. 1879, op. cit.

112 '*to send on the camp equipage*': Statement by Captain Alan Gardner, 26 Jan. 1879, Supplement to the *London Gazette*, 15 Mar. 1879.

112 '*I shall never forget*' . . . '*far away*': Hamilton-Browne, *Lost Legionary*, 126.

112–13 '*in case any Zulus*': Crealock's Statement to the Court of Inquiry, no date, Supplement to the *London Gazette*, 15 Mar. 1879.

113 *The terrified prisoner*: Hamilton-Browne, *Lost Legionary*, 127–8.

113 *'Beyond noticing'* . . . *'from the camp'*: Symons Account, op. cit., 9.

113 *'This hill was covered'*: Quoted in *Zulu Victory*, 178.

113 *'to fix upon a site'*: Chelmsford to Stanley, 27 Jan. 1879, op. cit.

114 *'I galloped up the hill'* . . . *who they were*: Brigadier-General H. G. Mainwaring to the editor of the *Morning Post*, *c.* 1921, SWB, ZC 2/3/14, 1957.60, 12.

114 *'where our lines'* . . . *'being out of it'*: Lieutenant Banister to his father, 27 Jan. 1879, SWB, 6/A/6, 1985.67.

114 *At the foot of the hill* . . . *sent for help*: Symons Account, op. cit., 11.

114 *'at once turned back'* . . . *'join the main body'*: Mainwaring, op. cit., 14.

114 *'wanted to know what we meant'*: Banister to his father, 27 Jan. 1879, op. cit.

114–15 *He also told Harness* . . . *thrown away*: Mainwaring, op. cit., 14.

115 *His official report*: Chelmsford to Stanley, 27 Jan. 1879, op. cit.

115 *'he had heard'* . . . *'ride into camp'*: Crealock's Statement, op. cit.

115 *'and some men were stationed'*: Lieutenant W. H. James, RE, 'The Isandlana Disaster', 21 Mar. 1879, RA VIC 0/34/23.

116 *The cavalry vedettes* . . . *'with the report'*: Account by Trooper W. W. Barker, in Stalker, *The Natal Carbineers*, 99.

117 *'to watch the enemy carefully'*: ibid.

117 *1,241 in all*: The troops left at Isandlwana on 22 Jan. 1879 were as follows: Staff – 13; N/5 Battery, RA – 2 officers and 70 men; 1/24th – 14 officers and 402 men; 2/24th – 4 officers and 170 men; 90th Regiment (attached to 1/24th) – 6 men; Army Service Corps – 3 men; Army Hospital Corps – 1 officer and 10 men; Mounted Infantry – 28 men; NMP – 34 men; Natal Carbineers – 2 officers and 26 men; Newcastle Mounted Rifles – 2 officers and 15 men; Buffalo Border Guard – 1 officer and 7 men; 1/3rd NNC – 11 officers and 200 men (30 Europeans); 2/3rd NNC – 9 officers and 200 men (30 Europeans); NNP – 1 officer and 10 men.

117 *'I got a message'*: *Curling Letters*, 89.

117 *'Column Alarm was sounded'*: Statement by Private J. Williams, in Holme, 195.

118 *'appearing on the extreme left'*: Lieutenant W. Higginson to Chelmsford, 17 Feb. 1879, SWB, ZB 3/41d, 990.314i.

118 *'numbers of Zulus'*: Account by Trooper Barker, op. cit.

118 '*Zulus showed in considerable force*': Brickhill Report, undated, SWB, ZC 2/4/1.

118 '*the enemy moving*': 2nd Chard Report, 21 Feb. 1880, in Holme, 270.

118 *The most alarming report . . . a Zulu attack*: T. E. Newmarch, 'Looking Back', KCAL, KCM 02/7/2/17.

118 '*collect all their oxen*': Brickhill Report, op. cit.

119 '*with all the force you have*' . . . '*attack at daybreak*': Lieutenant W. Cochrane to AAG, 8 Feb. 1879, in Emery, 78.

119 *a total of just 526 men*: The breakdown is as follows: Staff – 3 officers and 1 European NCO; Rocket Battery – 1 officer and 9 men; NNH – 6 officers and 259 men; NNC – 6 officers and 241 men (10 Europeans). Holme, 377.

119 *An old African hand . . . 'around the hat*': Droogleever, 178.

119–20 *As he climbed . . . without delay*: 2nd Chard Report, 21 Feb. 1880, in Holme, 270.

120 '*We found the troops*': Lieutenant C. Raw's report, no date, Chelmsford Papers, NAM, 6807-386-8-41.

120 '*saw a small body of Zulus*' . . . '*army was at hand*': Account by Jabez Molife, in Jackson & Whybra, 25.

120 '*Colonel Pulleine . . . gave over*': Evidence given by Lieutenant Cochrane at the Court of Inquiry, 27 Jan. 1879, Supplement to the *London Gazette*, 15 Mar. 1879.

121 '*The news was that a number*': Cochrane to AAG, 8 Feb. 1879, op. cit.

121 *This last message . . . 'follow them up*': Higginson to Chelmsford, 17 Feb. 1879, op. cit.

121 *Cochrane's version . . . 'my own men*': Cochrane to AAG, 8 Feb. 1879, op. cit.

122 '*drive the enemy*': Raw's report, no date, op. cit.

122 *Barton was accompanied . . . promised he would*: Droogleever, 206; Cochrane's evidence, 27 Jan. 1879, op. cit.

122 *to 'advance from the Camp*': Statement by Private H. Grant, in Holme, 193.

123 '*If they are going towards*' . . . '*attack the camp*': Account by Jabez Molife, op. cit., 26.

123 '*About two hundred*': Quoted in Stalker, *The Natal Carbineers*, 99–100.

123 *Durnford was furious . . . engaged the Zulus*: Account by Jabez Molife, op. cit., 26.

Chapter Seven: Isandlwana

124 'He said' . . . 'that their scouts': T. E. Newmarch, 'Looking Back', KCAL, KCM 02/7/2/17.

125 'We left camp': Lieutenant C. Raw's report, no date, Chelmsford Papers, NAM, 6807-386-8-41.

125 According to James Hamer . . . 'at 12,000': J. Hamer to his father, no date, NAM, 6807-386-8-14.

125–6 'A small herd of cattle' . . . 'remained where they were': Statement of a Zulu deserter, Supplement to the *London Gazette*, 21 Mar. 1879.

126 'a body of horse' . . . 'came up the hill': Emery, 86.

127 On hearing the sound . . . passed through it: Cochrane to AAG, 8 Feb. 1879, in Emery, 79.

127 The rocket battery . . . artillery horses: Statements by Privates H. Grant, D. Johnson and J. Trainer, in Holme, 193–4.

127 'There was a hand-to-hand engagement': Cochrane to AAG, 8 Feb. 1879, op. cit.

128 'as quick as possible': Statement by Private E. Wilson, in Holme, 196.

128 'Not one of us dreamt': Curling Letters, 89.

128 'But before Capt. S.' . . . 'driving our men this way': Brickhill Report, SWB, ZC 2/4/1.

128 'The General knows nothing of this': ibid.

129 'We both went to Colonel Pulleine': Evidence given by Captain A. Gardner, 27 Jan. 1879, published in the Supplement to the *London Gazette*, 15 Mar. 1879.

129 Pulleine had also . . . 'to left flank': Droogleever, 211.

130 'one or both flanks' . . . 'rear, of the enemy': Durnford Papers, REM, 4901-44/1.

131 'At about twelve o'clock': Captain Essex's Evidence, 24 Jan. 1879, Supplement to the *London Gazette*, 15 Mar. 1879.

131–2 'By the time these dispositions' . . . 'waver and bolted': Stafford Statement, NAM, 8406-49.

132 The auxiliaries . . . respite would be temporary: ibid.; J. Hamer to his father, op. cit.; Captain Essex's Evidence, 24 Jan. 1879, op. cit.

132 'into a huge mass': Curling Letters, 92.

132 'the first shell': Emery, 86.

132–3 'The Zulus soon split up': Curling Letters, 92–3.

133 'Never did his Majesty': Muziwentu, 'A Zulu Boy's Recollections of the Zulu War', *Natalia*, no. 8, Dec. 1978, 11.

133–4 'Here we made a long stand': Account by Jabez Molife, in Jackson & Whybra, 26.

134 'On the side of . . . hill': Quoted in Stalker, *The Natal Carbineers*, 105.

134 'ammunition was beginning': Statement by Private E. Wilson, op. cit., 196.

134–5 'The companies . . . first engaged': Captain Essex's Evidence, 24 Jan. 1879, op. cit.

135 'I, having no particular duty': Smith-Dorrien, *Memories*, 14.

135 'all who asked for it': Trooper Barker, in Stalker, *The Natal Carbineers*, 101.

135–6 'For heaven's sake' . . . 'do you?': Smith-Dorrien, *Memories*, 14.

136 he sent 'a messenger': Account by Jabez Molife, op. cit., 26.

136 'On seeing us retire': Quoted in Stalker, *The Natal Carbineers*, 105.

136 'There seemed to be': Account by Trooper Sparks, *Natal Mercury*, 22 Jan. 1929.

137 'The same remark': Evidence given by Captain A. Gardner, 27 Jan. 1879, op. cit.

137 'collect all the troops': Statement by Captain A. Gardner, 26 Jan. 1879, ibid.

137 'to hold the enemy': Captain Essex's Evidence, 24 Jan. 1879, op. cit.

137 'and rallied them' . . . 'in among the tents': 'Warrior of the uMbonambi', in Laband, *Fight Us in the Open*, 15.

137–8 'We limbered up' . . . 'two sergeants': Curling Letters, 93–5.

138 'Our ammunition failed': Knight, 101.

138 'The British soldier': Symons Account, SWB, 6/A/36.

138–9 'When the soldiers retired': Quoted in Laband, *Fight Us in the Open*, 16.

139 A graphic account . . . with his iKlwa: Holme, 248.

139 'Follow me' . . . never seen again: Brickhill Report, op. cit.

139–40 'The enemy attacked': Lieutenant C. Raw's Report, no date, op. cit.

140 'In a moment all was disorder': Quoted in Knight, 101.

140 *James Brickhill . . . making for the nek*: Brickhill Report, op. cit.

140 *'good Colonel Durnford'* . . . *'trying to escape'*: J. Hamer to his father, no date, op. cit.

141 *'I saw several white men'*: Emery, 85.

141 *'We worked round behind'*: ibid., 84.

141–2 *'completely blocked up by Zulus'* . . . *'had been killed'*: Lieutenant Curling's Report, 26 Jan. 1879, Supplement to the *London Gazette*, 15 Mar. 1879.

142 *'Have mercy on us'* . . . *'uSuthu!'*: Nzuzu, in Laband, *Fight Us in the Open*, 16–17.

142–3 *'No path, no track'* . . . *Queen's Colour of his battalion*: Brickhill Report, op. cit.

144 *'wearing a blue patrol jacket'* . . . *'his saddle'*: Smith-Dorrien, *Memories*, 16–17.

144 *'When I got down to the drift'*: Holme, 195–6.

144–5 *Smith-Dorrien took advantage* . . . *James Hamer*: Smith-Dorrien, *Memories*, 16–17.

145 *He had been kicked* . . . *'clean away'*: Quoted in Emery, 90.

145 *Smith-Dorrien struggled on* . . . *'expecting attack'*: Smith-Dorrien, *Memories*, 16; letter from Smith-Dorrien, quoted in Emery, 90.

145–6 *According to Higginson* . . . *letter to Lord Chelmsford*: Lieutenant W. Higginson to Chelmsford, 17 Feb. 1879, SWB, ZB 3/41d, 990.314i.

146–7 *But a very different account* . . . *black eye*: Account by Trooper W. W. Barker, in Stalker, *The Natal Carbineers*, 102–3; Denis Barker, 'The Last Colonial', FP.

147 *for assisting 'Melville & Coghill'*: Cambridge to Chelmsford, 10 Apr. 1879, RA VIC/Add E/1/8624.

147–8 *In complete contrast . . . and safety*: Greaves, *Rorke's Drift*, 320–21; *VC Register*, 327.

148 *Gardner had 'sent an order'*: Statement by Captain A. Gardner, 26 Jan. 1879, op. cit.

148 *'The Zulu army swept down'*: Account by Jabez Molife, op. cit., 26–7.

149 *'One fellow seized hold'*: Emery, 91.

149 *'His escape must have been'*: Lieutenant J. Maxwell, 'Reminiscences of the Zulu War', KCAL, F968, 3 Max, 23.

149–50 *'We were told'*: 'A Zulu Boy's Recollections', op. cit., 8–20.

150 '*They fought well*' . . . '*last to fall*': Quoted in Emery, 84.

151 *A Zulu eyewitness*: Quoted in Droogleever, 229.

151 '*It was a long time*': Knight, 103.

151 '*Some Zulus threw assegais*': Laband, *Fight Us in the Open*, 17.

151 '*Dum! Dum!*': ibid., 18.

151 '*the Zulus would have become swollen*': ibid.

152 *he died* '*early*': Captain Hallam Parr to Sir Bartle Frere, 24 Jan. 1879, RA VIC/o33/118.

152 '*strewn with empty cartridge cases*' . . . *round its neck*: Brigadier-General Mainwaring to the editor of the *Morning Post, c.* 1921, SWB, ZC 2/3/14, 1957.60, 9n.

152 '*Maize, bread stuffs*': Emery, 83.

152 '*over the veldt*': Nzuzi, quoted in Laband, *Fight Us in the Open*, 17.

152 '*Some of our men*' . . . '*black stuff in bottles*': Emery, 86.

153 *But all horses were killed*: Nzuzi, op. cit.

153 '*hastened by having seen*': Zulu deserter, in Emery, 83–4.

153 *Commandant Rupert* . . . '*fired rifles and missed*': Mainwaring, op. cit., 13n.

154 '*The Zulus have the camp*' . . . '*I have been into it*': Lieutenant-Colonel Crealock's Statement to the Court of Inquiry, no date, Supplement to the *London Gazette*, 15 Mar. 1879.

154 '*But I left 1,000 men*' . . . *some cheered*: Knight, 111.

154 *Chelmsford, meanwhile . . . possession of the camp*: Crealock's Statement, op. cit.

154 '*Twenty-fourth*': Symons Account, op. cit., 12–13.

154–5 *As the nervous British . . .* '*force to advance*': Mainwaring, op. cit., 15.

155 *Captain Harford . . .* '*up in clumps*': Harford Journal, 32.

155 *stumbling* '*over the naked*': Symons Account, op. cit., 13.

155 '*Everything had gone*': Harford Journal, 34.

155–6 '*I did not feel it much*': Colonel Henry Degacher to Captain Adeane, RN, 3 Feb. 1879, RA VIC/o34/19.

156 '*Everyone felt very anxious*': Harford Journal, 33–5.

156 '*The troops had no spare ammunition*': Chelmsford to Stanley, 27 Jan. 1879, NAM, 6807-386-8-30.

156–7 '*Most of the bodies*': Symons Account, op. cit., 37.

157 '*There were bullocks*': Letter of Sergeant W. E. Warren, in Emery, 94.

157 *'with his head cut clean off'*: Letter by a Natal Carbineer, *Natal Mercury*, 11 Feb. 1879.

157 *'The road wound through'* . . . *'squatting position'*: Maxwell, 'Reminiscences', op. cit., 22.

157 *Once across the Batshe* . . . *'I rode along'*: Hallam Parr to Frere, 24 Jan. 1879, op. cit.

158 *'When we reached the top'*: Lieutenant Banister to his father, 27 Jan. 1879, SWB, 6/A/6, 1985.67.

Chapter Eight: Rorke's Drift

159–60 *thirty-five patients*: 1st Chard Report, 25 Jan. 1879, NAM, 6309-115.

160 *The chapel* . . . *previous conflict*: Greaves, 235–6.

161 *Colonel Degacher* . . . *'everything except soldiering'*: Clery Letter, 16 May 1879, in ibid., 180.

162 *Of the 113 NCOs and men*: Holme, 321–69.

162 *'painfully thin'* . . . *'a very happy family'*: Bourne Account, *Listener*, 30 Dec. 1936.

163 *'dangerously ill'* . . . *'dying wife'*: *Natal Mercury*, 18 June 1879.

164 *Chard returned* . . . *quickly overwhelmed*: 2nd Chard Report, 21 Feb. 1880, in Holme, 270–71.

164 *Spalding decided*: Major Spalding's Report, Supplement to the *London Gazette*, 15 Mar. 1879.

164 *Chard had mounted* . . . *'this evening early'*: 2nd Chard Report, op. cit., 272.

165 *'shared the same fate'*: ibid.

165 *'advancing on Rorke's Drift'*: 1st Chard Report, op. cit.

165 *'at all costs'*: ibid.

165 *'orders were given'* . . . *'certain to be killed'*: Wood, 'An Account by Private Alfred Henry Hook, 2/24th Regiment', *Royal Magazine*, Feb. 1905.

166 *Dalton's 'energy'*: 2nd Chard Report, op. cit., 273.

166 *'Several fugitives'*: ibid.

166 *Shortly after Chard's arrival* . . . *He agreed*: 1st Chard Report, op. cit.

166 '*several casks of rum*': 2nd Chard Report, op. cit., 273.

166–7 *The first positive sighting* . . . '*approaching were Zulus*': Morris, 400–401; Reverend Otto Witt, 'The Disaster at Isandula', *The Times Weekly Edition*, 7 Mar. 1879.

168 *He admitted later*: Knight, 117.

168 '*Oh! Let us go*': Muziwentu, in Laband, *Fight Us in the Open*, 19.

168 *Having belatedly* . . . '*short distance*' *from the drift*: Witt, 'The Disaster at Isandula', op. cit.

168 '*the best parlour paper*' . . . '*mein children at Umsinga*': Trooper Harry Lugg, *North Devon Herald*, 24 Apr. 1879; Surgeon J. Reynolds, in Greaves, 108.

169 *He was not alone* . . . *within a mile*: Lugg, op. cit.

169 '*going off to Helpmakaar*': ibid.

169 *This was too much*: Wood, 'Hook Account', op. cit.

169 *The garrison had* . . . *been reduced*: 1st Chard Report, op. cit.

169 '*How many*' . . . '*for a few seconds*': Hitch Account, in Holme, 284.

170 '*Here they come!*': Interview with Roger Lane, Sergeant Gallagher's great-grandson, 'Zulu – The True Story', *Timewatch*, BBC2, 24 Oct. 2003.

170 *The defenders opened fire* . . . *to seek shelter*: Hitch Account, *Chums*, 11 Mar. 1908; 2nd Chard Report, op. cit., 274.

170 '*Our firing was very quick*': Emery, 134.

170 *Dalton, a former army*: *VC Register*, 81.

170–71 '*Had the Zulus taken the bayonet*' . . . *release his grip*: Hitch Account, in Holme, 284.

171–2 '*Each time*': 2nd Chard Report, op. cit., 274.

172 '*But the men continued to swear*': Hitch Account, *Chums*, op. cit.

173 '*one of the bravest men*': Wood, 'Hook Account', op. cit.

173 '*great coolness*': 2nd Chard Report, op. cit., 275.

173 '*The helpless patient*': Wood, 'Hook Account', op. cit.

173–5 *As Hook's room* . . . '*a heavy man*': ibid.

175 *Unwittingly they left* . . . *trod on him*: Account by Private John Waters, *Cambrian*, 13 June 1879.

175–6 '*dazed by the glare*': 2nd Chard Report, op. cit., 275.

176 *One other patient* . . . *found their mark*: Account by Private R. Jones, *Strand*, Jan.–June 1891.

176 *There was one other . . . and was killed*: 2nd Chard Report, op. cit., 278.

176 *'necessity for making'*: ibid., 275.

177 *'a bullet striking'*: ibid.

177 *'Then, when they were goaded'*: Wood, 'Hook Account', op. cit.

177 *Chard recorded the marksman*: 2nd Chard Report, op. cit., 275.

177 *'we' converted the two heaps . . . 'bullets went high'*: ibid., 273–5.

178 *One of the first men . . . biscuit boxes*: ibid., 275–6.

178–9 *'In one of these nasty' . . . mealie-bag redoubt*: Hitch Account, *Chums*, op. cit.; Holme, 284–5.

179–80 *'all except two' . . . if they carried on*: Major Spalding's Report, op. cit.

180 *much to the delight of Smith-Dorrien*: Smith-Dorrien, *Memories*, 18.

180 *'utterly worthless'*: Letter from Major Clery, 13 Apr. 1879, op. cit.

180 *seen the 'red-coats coming'*: 2nd Chard Report, op. cit., 276.

180 *'seeing the hospital'*: Hitch Account, *Chums*, op. cit.

180 *two companies 'did come down'*: 2nd Chard Report, op. cit., 276.

180–81 *According to Chard . . . renewed their attack*: ibid.; Wood, 'Hook Account', op. cit.

181 *Hook went out alone*: Wood, 'Hook Account', op. cit.

181 *'The enemy remained'*: 2nd Chard Report, op. cit., 277.

181–2 *Hook was in his shirtsleeves . . . 'what we had done'*: Wood, 'Hook Account', op. cit.

182 *'excellent services'*: Hitch Account, *Chums*, op. cit.

182 *he found 'old Gunny' . . . 'dead niggers everywhere'*: Lieutenant G. S. Banister to his father, 27 Jan. 1879, SWB, 6/A/6, 1985.67.

182 *Having told Lieutenant Mainwaring . . . 'got him in the end'*: Brigadier-General H. G. Mainwaring to the editor of the *Morning Post*, c. 1921, SWB, ZC 2/3/14, 1957.60, 17.

182 *'as if done by an axe' . . . 'back of his head'*: 2nd Chard Report, op. cit., 276.

182 *'his belly cut open'*: Sergeant G. Smith to his wife, 24 Jan. 1879, in Holme, 293.

183 *'still leaning'*: 2nd Chard Report, op. cit., 277.

183 *British casualties*: 1st Chard Report, op. cit.

183 *'proving to what an extent' . . . overheated rifle barrels*: Lieutenant J. Maxwell, 'Reminiscences of the Zulu War', KCAL, F968.3 Max, 22.

183 *a special committee*: Special Committee's Report, 15 Oct. 1885–19 Apr. 1886, NAM, 7805-26.

183 *'We did so much firing'*: Wood, 'Hook Account', op. cit.

183 *The official number of Zulu dead*: 2nd Chard Report, op. cit., 278.

183–4 *Lonsdale's men . . . and burnt*: Maxwell, 'Reminiscences', op. cit., 22.

184 *As Chard himself admitted*: 2nd Chard Report, op. cit., 278.

184 *'quite impossible' . . . 'friends or relations'*: *Harford Journal*, 36.

184 *'large number of wounded' . . . 'burned hospital'*: Hamilton-Browne, *Lost Legionary*, 152.

184 *Inspector George Mansel . . . 'to stop it'*: George Mansel to Fanny Colenso, 26 Mar. 1882, Colenso Papers, KZN, A204/6.

184 *'351 dead Zulus'*: Crealock Journal, 21 Jan. 1879, RA VIC 033/44.

184–5 *'In the morning we found'*: *Western Mail*, 11 May 1914.

185 *'killed and shot'*: Sergeant G. Smith to his wife, 24 Jan. 1879, in Holme, 293.

185 *An estimated 1,000 Zulus*: Laband, *Rise and Fall*, 239.

185 *'Remarkably few'*: Laband, *Fight Us in the Open*, 10.

186 *'Our people laughed'*: Muziwentu, 'A Zulu Boy's Recollections', *Natalia*, no. 8, Dec. 1978, 12–13.

186 *'The white men'*: ibid., 12.

186 *did not 'make a better fight of it'*: Laband, *Fight Us in the Open*, 20.

186 *'The Zulus had no desire'*: 'A Zulu Boy's Recollections', op. cit., 13.

186–7 *'The first news'*: Laband, *Fight Us in the Open*, 22.

187 *'If you think'*: Kumbeka, in ibid.

187 *'They told him' . . . 'on the ground'*: Ruscombe Poole, in ibid., 23.

187 *Back at Isandlwana . . . 'people's blood'*: 'A Zulu Boy's Recollections', op. cit., 13.

Chapter Nine: Wood and Pearson

188 *'He is clever & amusing'*: RA QVJ: 9 Sept. 1879.

189 *'attacked almost single-handed'*: *VC Register*, 338.

190 *'reserved & shy'*: RA QVJ: 9 Sept. 1879.

190 *'There is no stronger'*: Robinson (ed.), *Celebrities of the British Army*, 2.

191 *'quite useless'*: Buller to Wood, 22 Oct. 1878, KZN, A598/11/2/1.

191 *'never heard anything'*: Sir H. Ponsonby to the queen, 11 Sept. 1879, RA VIC/B62/10.

193–4 *'difficult stony cattle track'* . . . *continue the pursuit*: Knight, 129–30.

194 *The first Wood heard* . . . *mountain stronghold*: Wood, II, 30–31.

194–5 *Wood set out* . . . *He was not wrong*: ibid., 31.

195–6 *In the early hours* . . . *'disaster of Isandhlwana'*: ibid., 31–2.

196 *It would later emerge* . . . *'with a note'*: Gardner to Wood, Utrecht, 23 Jan. 1879, KCAL, KCM 89/9/27/3.

196 *Written at Helpmakaar* . . . *'this evening'*: Report by Captain Alan Gardner, 22 Jan. 1879, ibid., 89/9/27/2.

196 *Wood at once* . . . *he had received*: Wood, II, 32.

196–7 *Wood was in grave danger* . . . *'your column'*: ibid., 33.

197 *Wood replied* . . . *'save Natal'*: ibid.

197 *'I never slept'*: ibid., 34.

197–8 *'My spies informed me'* . . . *'our precautions'*: ibid., 34–5.

198 *'The Kafirs in it fled'*: Knight, 132–3.

198 *'We find it very dull'*: Lieutenant E. L. England to his sister, 11 Feb. 1879, SWB, ZC 2/1/6, L1953.22.

198 *'the Qulusi [were] utterly'*: Laband, *Fight Us in the Open*, 24.

199 *'they burnt down'* . . . *'sheep and goats'*: Report by Commandant F. Schermbrucker, in Knight, 133–4.

201 *'By 7.30 a.m.'*: Major McGregor, 'The Zulu War with Colonel Pearson at Ekowe', *Blackwood's Edinburgh Magazine*, no. 765, July 1879, vol. 126, 4.

201–2 *'I saw at once'*: Knight, 54.

202 *'I immediately'*: Emery, 186.

202 *All but one* . . . *'disappeared'*: Knight, 58.

203 *'On arriving'*: ibid., 60.

203 *'fled in all directions'*: ibid., 59.

203 *'As we advanced'*: Laband, *Fight Us in the Open*, 27.

203 *'I never thought'*: Emery, 185.

203–4 *'found dead Zulus'*: 'The Zulu War with Colonel Pearson', op. cit., 4.

204 *The British had just*: Young, *They Fell Like Stones*, 37–8.

204 *A Zulu informant* . . . *'no part at all'*: Laband, *Fight Us in the Open*, 25.

204 '*to leave our surplus*' . . . '*in Zululand!*': 'The Zulu War with Colonel Pearson', op. cit., 5–6.

205 '*Up this hill*' . . . '*and storehouses*': ibid., 6.

205 '*Durnford had met*' . . . '*previous orders*': Colonel Forestier Walker to Sir Bartle Frere, 29 Jan. 1879, RA VIC/033/118.

205–6 '*You must be prepared*' . . . *to the entrenchment*: 'The Zulu War with Colonel Pearson', op. cit., 6–9.

Chapter Ten: The Cover-up

207 '*a good staff officer*': Chelmsford to Wood, 23 Dec. 1878, KZN, A598/11/2/2.

208 '*The General had not*': Clery to Major-General Archibald Alison, DQMG, 23 Apr. 1879, in *Zulu Victory*, 245.

208 '*Lord C.'s staff*': George Mansel to Fanny Colenso, 26 Mar. 1882, Colenso Papers, KZN, A204/6.

209 *On 23 January* . . . '*effectual resistance*': Laband, 76–7.

209–10 '*Lieut. Colonel Pulleine*' . . . '*successful issue*': Chelmsford to Stanley, 27 Jan. 1879, NAM, 6807-386-8-30.

210 '*though greatly*' . . . '*took command*': Frere to Cambridge, 27 Jan. 1879, RA VIC/Add E/1/8514.

211 '*He built a fort*': Clery to Alison, 25 May 1879, in *Zulu Victory*, 251.

211 '*not over-fond of work*': Chelmsford to Wood, 23 Dec. 1879, KZN, A598/11/2/2.

211 '*loss of the camp*' . . . '*an opinion*': *Fraser's Magazine*, Apr. 1880.

211 '*The Court has very properly*': Chelmsford to Stanley, 8 Feb. 1879, Supplement to the *London Gazette*, 15 Mar. 1879.

212 '*From the statements*': Chelmsford Papers, NAM, 6807-386-8-44.

212–13 '*I consider*' . . . '*for the oxen*': 'Notes by Chelmsford on the findings of the Court of Inquiry', no date, in Laband, 93.

213 '*the most gallant*' . . . '*Lieut. Chard*': Chelmsford Papers, op. cit.

213 '*anxious to send*': Chelmsford to Glyn, 1 Feb. 1879, SWB, 1983.13.

213 *it made special mention*: 1st Chard Report, 25 Jan. 1879, NAM, 6309-15.

213–14 '*Remarkably,' writes Greaves*: Greaves, 176, 182.

214 '*The defeat of the Zulus*' . . . '*most valuable*': Chelmsford to Stanley, no date, in Greaves, 358.

214 '*especially distinguished*': Bromhead to Degacher, 15 Feb. 1879, TNA, WO32/7390.

214 '*Only two other letters*': Greaves, 179.

215 '*I was about a month*': ibid., 180.

215 '*Does this not deserve*': Degacher to Captain Adeane, RN, 3 Feb. 1879, RA VIC/034/19.

216 '*I promised you*' . . . '*Bromhead's light*': Lieutenant G. S. Banister to his father, 27 Jan. 1879, SWB, 6/A/6, 1985, 67.

216 '*I daresay the old fool*': 'Bob Head' (a pseudonym), 2/24th, to his brother, no date, SWB, ZC 2/1/8, L1948.48.

216 '*We have at once*': Cambridge Military Papers, RA VIC/Add E/1/8624.

216 '*It would seem*' . . . *Royal Engineers*: Chelmsford to Stanley, 27 Jan 1879, in Laband, 81–2.

217 *such numbers were* '*necessary*': Horse Guards' Memorandum, 11 Feb. 1879, RA VIC/033/91.

217 '[*The Zulus*] *are to be defeated*': *Illustrated London News*, 22 Feb. 1879.

217 *In a letter to Queen Victoria* . . . '*superseding him*': Stanley to the queen, 11 Feb. 1879, RA VIC/033/89.

217 '*Had a very distressed letter*': RA QVJ: 12 Feb. 1879.

218 '*The last thing*': Blake, *Disraeli*, 664.

218 '*It is to be hoped*': *Victoria Letters*, III, 11n.

219 '*was the condescending sympathy*': Disraeli to the queen, 8 Feb. 1880, in Blake, *Disraeli*, 547.

219 *She was horrified* . . . '*enticed away*': RA QVJ: 11 Feb. 1879.

219 '*I think it will turn out*': Ponsonby to his wife, 13 Feb. 1879, RA VIC/Add A36/18.

219 *she* '*sympathises most sincerely*': Ponsonby to Stanley, 11 Feb. 1879, *Victoria Letters*, III, 10–11.

220 '*deep feeling*': Hicks Beach to Ponsonby, 12 Feb. 1879, ibid., 11.

220 '*The force of so-called*': Horse Guards' Memorandum, 11 Feb. 1879, op. cit.

220 '*He does not seem*': RA VIC/033/92.

220–21 '*They are placed*': Cambridge Military Papers, RA VIC/E/1/ 8542.

221 '*officer of great knowledge*': Cambridge to Frere, 27 Feb. 1879, RA VIC/E1/8562.

221 '*It is a military disaster*' . . . '*had been applied for*': House of Lords, 13 Feb. 1879, Hansard, 3rd Series, vol. 243, 1,042.

221 *None of this*: duke of Richmond to the queen, 14 Feb. 1879, RA VIC/O33/107.

221 the '*terrible disaster*': Disraeli to Lady Chesterfield, 13 Feb. 1879, *Disraeli Letters*, 208.

222 '*No such disaster*': *Illustrated London News*, 8 Mar. 1879.

222 '*does not give the reasons*': RA QVJ: 1 Mar. 1879.

222 '*neither good or clear*': ibid., 4 Mar. 1879.

222 '*have left us*' . . . '*in doubt*': Cambridge to Frere, 6 Mar. 1879, RA VIC/Add E/1/8576.

222–3 '*How did it happen*': Ellice to Chelmsford, 6 Mar. 1879, Chelmsford Papers, NAM, 6807–386–8–56.

223 '*with the exception*' . . . '*carried the day*': RA QVJ: 12 Mar. 1879.

223 '*Lord Chelmsford has added*': Stanley to the queen, 14 Mar. 1879, RA VIC/O34/9.

224 '*any General*' . . . *motion was withdrawn*: Hansard, 3rd Series, vol. 244, 907.

224 '*the officers*': duke of Richmond to the queen, 15 Mar. 1879, RA VIC/O34/11.

224 '*Bartle Frere should*': Roberts, *Salisbury*, 226.

224–5 '*Had all gone successfully*' . . . '*towards Confederation*': Hicks Beach to Frere, 13 Mar. 1879, Hicks Beach Papers, GRO, D2455/PCC/23.

225 '*most impertinent*' . . . '*decidedly answered*': RA QVJ: 19 Mar. 1879.

225 *The explanation* . . . '*no common character*': Hansard, 3rd Series, vol. 244, 1,147.

225 '*do what he could*': RA QVJ: 23 Mar. 1879.

226 '*I do not understand*': Ponsonby to his wife, 26 Mar. 1879, RA VIC/ Add A36/18.

226 '*future contingencies*' . . . *down completely*: Laband, 102–3.

226 '*utterly destroyed*' . . . '*the Colony*': Ponsonby to his wife, 11 Sept. 1879, RA VIC/Add A36/18.

226–7 *'inclined to view'*: Cambridge Military Papers, RA VIC/Add E/1/ 8513.

227 *'I have had a long'*: Laband, 82–3.

227 *'I am fairly puzzled'*: Wood Papers, KZN, A598/II/2/2.

227–8 *'His Royal Highness'*: Wood Papers, KZN, A598/II/2/2.

228 *'memorable defence'*: 14 Mar. 1879, Hansard, 3rd Series, vol. 244, 907.

228 *'I have received'*: Greaves, 366.

228–9 *'Reputations are being made'*: Clery Letter, 16 May 1879, quoted in Greaves, 178–9.

229 *'It is very amusing'*: *Curling Letters*, 122.

229 *'I never met'*: Captain H. Watson to his family, 26 May 1879, KCAL, KCM 4275.

229 *'He is a* particularly nice': ibid., mid July 1879.

229 *'A more uninteresting'*: *Wolseley Journal*, 16 July 1879, TNA, WO 147/7.

229 *'He is a most amiable'*: Jones to his family, 2 Aug. 1879, in Emery, 241.

230 *'I have now given'*: *Wolseley Journal*, 16 July 1879, op. cit.

230 *'They spoke to me'*: Ponsonby to his wife, 11 Sept. 1879, RA VIC/ Add A36/18.

231 *'In your Cartoon'*: Greaves, 188–9.

231 Reynolds's case . . . *'Mr. Dunne'*: ibid., 187.

232 *'to maximize public appreciation'*: Roberts, *Salisbury*, 226.

232–3 *'The Lieutenant-General'*: Greaves, 310–11.

233 *'It is monstrous'*: *Wolseley Journal*, TNA, WO 147/7.

233–4 *'This gave special interest'* . . . *great emotion*: *Harford Journal*, 49–53.

234 the *'noble and heroic conduct'* . . . *'more noble'*: Glyn to Chelmsford, 21 Feb. 1879, SWB, 1983.13.

234–5 *'very touching'*: RA QVJ: 1 Mar. 1879.

235 *'pictorially and vividly'*: Harrington, *British Artists and War*, 187–8.

235–6 *'It is most probable'*: Chelmsford to Stanley, 14 May 1879, in Greaves, *Isandlwana*, 141.

236 *'I am sorry'*: *Wolseley Journal*, 3 Aug. 1879, op. cit.

236 *'Heroes have been made'*: ibid., 19 Mar. 1880.

236 that *'cling and stick to you'*: Banister to his father, 27 Jan. 1879, op. cit.

236 *'I wish I was back'*: Emery, 95.

237 '*I am now left*': Glyn to Chelmsford, 24 Jan. 1879, in Greaves, 147.

237 '*In this state of filth*': *Harford Journal*, 38.

237–8 '*We have lost everything*': Greaves, 145.

238 *Glyn could have relieved . . . 'mile or two*': *Harford Journal*, 39.

238 '*Poor Col. Glyn*': Captain Hallam Parr to Sir Bartle Frere, 24 Jan. 1879, RA VIC/033/118.

238 '*Colonel Glyn (our chief) does nothing*': Captain W. Parke Jones to his family, 25 Feb. 1879, in Emery, 142.

238 '*should be partially entrenched*': *Zulu Victory*, 271.

238–9 '*I have no desire*': Glyn Letters, SWB, 1983.13.

239 *a private letter . . . 'shoulders to his*': Clery to Major-General Alison, 11 Mar. 1879, in *Zulu Victory*, 268.

239 '*Odd the general*': ibid.

239 *More specifically . . . 'more supplies*': Glyn to Bellairs, 26 Feb. 1879, Glyn Letters, SWB, 1983.13.

239 *He also refuted . . . 'safety of the camp*': Glyn to Bellairs, 25 and 26 Feb. 1879, ibid.

240 '*his views of the relations*': ibid.

240 '*had kept a written order* . . . '*hold their tongues*': George Mansel to Fanny Colenso, 25 Mar. 1882, KZN, A204/6.

240 '*I cannot tell you*': Cambridge Military Papers, RA VIC/Add E/1/8514.

240 *Native reports . . . 'and fight well*': ibid.

240–41 '*asking for peace* . . . '*laid down*': Chelmsford to Wood, 3 Mar. 1879, in Laband, 116–17.

241 *series of dispatches*: Hicks Beach Papers, GRO, D2455/PCC/23.

Chapter Eleven: Yet More Disasters

243–4 '*broken down* . . . *as soon as he could*: Tucker to his father, 19 Mar. 1879, quoted in Emery, 157–8.

244–5 *Moriarty's subaltern . . . 'simply slaughtered*': ibid., 158–9.

245 '*I am done*': ibid., 161.

245–6 '*I saw the kaffirs*': Knight, 140–41.

246 '*Had it not been*': *VC Register*, 33.

246–7 *Harward's craven conduct . . . buried in a long trench*: Tucker to his father, 19 Mar. 1879, op. cit., 159–61.

247 *'not less than 4,000'*: Knight, 142.

248 *'The moment Harward'*: Tucker to his father, 19 Mar. 1879, op. cit., 159.

248 *'I endeavoured to rally'*: Knight, 141.

248 *'Lieutenant Harward saddled'*: ibid., 142–3.

248 *'Surely,' he wrote to Chelmsford*: Cambridge to Chelmsford, 16 Apr. 1879, RA VIC/Add E/1/8630.

249 *'Had I released this officer'*: Knight, 143.

249 *'It is difficult to convey' . . . 'great anxiety'*: Frere to Chelmsford, 20 Mar. 1879, RA VIC/Add E/1/8597.

249–50 *Pearson's decision . . . 'distrust in Zululand'*: Cambridge Military Papers, RA VIC/Add E/1/8589.

250 *'fit to undertake'*: Chelmsford to Wood, 19 Mar. 1879, Wood Papers, KZN, A598/II/2.

250 *'If you are in a position'*: Knight, 146.

250 *'strongly protected'*: Lock, *Blood on the Painted Mountain*, 18.

250 *The plan . . . 'severe loss'*: District After Order (signed by Captain R. Campbell), 26 Mar. 1879, Buller Papers, TNA, WO/132/1.

251 *'at all hazards'*: Buller to Aunt G., 30 Mar. 1879, Buller Papers, TNA, WO/132/1.

251 *'It is not intended'*: District After Order, 26 Mar. 1879, op. cit.

251 *Wood, however . . . 'coming here'*: Wood, II, 46.

252 *'watch the country'*: District After Order, 26 Mar. 1879, op. cit.

253 *'carrying a revolver'*: Lock, *Blood on the Painted Mountain*, 122.

254 *'I asked whether'*: Wood, II, 47.

254 *'swarmed up the hill'*: Knight, 149.

254–5 *'I was horrified' . . . 'horse down'*: Buller to Aunt G., 30 Mar. 1879, op. cit.

255 *'On each side'*: ibid.

255 *'The natives'*: Knight, 150.

255–6 *Russell had left . . . 'to be gained'*: ibid., 151.

257 *One of them asked . . . 'parents or wife'*: Wood, II, 48.

257–8 *A little further . . . 'already set'*: ibid., 49–50.

258 *Wood now told Campbell . . . answered the call*: Wood to the military secretary, 25 July 1881, in Emery, 177.

258 'half blown off ': RA QVJ: 9 Sept. 1879.

258–9 *Without hesitating . . .* 'column had fared': Wood, II, 50–51.

259 'finding the Zulus': Buller to Aunt G., 30 Mar. 1879, op. cit.

259 'On arrival there': Knight, 152.

259 'dear good honest' . . . *Zulu army*: Buller to Aunt G., 30 Mar. 1879, op. cit.

259–60 'The English forces': Laband, *Fight Us in the Open, 35.*

260 'We were 30 miles': Buller to Aunt G., 30 Mar. 1879, op. cit.

260 'extremely steep': Knight, 158.

261 'but finding the enemy': ibid.

261 'I could not let anyone else': Wood, II, 54–5n.

261–2 'Cantering up' . . . 'Inhlobana': Knight, 156.

262 *Buller knew . . .* 'uncovered': Buller to Aunt G., 30 Mar. 1879, op. cit.

262–3 'an almost perpendicular': Knight, 159.

263 'We had to get down': Buller to Aunt G., 30 Mar. 1879, op. cit.

263 *Captain Cecil D'Arcy . . .* 'heavy boots': Emery, 168.

263 'We could not hit them': ibid., 170.

263–4 'When I got to the bottom' . . . 'ever met': Buller to Aunt G., 30 Mar. 1879, op. cit.

264 'loud shouts' . . . *off to safety*: Knight, 160–61.

264 'Had it not been': Emery, 166.

265 'Perhaps not' . . . 'African fighting': Ponsonby to his wife, 13 Sept. 1879, RA VIC/Add A36/18.

265 *Buller told Wood . . . Browne*: Wood to Chelmsford, 10 Apr. 1879, KZN, A598/II/3/1.

265 'unable to act': Ponsonby to his wife, 13 Sept. 1879, op. cit.

265 'There is no want': Wood to Chelmsford, 10 Apr. 1879, op. cit.

265–6 *Wood and his tiny escort . . . Border Horse*: Wood, II, 54.

266 'wonderful' what Buller 'had done': RA QVJ: 9 Sept. 1879.

266 'With any other leader' . . . 'but himself ': Chelmsford to Cambridge, 5 May 1879, RA VIC/Add E/1/8651.

266 'a defeat': Ponsonby to his wife, 13 Sept. 1879, op. cit.

266 'a hundred to one': ibid.

266–7 'I am quite sure': Chelmsford to Cambridge, 5 May 1879, op. cit.

Chapter Twelve: The Tide Turns

268 *'to stop a rush'* . . . *'human bodies'*: Wood, II, 53.

268–9 *Despite the losses . . . cattle laager*: Laband, *Rise and Fall*, 268–9.

269 *At dawn* . . . *'Alert'*: Wood, II, 57–9.

270 *Cetshwayo later claimed* . . . *'army'*: Cetshwayo to Ruscombe Poole, in Laband, *Fight Us in the Open*, 35–6.

270 *'They did not stand'*: Buller to Aunt G., 30 Mar. 1879, Buller Papers, TNA, WO/132/1.

271 *'We thought the Zulu'*: Knight, 166.

271 *'a fine tall Chief '* . . . *'all three were killed'*: Wood, II, 60.

271 *'Everyone in the iNgobamakhosi'*: Laband, *Fight Us in the Open*, 36.

271 *'It was evident'*: Buller to Aunt G., 30 Mar. 1879, op. cit.

271–2 *'The izinduna'*: Laband, *Fight Us in the Open*, 36.

272 *'Really it isn't your place'*: Wood, II, 61.

272–3 *'I was now left alone'*: Slade to his mother, 29 Mar. 1879, NAM, 1968-07-235.

273 *As the battle . . . deliberately low*: Wood, II, 61–2.

274 *'At first the advance'*: Captain Woodgate's Diary, in Emery, 175.

274 *'cheerily'* . . . *'rough and tumble'*: Wood, II, 62–3.

274 *'about to retreat'* . . . *'assegaiing our men'*: Slade to his mother, 29 Mar. 1879, op. cit.

274 *'where they did great execution'*: Wood, II, 63.

274 *'We were up & at them'*: Buller to Aunt G., 30 Mar. 1879, op. cit.

274 *'[We] followed them'*: Emery, 169.

274–5 *'unable from physical fatigue'* . . . *'get away fast'*: Chelmsford to Cambridge, 5 May 1879, RA VIC/Add E/1/8651.

275 *A further 785 Zulu bodies . . . 'lead on their men'*: Laband, *Rise and Fall*, 276–7.

275 *'large numbers'* . . . *Enfield rifles*: Captain Woodgate's Diary, in Emery, 175.

275 *British losses*: Laband, *Rise and Fall*, 276.

275 *'On March 30th'*: Emery, 173.

275 *'The whole of the infantry'*: ibid., 22.

276 *Wood later commended* . . . *'was struck'*: Wood, II, 64.

276 *'The King was very angry'*: Laband, *Fight Us in the Open*, 37.

277 *On the same day . . . going to be enough*: Knight, 197.

277 *One in particular . . . 'confusion prevails'*: ibid., 194–5.

278 *he informed Colonel Stanley . . . 'into consideration'*: Cambridge to Stanley, 25 Mar. 1879, in Laband, 130–31.

278 *memorandum . . . in the vicinity*: Chelmsford Memorandum, no date, ibid., 132–3.

279 *The advance began . . . half-brothers*: Chelmsford to Stanley, 10 Apr. 1879, in ibid., 134–5.

279 *'bushy and very difficult'*: ibid., 135–6.

280 *'I passed a very wretched'*: Dawnay Journal, 12.

280 *'No preparation'*: Chelmsford to Stanley, 10 Apr. 1879, op. cit., 136.

281 *'send out scouts' . . . 'before attacking'*: Laband, *Fight Us in the Open*, 31.

281 *'It was the Zulu intention'*: Major McGregor, 'The Zulu War with Colonel Pearson at Ekowe', *Blackwood's Edinburgh Magazine*, no. 765, July 1879, vol. 126.

281 *'Impi' . . . 'Zulu army!'*: Knight, 203.

282 *'No whites ever'*: ibid., 203–4.

282 *'Soon the Zulus' . . . 'left arm'*: W. G. Ransley, 'On Service', NAM, 7208-73.

283 *'Our men'*: A. C. B. Mynors, in Knight, 143.

283 *'We kept up a heavy fire'*: Dawnay Journal, 14–15.

283–4 *'All the other officers'*: ibid., 15.

284 *'drew swords' . . . 'Umisi Hill'*: Knight, 206.

284 *Chelmsford estimated . . . artillery fire*: Chelmsford to Stanley, 10 Apr. 1879, op. cit., 136.

284 *British casualties*: Laband, *Rise and Fall*, 282.

284–5 *'A Zulu is hideous'*: Milne to his father, 14 Apr. 1879, RA VIC/034/45.

285 *'all future operations'*: 'The Zulu War with Pearson at Ekowe', op. cit., 26.

285 *'Who is he?'*: ibid., 27.

286 *'All was excitement'*: W. G. Ransley, 'On Service', op. cit.

286 *'There were mounted infantry'*: Charles E. Fripp, 'Reminiscences of the Zulu War', *Pall Mall Magazine*, vol. 20, 1900, 549–50.

286–7 *'little puffs' . . . 'having a match'*: ibid., 550.

287–8 *His intention* . . . *'I have asked for'*: Chelmsford to Cambridge, 11 Apr. 1879, in Laband, 145–8.

288–9 *'He said,' wrote Clifford* . . . *'false moves'*: Clifford to Cambridge, 17 Apr. 1879, RA VIC/Add E/1/8633.

289 *'I fear the cost'*: ibid., 21 Apr. 1879, E/1/8636.

289–90 *'Butler writes'*: ibid., 2 May 1879, E/1/8648.

290 *'The difficulties'*: Cambridge Military Papers, RA VIC/Add E/1/8641.

290 *Six days later* . . . *'for doing so'*: ibid., RA VIC/E/1/8642.

Chapter Thirteen: Sir Garnet Wolseley

291 *'unfavourable news'*: RA QVJ: 8 Apr. 1879.

291 *'Such a great thing'*: ibid., 22 Apr. 1879.

291 *'still much'* . . . *'great misfortune'*: RA VIC/Add B60/49.

291 *'The news from the Cape'*: RA QVJ: 28 Apr. 1879.

291 *'speedy close'*: Northcote to the queen, 4 Apr. 1879, RA VIC/O34/35.

292 *'got over'*: RA QVJ: 28 Apr. 1879.

292 *'want of energy'* . . . *'at Cyprus'*: RA VIC/Add T7/78.

292 *'He had not put Rorke's Drift'*: Chelmsford Papers, NAM, 6807-386-8-56.

294 *'You have no lateral'*: Cambridge Military Papers, RA VIC/Add E/1/8658.

294 *'The news from the Cape'*: Disraeli Letters, 216.

294 *'bona fide overtures'*: Hicks Beach Papers, GRO, D2455/PCC/13.

294 *'shameful'* . . . *'views of Government'*: RA QVJ: 18 May 1879.

295 *'abundance of private'* . . . *'general settlement'*: Disraeli to the queen, 19 May 1879, RA VIC/Add B61/7.

295 *'long talk'* . . . *'being recalled'*: Wolseley Journal, 25–6.

296 *'no mercy'* . . . *'over Him'*: ibid., 26.

296 *the Cabinet decided* . . . *'real secret'*: ibid., 27.

296–7 *Wolseley next went* . . . *queen's sanction*: ibid.

297 *'The Cabinet is of opinion'* . . . *'time is precious'*: RA QVJ: 26 May 1879.

297 *The queen . . . two grandchildren*: ibid., 23 May 1879.

298 '*If the Cabinet*': Queen to Disraeli, 23 May 1879, RA VIC/034/87.

298 *Disraeli had already . . . being recalled*: RA VIC/034/88.

298 '*master of the situation*' . . . '*Colonial Government*': RA VIC/034/85.

298 '*on information derived*': Queen to Disraeli, 24 May 1879, RA VIC/034/84.

298 '*not having received*': RA QVJ: 26 May 1879.

299 *She immediately sent . . . did this mean?*: Abstract of Correspondence on the subject of Wolseley's appointment, RA VIC/034/84.

299 '*Whatever fault*': RA VIC/034/95.

299 *he replied by cipher*: RA QVJ: 27 May 1879.

299–300 '*long and deep*' . . . '*were necessary*': RA VIC/034/97.

300 *a 'satisfactory' one . . . 'etc.'*: RA QVJ: 28 May 1879.

300 '*We have had a terrible time*': Disraeli to Lady Chesterfield, 28 May 1879, *Disraeli Letters*, 218.

300–301 '*Dizzy was very complimentary*' . . . *in Parliament*: *Wolseley Journal*, 33.

301 '*It is the desire*': Hicks Beach to Wolseley, 29 May 1879, RA VIC/035/44.

302 *Wolseley took his leave . . . for South Africa*: *Wolseley Journal*, 33–4.

303 '*eager to march back*': *Harford Journal*, 45.

303 *assured Colonel Glyn*: Glyn Letters, SWB, 1893.13.

303 *On 3 March . . . move down?*: ibid.

303 '*I am inclined to think*' . . . '*proper line*': ibid.

304 '*There were bodies*' . . . *unscathed*: Lieutenant J. Maxwell, 'Reminiscences of the Zulu War', KCAL, F968.3 Max, 24.

304 '*several of the general's papers*': Jackson & Whybra, 30.

304 '*sickening*' *stench*: Chelmsford to Wood, 24 Mar. 1879, KZN, A598/II/2/2.

304 '*This column ought*': Emery, 143.

305–6 '*No Zulus were seen*' . . . '*broad belt*': *Illustrated London News*, 12 July 1879.

306 '*In all the seven campaigns*': ibid.

306–7 '*near the right*' . . . '*along the front*': ibid.

308 '*We fired the kraals*': Clark Letter, 22 May 1879, NAM, 6610-54.

308 '*desolate camp*' . . . '*No firearms*': *Illustrated London News*, 12 July 1879.

308–9 '*besides a cart*' . . . '*day's work*': Dawnay Journal, 35.

309 '*The objective*': Laband, 149–50.

309 '*unconquerable horror*': Ponsonby to his wife, 11 Sept. 1879, RA VIC/Add A36/18.

310 '*treat for peace*' . . . *annual instalments*: Knight, 228–9.

310 '*But we got no breakfast*': Roe Diary, NAM, 7504-18.

Chapter Fourteen: The Prince Imperial

311–12 '*clever fellow*' . . . '*cannot say*': Ponsonby to his wife, 21 Oct. 1879, RA VIC/Add A36/18.

313 '*thirsting to smell powder*': Knight, 91.

313 '*called upon to go*' . . . '*motives*': RA VIC/Add E/1/8551.

313 *On 21 February* . . . '*an old friend*': RA VIC/Add E/1/8552.

313 '*Heard from George C.*': RA QVJ: 24 Feb. 1879.

313 '*to see as much as he can*': Cambridge to Frere, 25 Feb. 1879, RA VIC/Add E/1/8558.

314 '*He is a fine young fellow*': Cambridge to Chelmsford, ibid., E/1/8559.

314 '*Heard the Prince Imperial*': RA QVJ: 27 Feb. 1879.

314 '*I am quite mystified*': Blake, *Disraeli*, 670–71.

314 '*I am as puzzled*': Roberts, *Salisbury*, 227.

314–15 '*Tomorrow I leave*': Knight, *With His Face to the Foe*, 119.

315 '*he himself was anxious*' . . . '*look after the Prince*': ibid., 146.

315 '*The Prince was a charming*': ibid., 144–5.

316 '*a Frenchman*': ibid., 161.

316 '*I said I would do*': ibid., 162.

317 '*high testimonials*' . . . '*for surveying the route*': ibid., 124–32.

317 '*After galloping about*': ibid., 170–71.

318 '*When we were on the move*': ibid., 171.

318 *would not allow* '*the Prince*': RA QVJ: 24 Aug. 1879.

318 '*immediate precincts*' . . . '*when on the march*': Knight, *With His Face to the Foe*, 178.

318 *But on 29 May* . . . '*surprised*': Watson Papers, KCAL, KCM 4275, 27, 99.

318–19 'You are right' . . . 'rather neatly': Molyneux, *Campaigning in South Africa and Egypt*, 159.

319–20 Meanwhile Carey . . . prescient patrol: Watson Papers, KCAL, KCM 4275, 27, 99–104.

320 That evening . . . 'proper escort: Knight, *With His Face to the Foe*, 185.

321 'Is the horse too high' . . . 'too tight': RA QVJ: 24 Aug. 1879.

322 'specially ordered' . . . 'without them': Harrison, *Recollections*, 172

322 'Oh no we are quite strong': Carey, 'Report to Harrison', 1 June 1879, RA VIC/R5/18.

322 'The Prince': Drummond to his father, 11 June 1879, RA VIC/R5/29.

322 'preferred to do so': Carey, 'Report to Harrison', op. cit.

322–3 it 'was one of the very kraals' . . . 'being perceived': Watson Papers, op. cit., 141.

323 'They had no business': Drummond to his father, 11 June 1879, op. cit.

323 It was now 2.40 p.m. . . . 'with a shout': Carey, 'Report to Harrison', op. cit.

323–4 On hearing the shots . . . without his owner: Knight, *With His Face to the Foe*, 202–4.

324–5 Carey, Cochrane . . . his brain: ibid., 205–6.

326 'waving their arms': Slade to his father, 2 June 1879, NAM, 1968-07-235.

326 Recognizing Carey . . . 'his life': RA QVJ: 24 Aug. 1857.

326 'could only discover' . . . 'unsafe': ibid., 9 Sept. 1857.

326–7 An incredulous Harrison . . . "lose you too": Harrison, *Recollections*, 173.

327 William Drummond . . . 'in the dark': Drummond to his father, 11 June 1879, op. cit.

327 saw him 'in his tent': Knight, *With His Face to the Foe*, 211.

327 'You know the dreadful': ibid., 213–14.

328 'both assegaied': Drummond to his father, 11 June 1879, op. cit.

328 'It was stripped': Scott to Chelmsford, 3 June 1879, NAM, 6312-180.

329 'Around the body': Knight, *With His Face to the Foe*, 219–20.

329 'Poor little fellow': Lieutenant J. MacSwiney to his sister, 1 June 1879, NAM, 6406-16.

329–30 *a more detailed letter . . . 'and risky'*: Chelmsford to Frere, 2 June 1879, RA VIC/Zulu War Papers.

330 *'The indignation'*: Captain S. N. McLeod Nairne, 'The Death of the Prince Imperial', *Journal of the Royal United Services Institute*, vol. 79, Feb. 1934, no. 513, 750.

330 *'Neither Carey'*: Slade to his mother, 2 June 1879, NAM, 1968-07-235.

331 *'most disgraceful' . . . 'on the Service'*: Watson Papers, op. cit., 108–9.

331 *Its conclusion . . . court martial*: Knight, *With His Face to the Foe*, 230–31.

331–2 *'regular blaze' . . . 'false alarm'*: ibid., 232–3.

332–3 *The charge . . . 'circumstances demanded'*: ibid., 238–46.

333 *'remain under arrest'*: ibid. 247.

333 *'This is terrible' . . . 'obstinate women'*: Weintraub, *Victoria*, 435.

333 *'The young French Prince'*: ibid., 436.

333–4 *'No, no' . . . 'did I get'*: RA QVJ: 19 June 1879.

334 *'What is it?' . . . been prevented'*: RA QVJ: 21 June 1879.

334 *'too plucky' . . . 'possibly be made'*: RA VIC/R5/76B.

335 *'After all'*: Disraeli to Lady Chesterfield, 22 June 1879, *Disraeli Letters*, 224.

335 *'She came towards me'*: RA QVJ: 12 July 1879.

335 *'I hope the French'*: Disraeli to Lady Chesterfield, 12 July 1879, *Disraeli Letters*, 226.

335 *'painful' evidence . . . 'precious life'*: RA QVJ: 14 July 1879.

335 *prince's 'own eagerness'*: Queen's Account of her conversation with Colonel Pemberton, 14 July 1879, RA VIC/R7/1.

336 *'It will be splendid'*: RA QVJ: 16 Dec. 1879.

Chapter Fifteen: Ulundi

337 *'Is the war over?' . . . 'not be sorry'*: Wolseley Journal, 42,

338 *latest conditions . . . 'final terms of peace'*: Laband, 184.

338 *'as there will be'*: Laband, *Rise and Fall*, 297.

339 *'take the consequences'*: Knight, 248.

339 *'would have to fight'*: Laband, *Rise and Fall*, 298.

339–40 *In his long reply . . .* 'longing for': Laband, 200–203.

340 '*Crealock & Chelmsford*': *Wolseley Journal*, 44.

340 '*To hear he was coming*': Watson Papers, KCAL, KCM 4275, 127.

340–41 *Wolseley and his staff . . .* 'in the field': *Wolseley Journal*, 46–7.

341 '*Position of army*' . . . '*daily from you*': Wolseley to Stanley, 30 June 1879, MS WOL, KCM 53176.

341–2 *Wolseley left . . . by land*: *Wolseley Journal*, 45, 50–51.

342 '*All this puts me out*': Wolseley Letters, 40.

342 '*to enable my men*': Laband, 203–4.

343 '*We set to work*': MacSwiney to his mother, 7 July 1879, NAM, 6406-16.

344–5 *Lord William Beresford . . . and galloped off*: RA QVJ: 24 Aug. 1879; *VC Register*, 29, 83, 246.

345 '*infernal war song*': Private G. Turnham to his parents, 7 July 1879, NAM, 8307–23.

345 '*With ever increasing*': Charles E. Fripp, 'Reminiscences of the Zulu War', *Pall Mall Magazine*, vol. 20, 1900, 555.

346 '*all were not confident*': Wood to General Sir Alfred Horsford, 13 July 1879, KCAL, KCM, 89/9/28/7.

346 '*Dark clusters*': Chelmsford to Stanley, 6 July 1879, in Laband, 210.

346 '*high ground*' . . . '*round us*': ibid., 210–11.

347 '*We set fire*': Turnham to his parents, 18 July 1879, NAM, 8307-23.

347–8 '*The fire opened*': Roe Diary, 4 July 1879, NAM, 7504-18.

348 '*the only really thick mass*' . . . '*the square*': *Dawnay Journal*, 67.

348 '*It was a fearful sight*': Roe Diary, 4 July 1879, op. cit.

348–9 '*A bullet went through*': MacSwiney to his mother, 7 July 1879, op. cit.

349 '*Our fire was so hot*': Slade Letters, NAM, 1968-07-235.

349 '*the enemy did not come on*': ibid.

349 '*I was rather disgusted*': Wood to Horsford, 13 July 1879, op. cit.

349 '*severe lesson*': Laband, *Fight Us in the Open*, 43.

349–50 '*It was a grand moment*' . . . *to the square*: *Dawnay Journal*, 65–71.

350 *Zulu dead*: Chelmsford to Stanley, 6 July 1879, op. cit.

350 *British casualties*: Laband, *Ulundi*, 44.

350 '*in a huff* ' . . . '*quite off his head*': Queen's conversation with Beresford, 26 Aug. 1879, RA VIC/R8/56.

350 *His body was found*: Wolseley Journal, 17 Aug. 1879, 89.

350 *'very odd mannered'* . . . *'try to catch'*: Queen's conversation with Buller, 9 Sept. 1879, RA VIC/R8/82.

350–51 *'We galloped up'*: Dawnay Journal, 65–71.

351 *'In a very short time'*: Roe Diary, 4 July 1879, op. cit.

351 *'It was a grand sight'*: Slade Letters, op. cit.

351 *'good conduct'*: ibid.

352 *After a gruelling ride*: Dawnay Journal, 72.

352 *a lengthy dispatch* . . . *'favourably received'*: Chelmsford to Stanley, 6 July 1879, op. cit., 212–14.

353 *'I think this ought'*: Wolseley Journal, 51–2.

353 *'He came out to meet us'*: ibid., 52.

353 *'power in Zululand'* . . . *not yet decided*: ibid., 53.

354 *With your approval*: Laband, 215.

354 *'I hope to reach Saint Paul's'*: ibid., 216.

354–5 *'I am anxious to maintain'* . . . *'little delay as possible'*: ibid., 217–18.

355 *'He is evidently'*: Wolseley Letters, 41.

355 *eighteen months of 'constant work'*: Wood Papers, KZN, A598/II/3/4.

355 *'extremely sorry'* . . . *increasingly fractious*: Wolseley Journal, 54.

355 *'both seedy'*: Wolseley to Wood, 13 July 1879, KZN, A598/II/2/2.

355 *'You and Buller'*: Wood, II, 82.

355–6 *'As I rode up'* . . . *'going home'*: Wolseley Journal, 56.

356 *'not fit to be a Corporal'*: ibid.

356 *'Wood would have stayed'* . . . *'at Ulundi'*: Ponsonby to his wife, 11 Sept. 1879, RA VIC/Add A36/18.

356 *'It marched past'*: Wolseley Journal, 57.

356 *'When we marched past'*: Wood, II, 82.

357 *'I haven't had'* . . . *'Natal sores'*: ibid., 83.

357 *'In notifying the Army'*: ibid.

357–8 *'God speed you'* . . . *'never forgotten'*: ibid., 84.

358 *not with happy results*: Wood took command of British forces in South Africa after Major-General Sir Pomeroy Colley had been killed at the Battle of Majuba during the Transvaal (or First Anglo-Boer) War of 1881 and was forced by the British government to conclude a humiliating peace that effectively gave the province back its inde-

pendence. Buller was replaced as commander-in-chief by Field Marshal Lord Roberts after a string of defeats in the first months of the South African, or Second Anglo-Boer, War of 1899–1902.

Chapter Sixteen: The Aftermath

359 '*Thank God!*': RA QVJ: 24 July 1879.

359 '*combined with*' . . . '*successful*': Disraeli to the queen, 24 July 1879, RA VIC/B61/25.

359 '*How sad*': RA QVJ: 23 July 1879.

360 '*The evidence is much*': ibid., 26 July 1879.

360 *while* '*legally*': Queen to Cambridge, 26 July 1879, RA VIC/R7/82.

360 *concurred with* '*every word*': Cambridge to the queen, 12 Aug. 1879, RA VIC/R8/24.

360–61 '*no doubt*' . . . '*martyr of him*': RA QVJ: 30 July 1879.

361–2 '*His orders*' . . . *rejoin his regiment*: Knight, *With His Face to the Foe*, 262–3.

362 '*strongly advised*' . . . '*keep quiet*': RA QVJ: 22 Aug. 1879.

362 '*As I have done nothing*': *Morning Post*, 29 Aug. 1879.

363 '*a totally different account*' . . . '*sickening cant*': RA QVJ: 28 Aug. 1879.

363 '*They have been copying*' . . . '*in his favour*': Ponsonby to his wife, 30 Aug. 1879, RA VIC/Add A36/18.

364 *so* '*remove the stain*': ibid., 1 Sept. 1879.

364 '*a history*' . . . '*would be best*': ibid., 10 Sept. 1879.

364 *Eugénie had come*: ibid., 14 Sept. 1879.

365 *He was* '*not guilty*': ibid., 15 Sept. 1879.

365 '*very much put out*' . . . '*suit him*': *Wolseley Journal*, 126–7.

365 '*precipitate retreat*' . . . '*around him*': ibid., 57.

366 '*never settle down*' . . . '*considered over*': ibid.

366 '*I shall thus*': ibid., 18 July 1879, 58.

366 *Before moving north* . . . '*had heard*': ibid., 19 July 1879, 59.

366–7 '*some amiable assassin*': ibid., 18 July 1879, 58.

367 '*never killed*' . . . *nothing more*: ibid., 7 Aug. 1879, 75–6.

367 *Later that day* . . . *on the 10th*: ibid., 77.

367 '*If you will take*': ibid., 10 Aug. 1879, 80–81.

368 *Vijn . . . no sign*: ibid., 12 Aug. 1879, 84–5.

368 *The following day . . . the attempt*: ibid., 13 Aug. 1879, 87.

368 *On 14 August Barrow. . .* 'depends upon it': ibid., 16 Aug. 1879, 88–9.

368 *That was not strictly . . . cattle confiscated*: ibid., 20 Aug. 1879, 92.

369 '[*Dunn*] has never been': ibid., 22 Aug. 1879, 93–4.

369 '*should have nothing*': ibid., 29 Aug. 1879.

370 '*take any risks*' . . . '*being captured*': Watson Papers, KCAL, KCM 4275, 162, 174–5.

370 '*They've caught him*' . . . '*Robin Island*': Wolseley Journal, 29 Aug. 1879, 100.

371 '*Although he did not*': W. G. Ransley, 'On Service', NAM, 7208-73.

371 '*as if he was the Conqueror*': Watson Papers, op. cit., 176–7.

371 '*very wise countenance*': Wolseley Journal, 31 Aug. 1879, 103.

371–2 '*series of other lies*' . . . '*coloured tablecloth*': ibid., 104.

372–3 *Cetshwayo's capture . . . live to regret*: Laband, *Rise and Fall*, 335–8.

375 '*Cetewayo is a very fine man*': RA QVJ: 14 Aug. 1882.

377 *Chief Mangosuthu Buthelezi is convinced*: Interview with Buthelezi, 'Zulu – The True Story', *Timewatch*, BBC2, 24 Oct. 2003.

Epilogue: '*I trust I may never serve under him again*'

378 '*tall, very thin*' . . . '*gentlemanlike*': RA QVJ: 2 Sept. 1879.

378 '*This one,*' *she recorded*: ibid., 3 Sept. 1879.

378–9 '*With regard to* [*Isandlwana*]': ibid., 5 Sept. 1879.

379–80 '*Every one must like him*': Ponsonby to his wife, 7 Sept. 1879, RA VIC/Add A36/18.

380 '*Sir Evelyn,*' *she noted*: RA QVJ: 9 Sept. 1879.

380 '*Lord Chelmsford is the kindest*': Memo of queen's conversation with Sir E. Wood, Very Confidential, 10 Sept. 1879, RA VIC/Z169/5.

380 '[*Buller*] *thinks*': Memo of queen's conversation with Buller and Wood, 11 Sept. 1879, Very Confidential, RA VIC/Z169/6.

380–81 '*As we walked*' . . . '*as a General*': Ponsonby to his wife, 11 Sept. 1879, RA VIC/Add A36/18.

381–2 *An* '*official interview*' . . . '*crowning mistake*': RA VIC/B61/37.

382 'He *has obtained*' . . . '*contend with*': Queen to Beaconsfield, 1 Sept. 1879, RA VIC/B61/39.

382 *This took place*: Beaconsfield to the queen, 7 Oct. 1879, RA VIC/B62/21.

382 '*delighted*' *with the general's visit*: Pickard to Wood, 26 Sept. 1879, KZN, A598/II/2/6.

382–3 '*Having very carefully*': TNA, WO 30/129/56316.

383–4 '*The advance from Rorke's Drift*': ibid.

384 '*they would have gone down*' . . . '*idea*': Shepstone to Fanny Colenso, 7 Aug. 1881, KZN, A204/6.

384 '*I was rather struck*': Fanny Colenso's Account of the removal of papers from Colonel Durnford's body, no date, Colenso Papers, KZN, A204/8.

385 '*mistake*' . . . '*coat pocket*': ibid.

385 '*exceedingly puzzled*': ibid.

385 '*I believe*' . . . '*wore a coat*': Longhurst to Edward Durnford, 13 Nov. 1882, ibid.

385 *A separate witness*: D. B. Scott to Edward Durnford, 20 Aug. 1882, ibid.

385 '*Capt. Longhurst's statement*': Shepstone to Fanny Colenso, 20 April 1882, ibid.

386 '*Lord Chelmsford has not*': Fanny Colenso's Account of the removal of papers, op. cit.

386 '*he wished to look up*': Statham to Fanny Colenso, 6 Mar. 1883, ibid.

386 '*apparently with a knife*': Fanny Colenso's Account of the removal of papers, op. cit.

386–7 '*I have taken measures*': Droogleever, 246.

387 '— *tells me*': ibid.

387–8 '*I write to inform you*' . . . *Isandlwana*: Jackson & Whybra, 19–20.

388 '*to march to this Camp*' . . . '*for official use*': ibid., 27–9.

389 '*Col. Durnford*': ibid., 27.

389 '*A mark of admiration*': Greaves, 233.

Index

Ranks and titles are generally the highest mentioned in the text